THE MUELLER REPORT

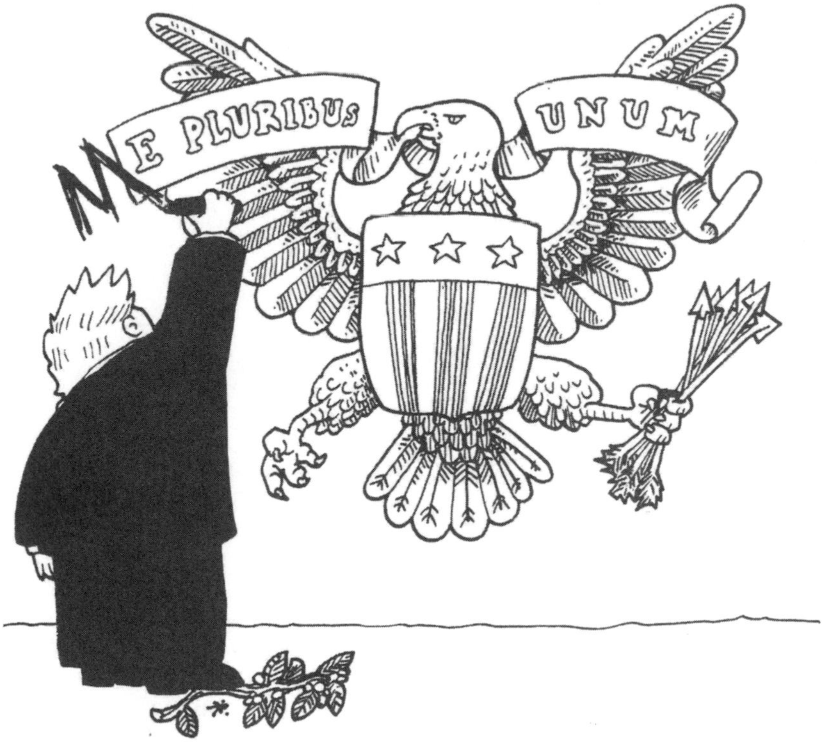
E PLURIBUS
UNUM

Shannon Wheeler

Steve Duin

To Robert S. Mueller III, for his patience and perseverance.

Written by Steve Duin and Shannon Wheeler
Illustrated by Shannon Wheeler
Edited by Justin Eisinger
Design by Chris Ross

Chris Ryall, President & Publisher/CCO
Cara Morrison, Chief Financial Officer
Matthew Ruzicka, Chief Accounting Officer
John Barber, Editor-in-Chief
Justin Eisinger, Editorial Director, Graphic Novels and Collections
Jerry Bennington, VP of New Product Development
Lorelei Bunjes, VP of Technology & Information Services
Jud Meyers, Sales Director
Anna Morrow, Marketing Director
Tara McCrillis, Director of Design & Production
Mike Ford, Director of Operations
Rebekah Cahalin, General Manager

Ted Adams and Robbie Robbins, IDW Founders

ISBN: 978-1-68405-668-2

20   21   22   23   4   3   2   1

TABLE OF CONTENTS

CHAPTER 1

INTRODUCTION

MY REPORT ARRIVES IN TWO PARTS.
INTRO
RUSSIA
TRUMP
THE MUELLER REPORT
IN PART ONE, WE INVESTIGATED RUSSIA'S INTRUSIVE MANEUVERS HELPING DONALD TRUMP DEFEAT HILLARY CLINTON. DID THE TRUMP CAMPAIGN CONSPIRE WITH THE RUSSIANS?

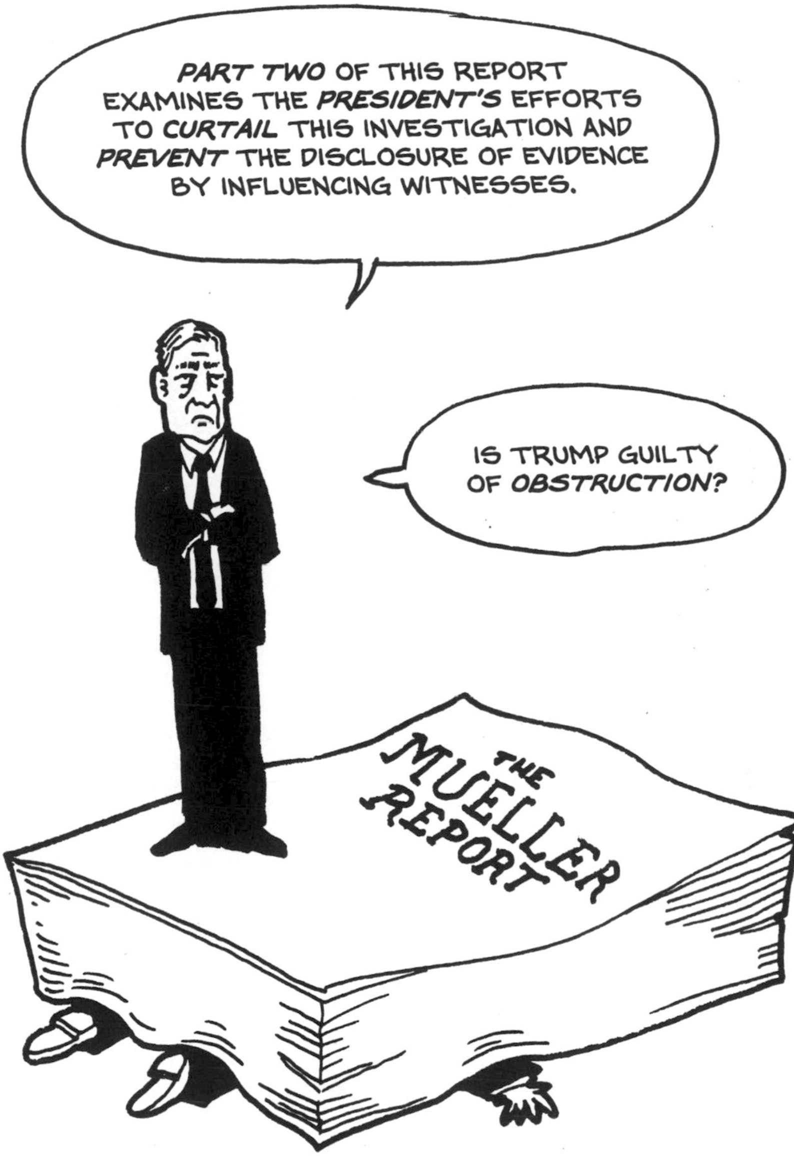

PART TWO OF THIS REPORT EXAMINES THE *PRESIDENT'S* EFFORTS TO *CURTAIL* THIS INVESTIGATION AND *PREVENT* THE DISCLOSURE OF EVIDENCE BY INFLUENCING WITNESSES.
IS TRUMP GUILTY OF *OBSTRUCTION?*
THE MUELLER REPORT

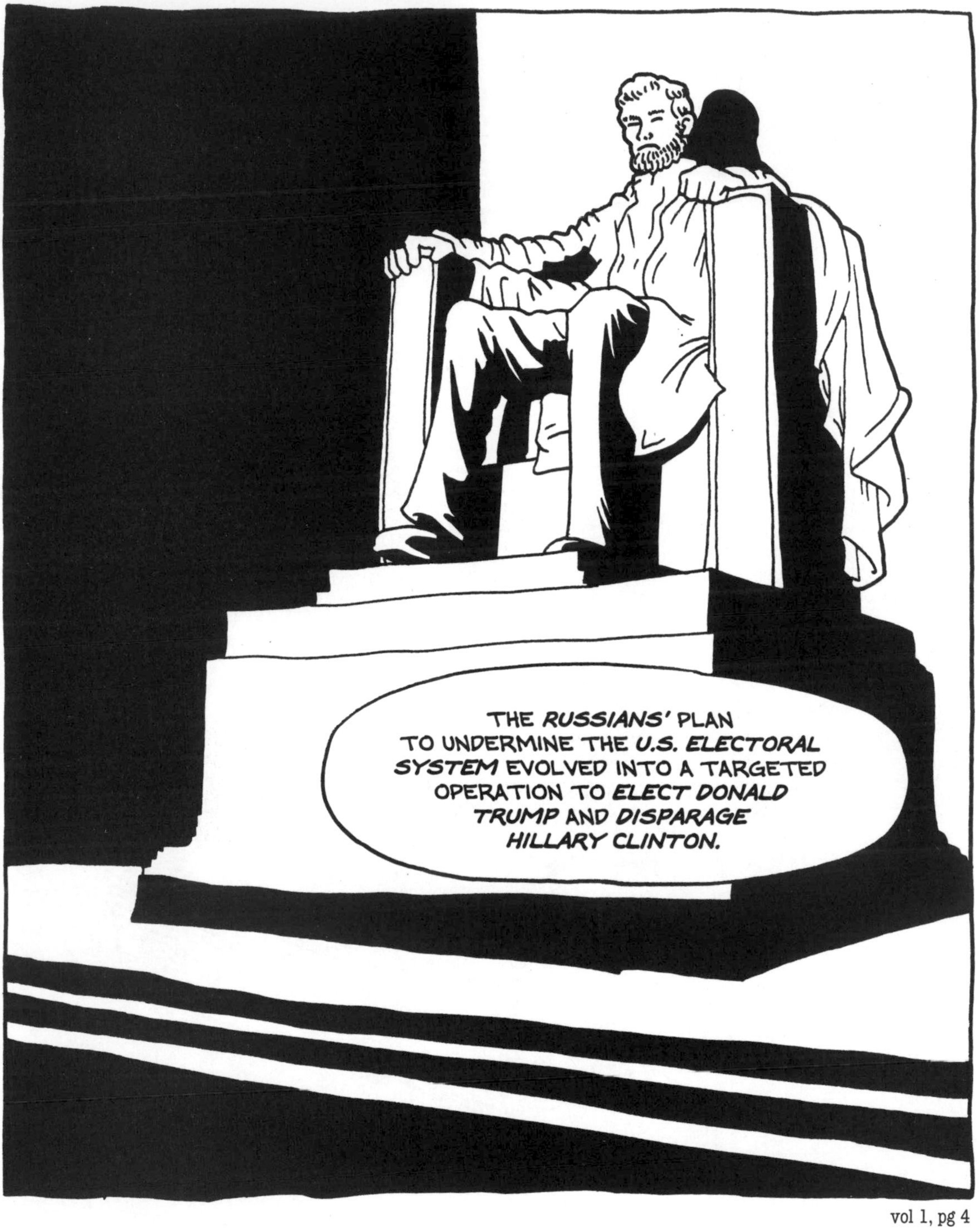
THE *RUSSIANS'* PLAN TO UNDERMINE THE *U.S. ELECTORAL SYSTEM* EVOLVED INTO A TARGETED OPERATION TO *ELECT DONALD TRUMP* AND *DISPARAGE HILLARY CLINTON.*

vol 1, pg 4

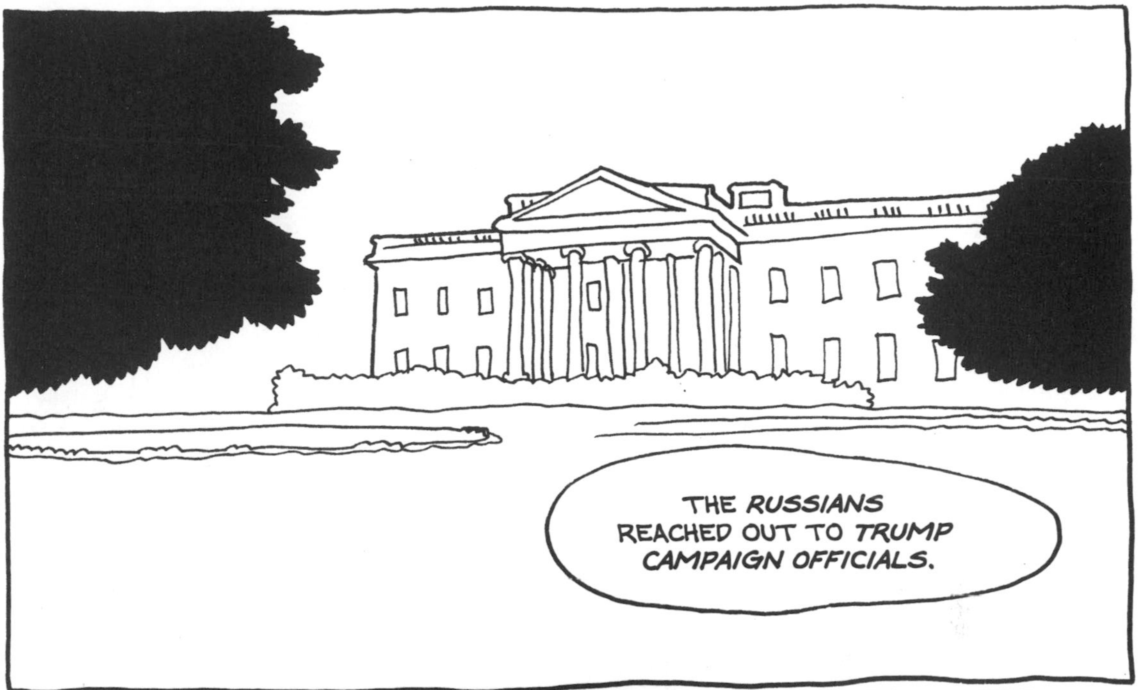
THE RUSSIANS REACHED OUT TO TRUMP CAMPAIGN OFFICIALS.

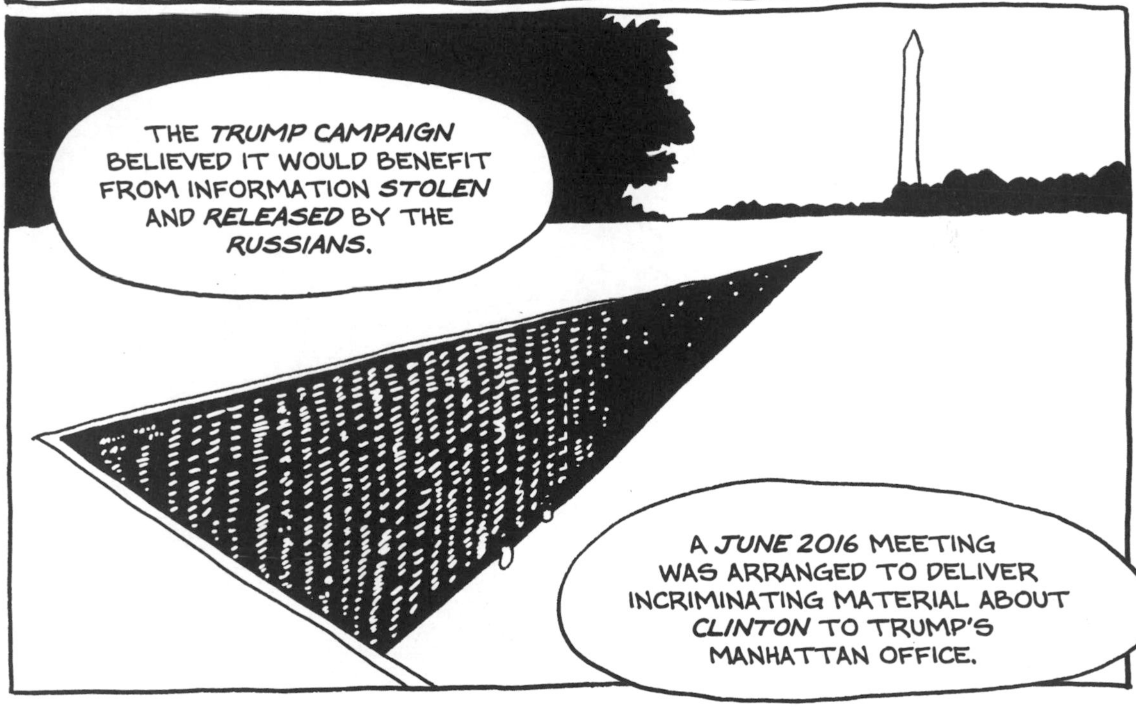
THE TRUMP CAMPAIGN BELIEVED IT WOULD BENEFIT FROM INFORMATION STOLEN AND RELEASED BY THE RUSSIANS.
A JUNE 2016 MEETING WAS ARRANGED TO DELIVER INCRIMINATING MATERIAL ABOUT CLINTON TO TRUMP'S MANHATTAN OFFICE.

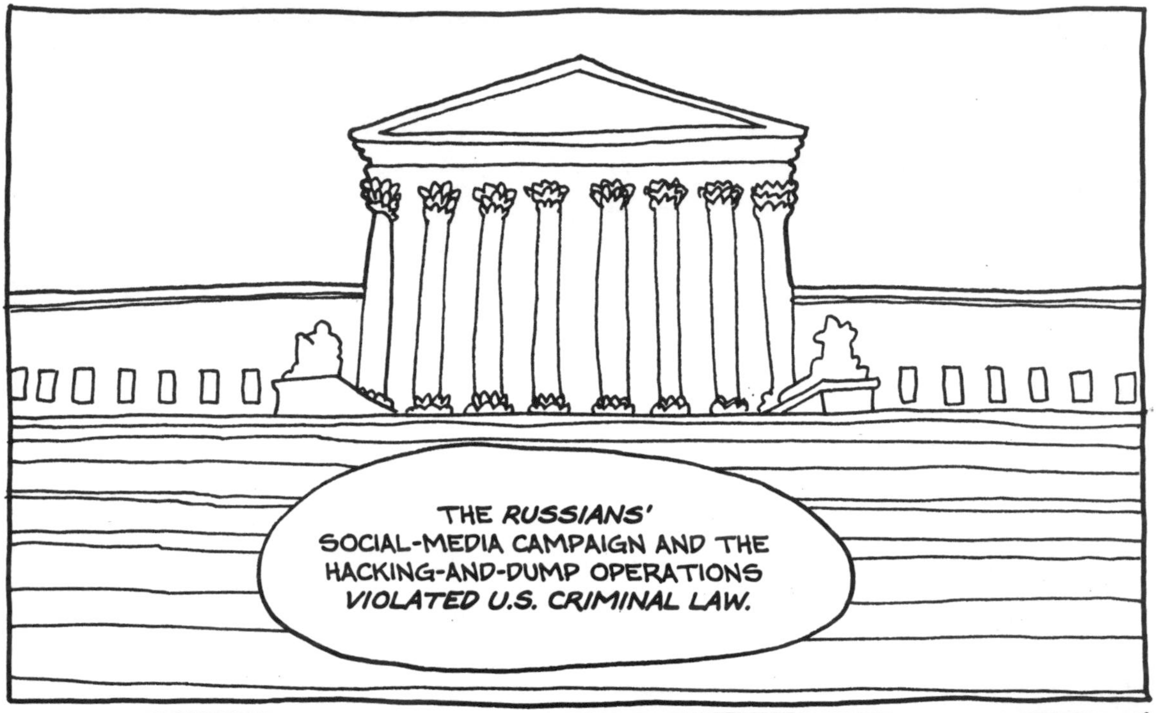
THE *RUSSIANS'* SOCIAL-MEDIA CAMPAIGN AND THE HACKING-AND-DUMP OPERATIONS *VIOLATED U.S. CRIMINAL LAW.*

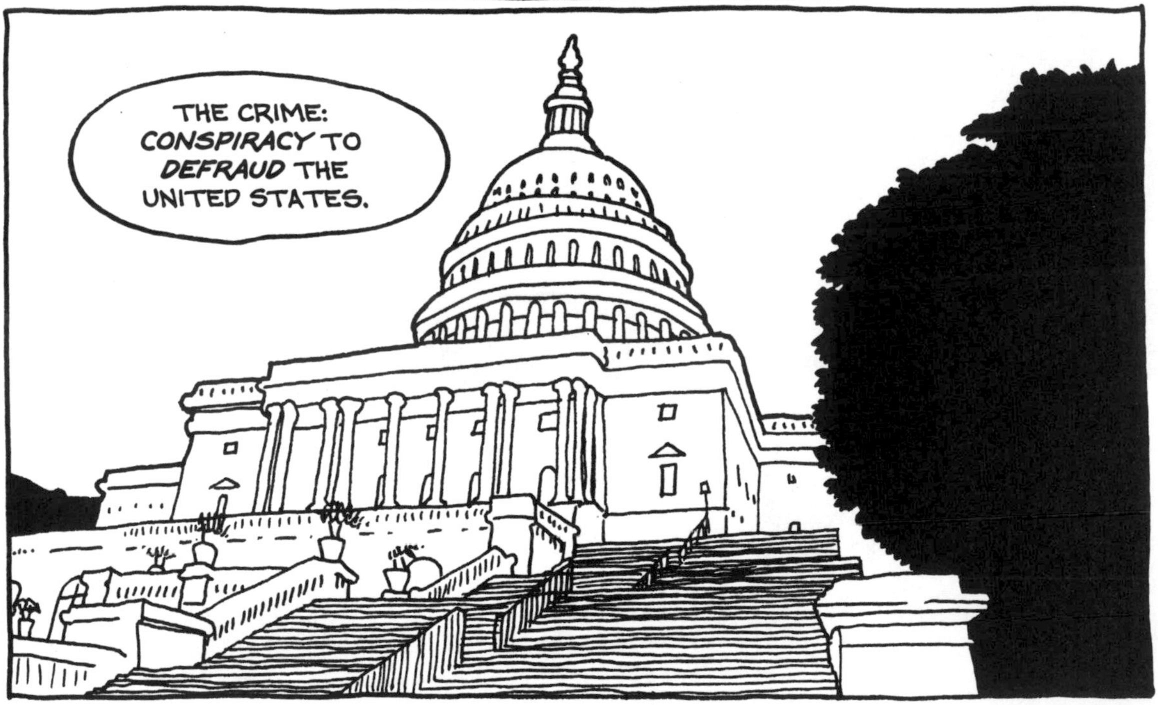
THE CRIME: *CONSPIRACY* TO *DEFRAUD* THE UNITED STATES.

vol 1, pg 9

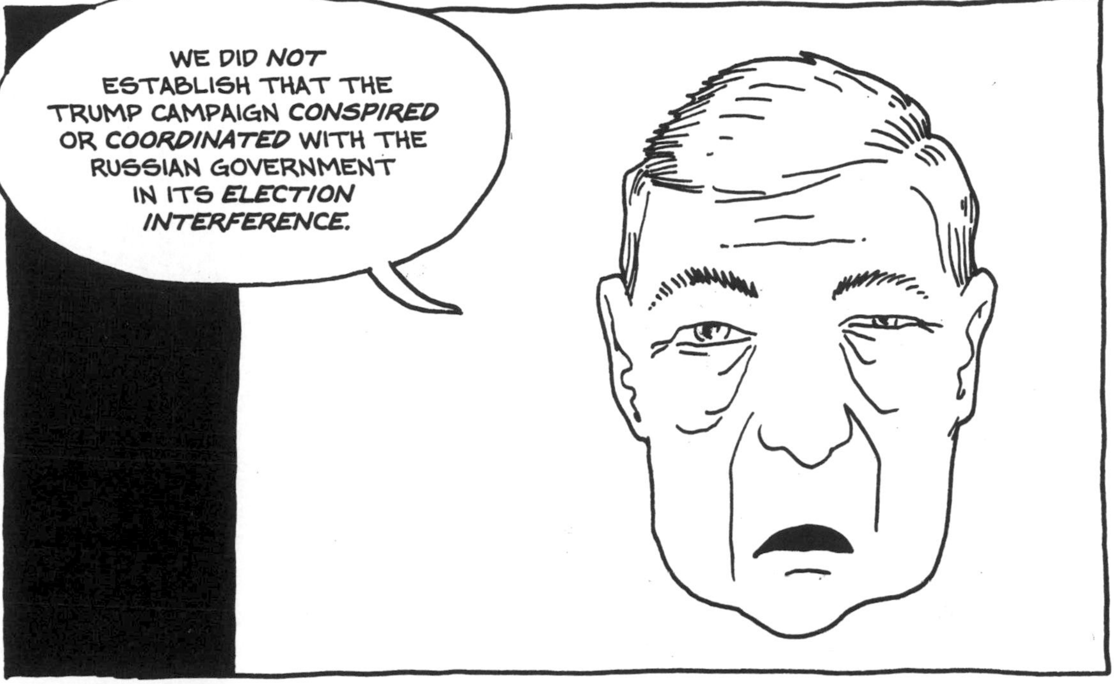
WE DID NOT ESTABLISH THAT THE TRUMP CAMPAIGN CONSPIRED OR COORDINATED WITH THE RUSSIAN GOVERNMENT IN ITS ELECTION INTERFERENCE.

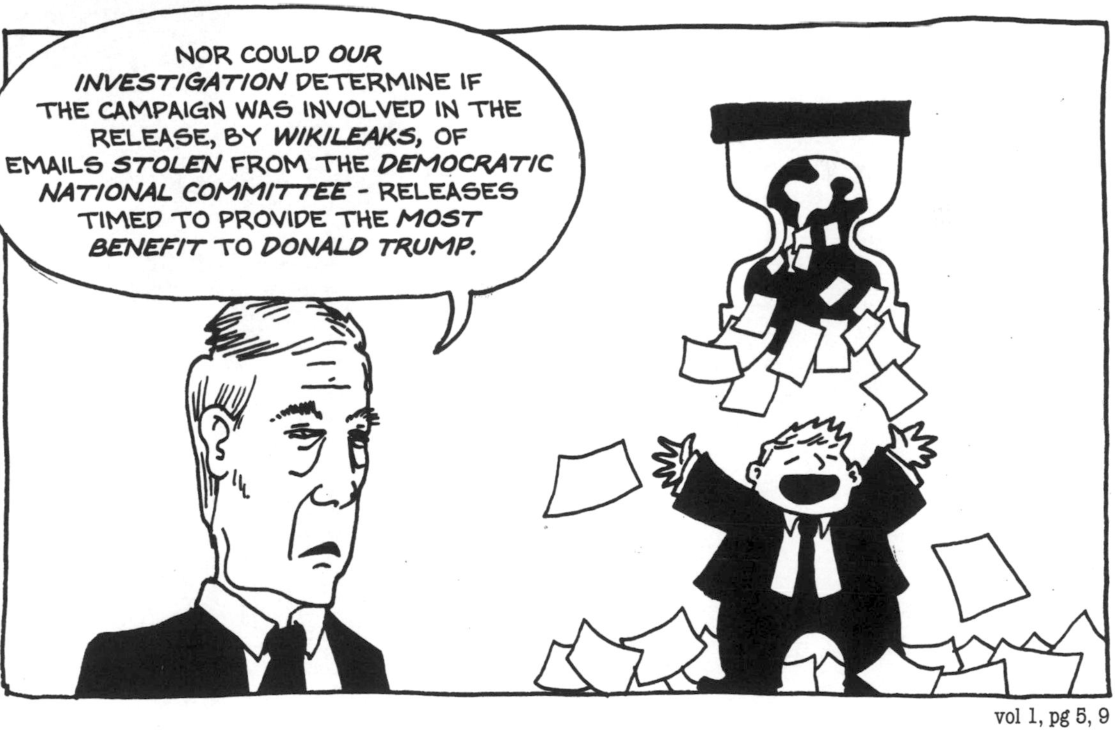
NOR COULD OUR INVESTIGATION DETERMINE IF THE CAMPAIGN WAS INVOLVED IN THE RELEASE, BY WIKILEAKS, OF EMAILS STOLEN FROM THE DEMOCRATIC NATIONAL COMMITTEE - RELEASES TIMED TO PROVIDE THE MOST BENEFIT TO DONALD TRUMP.

vol 1, pg 5, 9

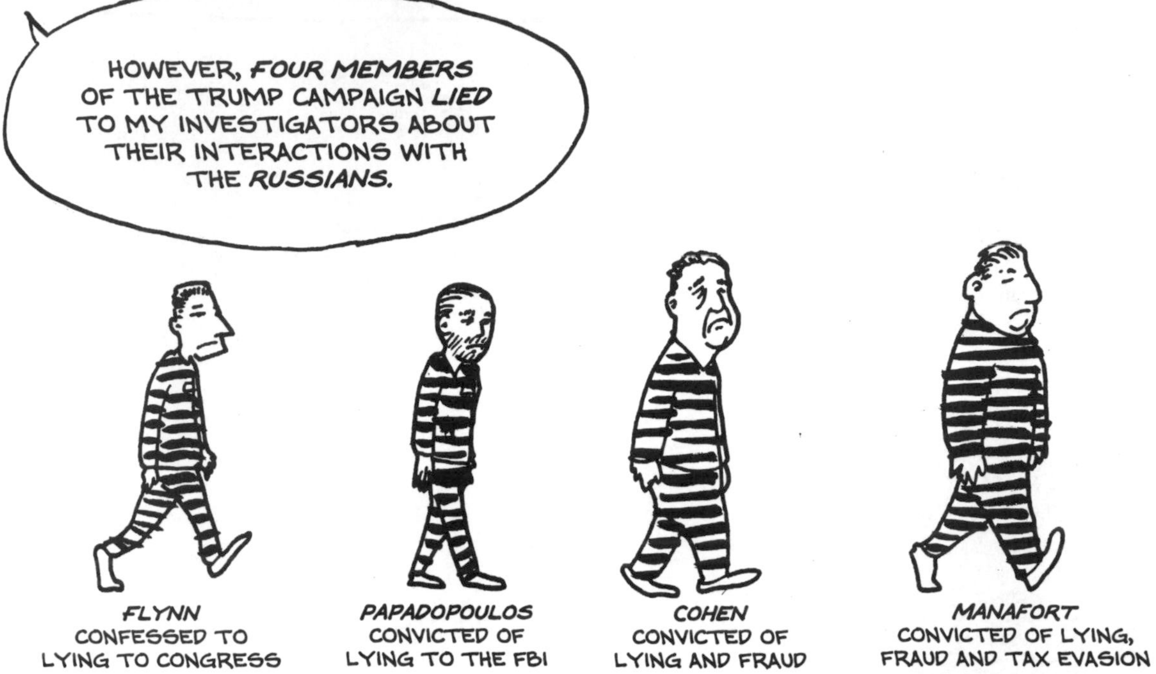
HOWEVER, *FOUR MEMBERS* OF THE TRUMP CAMPAIGN *LIED* TO MY INVESTIGATORS ABOUT THEIR INTERACTIONS WITH THE *RUSSIANS.*
FLYNN
CONFESSED TO LYING TO CONGRESS
PAPADOPOULOS
CONVICTED OF LYING TO THE FBI
COHEN
CONVICTED OF LYING AND FRAUD
MANAFORT
CONVICTED OF LYING, FRAUD AND TAX EVASION

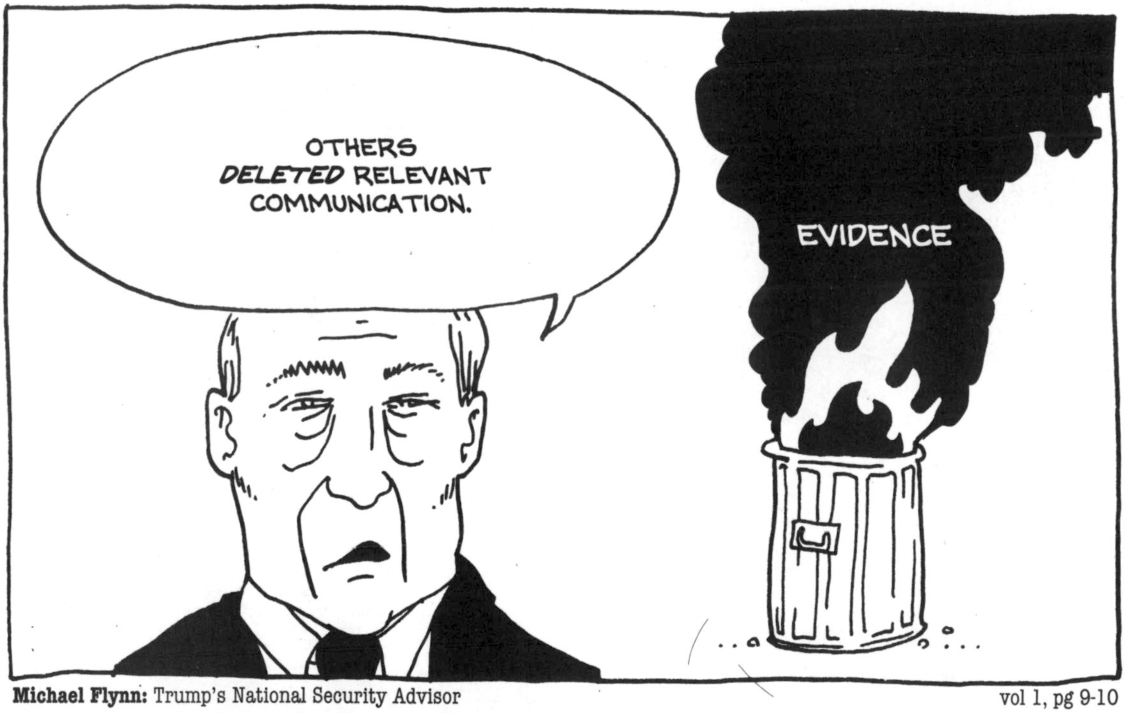
OTHERS *DELETED* RELEVANT COMMUNICATION.
EVIDENCE

Michael Flynn: Trump's National Security Advisor
George Papadopoulos: Trump's Foreign Policy Advisor, 2017
Michael Cohen: Trump's personal counsel, 2006-2018
Paul Manafort: Trump Presidential campaign team Jun-Aug 2016

vol 1, pg 9-10

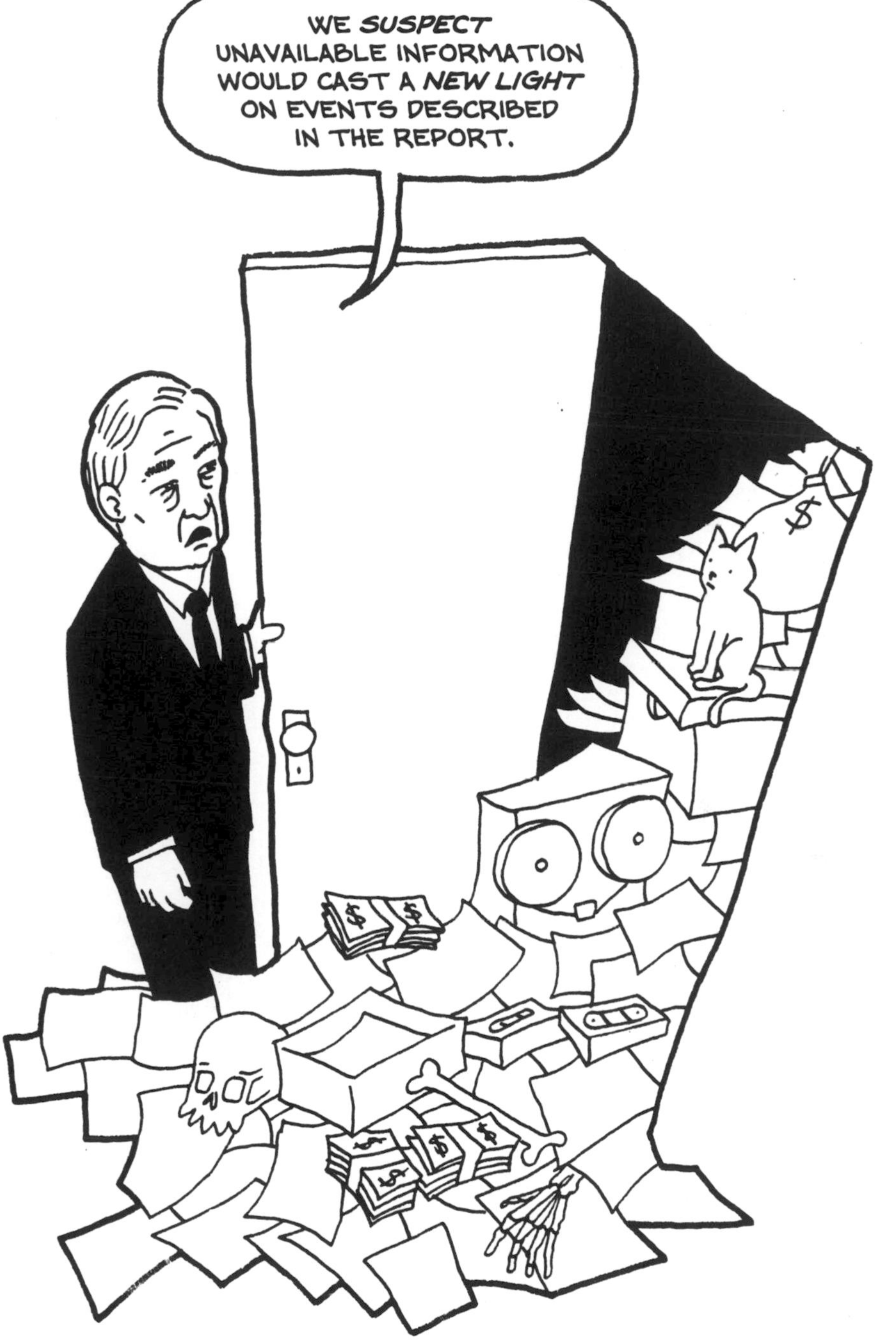
WE *SUSPECT* UNAVAILABLE INFORMATION WOULD CAST A *NEW LIGHT* ON EVENTS DESCRIBED IN THE REPORT.

vol 1, pg 10

CHAPTER 2

RUSSIAN HACKERS, WIKILEAKS, AND MEDIA MANIPULATION

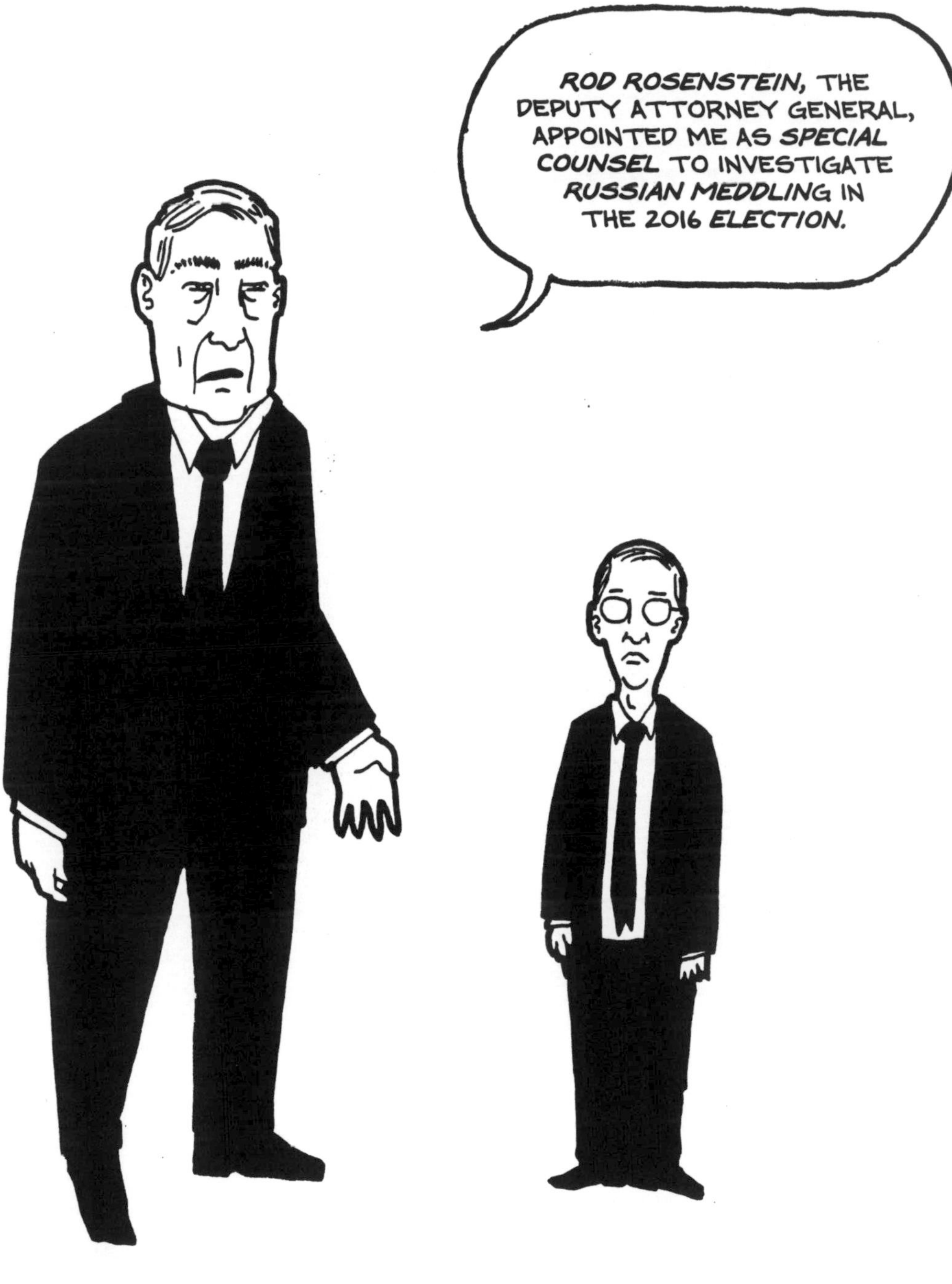
ROD ROSENSTEIN, THE DEPUTY ATTORNEY GENERAL, APPOINTED ME AS *SPECIAL COUNSEL* TO INVESTIGATE *RUSSIAN MEDDLING* IN THE 2016 *ELECTION.*

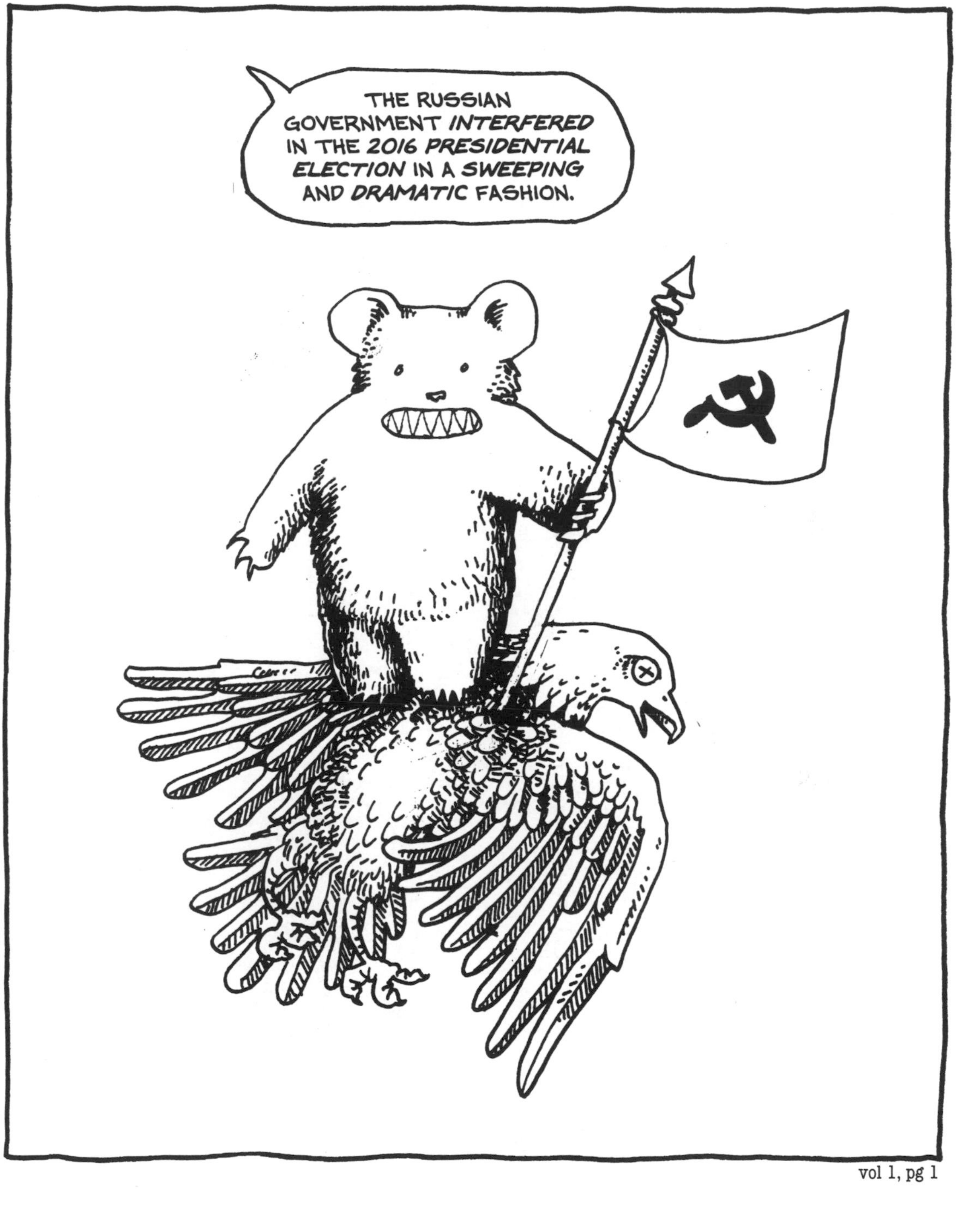
THE RUSSIAN GOVERNMENT *INTERFERED* IN THE *2016 PRESIDENTIAL ELECTION* IN A *SWEEPING* AND *DRAMATIC* FASHION.

vol 1, pg 1

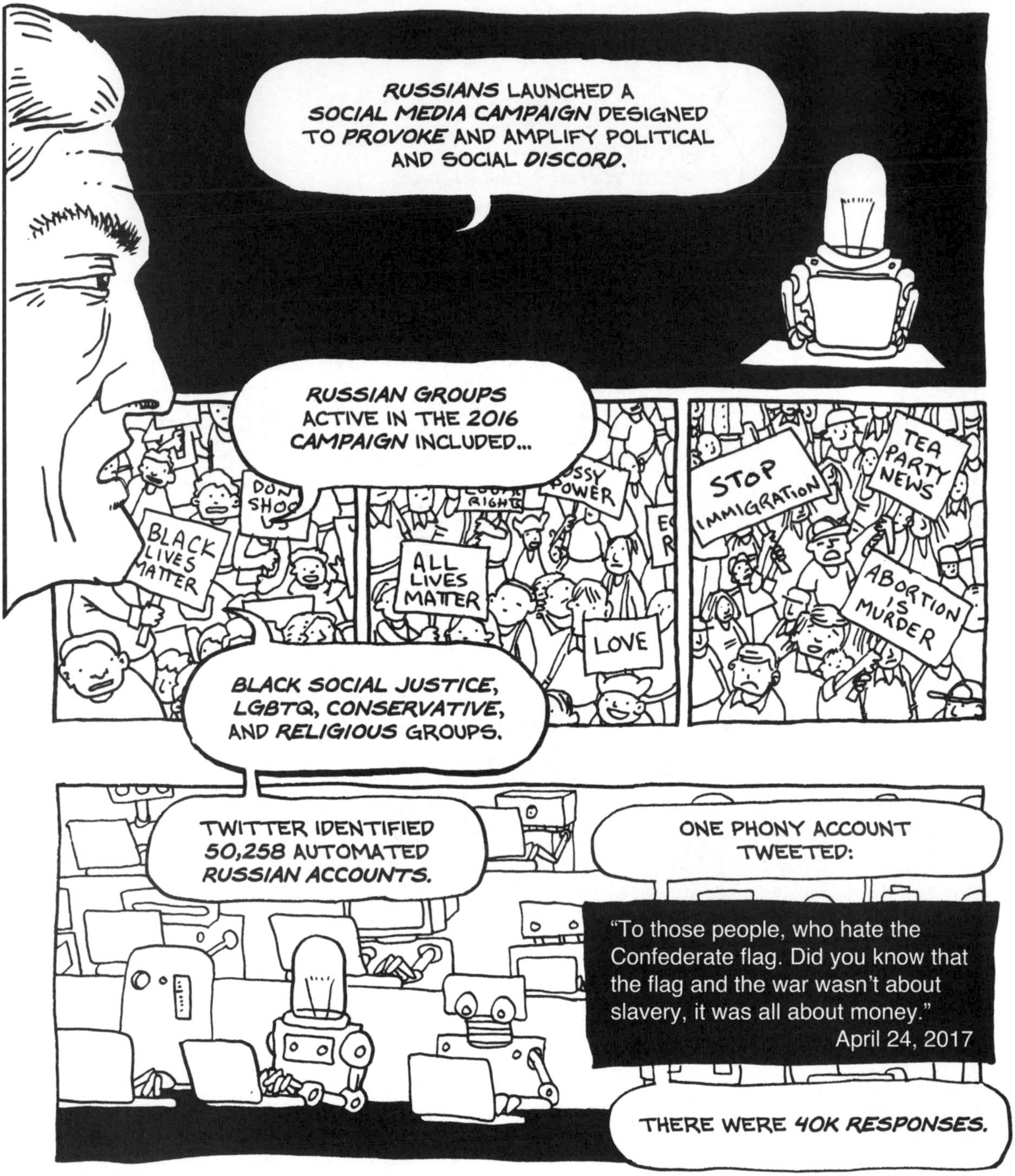
RUSSIANS LAUNCHED A SOCIAL MEDIA CAMPAIGN DESIGNED TO PROVOKE AND AMPLIFY POLITICAL AND SOCIAL DISCORD.
RUSSIAN GROUPS ACTIVE IN THE 2016 CAMPAIGN INCLUDED...
BLACK LIVES MATTER
ALL LIVES MATTER
LOVE
STOP IMMIGRATION
TEA PARTY NEWS
ABORTION IS MURDER
BLACK SOCIAL JUSTICE, LGBTQ, CONSERVATIVE, AND RELIGIOUS GROUPS.
TWITTER IDENTIFIED 50,258 AUTOMATED RUSSIAN ACCOUNTS.
ONE PHONY ACCOUNT TWEETED:
"To those people, who hate the Confederate flag. Did you know that the flag and the war wasn't about slavery, it was all about money."
April 24, 2017
THERE WERE 40K RESPONSES.

vol 1, pg 4, 24-25, 27, 29, footnote 70, 80

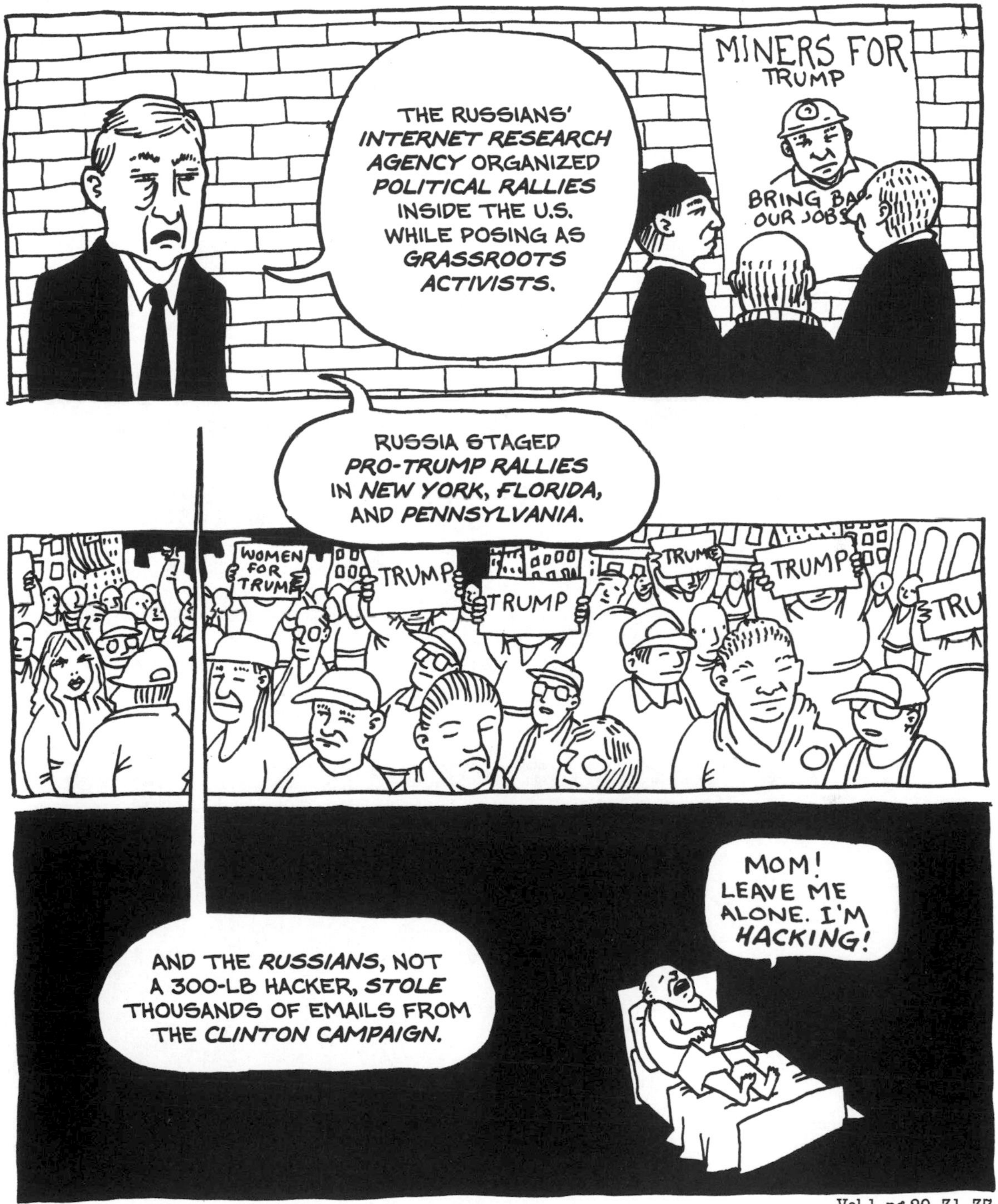
MINERS FOR TRUMP
THE RUSSIANS' *INTERNET RESEARCH AGENCY* ORGANIZED *POLITICAL RALLIES* INSIDE THE U.S. WHILE POSING AS *GRASSROOTS ACTIVISTS*.
RUSSIA STAGED *PRO-TRUMP RALLIES* IN *NEW YORK*, *FLORIDA*, AND *PENNSYLVANIA*.
WOMEN FOR TRUMP
TRUMP
TRUMP
TRUMP
AND THE *RUSSIANS*, NOT A 300-LB HACKER, *STOLE* THOUSANDS OF EMAILS FROM THE *CLINTON CAMPAIGN*.
MOM! LEAVE ME ALONE. I'M *HACKING*!

Vol 1, pg 29, 31, 37

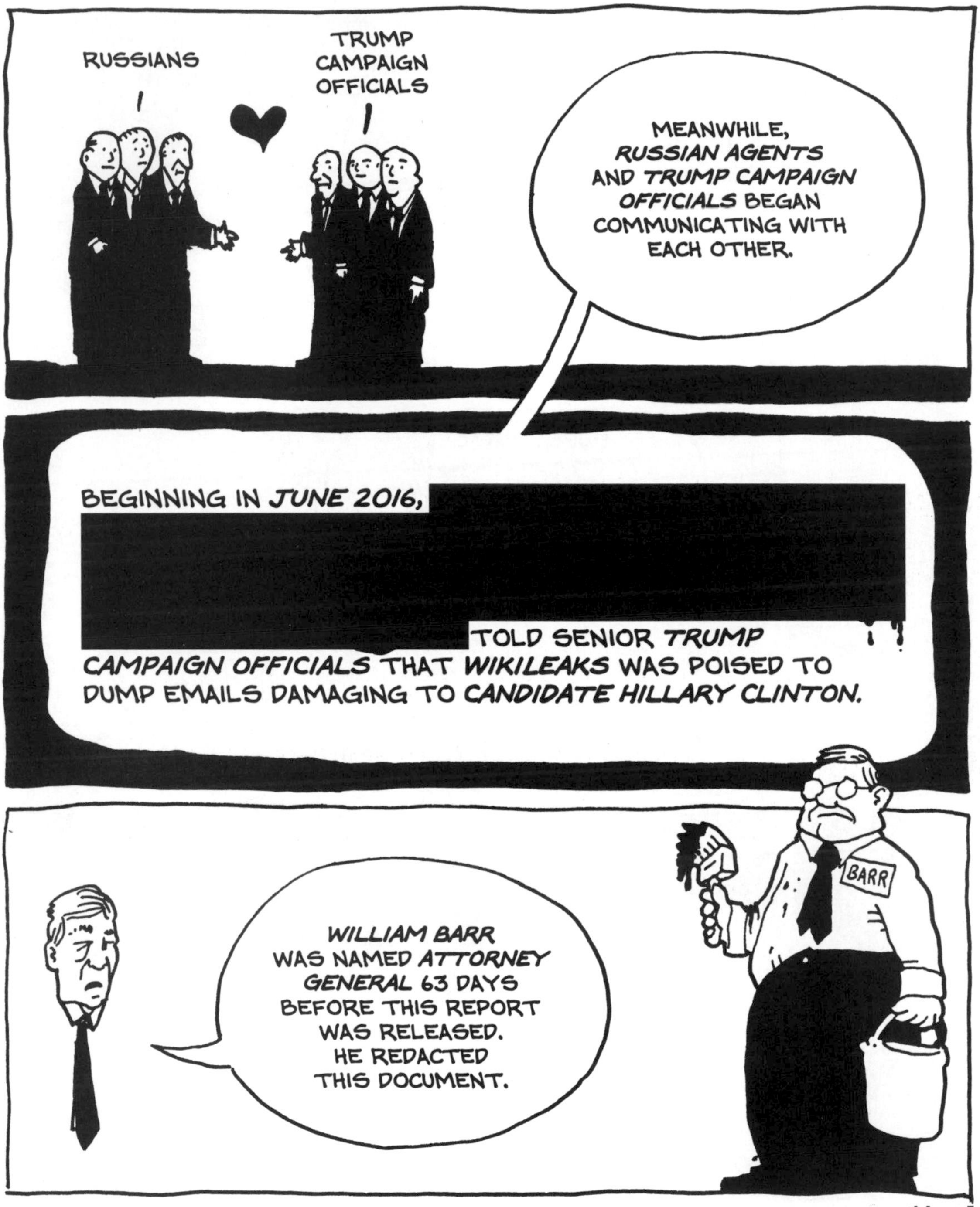
RUSSIANS
TRUMP CAMPAIGN OFFICIALS
MEANWHILE, RUSSIAN AGENTS AND TRUMP CAMPAIGN OFFICIALS BEGAN COMMUNICATING WITH EACH OTHER.
BEGINNING IN JUNE 2016, [redacted] TOLD SENIOR TRUMP CAMPAIGN OFFICIALS THAT WIKILEAKS WAS POISED TO DUMP EMAILS DAMAGING TO CANDIDATE HILLARY CLINTON.
WILLIAM BARR WAS NAMED ATTORNEY GENERAL 63 DAYS BEFORE THIS REPORT WAS RELEASED. HE REDACTED THIS DOCUMENT.
BARR

vol 1, pg 5

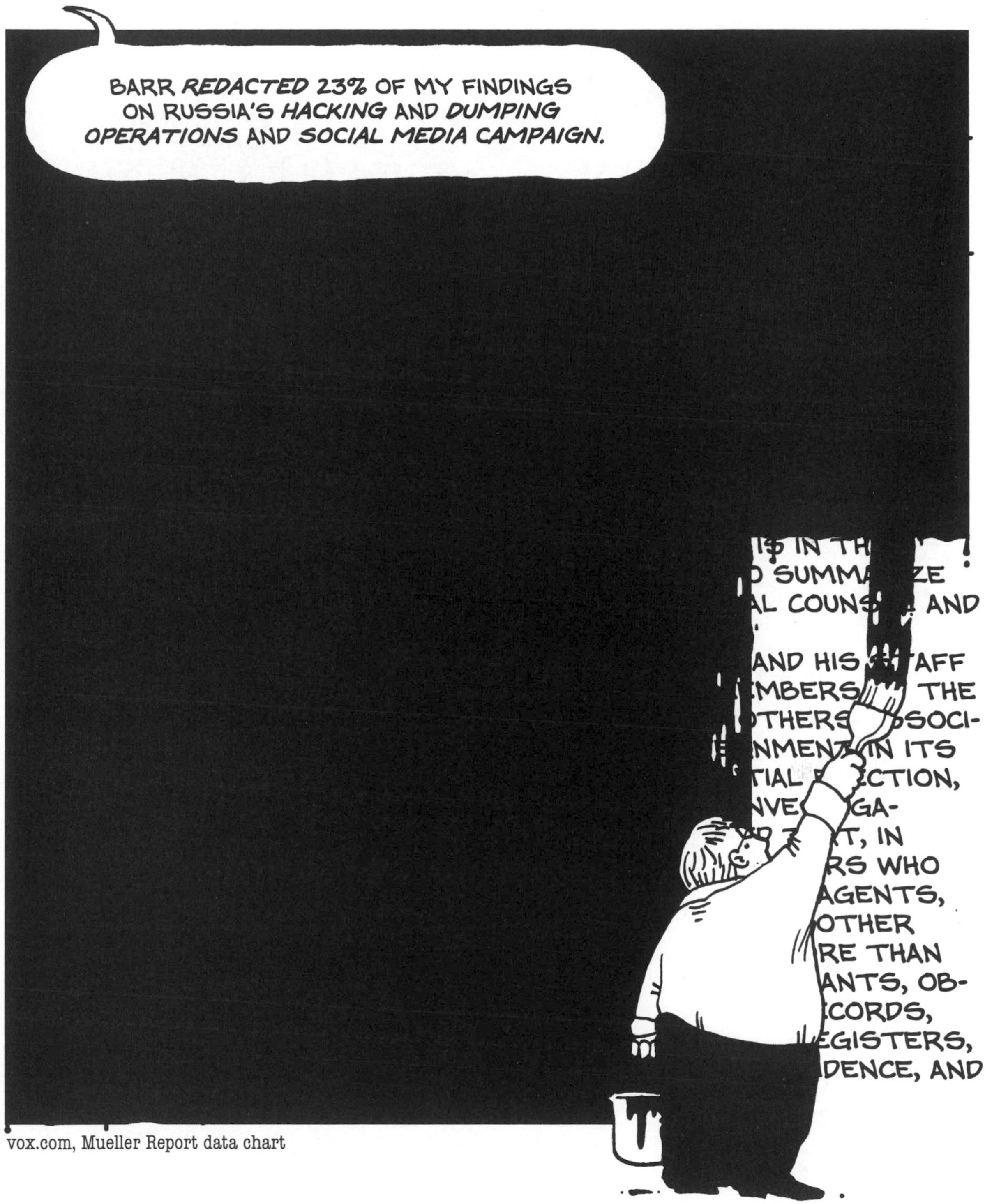

vox.com, Mueller Report data chart

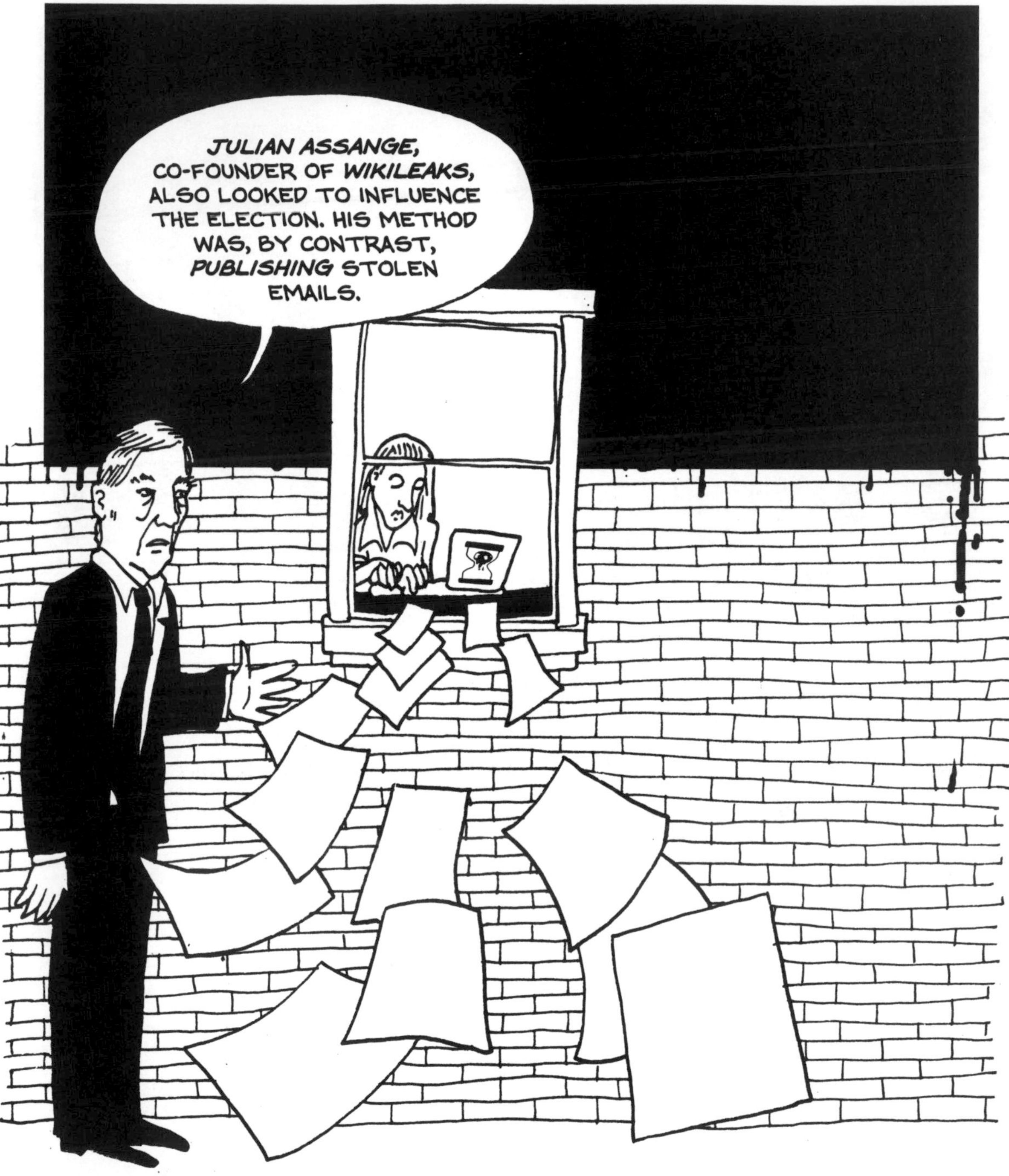
JULIAN ASSANGE, CO-FOUNDER OF WIKILEAKS, ALSO LOOKED TO INFLUENCE THE ELECTION. HIS METHOD WAS, BY CONTRAST, PUBLISHING STOLEN EMAILS.

Wikileaks: Publisher of leaked, anonymously sourced "news" vol 1, pg 44

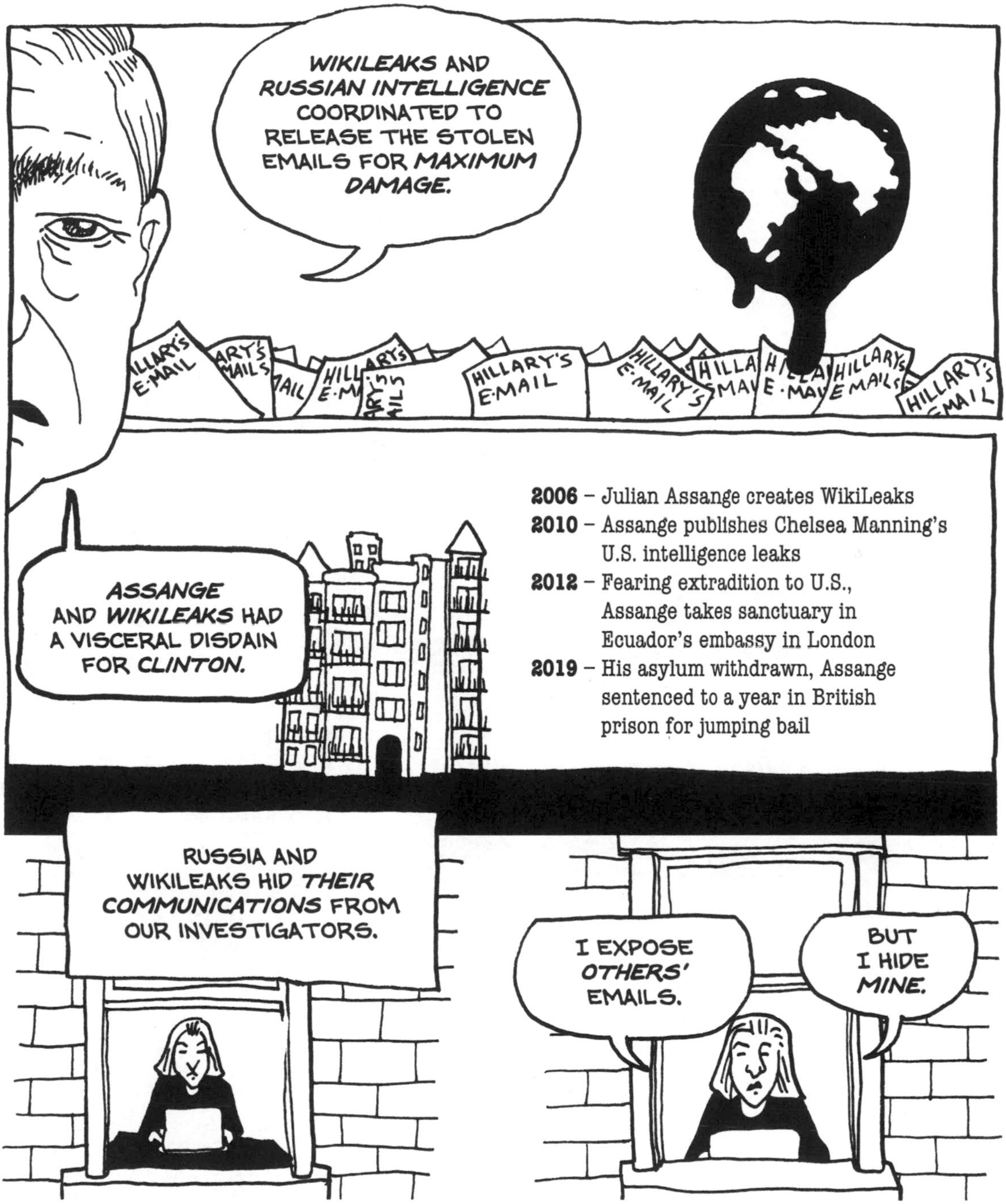
WIKILEAKS AND RUSSIAN INTELLIGENCE COORDINATED TO RELEASE THE STOLEN EMAILS FOR MAXIMUM DAMAGE.
HILLARY'S E-MAIL
ASSANGE AND WIKILEAKS HAD A VISCERAL DISDAIN FOR CLINTON.
2006 – Julian Assange creates WikiLeaks
2010 – Assange publishes Chelsea Manning's U.S. intelligence leaks
2012 – Fearing extradition to U.S., Assange takes sanctuary in Ecuador's embassy in London
2019 – His asylum withdrawn, Assange sentenced to a year in British prison for jumping bail
RUSSIA AND WIKILEAKS HID THEIR COMMUNICATIONS FROM OUR INVESTIGATORS.
I EXPOSE OTHERS' EMAILS.
BUT I HIDE MINE.

vol 1, pg 45, footnote 158

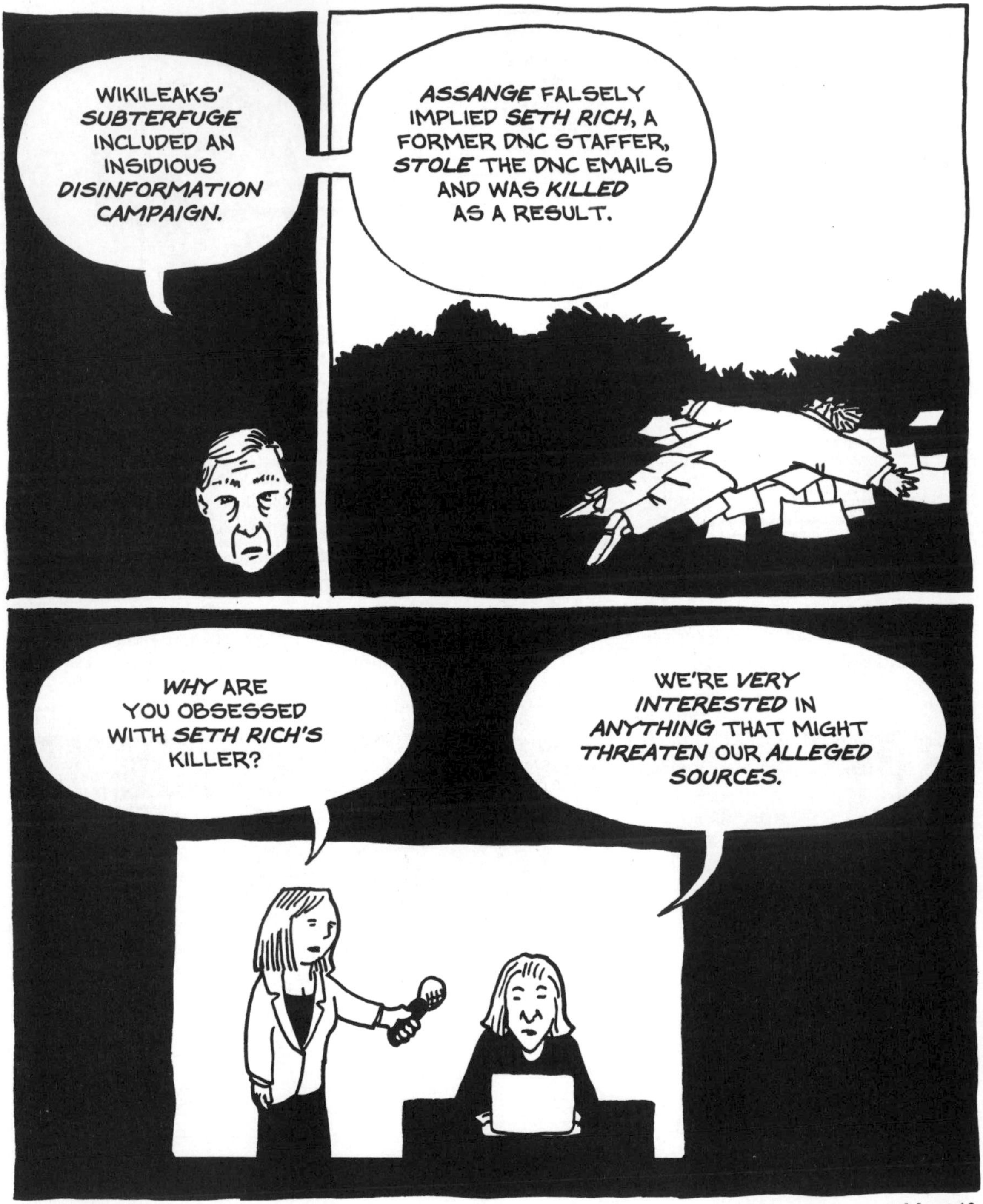
WIKILEAKS' SUBTERFUGE INCLUDED AN INSIDIOUS DISINFORMATION CAMPAIGN.
ASSANGE FALSELY IMPLIED SETH RICH, A FORMER DNC STAFFER, STOLE THE DNC EMAILS AND WAS KILLED AS A RESULT.
WHY ARE YOU OBSESSED WITH SETH RICH'S KILLER?
WE'RE VERY INTERESTED IN ANYTHING THAT MIGHT THREATEN OUR ALLEGED SOURCES.

vol 1, pg 48

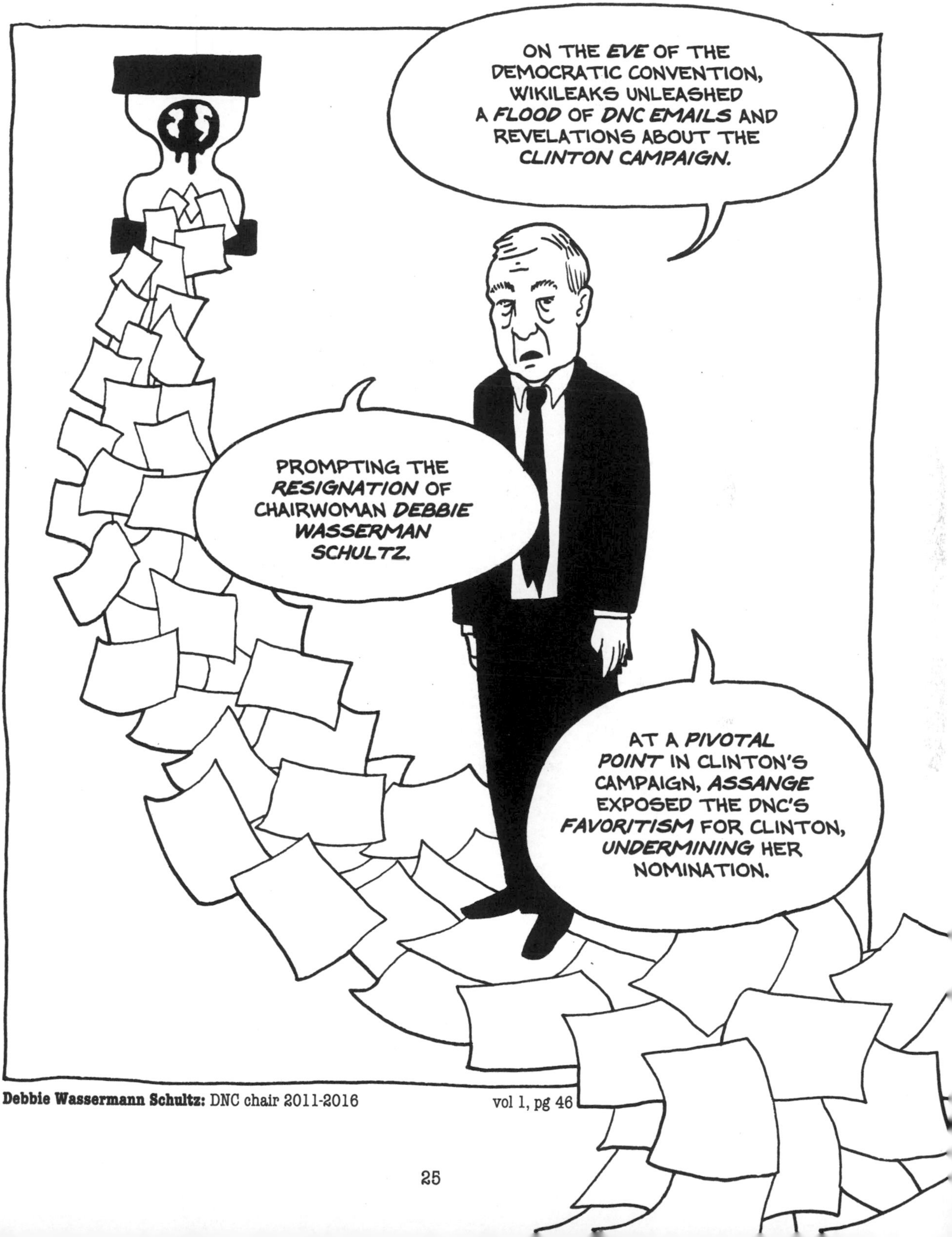
ON THE EVE OF THE DEMOCRATIC CONVENTION, WIKILEAKS UNLEASHED A FLOOD OF DNC EMAILS AND REVELATIONS ABOUT THE CLINTON CAMPAIGN.
PROMPTING THE RESIGNATION OF CHAIRWOMAN DEBBIE WASSERMAN SCHULTZ.
AT A PIVOTAL POINT IN CLINTON'S CAMPAIGN, ASSANGE EXPOSED THE DNC'S FAVORITISM FOR CLINTON, UNDERMINING HER NOMINATION.

Debbie Wassermann Schultz: DNC chair 2011-2016 vol 1, pg 46

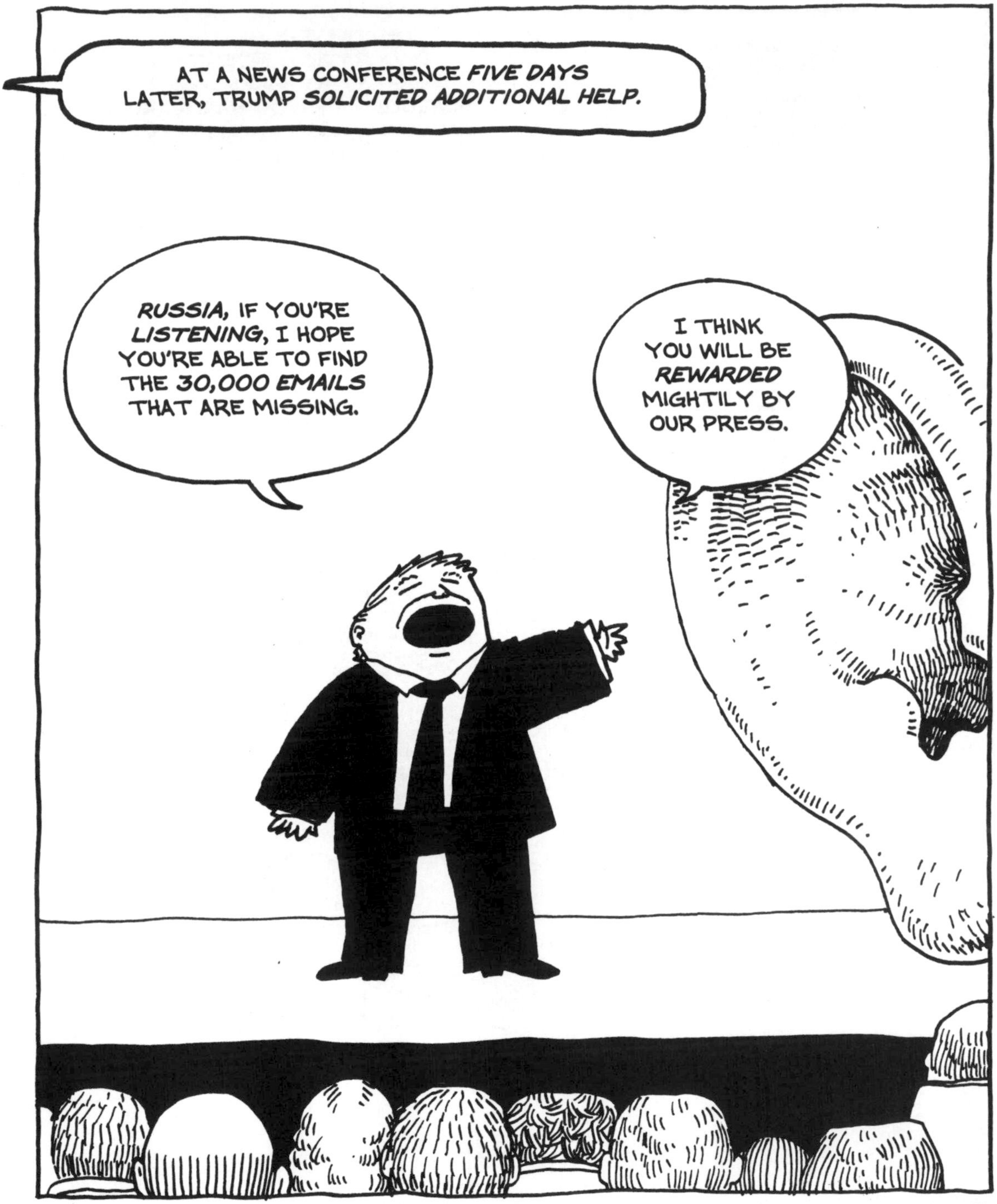
AT A NEWS CONFERENCE FIVE DAYS LATER, TRUMP SOLICITED ADDITIONAL HELP.
RUSSIA, IF YOU'RE LISTENING, I HOPE YOU'RE ABLE TO FIND THE 30,000 EMAILS THAT ARE MISSING.
I THINK YOU WILL BE REWARDED MIGHTILY BY OUR PRESS.

vol 1, pg 62

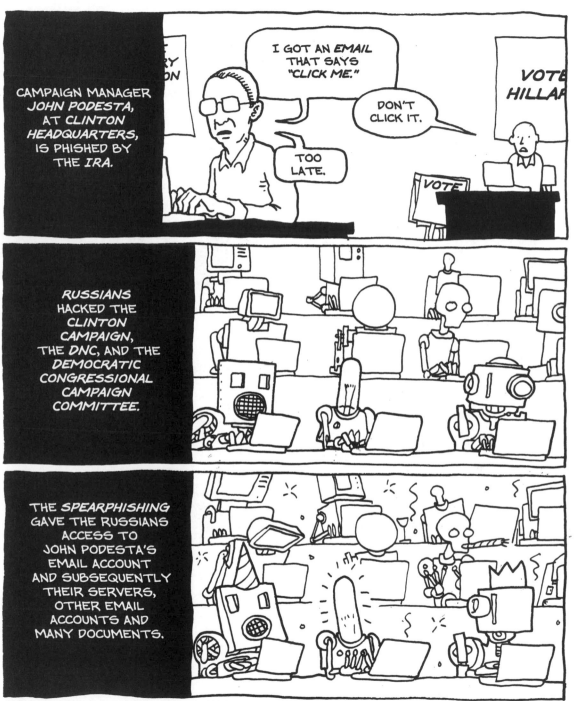

CAMPAIGN MANAGER *JOHN PODESTA*, AT *CLINTON HEADQUARTERS*, IS PHISHED BY THE *IRA*.

I GOT AN *EMAIL* THAT SAYS "CLICK ME."

DON'T CLICK IT.

TOO LATE.

RUSSIANS HACKED THE *CLINTON CAMPAIGN*, THE *DNC*, AND THE *DEMOCRATIC CONGRESSIONAL CAMPAIGN COMMITTEE*.

THE *SPEARPHISHING* GAVE THE RUSSIANS ACCESS TO JOHN PODESTA'S EMAIL ACCOUNT AND SUBSEQUENTLY THEIR SERVERS, OTHER EMAIL ACCOUNTS AND MANY DOCUMENTS.

John Podesta: Chairman of Hillary Clinton's 2016 presidential campaign
IRA: Internet Research Agency, based in Russia

vol 1, pg 37, 40

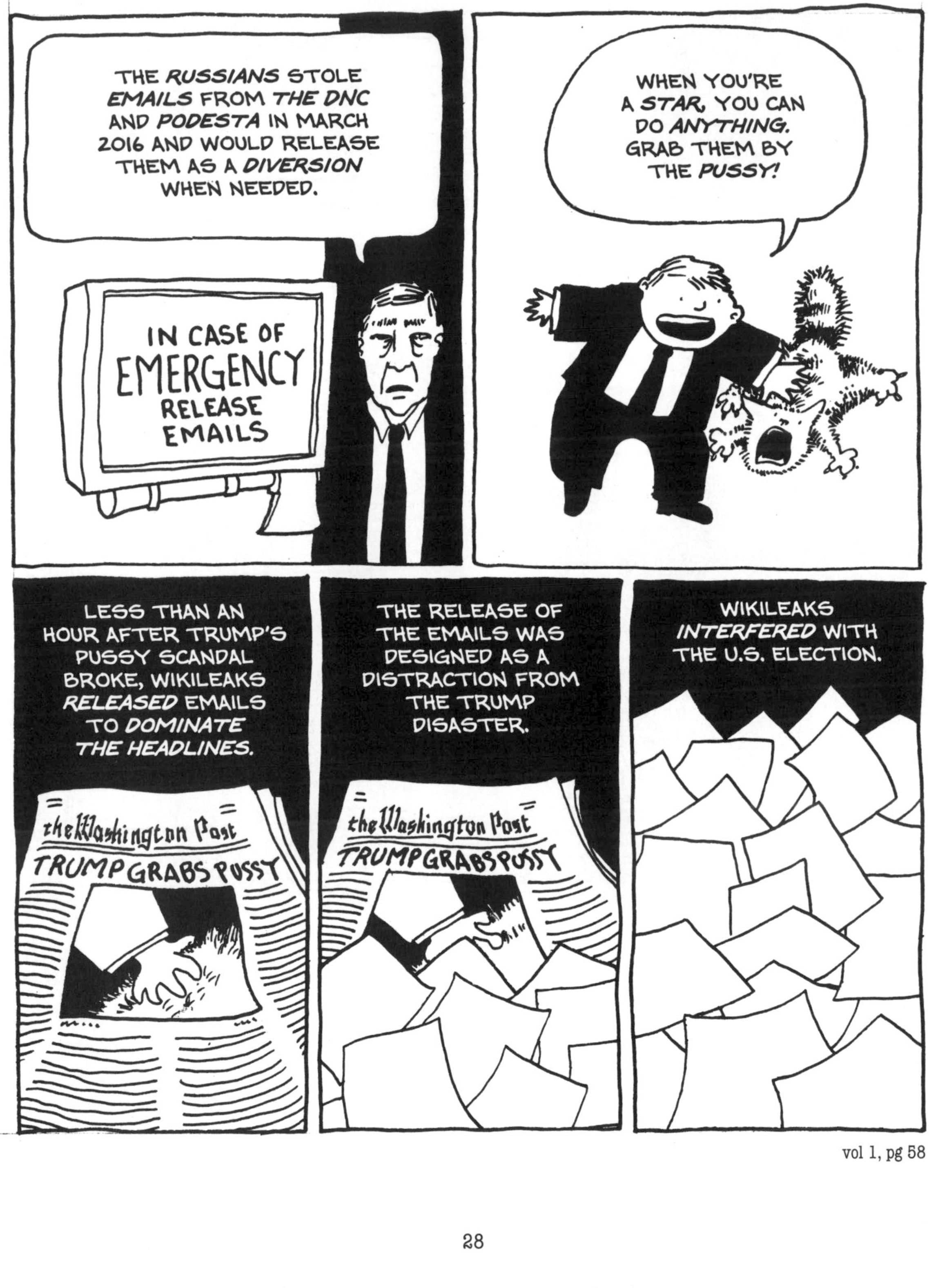
THE RUSSIANS STOLE EMAILS FROM THE DNC AND PODESTA IN MARCH 2016 AND WOULD RELEASE THEM AS A DIVERSION WHEN NEEDED.
IN CASE OF EMERGENCY RELEASE EMAILS
WHEN YOU'RE A STAR, YOU CAN DO ANYTHING. GRAB THEM BY THE PUSSY!
LESS THAN AN HOUR AFTER TRUMP'S PUSSY SCANDAL BROKE, WIKILEAKS RELEASED EMAILS TO DOMINATE THE HEADLINES.
the Washington Post
TRUMP GRABS PUSSY
THE RELEASE OF THE EMAILS WAS DESIGNED AS A DISTRACTION FROM THE TRUMP DISASTER.
the Washington Post
TRUMP GRABS PUSSY
WIKILEAKS INTERFERED WITH THE U.S. ELECTION.

vol 1, pg 58

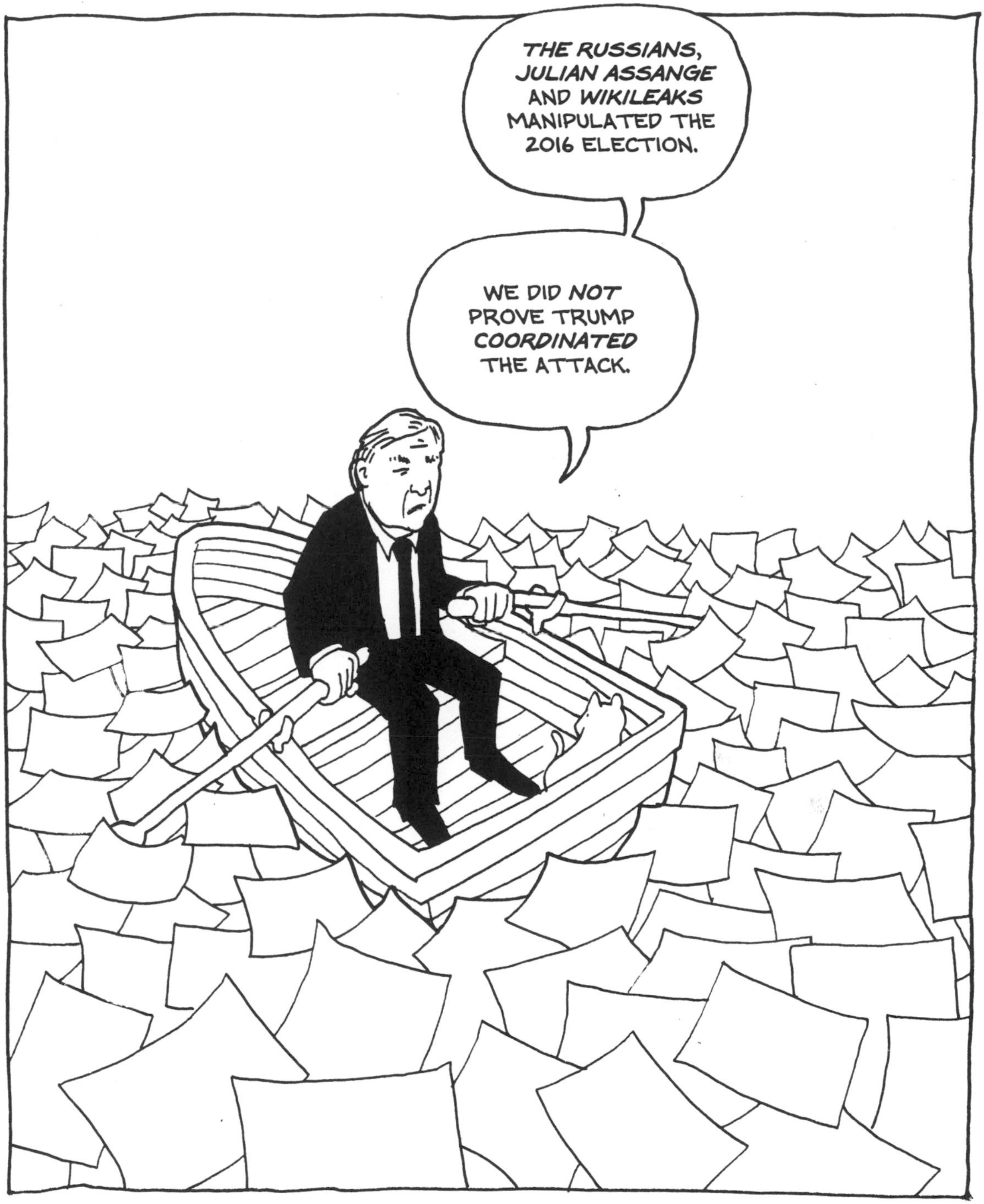

THE RUSSIANS, JULIAN ASSANGE AND *WIKILEAKS* MANIPULATED THE 2016 ELECTION.
WE DID *NOT* PROVE TRUMP *COORDINATED* THE ATTACK.

vol 1, pg 59

CHAPTER 3

RUSSIAN OUTREACH

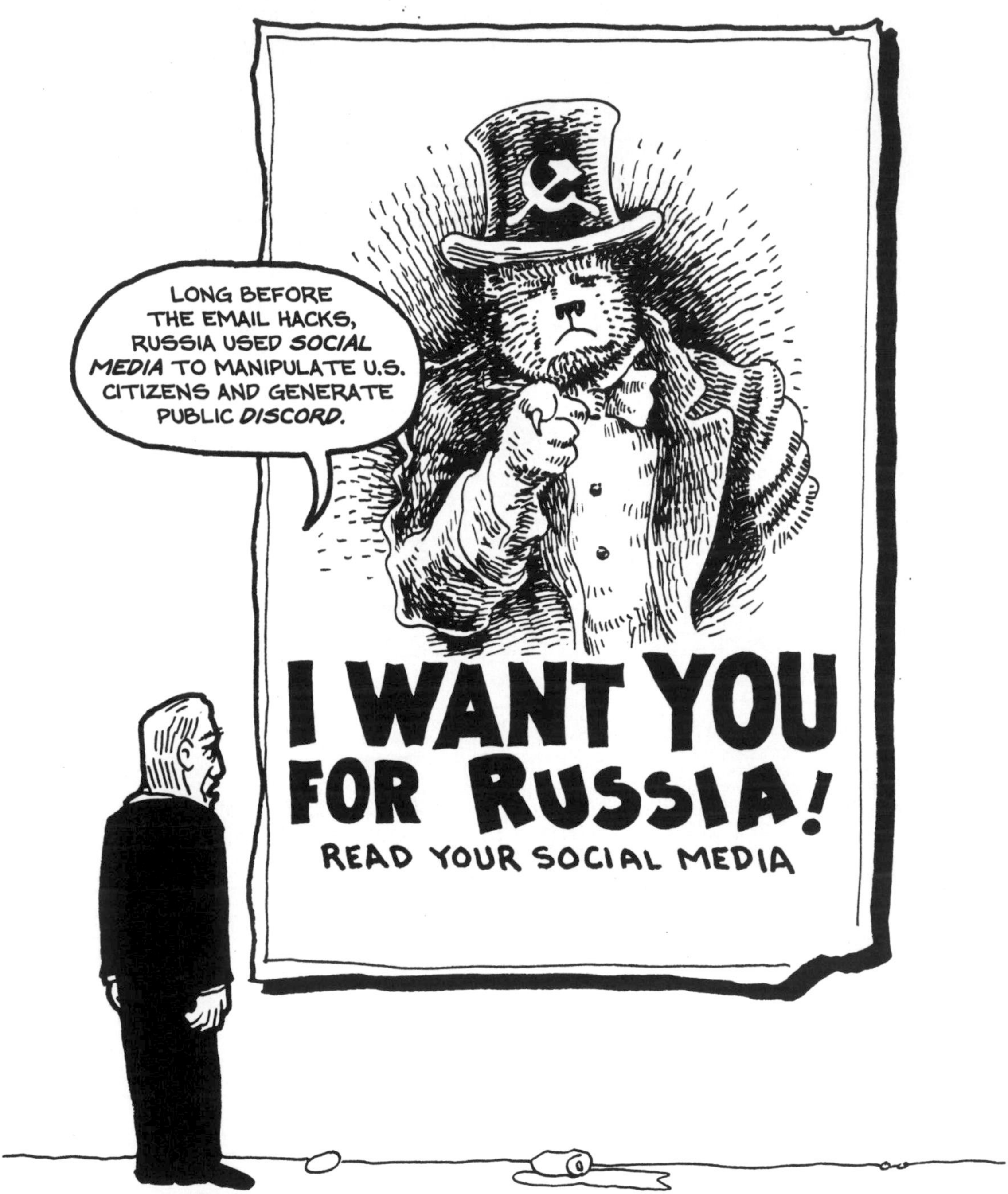
LONG BEFORE THE EMAIL HACKS, RUSSIA USED *SOCIAL MEDIA* TO MANIPULATE U.S. CITIZENS AND GENERATE PUBLIC *DISCORD.*
I WANT YOU FOR RUSSIA!
READ YOUR SOCIAL MEDIA

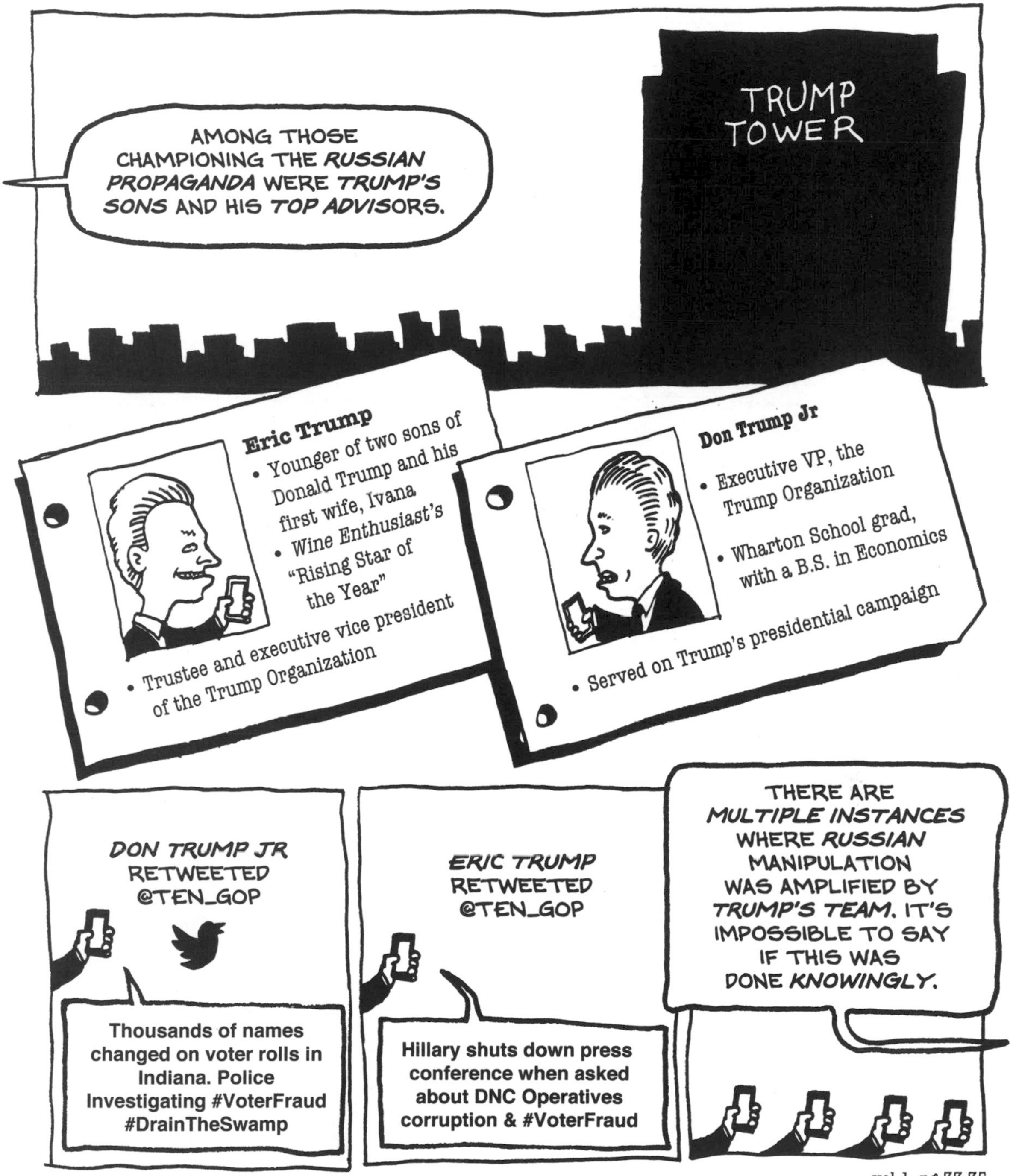
AMONG THOSE CHAMPIONING THE *RUSSIAN PROPAGANDA* WERE *TRUMP'S SONS* AND HIS *TOP ADVISORS*.
TRUMP TOWER
Eric Trump
• Younger of two sons of Donald Trump and his first wife, Ivana
• Wine Enthusiast's "Rising Star of the Year"
• Trustee and executive vice president of the Trump Organization
Don Trump Jr
• Executive VP, the Trump Organization
• Wharton School grad, with a B.S. in Economics
• Served on Trump's presidential campaign
DON TRUMP JR RETWEETED @TEN_GOP
Thousands of names changed on voter rolls in Indiana. Police Investigating #VoterFraud #DrainTheSwamp
ERIC TRUMP RETWEETED @TEN_GOP
Hillary shuts down press conference when asked about DNC Operatives corruption & #VoterFraud
THERE ARE *MULTIPLE INSTANCES* WHERE *RUSSIAN* MANIPULATION WAS AMPLIFIED BY *TRUMP'S TEAM*. IT'S IMPOSSIBLE TO SAY IF THIS WAS DONE *KNOWINGLY*.

vol 1, pg 33-35

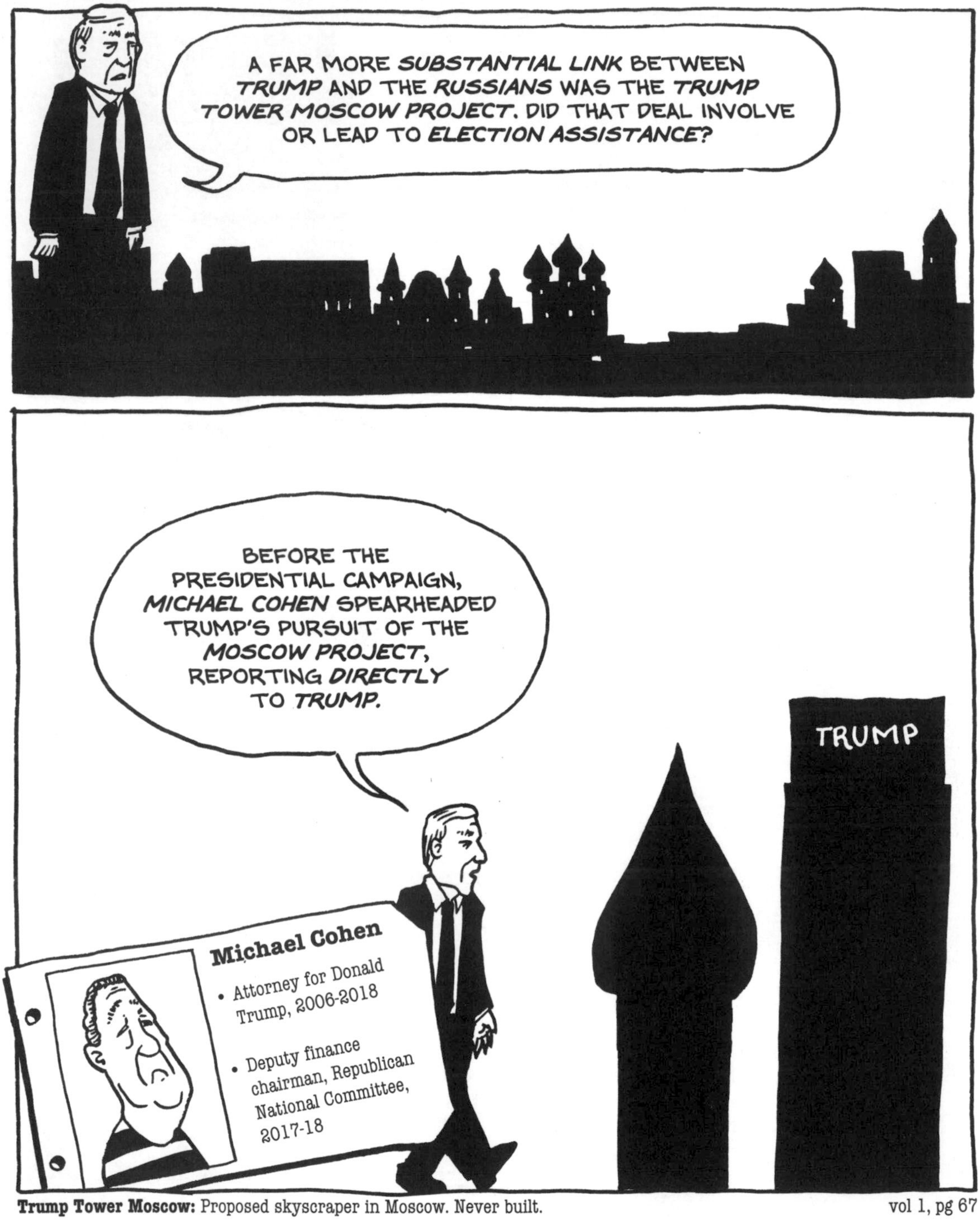
A FAR MORE SUBSTANTIAL LINK BETWEEN TRUMP AND THE RUSSIANS WAS THE TRUMP TOWER MOSCOW PROJECT. DID THAT DEAL INVOLVE OR LEAD TO ELECTION ASSISTANCE?
BEFORE THE PRESIDENTIAL CAMPAIGN, MICHAEL COHEN SPEARHEADED TRUMP'S PURSUIT OF THE MOSCOW PROJECT, REPORTING DIRECTLY TO TRUMP.
TRUMP
Michael Cohen
• Attorney for Donald Trump, 2006-2018
• Deputy finance chairman, Republican National Committee, 2017-18

Trump Tower Moscow: Proposed skyscraper in Moscow. Never built. vol 1, pg 67

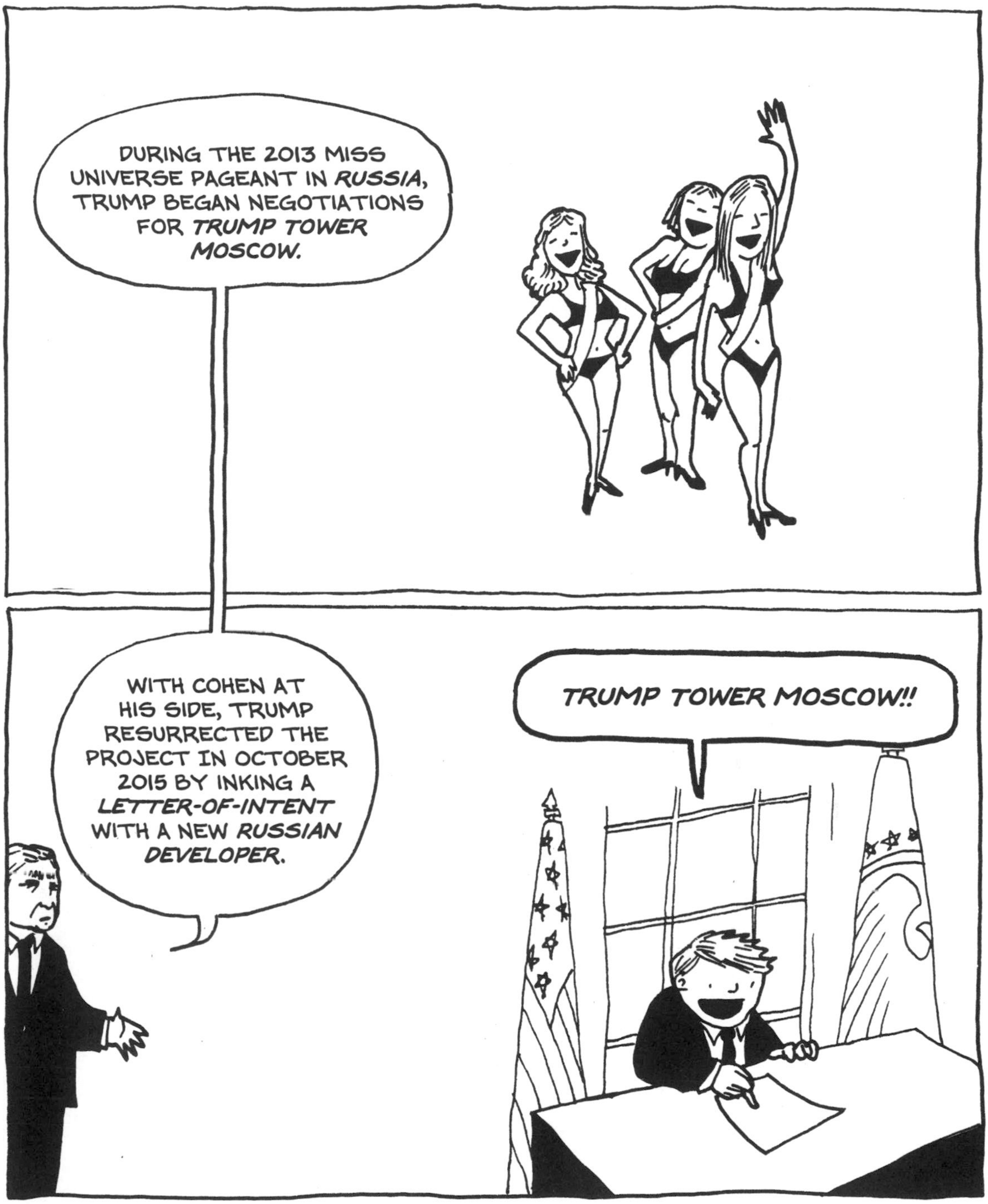
DURING THE 2013 MISS UNIVERSE PAGEANT IN *RUSSIA*, TRUMP BEGAN NEGOTIATIONS FOR *TRUMP TOWER MOSCOW.*
WITH COHEN AT HIS SIDE, TRUMP RESURRECTED THE PROJECT IN OCTOBER 2015 BY INKING A *LETTER-OF-INTENT* WITH A NEW *RUSSIAN DEVELOPER*.
TRUMP TOWER MOSCOW!!

vol 1, pg 67, 70

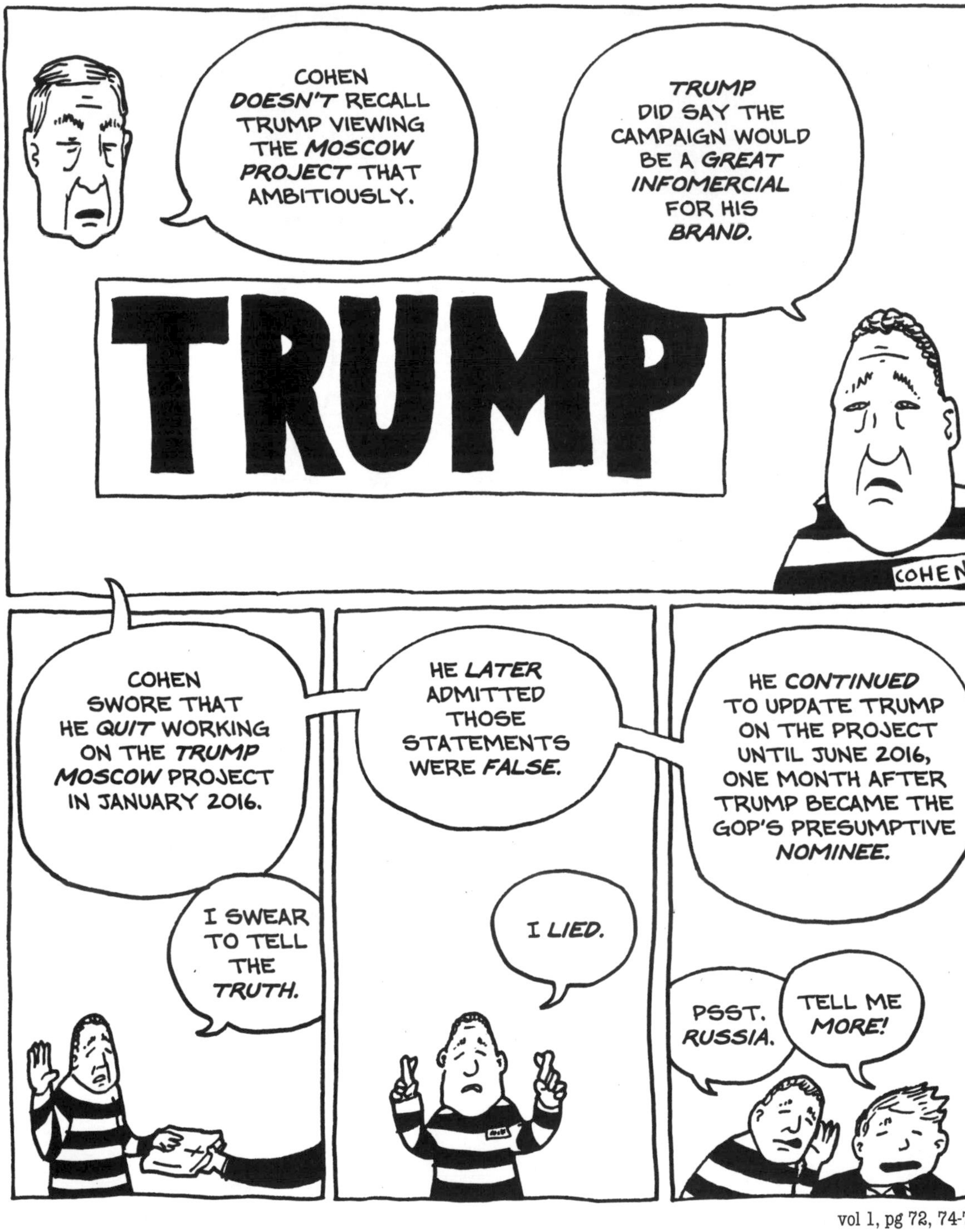
COHEN DOESN'T RECALL TRUMP VIEWING THE MOSCOW PROJECT THAT AMBITIOUSLY.
TRUMP DID SAY THE CAMPAIGN WOULD BE A GREAT INFOMERCIAL FOR HIS BRAND.
TRUMP
COHEN
COHEN SWORE THAT HE QUIT WORKING ON THE TRUMP MOSCOW PROJECT IN JANUARY 2016.
I SWEAR TO TELL THE TRUTH.
HE LATER ADMITTED THOSE STATEMENTS WERE FALSE.
I LIED.
HE CONTINUED TO UPDATE TRUMP ON THE PROJECT UNTIL JUNE 2016, ONE MONTH AFTER TRUMP BECAME THE GOP'S PRESUMPTIVE NOMINEE.
PSST. RUSSIA.
TELL ME MORE!

vol 1, pg 72, 74-75

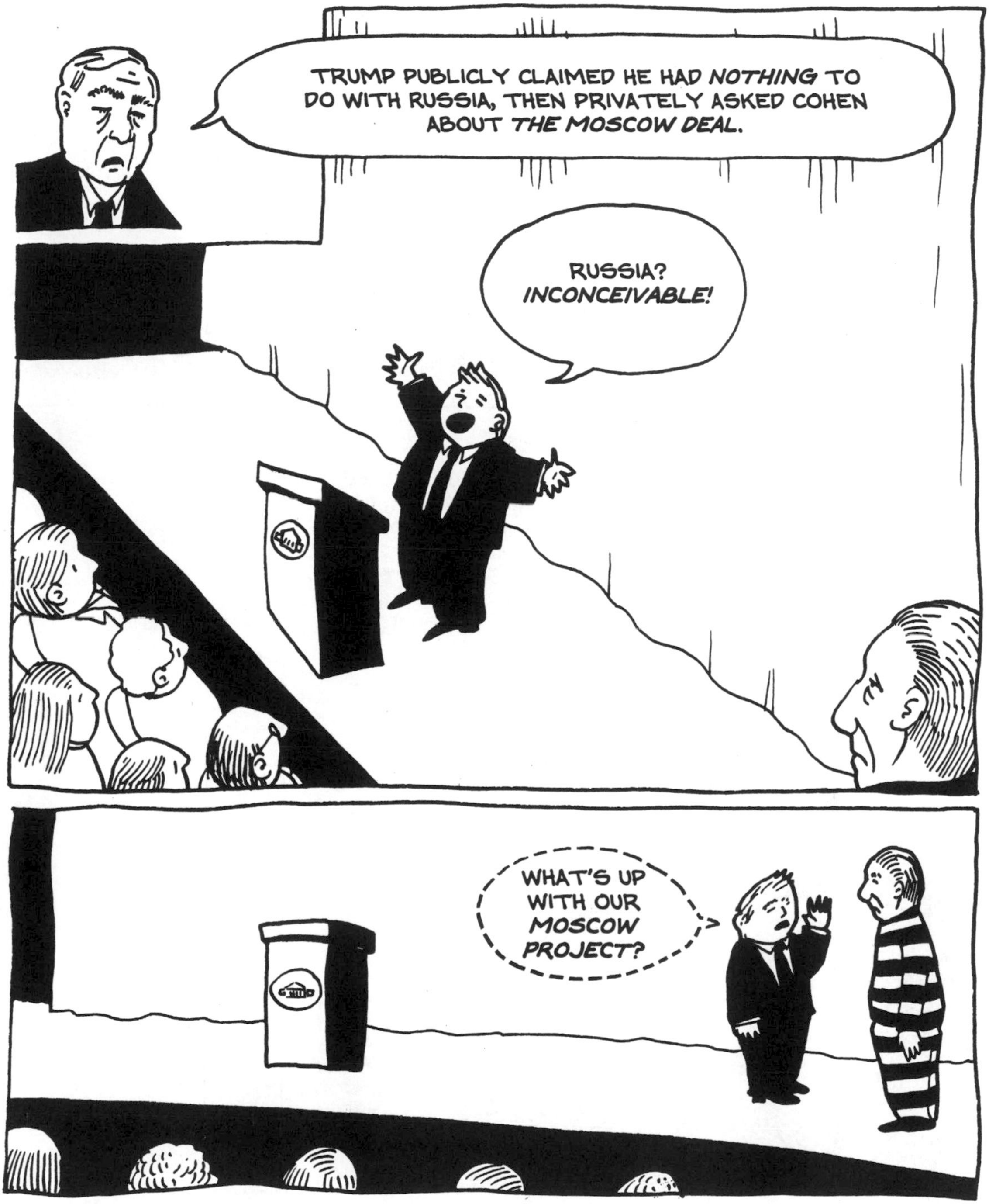
TRUMP PUBLICLY CLAIMED HE HAD NOTHING TO DO WITH RUSSIA, THEN PRIVATELY ASKED COHEN ABOUT THE MOSCOW DEAL.
RUSSIA? INCONCEIVABLE!
WHAT'S UP WITH OUR MOSCOW PROJECT?

vol 2, pg 137

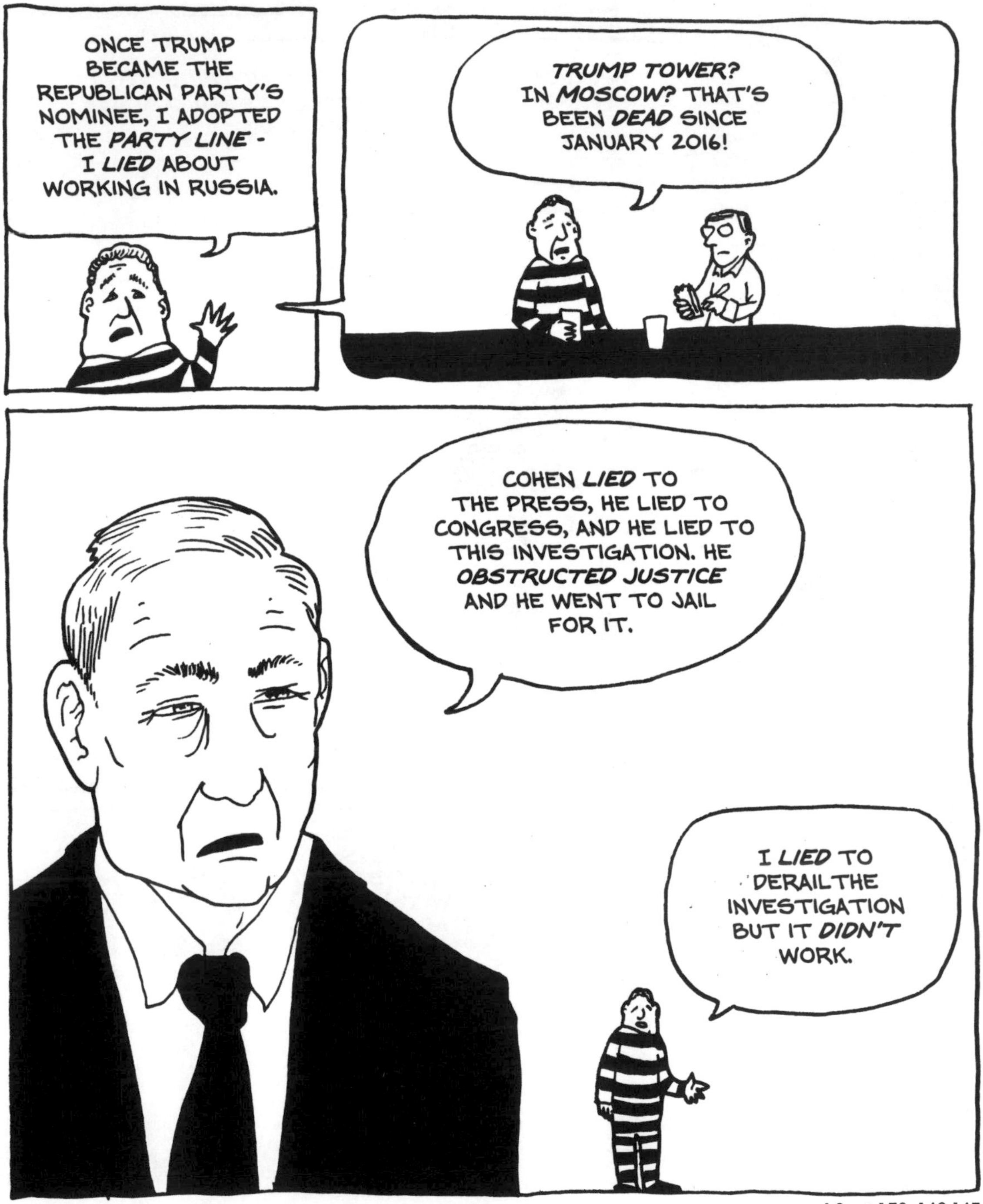
ONCE TRUMP BECAME THE REPUBLICAN PARTY'S NOMINEE, I ADOPTED THE *PARTY LINE* - I *LIED* ABOUT WORKING IN RUSSIA.
TRUMP TOWER? IN *MOSCOW?* THAT'S BEEN *DEAD* SINCE JANUARY 2016!
COHEN *LIED* TO THE PRESS, HE LIED TO CONGRESS, AND HE LIED TO THIS INVESTIGATION. HE *OBSTRUCTED JUSTICE* AND HE WENT TO JAIL FOR IT.
I *LIED* TO DERAIL THE INVESTIGATION BUT IT *DIDN'T* WORK.

vol 2, pg 138, 142-143

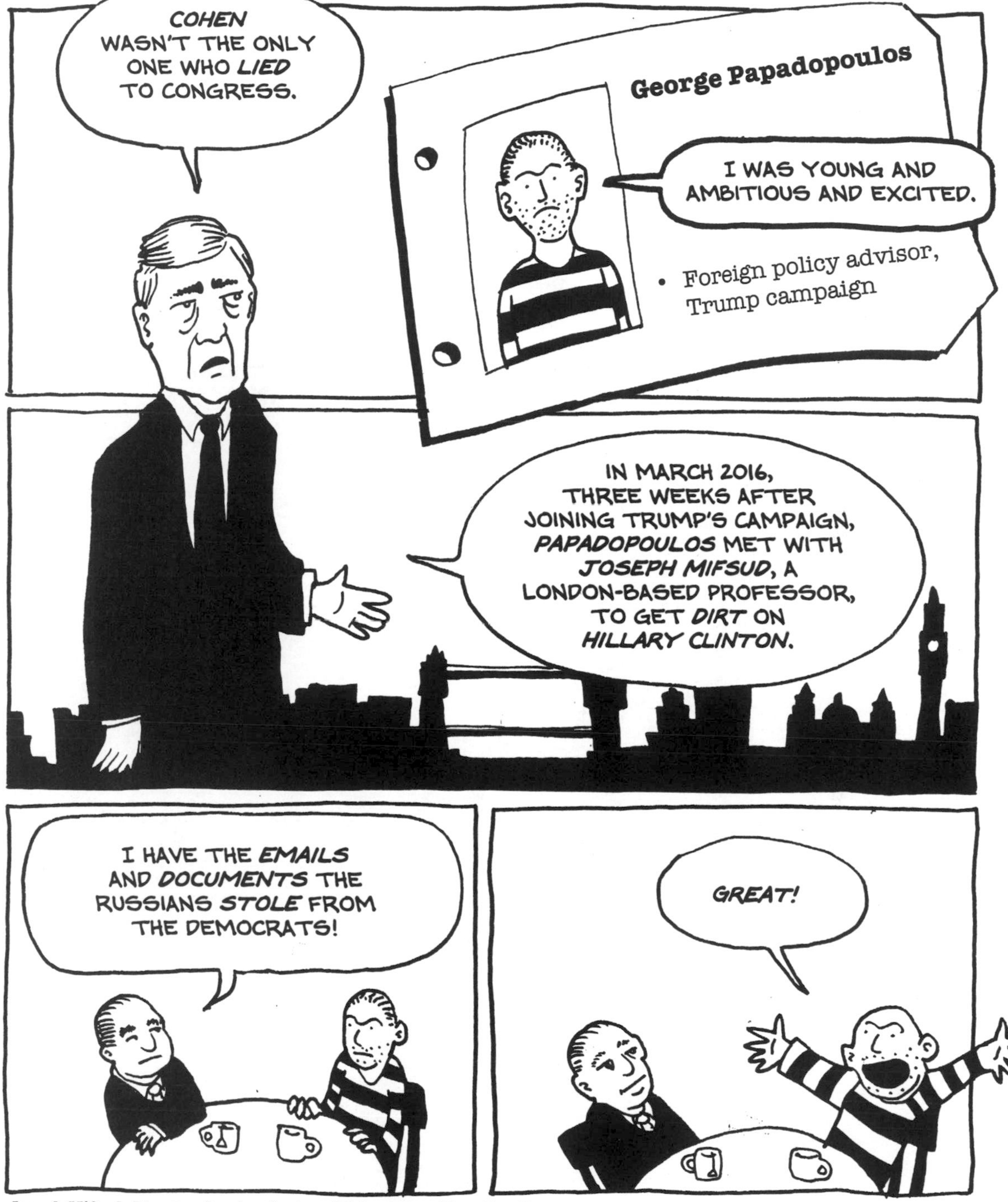
COHEN WASN'T THE ONLY ONE WHO LIED TO CONGRESS.
George Papadopoulos
I WAS YOUNG AND AMBITIOUS AND EXCITED.
• Foreign policy advisor, Trump campaign
IN MARCH 2016, THREE WEEKS AFTER JOINING TRUMP'S CAMPAIGN, PAPADOPOULOS MET WITH JOSEPH MIFSUD, A LONDON-BASED PROFESSOR, TO GET DIRT ON HILLARY CLINTON.
I HAVE THE EMAILS AND DOCUMENTS THE RUSSIANS STOLE FROM THE DEMOCRATS!
GREAT!

Joseph Mifsud: Director, London Center of International Law Practice

vol 1, pg 81

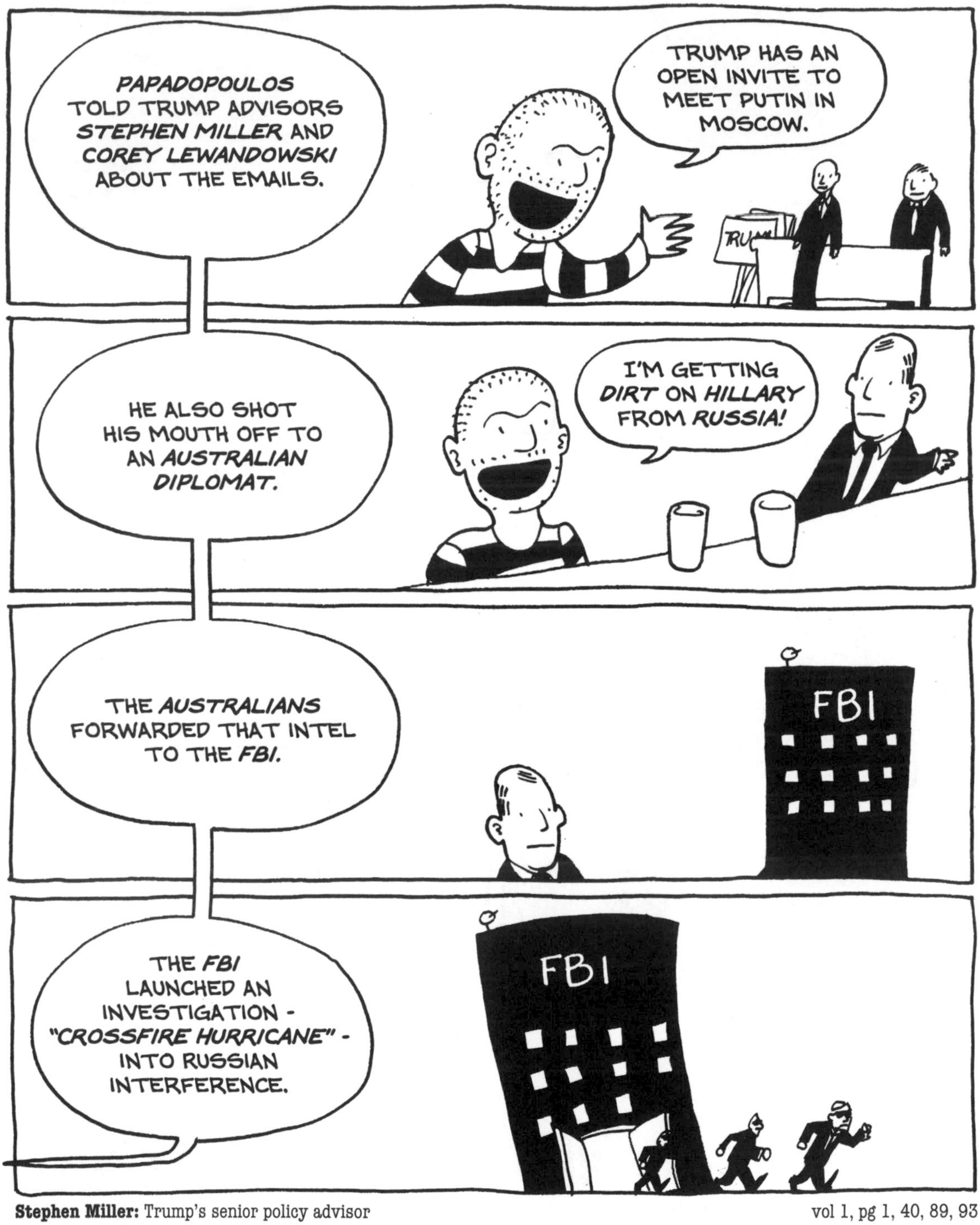
PAPADOPOULOS TOLD TRUMP ADVISORS STEPHEN MILLER AND COREY LEWANDOWSKI ABOUT THE EMAILS.
TRUMP HAS AN OPEN INVITE TO MEET PUTIN IN MOSCOW.
HE ALSO SHOT HIS MOUTH OFF TO AN AUSTRALIAN DIPLOMAT.
I'M GETTING DIRT ON HILLARY FROM RUSSIA!
THE AUSTRALIANS FORWARDED THAT INTEL TO THE FBI.
FBI
THE FBI LAUNCHED AN INVESTIGATION - "CROSSFIRE HURRICANE" - INTO RUSSIAN INTERFERENCE.
FBI

Stephen Miller: Trump's senior policy advisor
Corey Lewandowski: Trump's campaign manager, Jan 2015-Jun 2016

vol 1, pg 1, 40, 89, 93

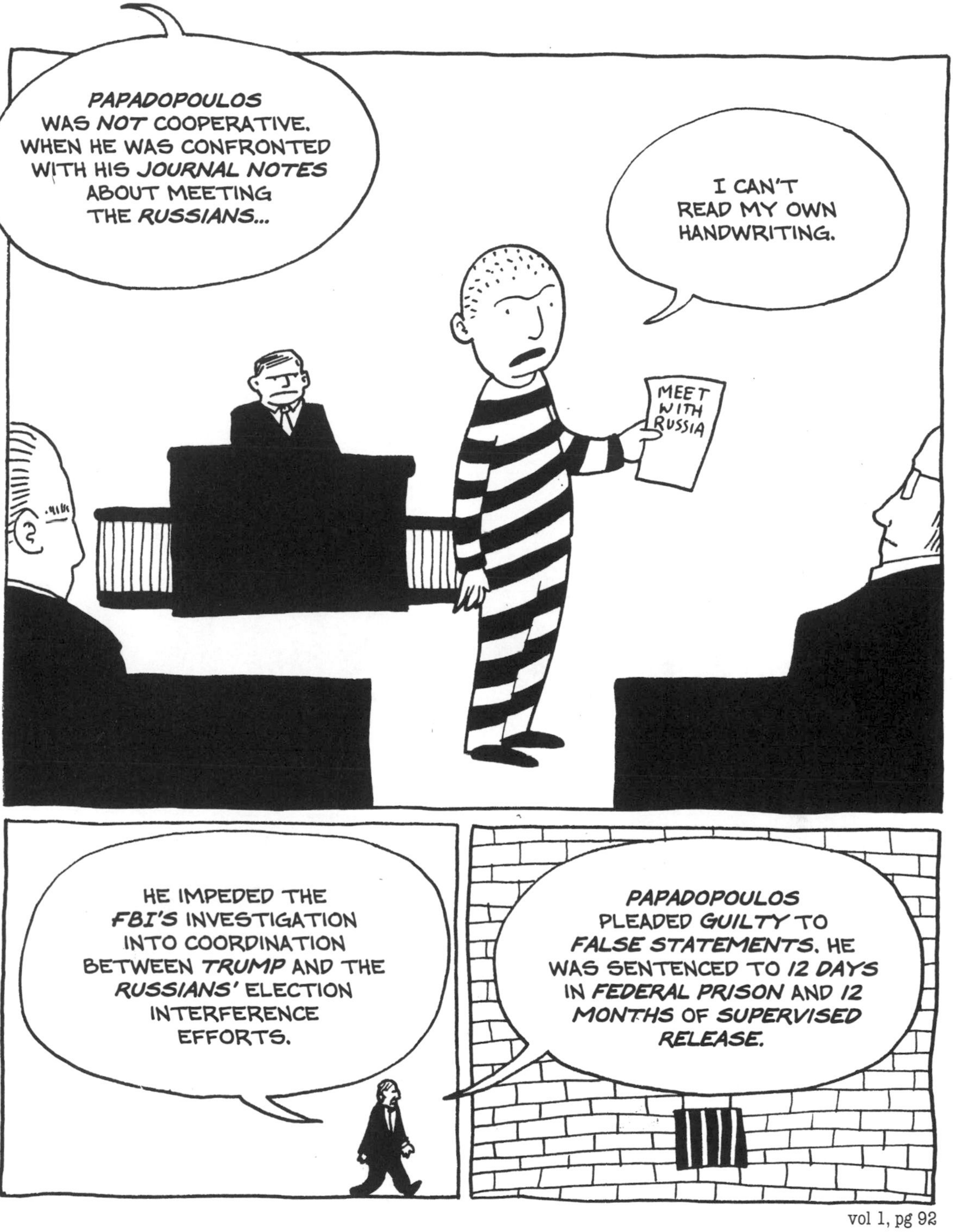
PAPADOPOULOS WAS NOT COOPERATIVE. WHEN HE WAS CONFRONTED WITH HIS JOURNAL NOTES ABOUT MEETING THE RUSSIANS...
I CAN'T READ MY OWN HANDWRITING.
MEET WITH RUSSIA
HE IMPEDED THE FBI'S INVESTIGATION INTO COORDINATION BETWEEN TRUMP AND THE RUSSIANS' ELECTION INTERFERENCE EFFORTS.
PAPADOPOULOS PLEADED GUILTY TO FALSE STATEMENTS. HE WAS SENTENCED TO 12 DAYS IN FEDERAL PRISON AND 12 MONTHS OF SUPERVISED RELEASE.

vol 1, pg 92

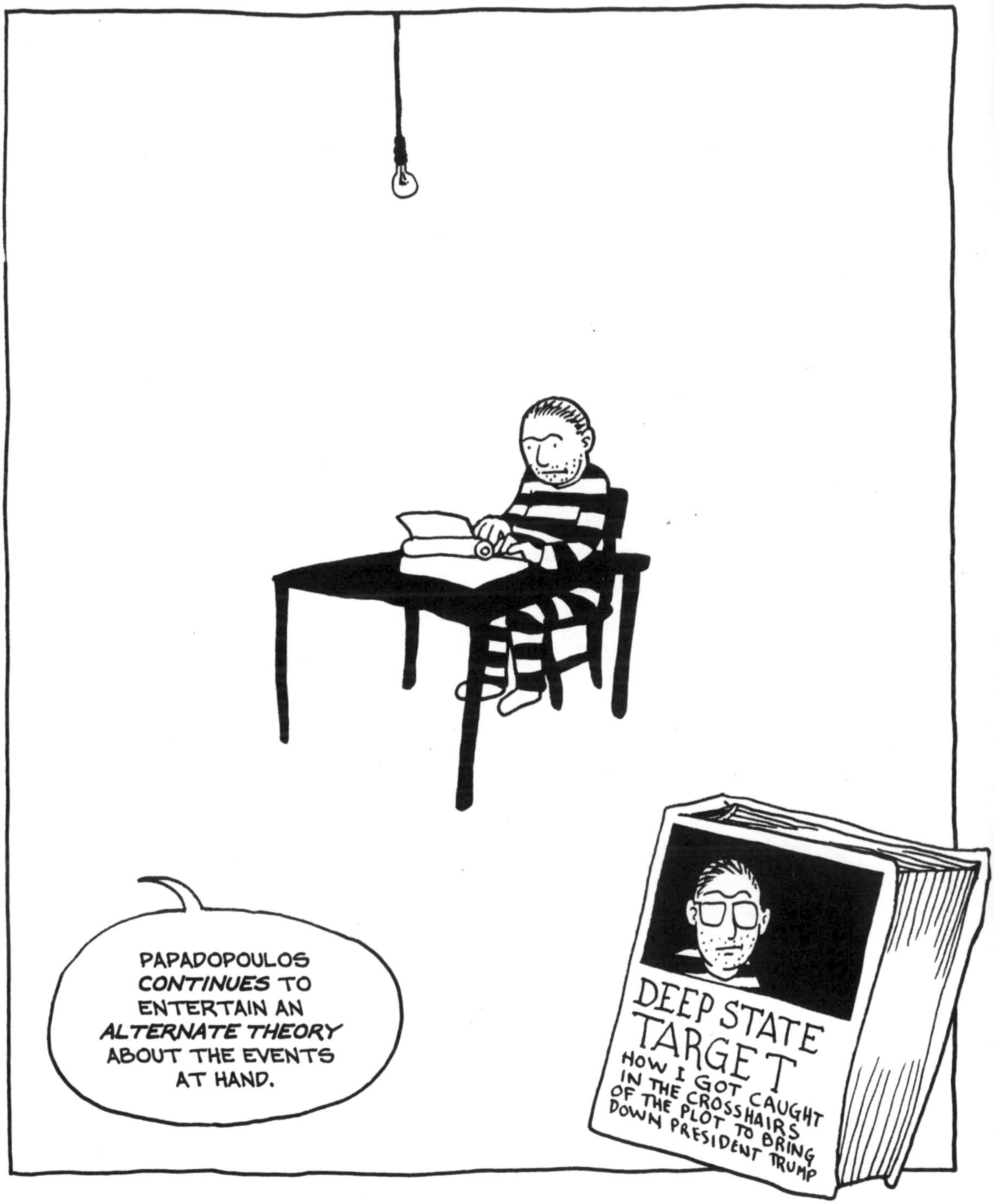
PAPADOPOULOS *CONTINUES* TO ENTERTAIN AN *ALTERNATE THEORY* ABOUT THE EVENTS AT HAND.
DEEP STATE TARGET
HOW I GOT CAUGHT IN THE CROSSHAIRS OF THE PLOT TO BRING DOWN PRESIDENT TRUMP

CHAPTER 4

JUNE 9TH
AT TRUMP TOWER

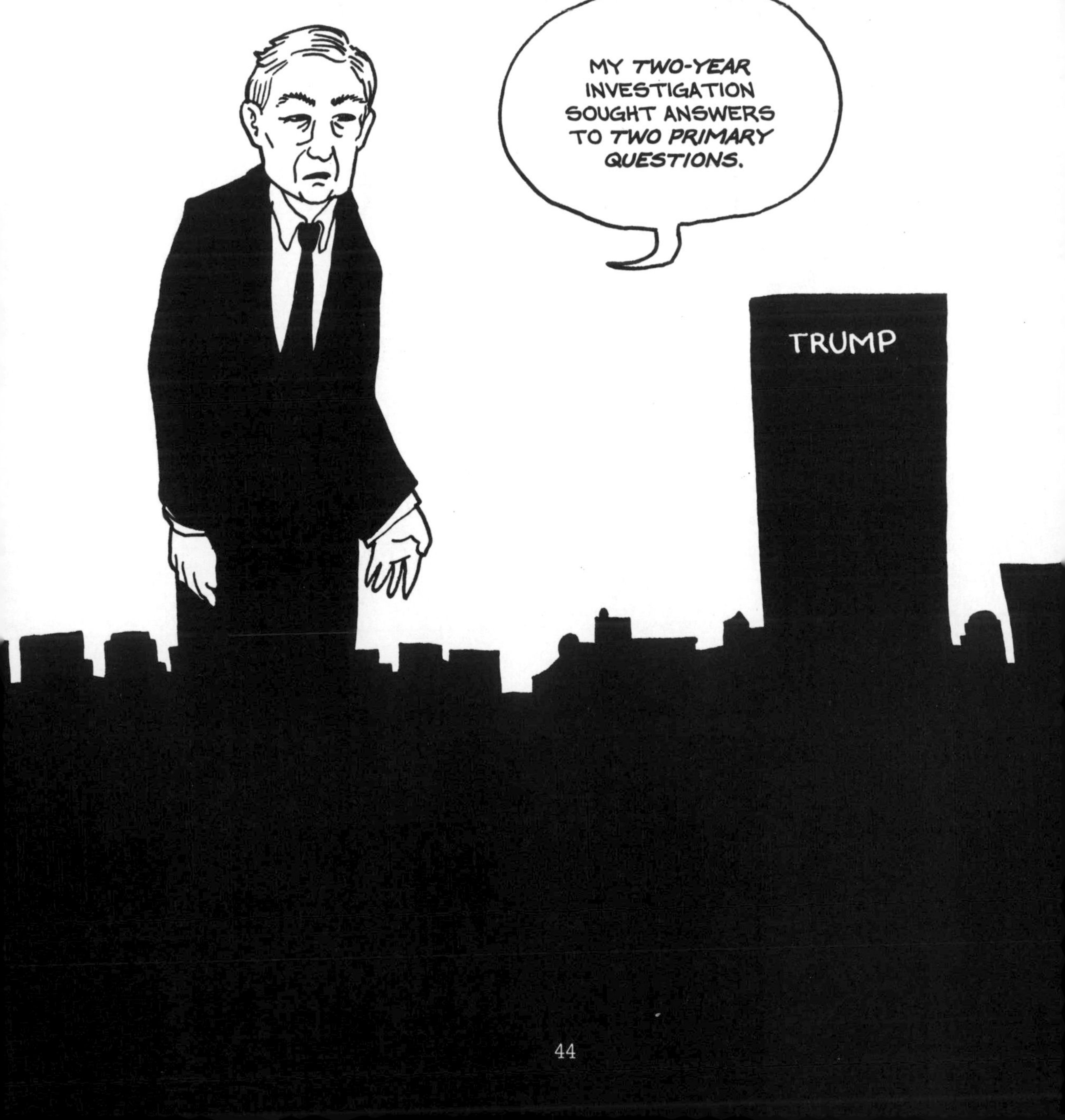
MY *TWO-YEAR* INVESTIGATION SOUGHT ANSWERS TO *TWO PRIMARY QUESTIONS.*
TRUMP

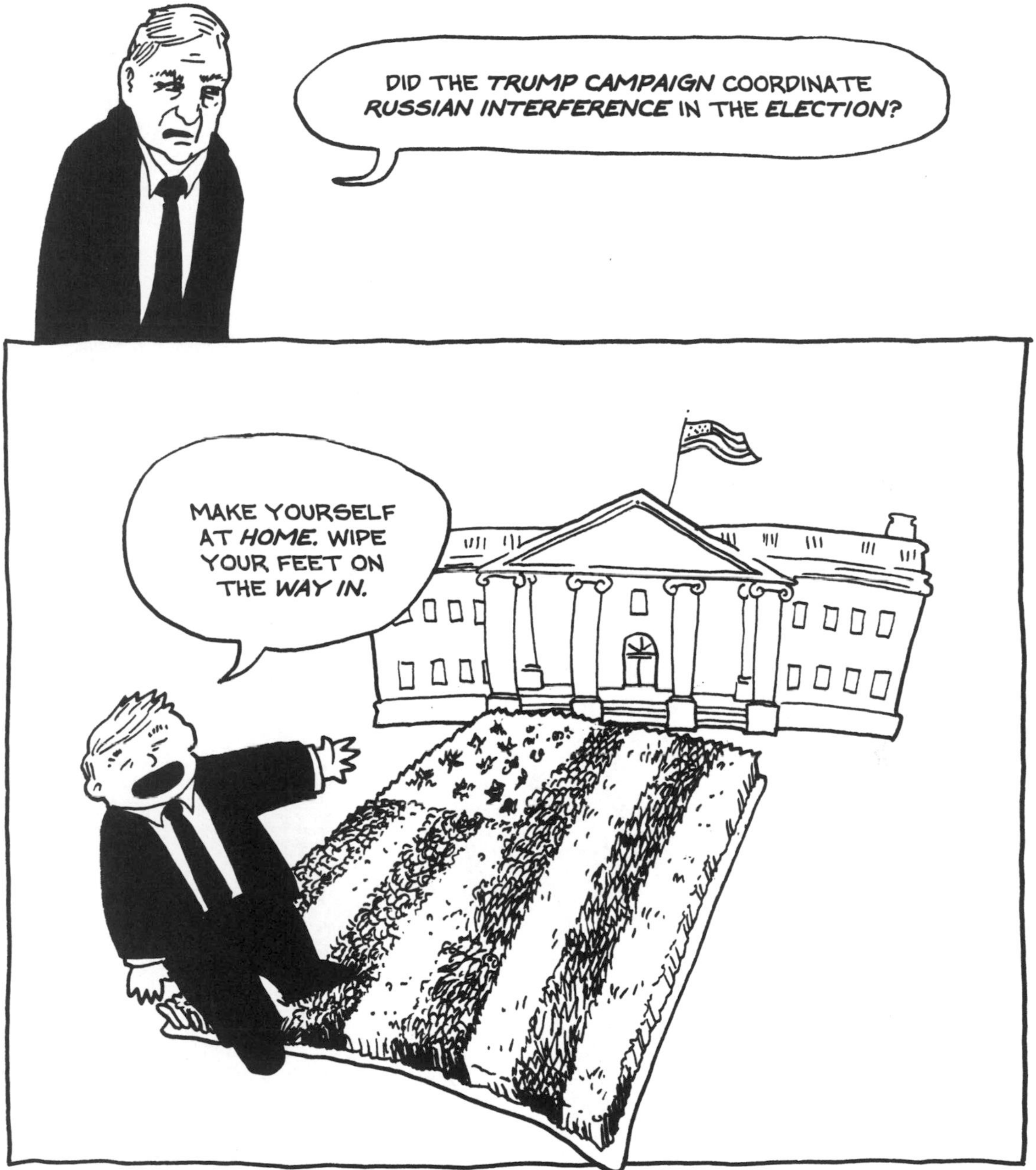
DID THE TRUMP CAMPAIGN COORDINATE RUSSIAN INTERFERENCE IN THE ELECTION?
MAKE YOURSELF AT HOME. WIPE YOUR FEET ON THE WAY IN.

vol 1, pg 131

AND DID TRUMP *OBSTRUCT JUSTICE* RESPONDING TO MY INVESTI
GATI
THERE'S *NOTHING* TO SEE HERE!

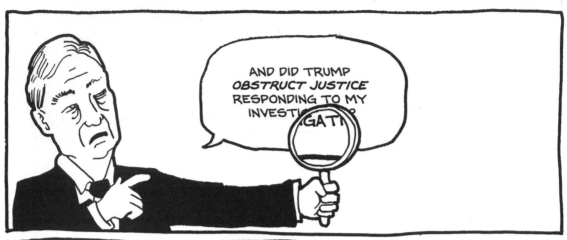

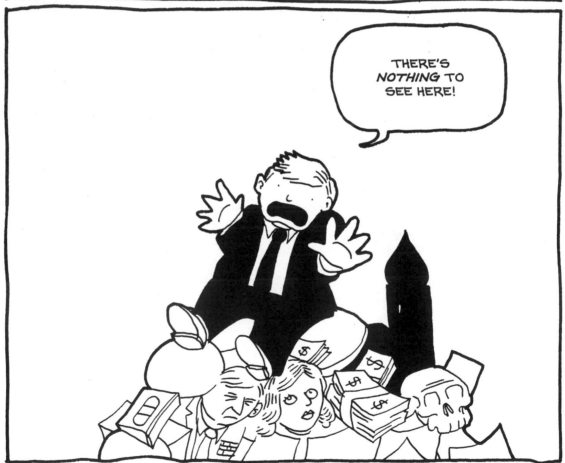

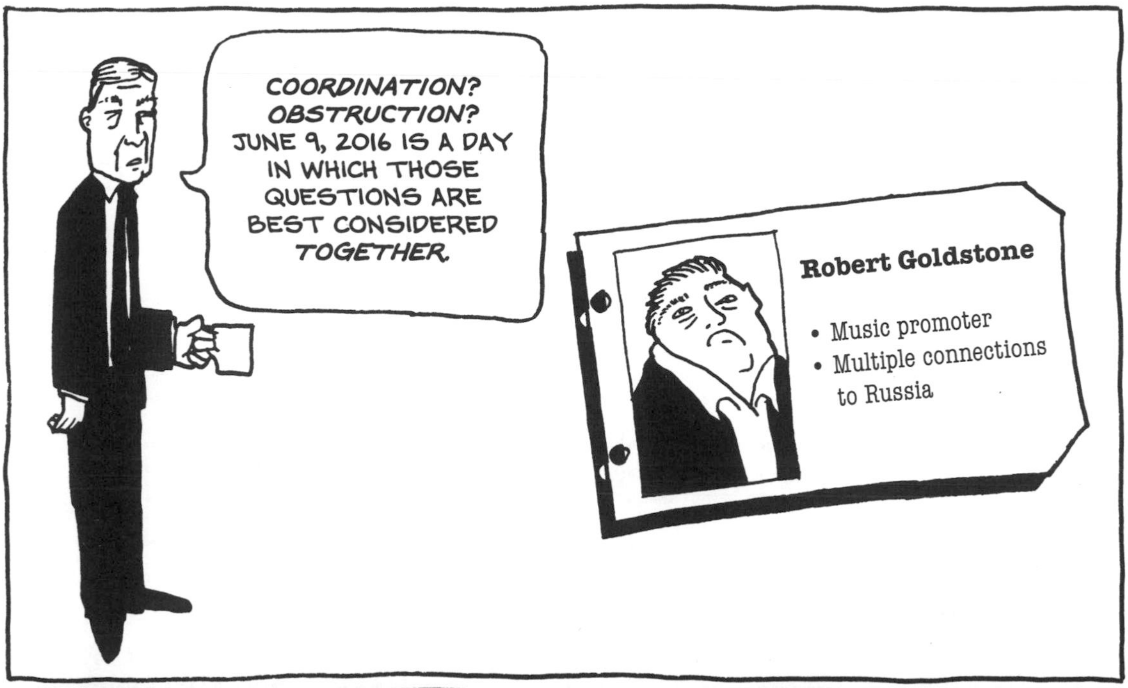
COORDINATION? OBSTRUCTION? JUNE 9, 2016 IS A DAY IN WHICH THOSE QUESTIONS ARE BEST CONSIDERED TOGETHER.
Robert Goldstone
• Music promoter
• Multiple connections to Russia

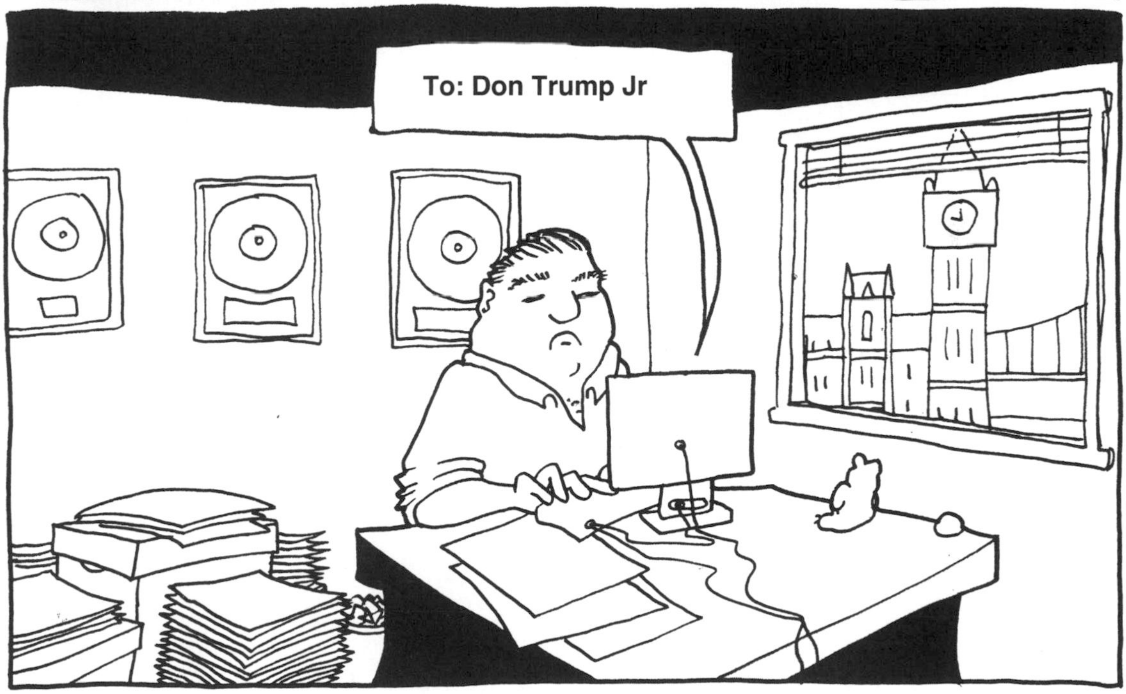
To: Don Trump Jr

vol 1, pg 99, 111, 113

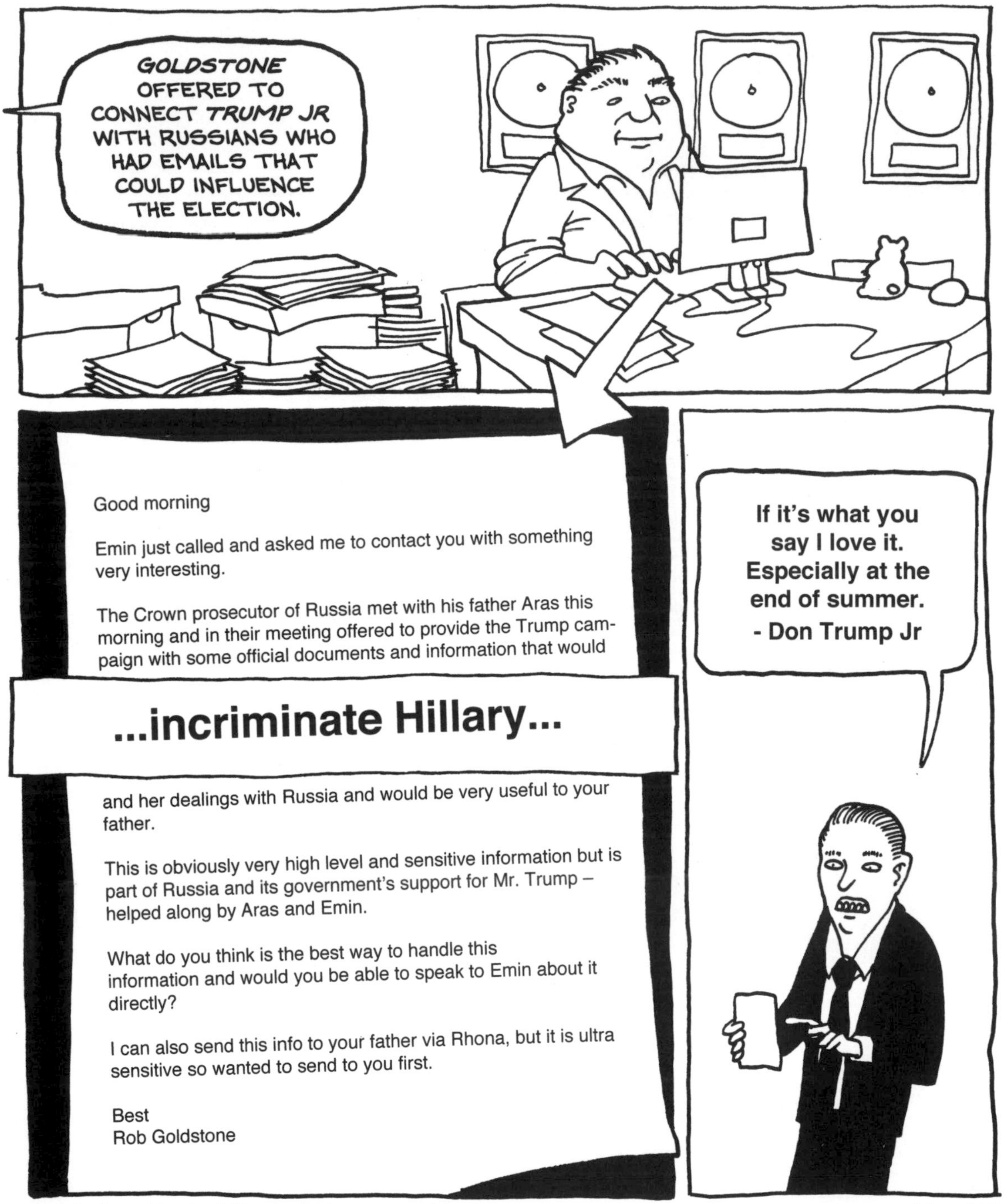
GOLDSTONE OFFERED TO CONNECT TRUMP JR WITH RUSSIANS WHO HAD EMAILS THAT COULD INFLUENCE THE ELECTION.
Good morning
Emin just called and asked me to contact you with something very interesting.
The Crown prosecutor of Russia met with his father Aras this morning and in their meeting offered to provide the Trump campaign with some official documents and information that would
...incriminate Hillary...
and her dealings with Russia and would be very useful to your father.
This is obviously very high level and sensitive information but is part of Russia and its government's support for Mr. Trump – helped along by Aras and Emin.
What do you think is the best way to handle this information and would you be able to speak to Emin about it directly?
I can also send this info to your father via Rhona, but it is ultra sensitive so wanted to send to you first.
Best
Rob Goldstone
If it's what you say I love it. Especially at the end of summer. - Don Trump Jr

Aras Agalarov: Russian billionaire businessman and developer
Emin Agalarov: Russian pop singer, son of Aras Agalarov

vol 1, pg 113

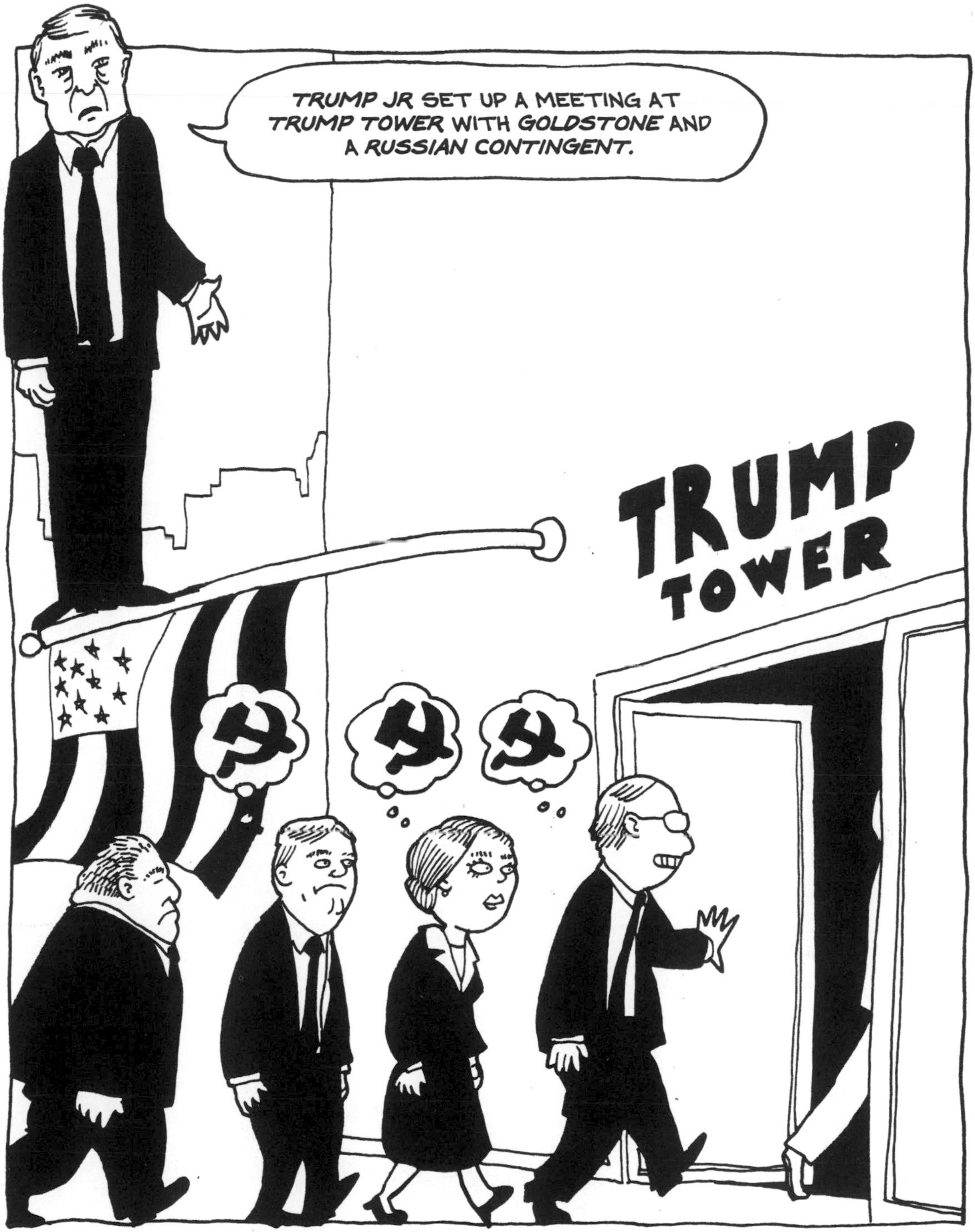
TRUMP JR SET UP A MEETING AT TRUMP TOWER WITH GOLDSTONE AND A RUSSIAN CONTINGENT.
TRUMP TOWER

vol 1, pg 114

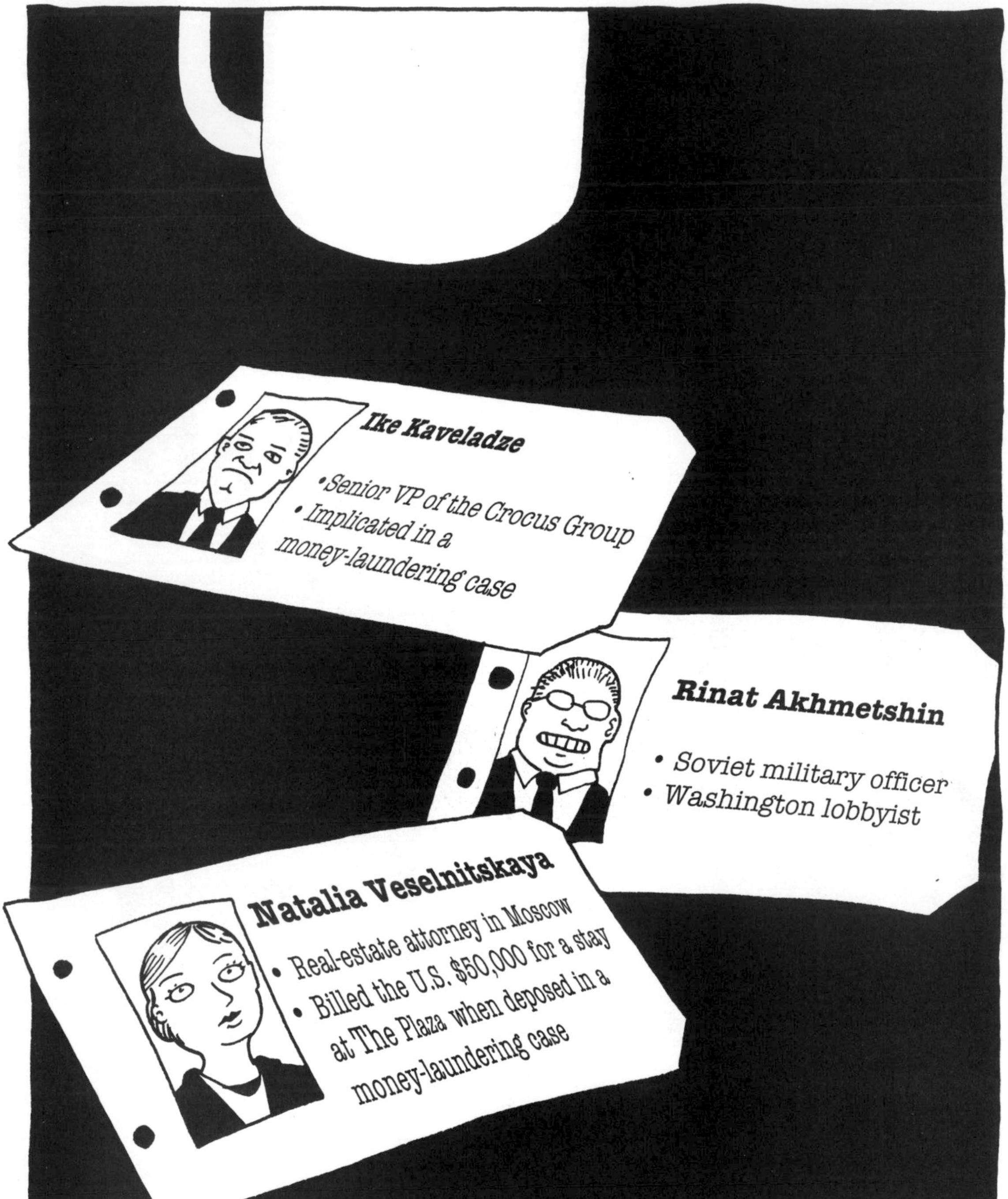
Ike Kaveladze
•Senior VP of the Crocus Group
• Implicated in a money-laundering case
Rinat Akhmetshin
• Soviet military officer
• Washington lobbyist
Natalia Veselnitskaya
• Real-estate attorney in Moscow
• Billed the U.S. $50,000 for a stay at The Plaza when deposed in a money-laundering case

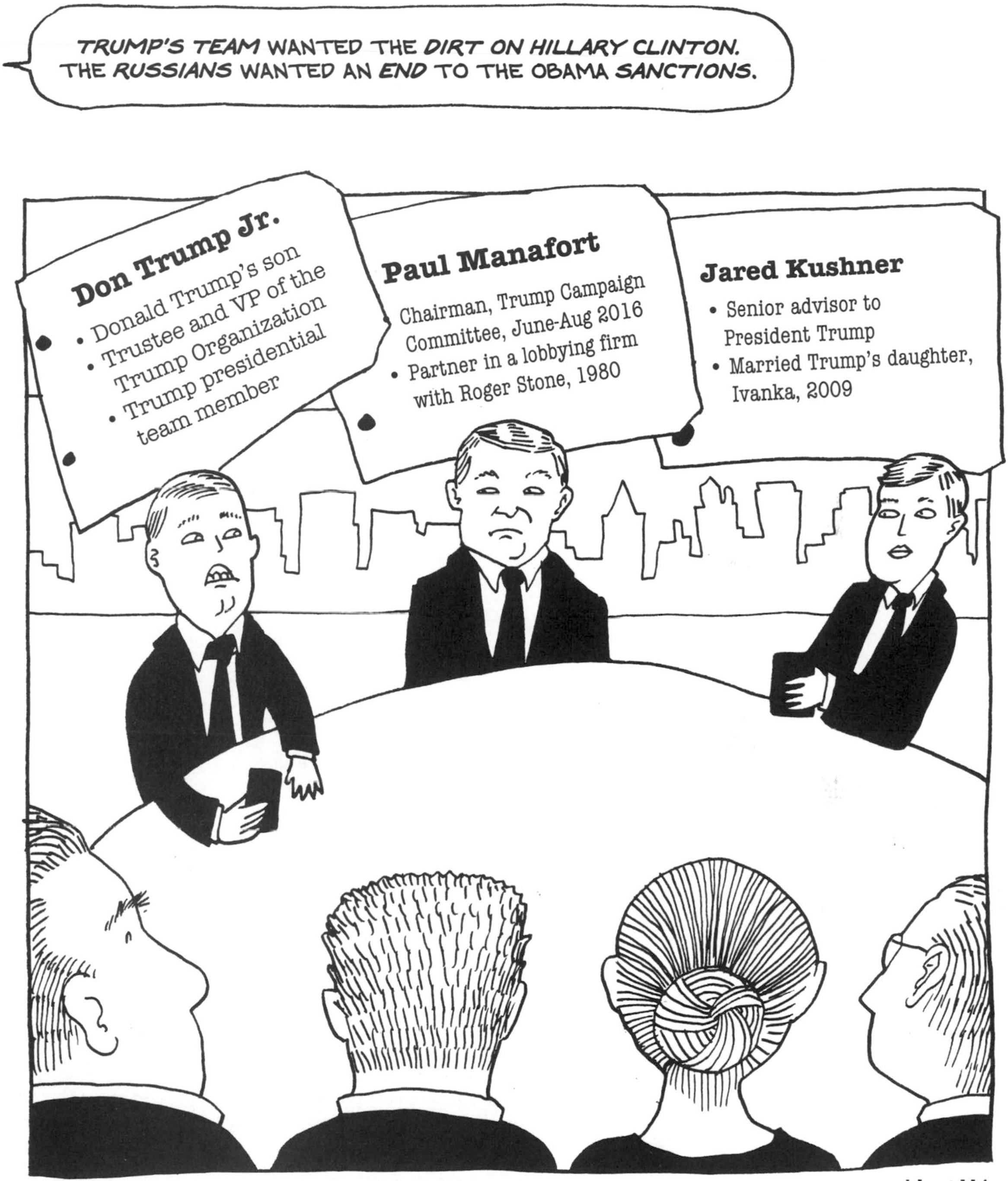
TRUMP'S TEAM WANTED THE DIRT ON HILLARY CLINTON. THE RUSSIANS WANTED AN END TO THE OBAMA SANCTIONS.
Don Trump Jr.
• Donald Trump's son
• Trustee and VP of the Trump Organization
• Trump presidential team member
Paul Manafort
Chairman, Trump Campaign Committee, June-Aug 2016
• Partner in a lobbying firm with Roger Stone, 1980
Jared Kushner
• Senior advisor to President Trump
• Married Trump's daughter, Ivanka, 2009

vol 1, pg 114

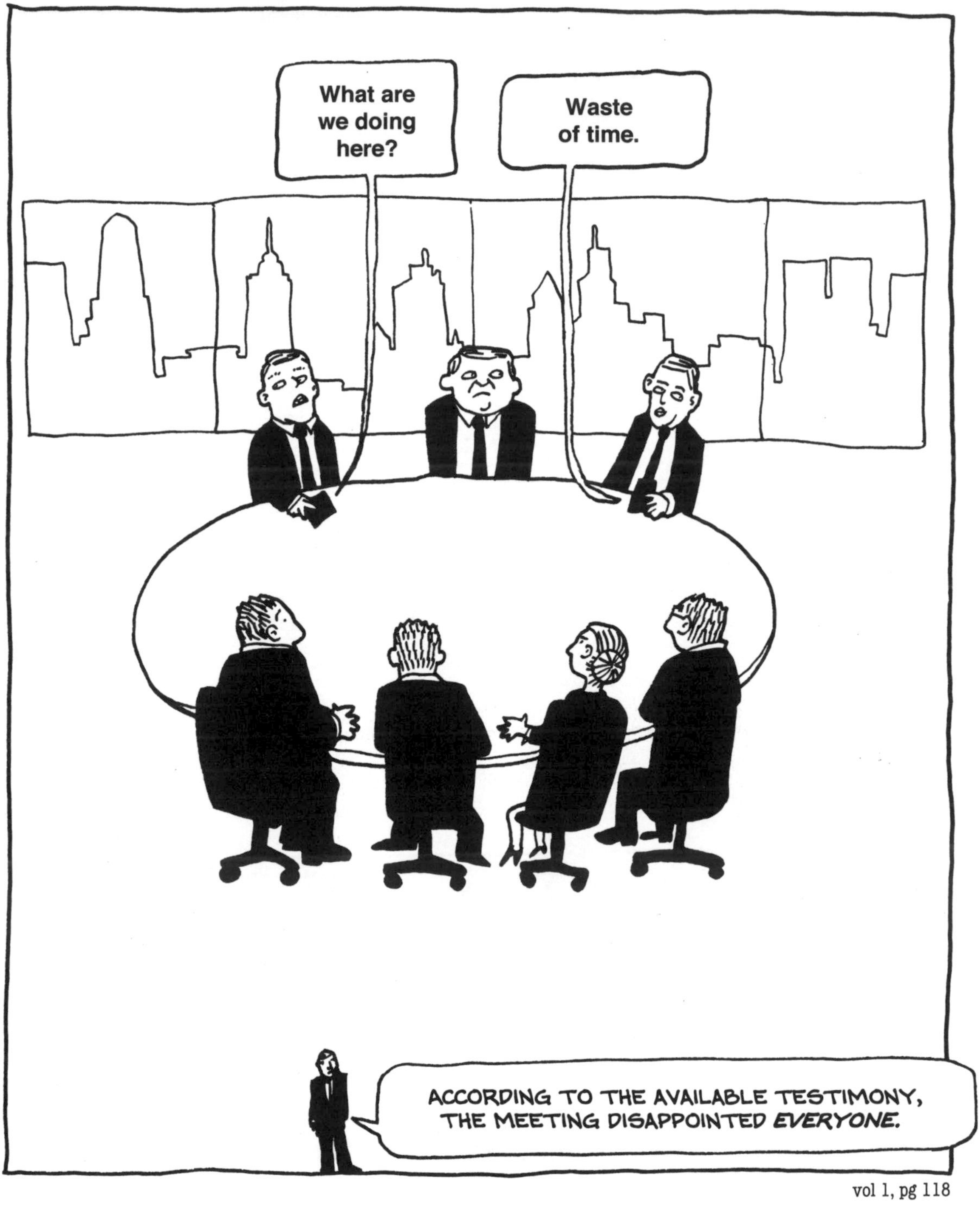
What are we doing here?
Waste of time.
ACCORDING TO THE AVAILABLE TESTIMONY, THE MEETING DISAPPOINTED *EVERYONE.*

vol 1, pg 118

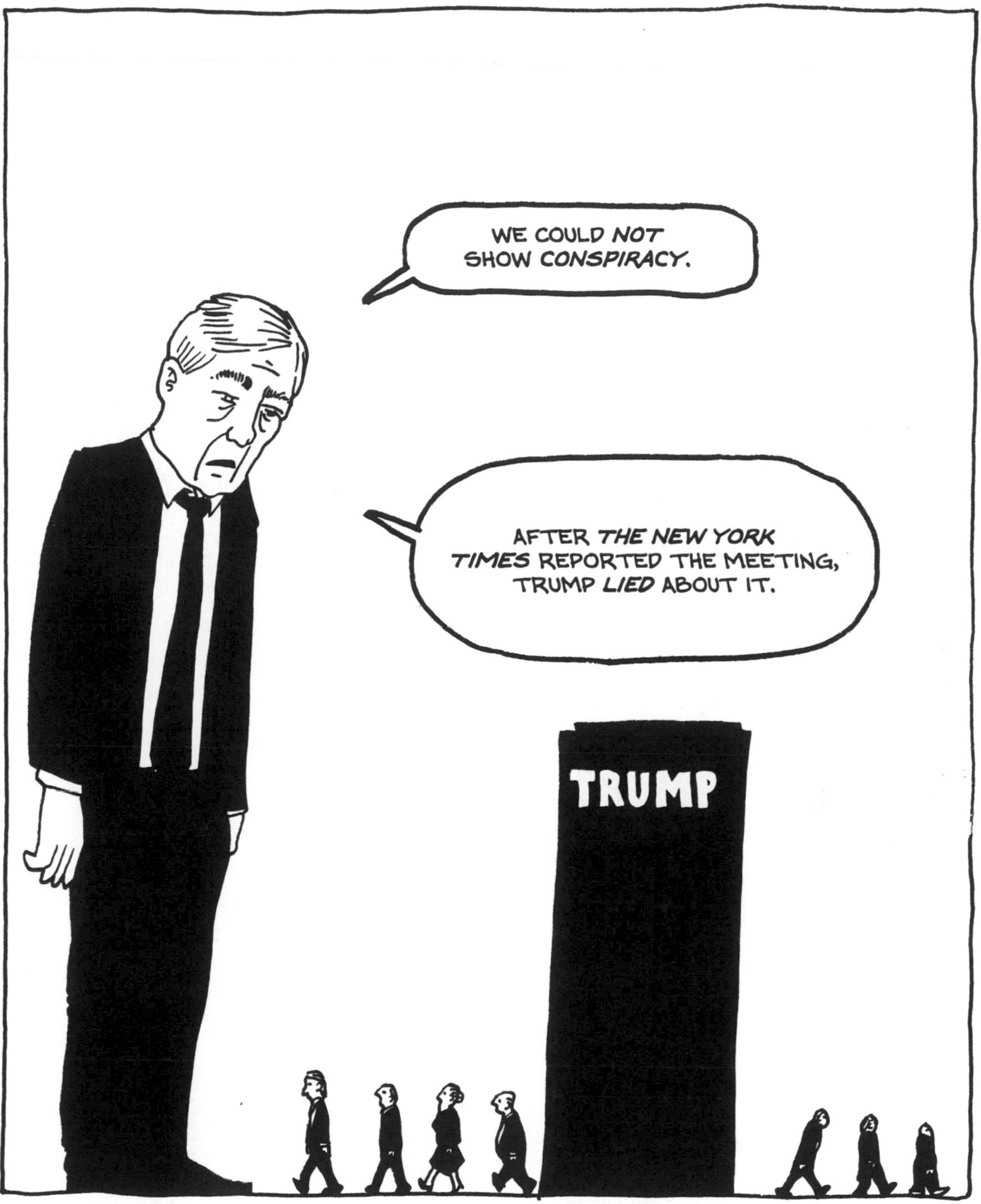
WE COULD *NOT* SHOW *CONSPIRACY*.
AFTER *THE NEW YORK TIMES* REPORTED THE MEETING, TRUMP *LIED* ABOUT IT.
TRUMP

vol. 1, pg 121-122, 181

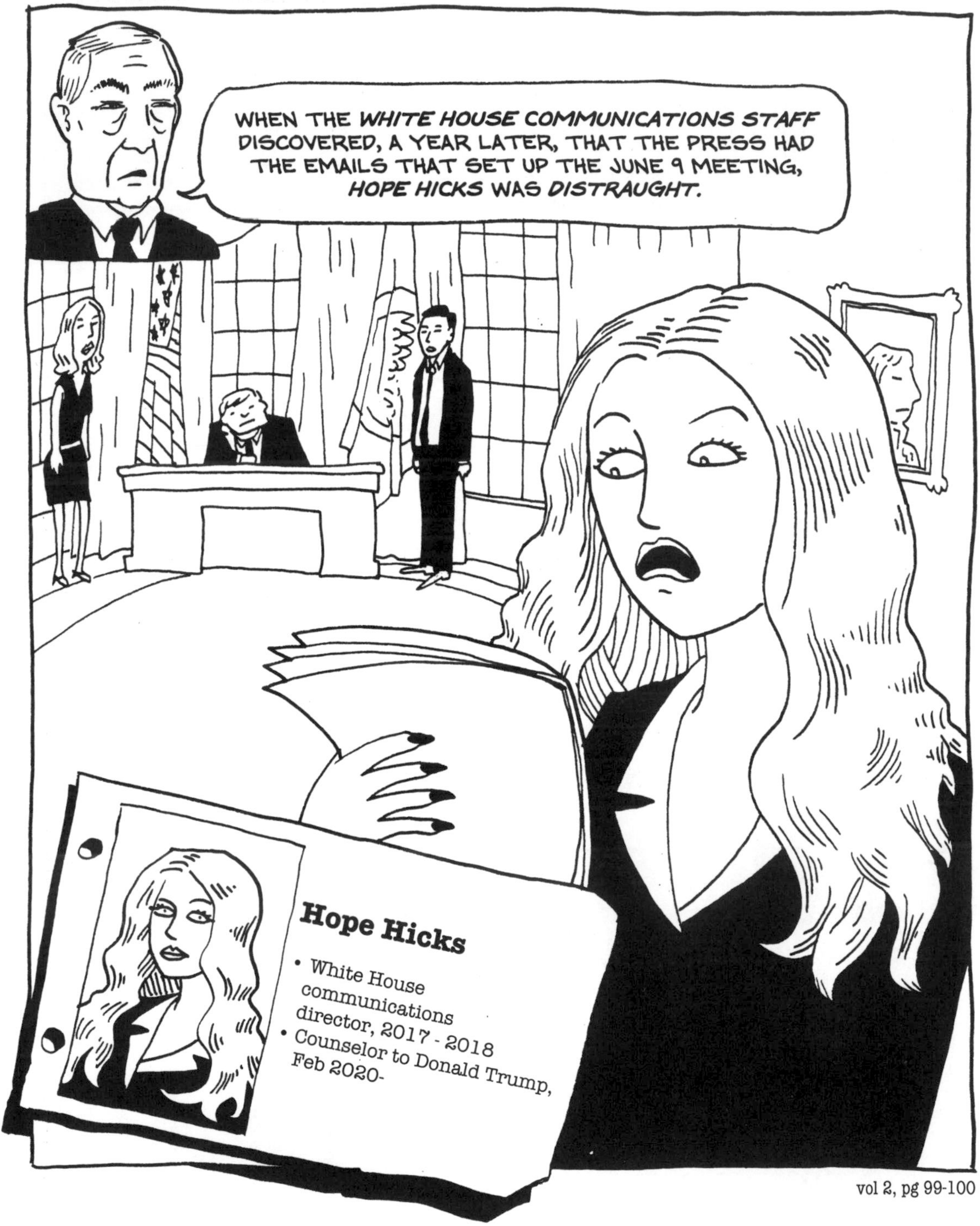
WHEN THE *WHITE HOUSE COMMUNICATIONS STAFF* DISCOVERED, A YEAR LATER, THAT THE PRESS HAD THE EMAILS THAT SET UP THE JUNE 9 MEETING, *HOPE HICKS* WAS *DISTRAUGHT*.
Hope Hicks
• White House communications director, 2017 - 2018
• Counselor to Donald Trump, Feb 2020-

vol 2, pg 99-100

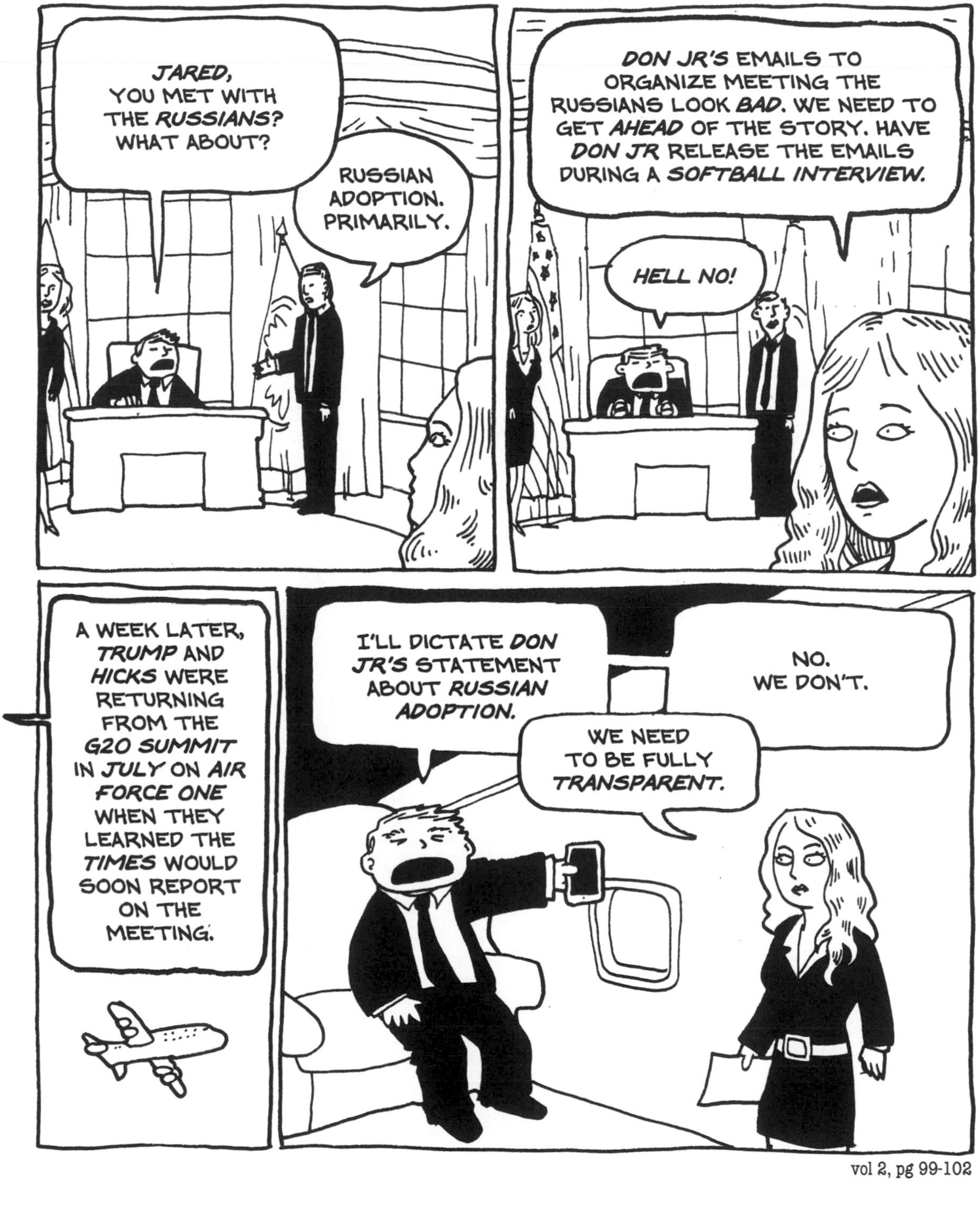
JARED, YOU MET WITH THE RUSSIANS? WHAT ABOUT?
RUSSIAN ADOPTION. PRIMARILY.
DON JR'S EMAILS TO ORGANIZE MEETING THE RUSSIANS LOOK BAD. WE NEED TO GET AHEAD OF THE STORY. HAVE DON JR RELEASE THE EMAILS DURING A SOFTBALL INTERVIEW.
HELL NO!
A WEEK LATER, TRUMP AND HICKS WERE RETURNING FROM THE G20 SUMMIT IN JULY ON AIR FORCE ONE WHEN THEY LEARNED THE TIMES WOULD SOON REPORT ON THE MEETING.
I'LL DICTATE DON JR'S STATEMENT ABOUT RUSSIAN ADOPTION.
NO. WE DON'T.
WE NEED TO BE FULLY TRANSPARENT.

vol 2, pg 99-102

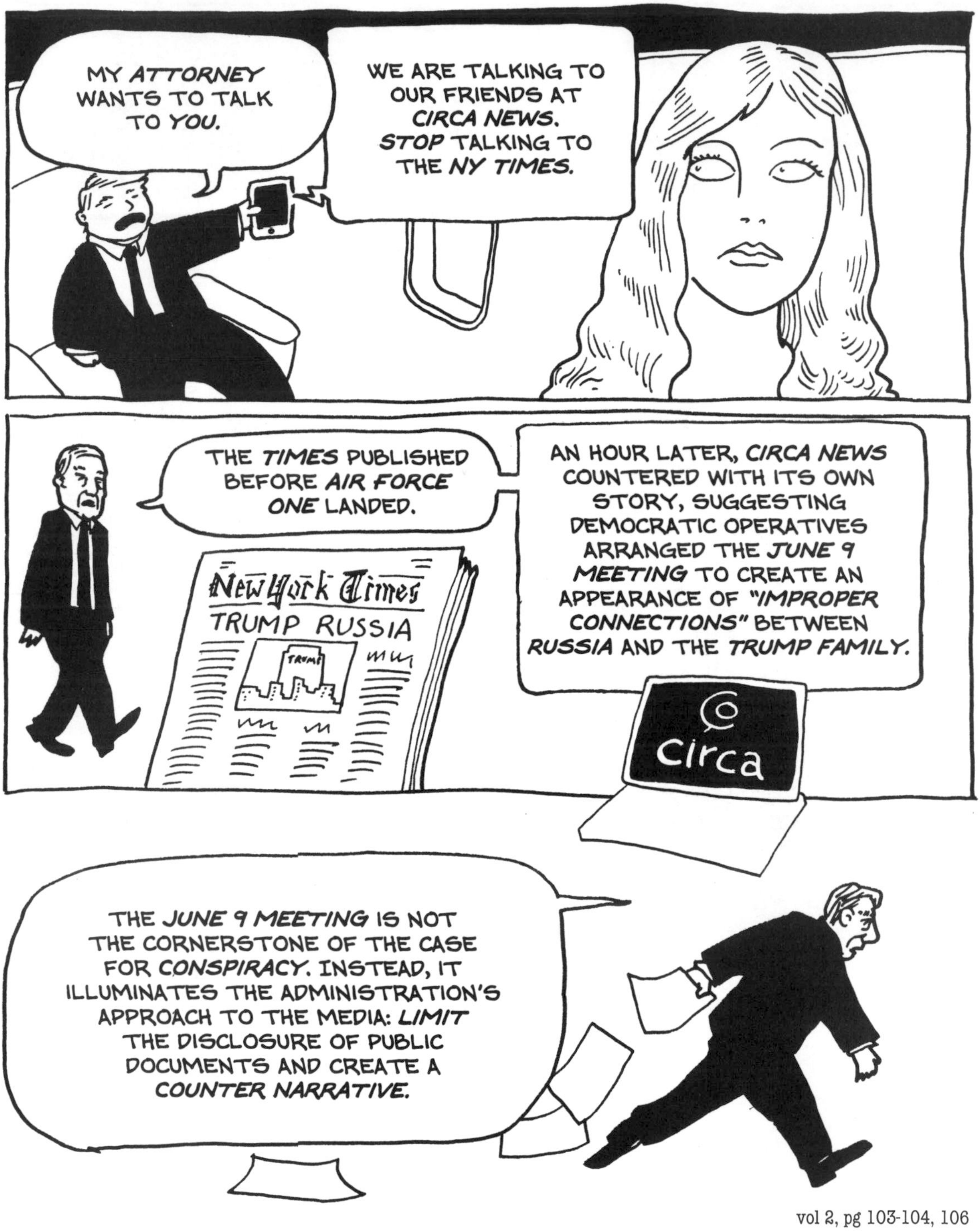

MY ATTORNEY WANTS TO TALK TO YOU.
WE ARE TALKING TO OUR FRIENDS AT CIRCA NEWS. STOP TALKING TO THE NY TIMES.
THE TIMES PUBLISHED BEFORE AIR FORCE ONE LANDED.
New York Times
TRUMP RUSSIA
TRUMP
AN HOUR LATER, CIRCA NEWS COUNTERED WITH ITS OWN STORY, SUGGESTING DEMOCRATIC OPERATIVES ARRANGED THE JUNE 9 MEETING TO CREATE AN APPEARANCE OF "IMPROPER CONNECTIONS" BETWEEN RUSSIA AND THE TRUMP FAMILY.
circa
THE JUNE 9 MEETING IS NOT THE CORNERSTONE OF THE CASE FOR CONSPIRACY. INSTEAD, IT ILLUMINATES THE ADMINISTRATION'S APPROACH TO THE MEDIA: LIMIT THE DISCLOSURE OF PUBLIC DOCUMENTS AND CREATE A COUNTER NARRATIVE.

vol 2, pg 103-104, 106

CHAPTER 5

PAUL MANAFORT

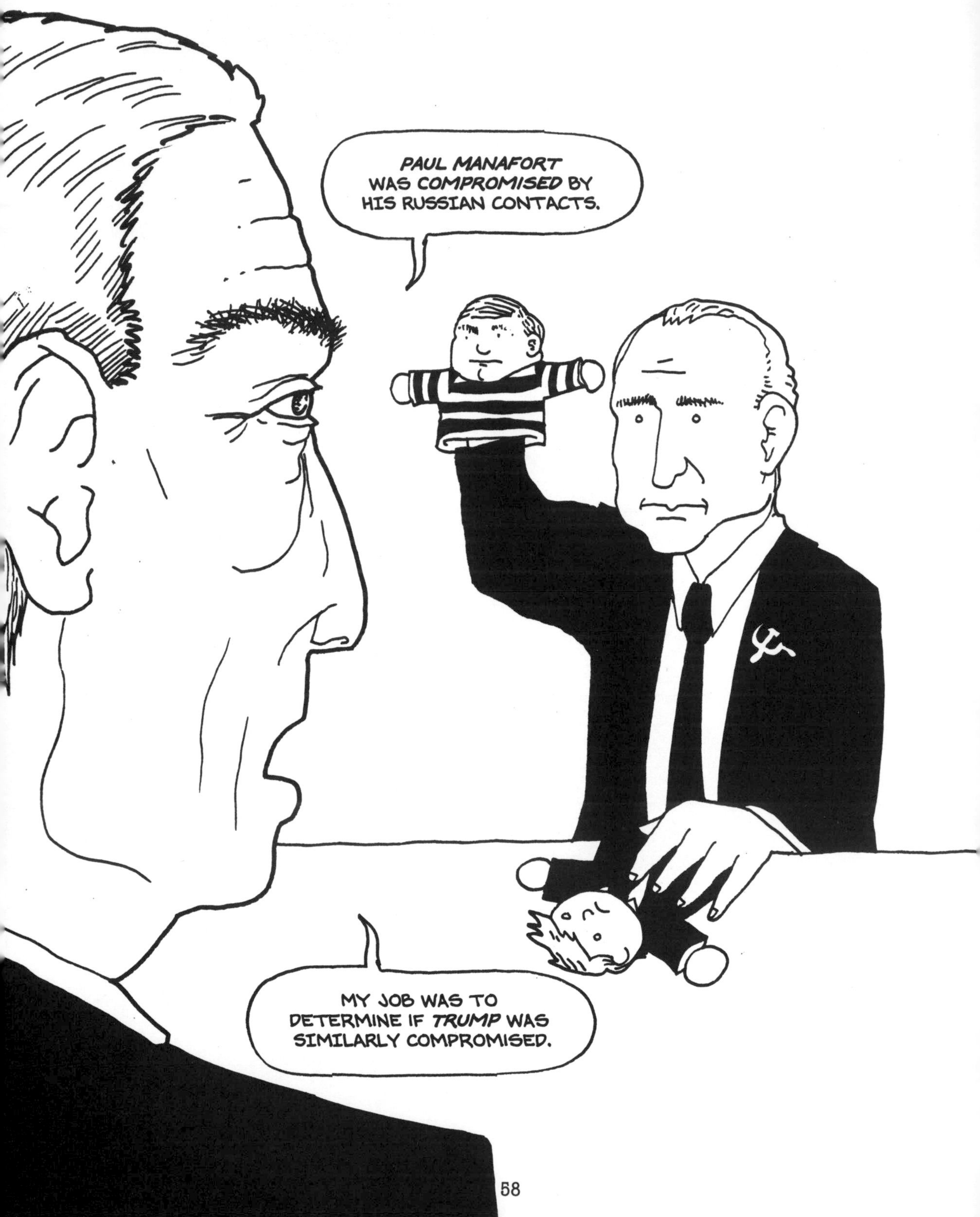
PAUL MANAFORT WAS *COMPROMISED* BY HIS RUSSIAN CONTACTS.
MY JOB WAS TO DETERMINE IF *TRUMP* WAS SIMILARLY COMPROMISED.

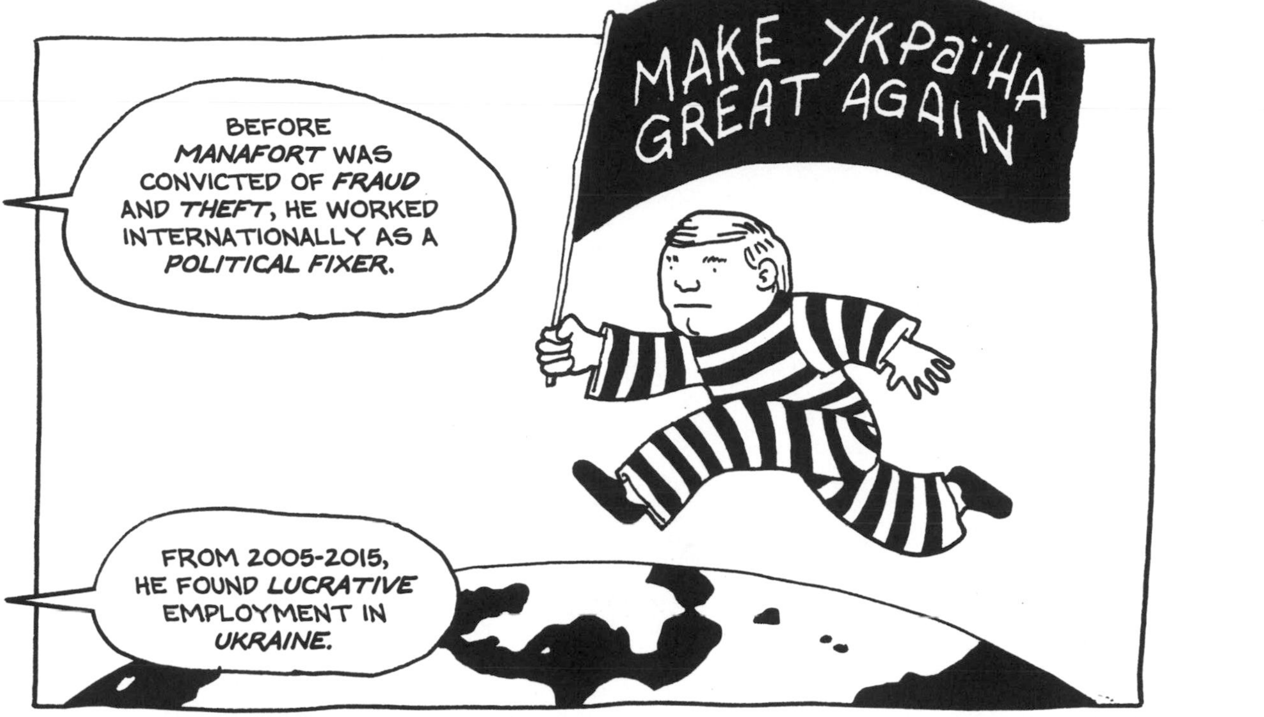
MAKE УКРаїНА GREAT AGAIN
BEFORE *MANAFORT* WAS CONVICTED OF *FRAUD* AND *THEFT*, HE WORKED INTERNATIONALLY AS A *POLITICAL FIXER*.
FROM 2005-2015, HE FOUND *LUCRATIVE* EMPLOYMENT IN *UKRAINE*.

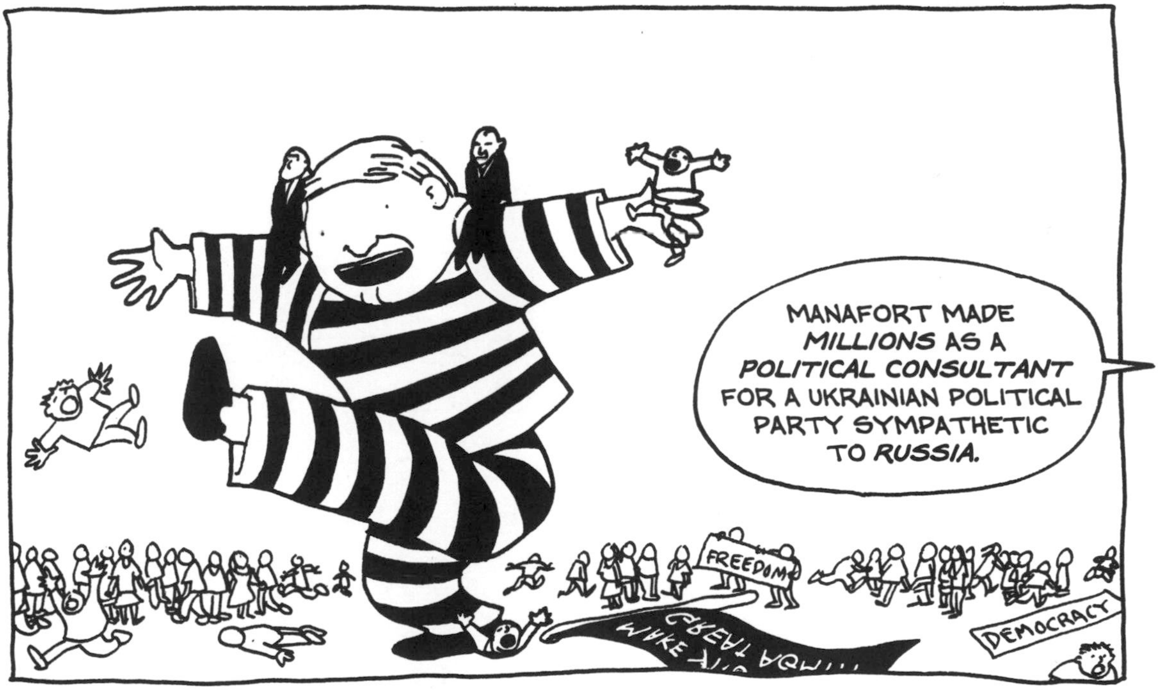
MANAFORT MADE *MILLIONS* AS A *POLITICAL CONSULTANT* FOR A UKRAINIAN POLITICAL PARTY SYMPATHETIC TO *RUSSIA*.
FREEDOM
DEMOCRACY

vol 1, pg 129, 132

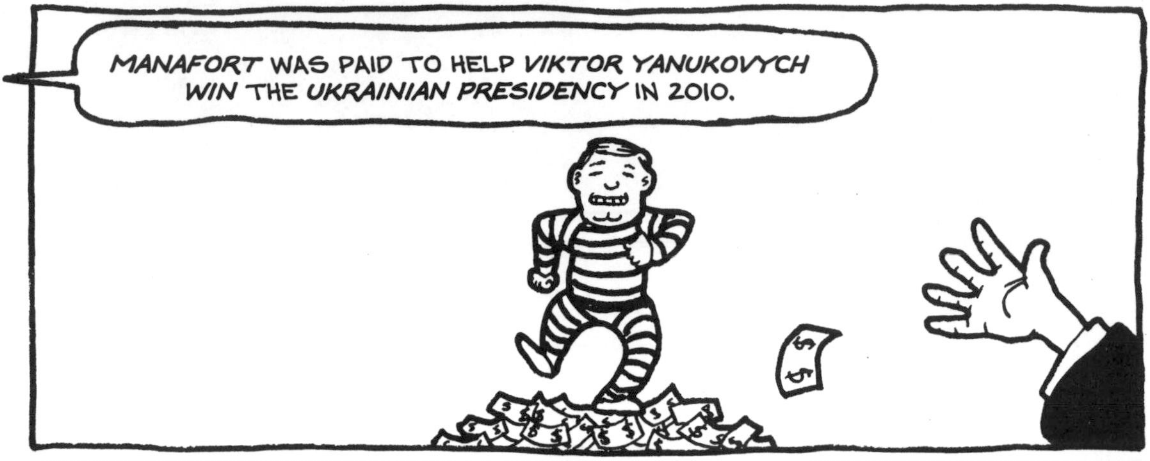
MANAFORT WAS PAID TO HELP VIKTOR YANUKOVYCH WIN THE UKRAINIAN PRESIDENCY IN 2010.

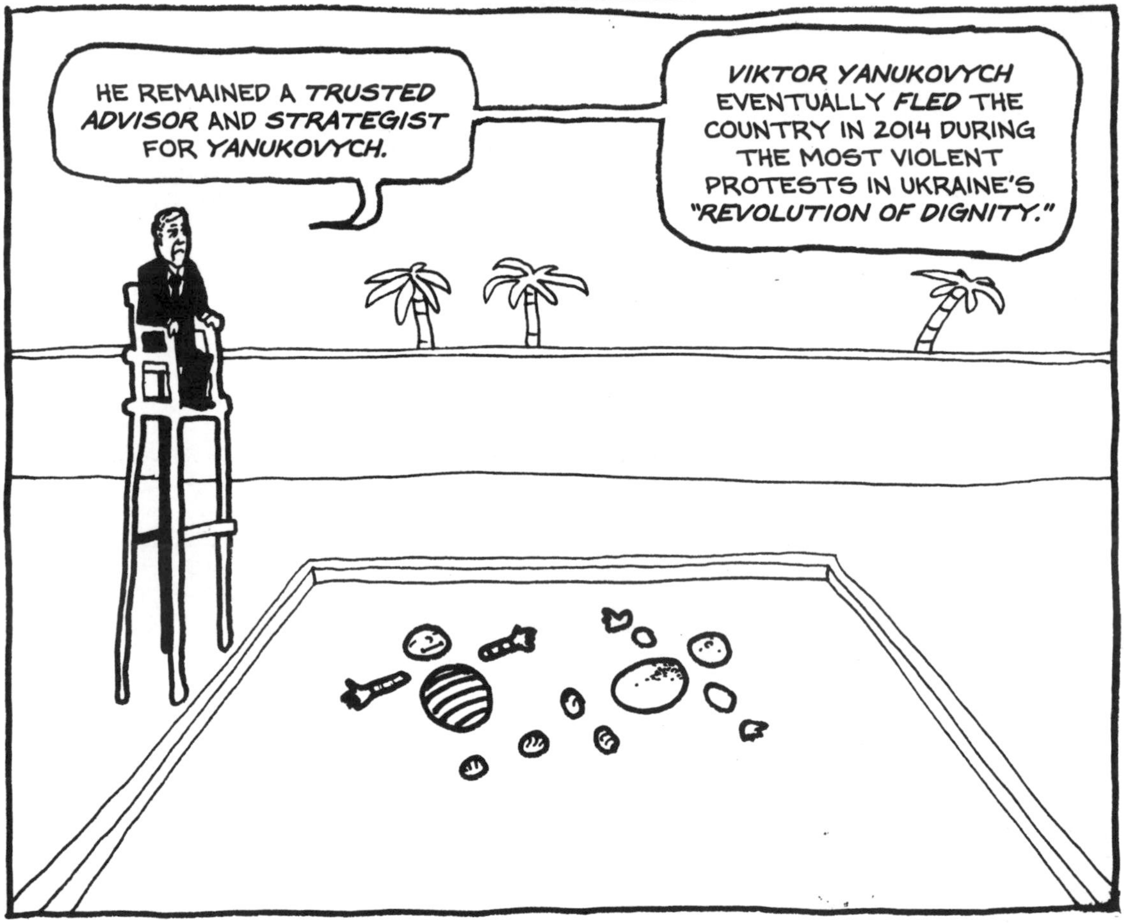
HE REMAINED A TRUSTED ADVISOR AND STRATEGIST FOR YANUKOVYCH.
VIKTOR YANUKOVYCH EVENTUALLY FLED THE COUNTRY IN 2014 DURING THE MOST VIOLENT PROTESTS IN UKRAINE'S "REVOLUTION OF DIGNITY."

vol 1, pg 132

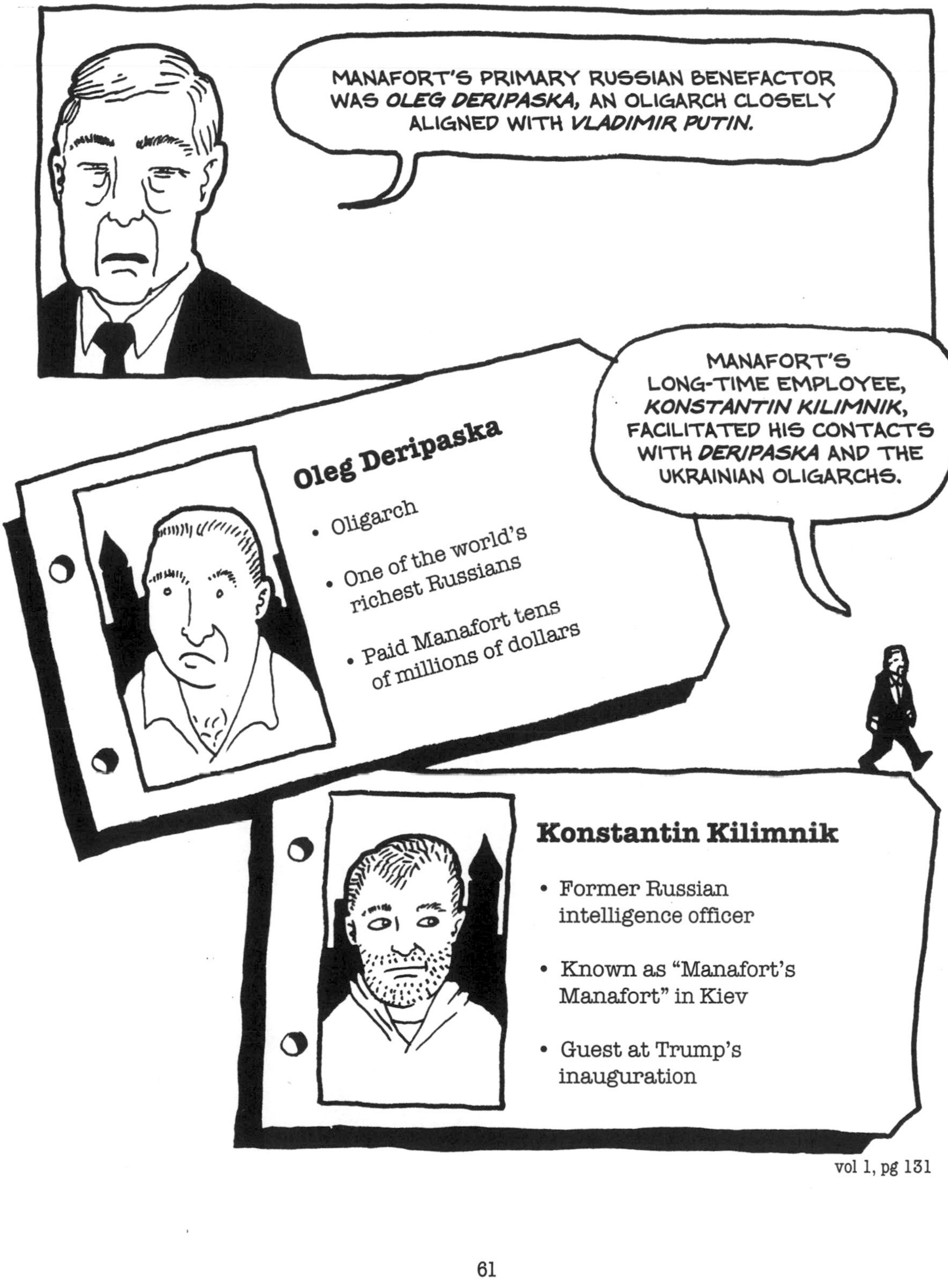
MANAFORT'S PRIMARY RUSSIAN BENEFACTOR WAS OLEG DERIPASKA, AN OLIGARCH CLOSELY ALIGNED WITH VLADIMIR PUTIN.
Oleg Deripaska
• Oligarch
• One of the world's richest Russians
• Paid Manafort tens of millions of dollars
MANAFORT'S LONG-TIME EMPLOYEE, KONSTANTIN KILIMNIK, FACILITATED HIS CONTACTS WITH DERIPASKA AND THE UKRAINIAN OLIGARCHS.
Konstantin Kilimnik
• Former Russian intelligence officer
• Known as "Manafort's Manafort" in Kiev
• Guest at Trump's inauguration

vol 1, pg 131

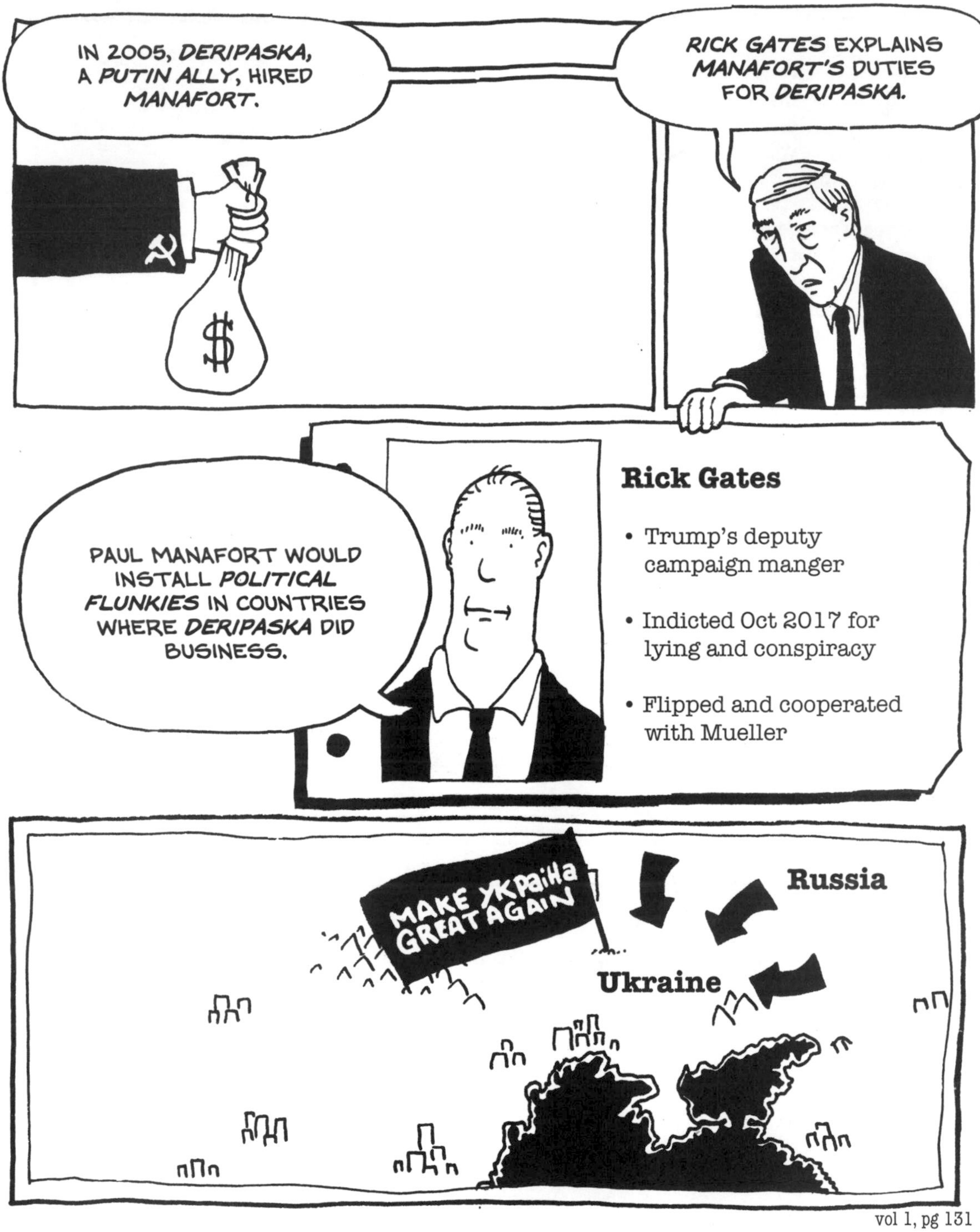
IN 2005, *DERIPASKA*, A *PUTIN ALLY*, HIRED *MANAFORT*.
RICK GATES EXPLAINS *MANAFORT'S* DUTIES FOR *DERIPASKA*.
PAUL MANAFORT WOULD INSTALL *POLITICAL FLUNKIES* IN COUNTRIES WHERE *DERIPASKA* DID BUSINESS.
Rick Gates
• Trump's deputy campaign manger
• Indicted Oct 2017 for lying and conspiracy
• Flipped and cooperated with Mueller
MAKE УКраїна GREAT AGAIN
Russia
Ukraine

vol 1, pg 131

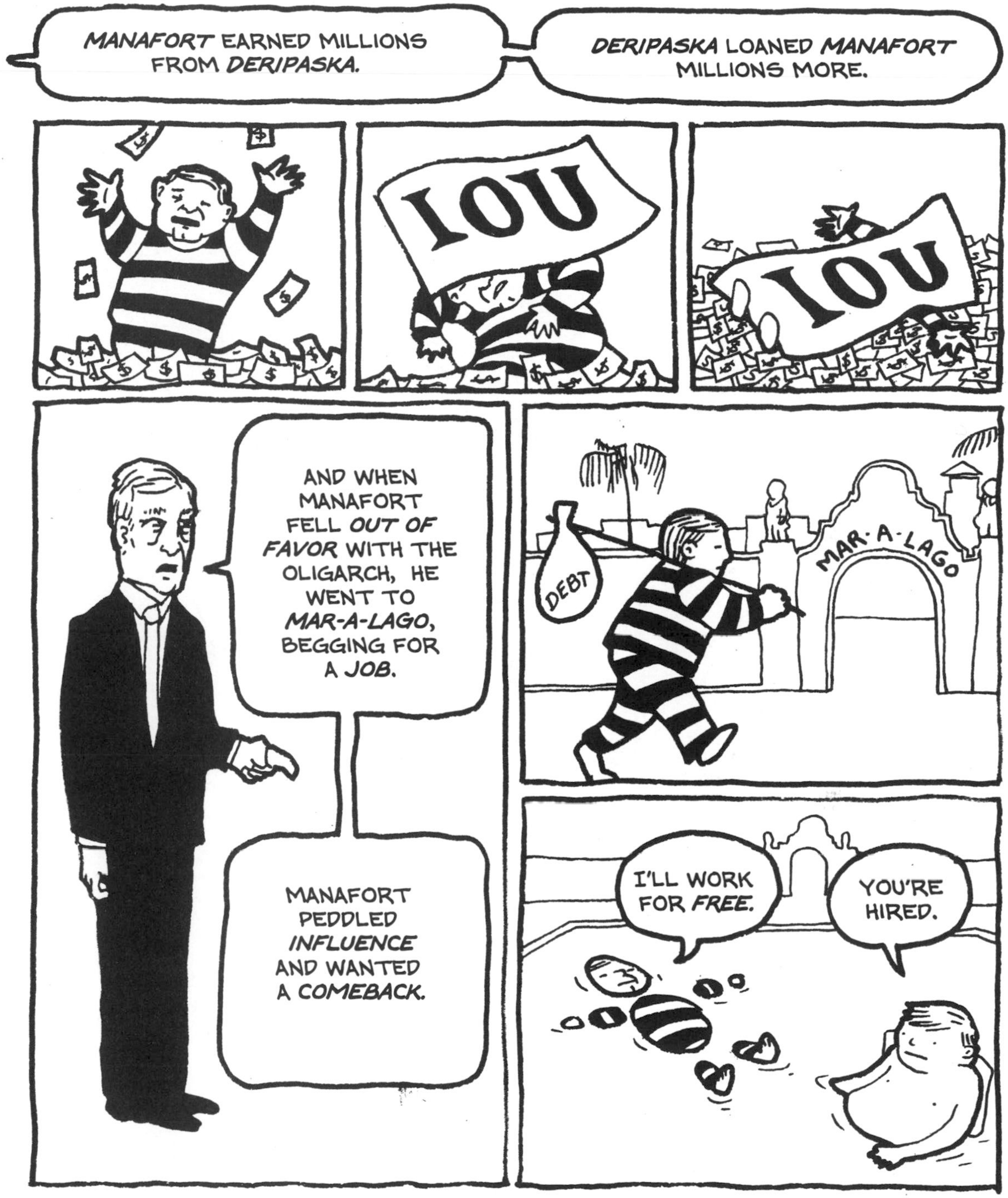
MANAFORT EARNED MILLIONS FROM DERIPASKA.
DERIPASKA LOANED MANAFORT MILLIONS MORE.
IOU
IOU
AND WHEN MANAFORT FELL OUT OF FAVOR WITH THE OLIGARCH, HE WENT TO MAR-A-LAGO, BEGGING FOR A JOB.
MANAFORT PEDDLED INFLUENCE AND WANTED A COMEBACK.
DEBT
MAR-A-LAGO
I'LL WORK FOR FREE.
YOU'RE HIRED.

vol 1, pg 131, 135

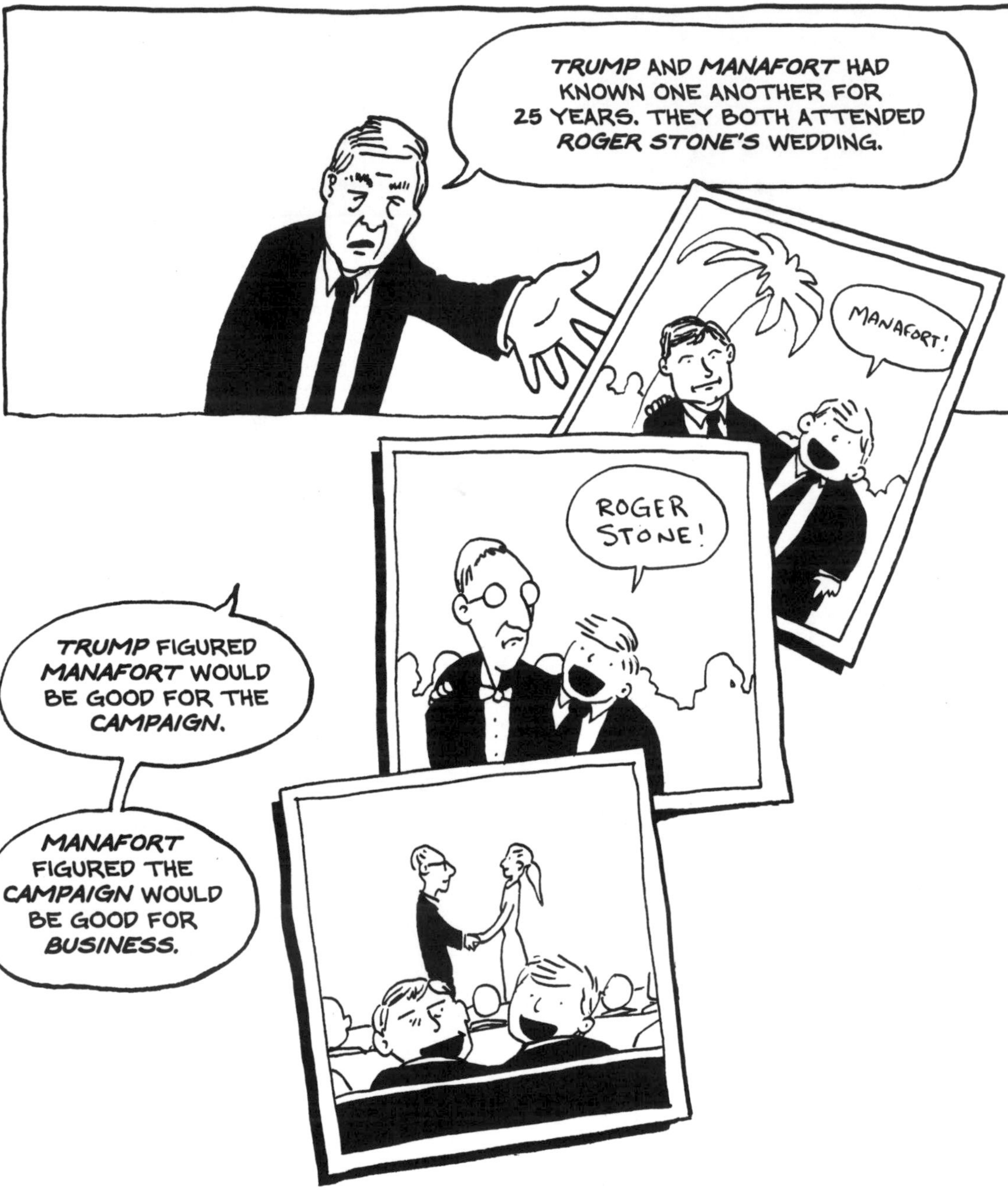
TRUMP AND MANAFORT HAD KNOWN ONE ANOTHER FOR 25 YEARS. THEY BOTH ATTENDED ROGER STONE'S WEDDING.
MANAFORT!
ROGER STONE!
TRUMP FIGURED MANAFORT WOULD BE GOOD FOR THE CAMPAIGN.
MANAFORT FIGURED THE CAMPAIGN WOULD BE GOOD FOR BUSINESS.

vol 1, pg 134-135

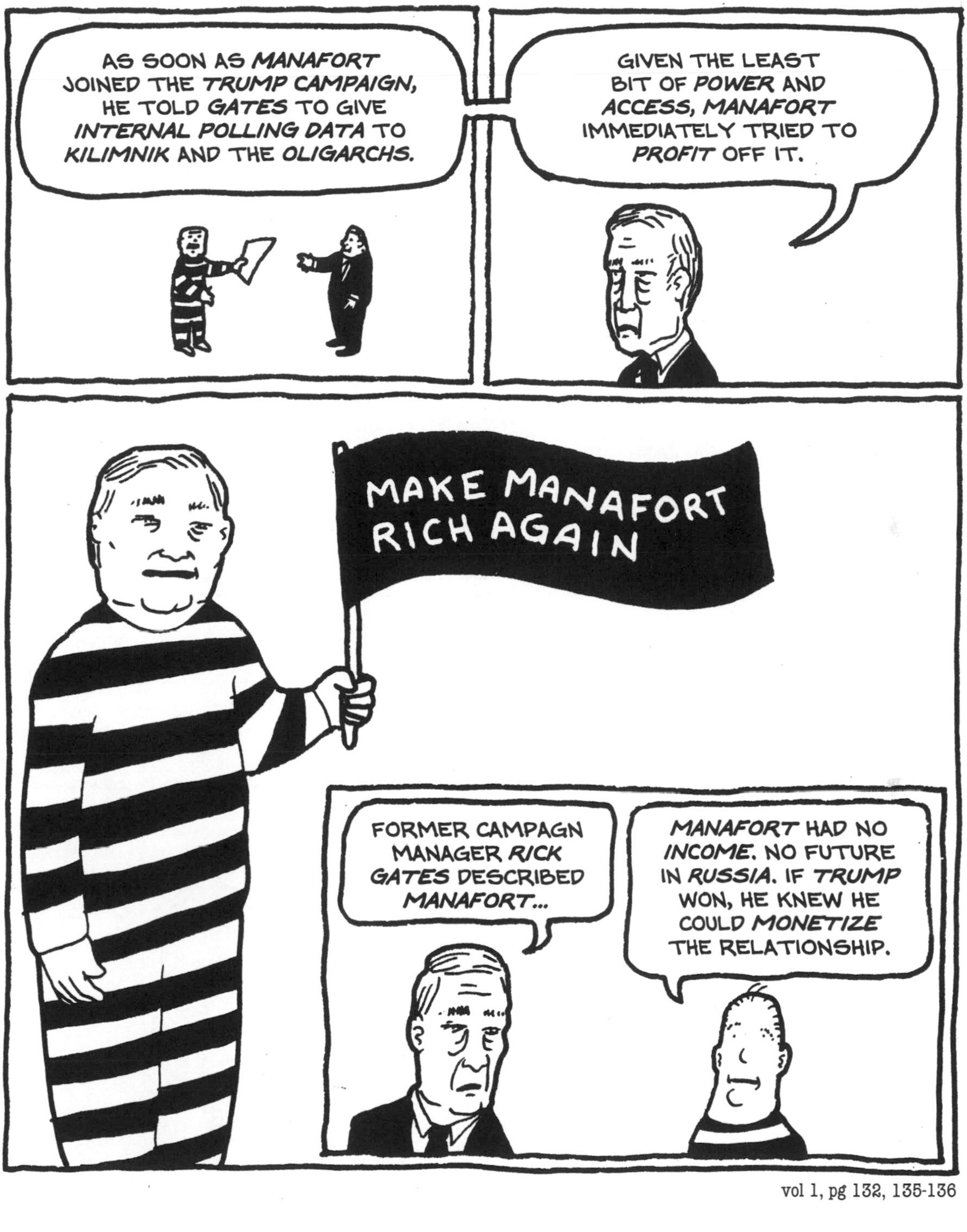
AS SOON AS MANAFORT JOINED THE TRUMP CAMPAIGN, HE TOLD GATES TO GIVE INTERNAL POLLING DATA TO KILIMNIK AND THE OLIGARCHS.
GIVEN THE LEAST BIT OF POWER AND ACCESS, MANAFORT IMMEDIATELY TRIED TO PROFIT OFF IT.
MAKE MANAFORT RICH AGAIN
FORMER CAMPAGN MANAGER RICK GATES DESCRIBED MANAFORT...
MANAFORT HAD NO INCOME. NO FUTURE IN RUSSIA. IF TRUMP WON, HE KNEW HE COULD MONETIZE THE RELATIONSHIP.

vol 1, pg 132, 135-136

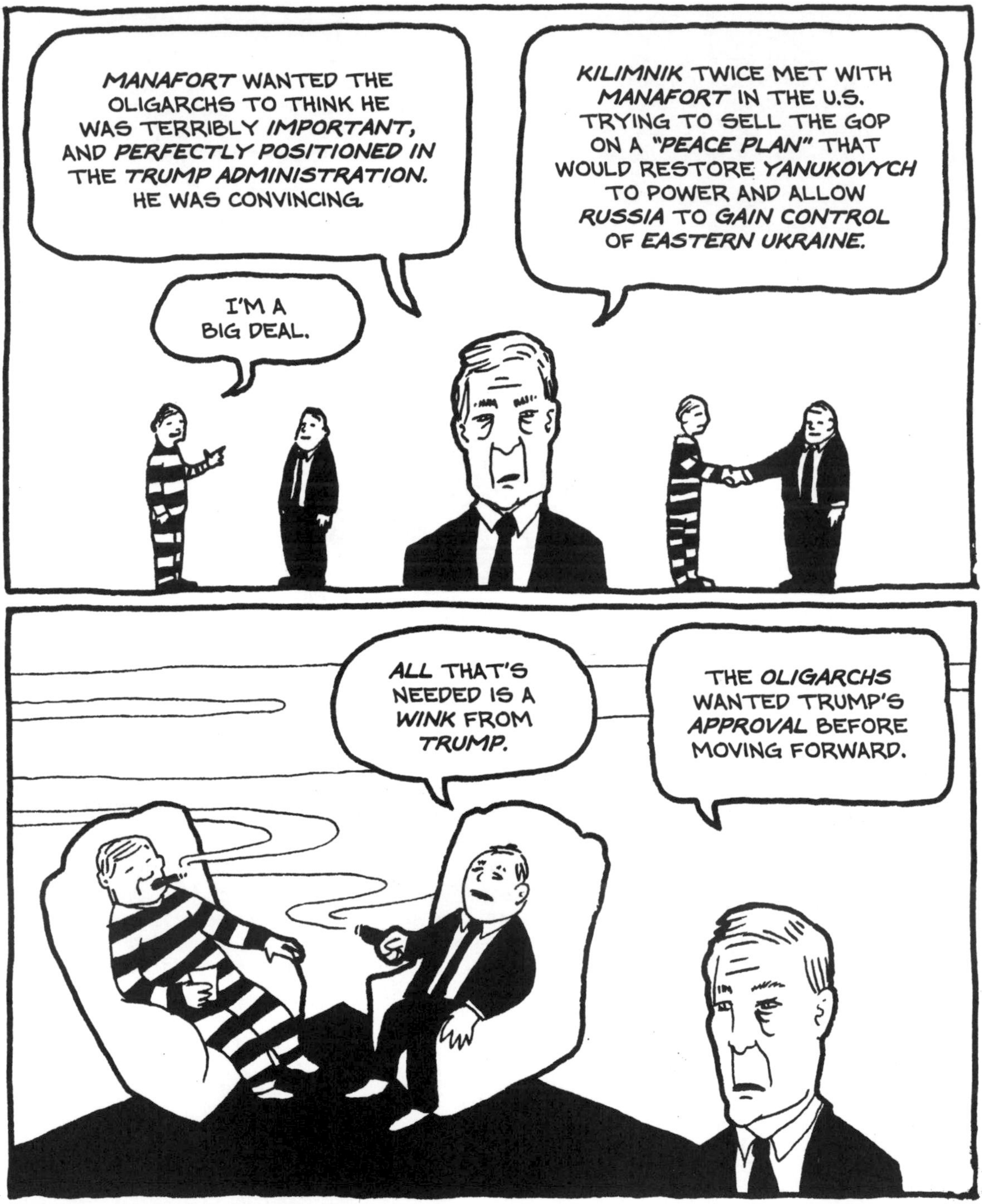
MANAFORT WANTED THE OLIGARCHS TO THINK HE WAS TERRIBLY IMPORTANT, AND PERFECTLY POSITIONED IN THE TRUMP ADMINISTRATION. HE WAS CONVINCING.
KILIMNIK TWICE MET WITH MANAFORT IN THE U.S. TRYING TO SELL THE GOP ON A "PEACE PLAN" THAT WOULD RESTORE YANUKOVYCH TO POWER AND ALLOW RUSSIA TO GAIN CONTROL OF EASTERN UKRAINE.
I'M A BIG DEAL.
ALL THAT'S NEEDED IS A WINK FROM TRUMP.
THE OLIGARCHS WANTED TRUMP'S APPROVAL BEFORE MOVING FORWARD.

Viktor Yanukovych: Ukraine President, 2010-2014 vol 1, pg 138-140

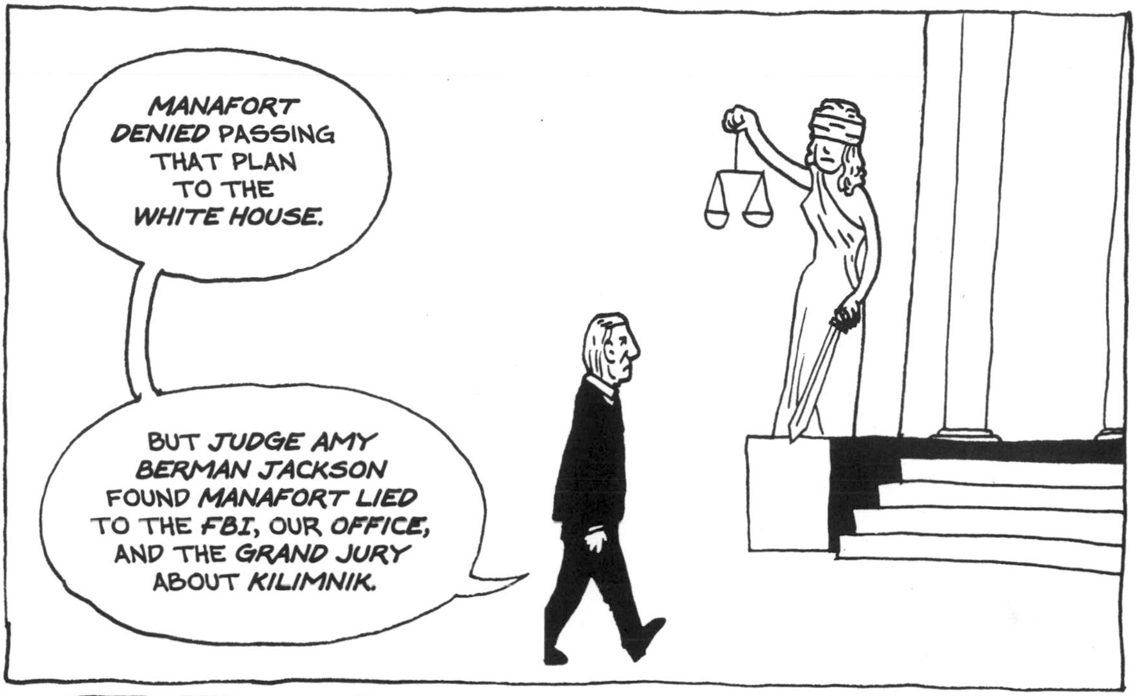
MANAFORT DENIED PASSING THAT PLAN TO THE WHITE HOUSE.
BUT JUDGE AMY BERMAN JACKSON FOUND MANAFORT LIED TO THE FBI, OUR OFFICE, AND THE GRAND JURY ABOUT KILIMNIK.

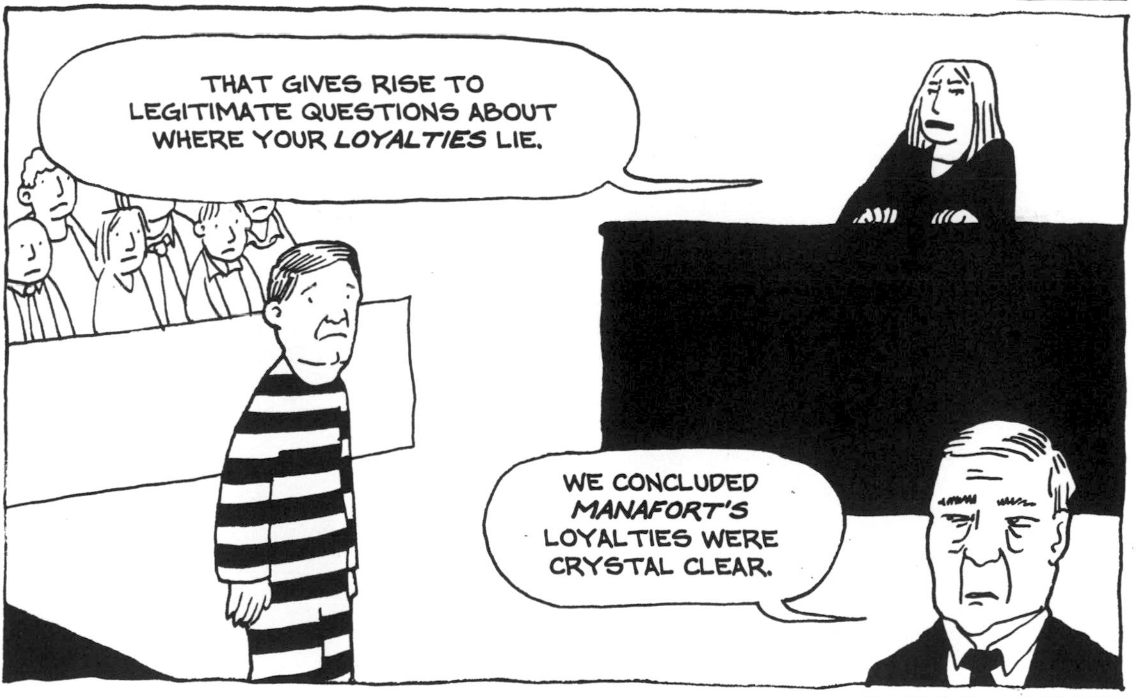
THAT GIVES RISE TO LEGITIMATE QUESTIONS ABOUT WHERE YOUR LOYALTIES LIE.
WE CONCLUDED MANAFORT'S LOYALTIES WERE CRYSTAL CLEAR.

New York Times, 2/15/2019

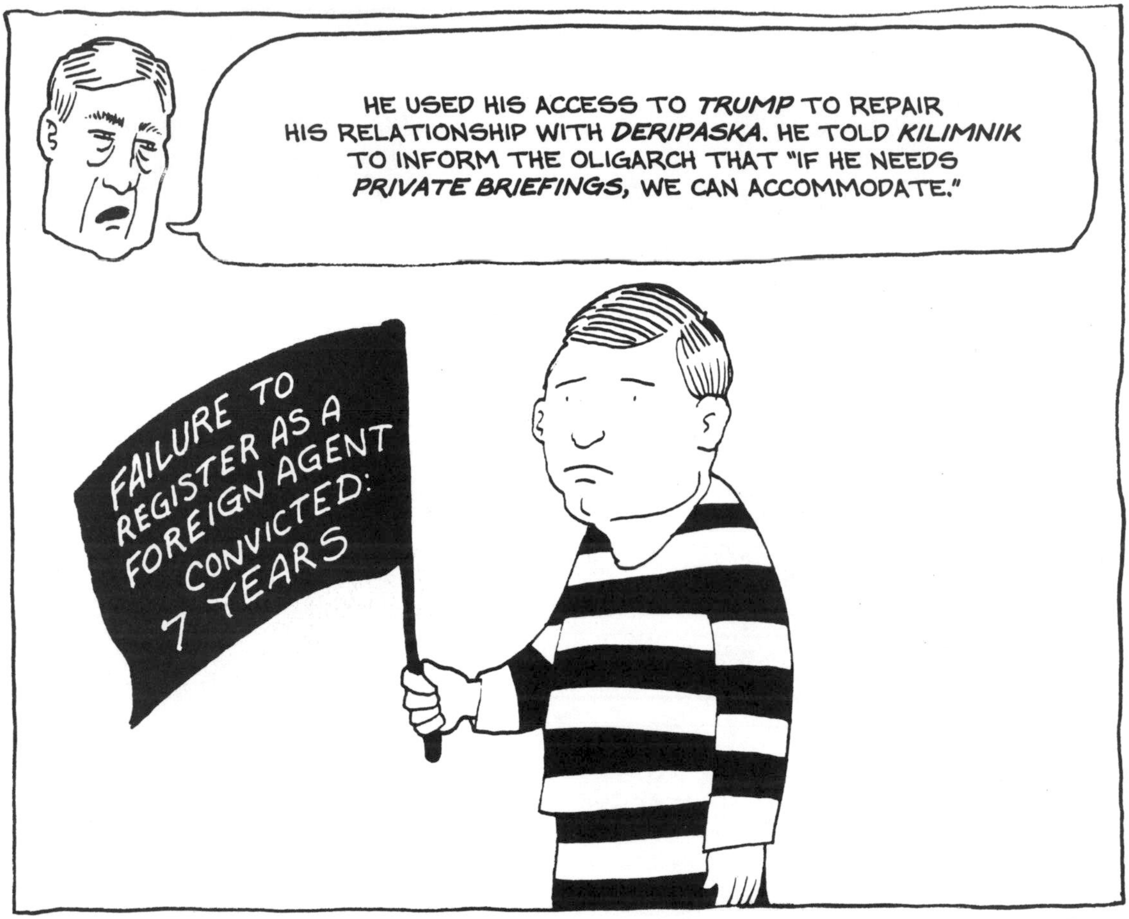
HE USED HIS ACCESS TO *TRUMP* TO REPAIR HIS RELATIONSHIP WITH *DERIPASKA*. HE TOLD *KILIMNIK* TO INFORM THE OLIGARCH THAT "IF HE NEEDS *PRIVATE BRIEFINGS*, WE CAN ACCOMMODATE."
FAILURE TO REGISTER AS A FOREIGN AGENT CONVICTED: 7 YEARS

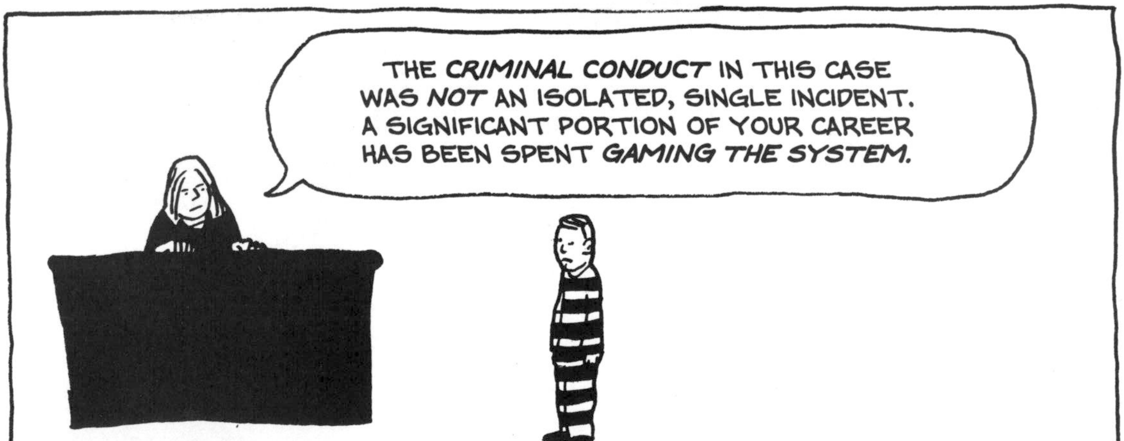
THE *CRIMINAL CONDUCT* IN THIS CASE WAS *NOT* AN ISOLATED, SINGLE INCIDENT. A SIGNIFICANT PORTION OF YOUR CAREER HAS BEEN SPENT *GAMING THE SYSTEM*.

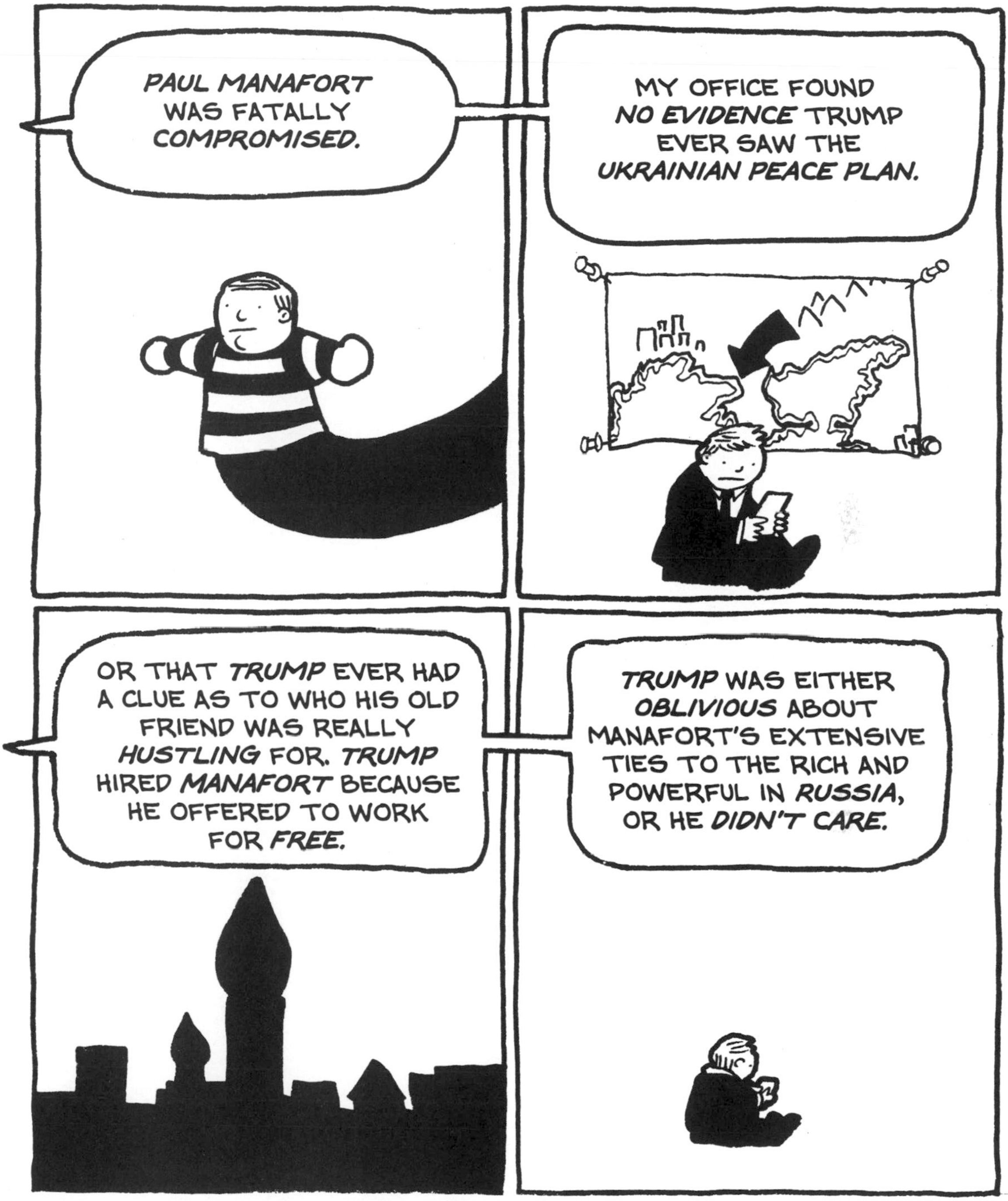
PAUL MANAFORT WAS FATALLY COMPROMISED.
MY OFFICE FOUND NO EVIDENCE TRUMP EVER SAW THE UKRAINIAN PEACE PLAN.
OR THAT TRUMP EVER HAD A CLUE AS TO WHO HIS OLD FRIEND WAS REALLY HUSTLING FOR. TRUMP HIRED MANAFORT BECAUSE HE OFFERED TO WORK FOR FREE.
TRUMP WAS EITHER OBLIVIOUS ABOUT MANAFORT'S EXTENSIVE TIES TO THE RICH AND POWERFUL IN RUSSIA, OR HE DIDN'T CARE.

vol 1, pg 144

CHAPTER 6

MICHAEL FLYNN

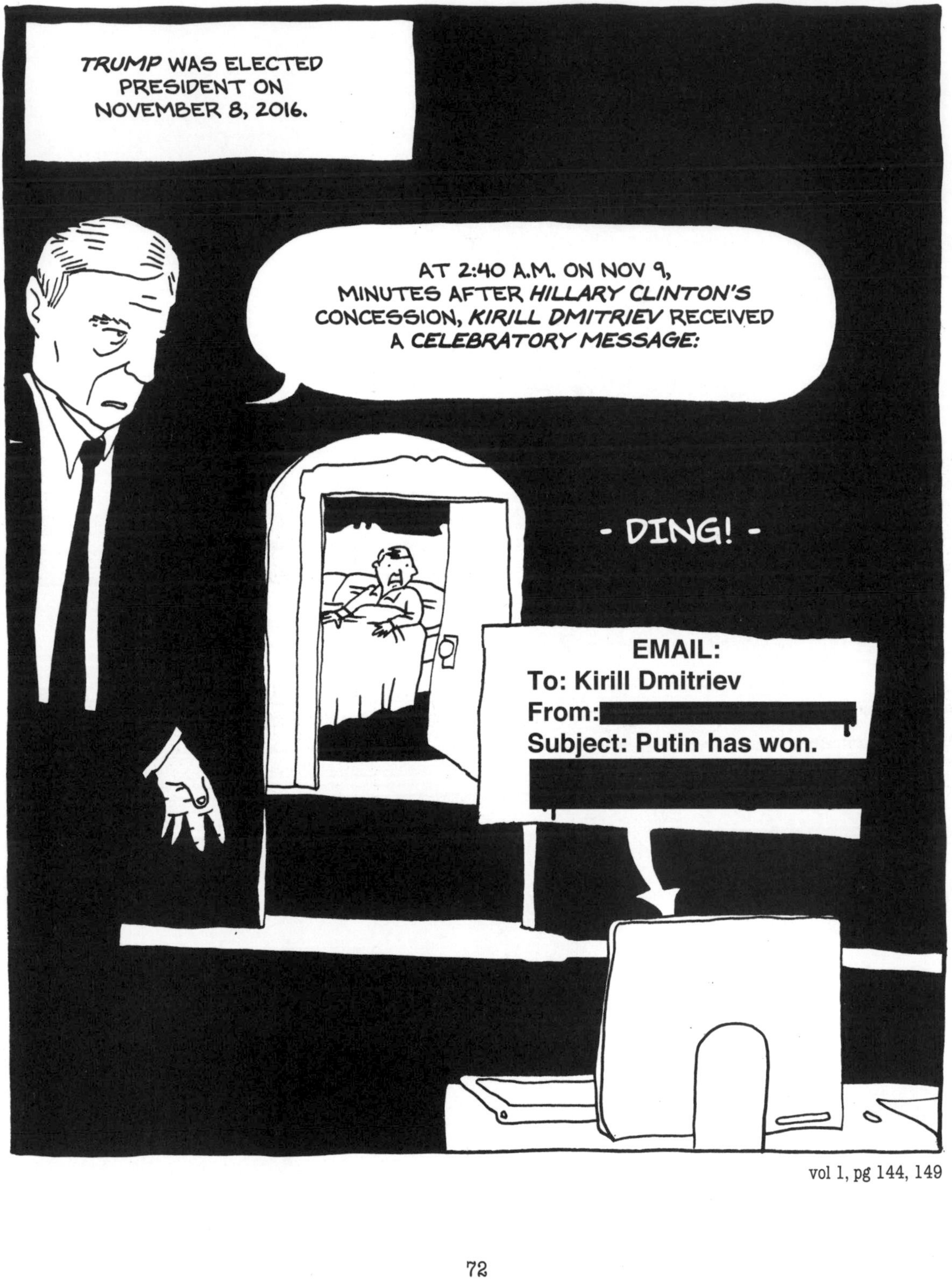
TRUMP WAS ELECTED PRESIDENT ON NOVEMBER 8, 2016.
AT 2:40 A.M. ON NOV 9, MINUTES AFTER HILLARY CLINTON'S CONCESSION, KIRILL DMITRIEV RECEIVED A CELEBRATORY MESSAGE:
- DING! -
EMAIL:
To: Kirill Dmitriev
From: [redacted]
Subject: Putin has won.
[redacted]

vol 1, pg 144, 149

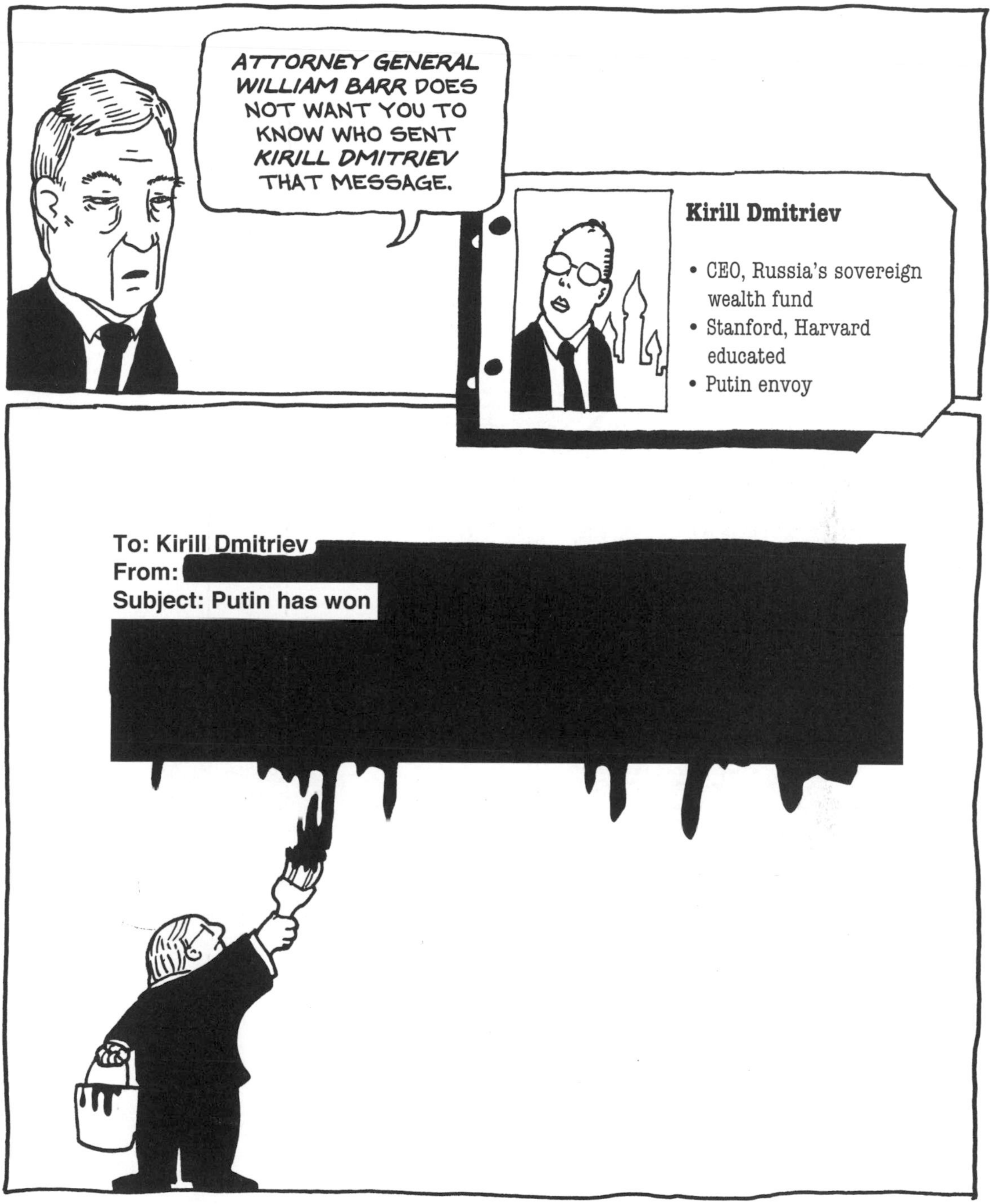
ATTORNEY GENERAL WILLIAM BARR DOES NOT WANT YOU TO KNOW WHO SENT KIRILL DMITRIEV THAT MESSAGE.
Kirill Dmitriev
• CEO, Russia's sovereign wealth fund
• Stanford, Harvard educated
• Putin envoy
To: Kirill Dmitriev [redacted]
From: [redacted]
Subject: Putin has won
[redacted]

Part 1, pg 149 classified as "Investigative Technique"

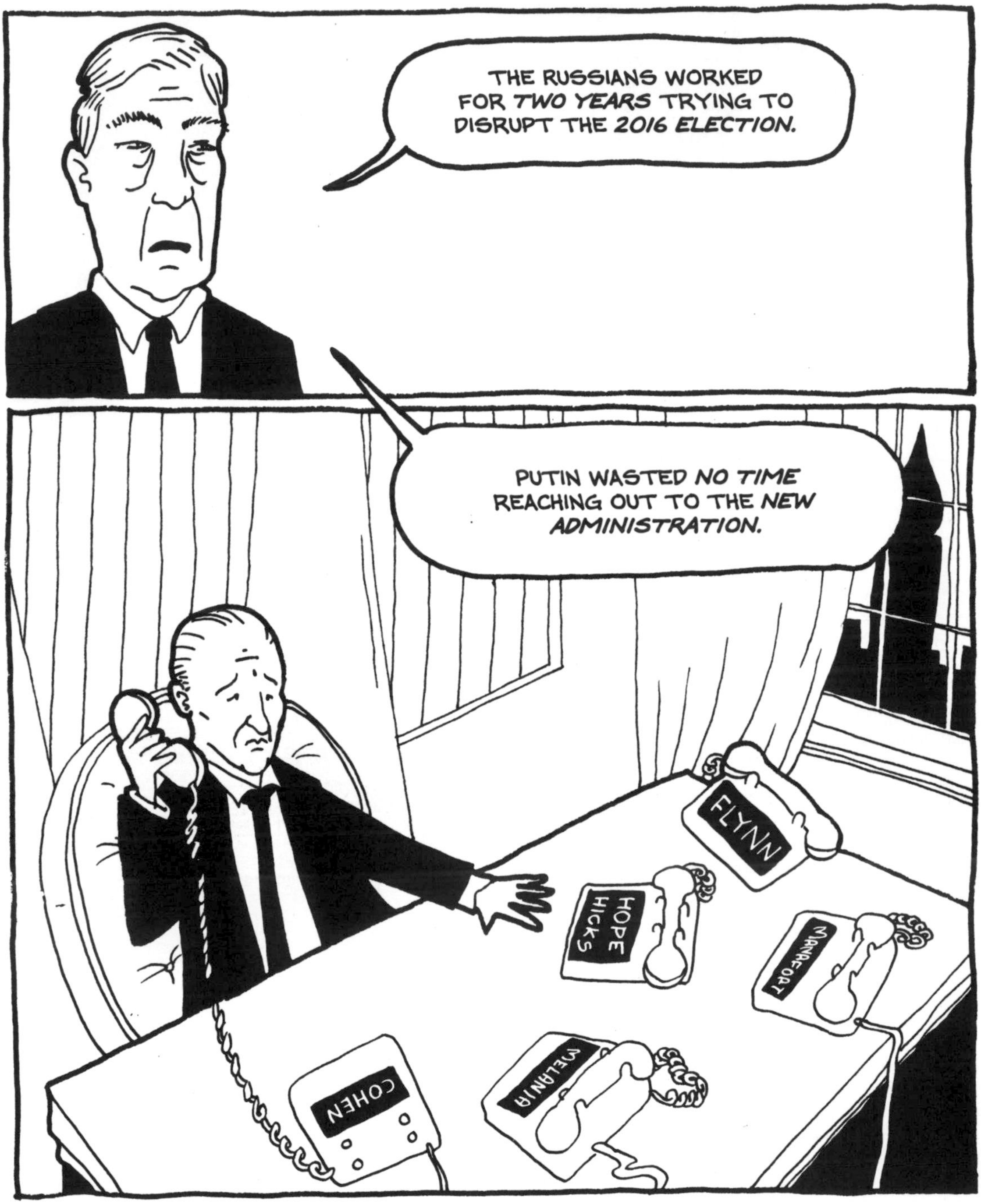
THE RUSSIANS WORKED FOR *TWO YEARS* TRYING TO DISRUPT THE *2016 ELECTION.*
PUTIN WASTED *NO TIME* REACHING OUT TO THE *NEW ADMINISTRATION.*
FLYNN
HOPE HICKS
MANAFORT
MELANIA
COHEN

Vladimir Putin: President of Russia

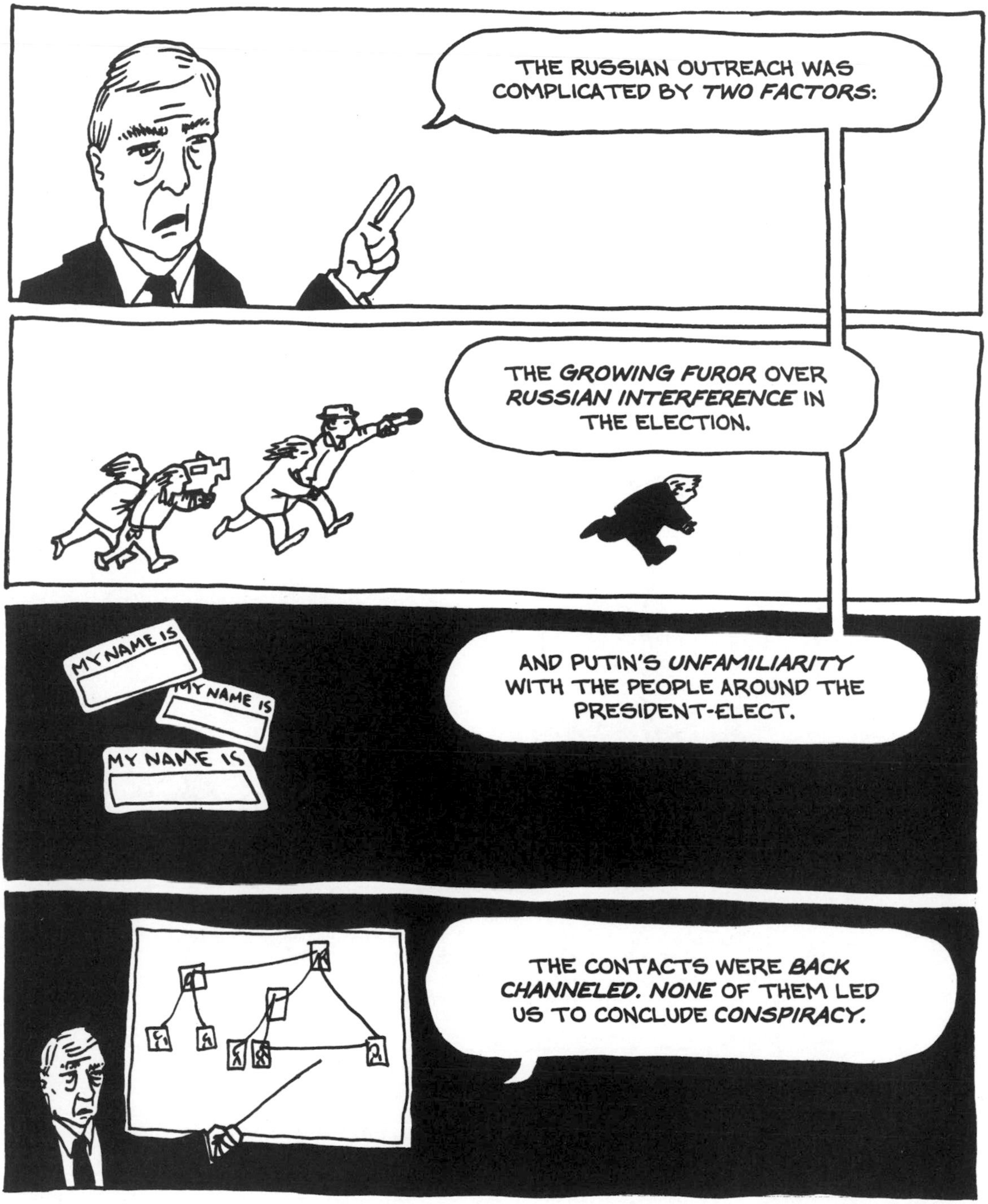

THE RUSSIAN OUTREACH WAS COMPLICATED BY *TWO FACTORS*:
THE *GROWING FUROR* OVER *RUSSIAN INTERFERENCE* IN THE ELECTION.
MY NAME IS
MY NAME IS
MY NAME IS
AND PUTIN'S *UNFAMILIARITY* WITH THE PEOPLE AROUND THE PRESIDENT-ELECT.
THE CONTACTS WERE *BACK CHANNELED. NONE* OF THEM LED US TO CONCLUDE *CONSPIRACY.*

vol 1, pg 147, 173

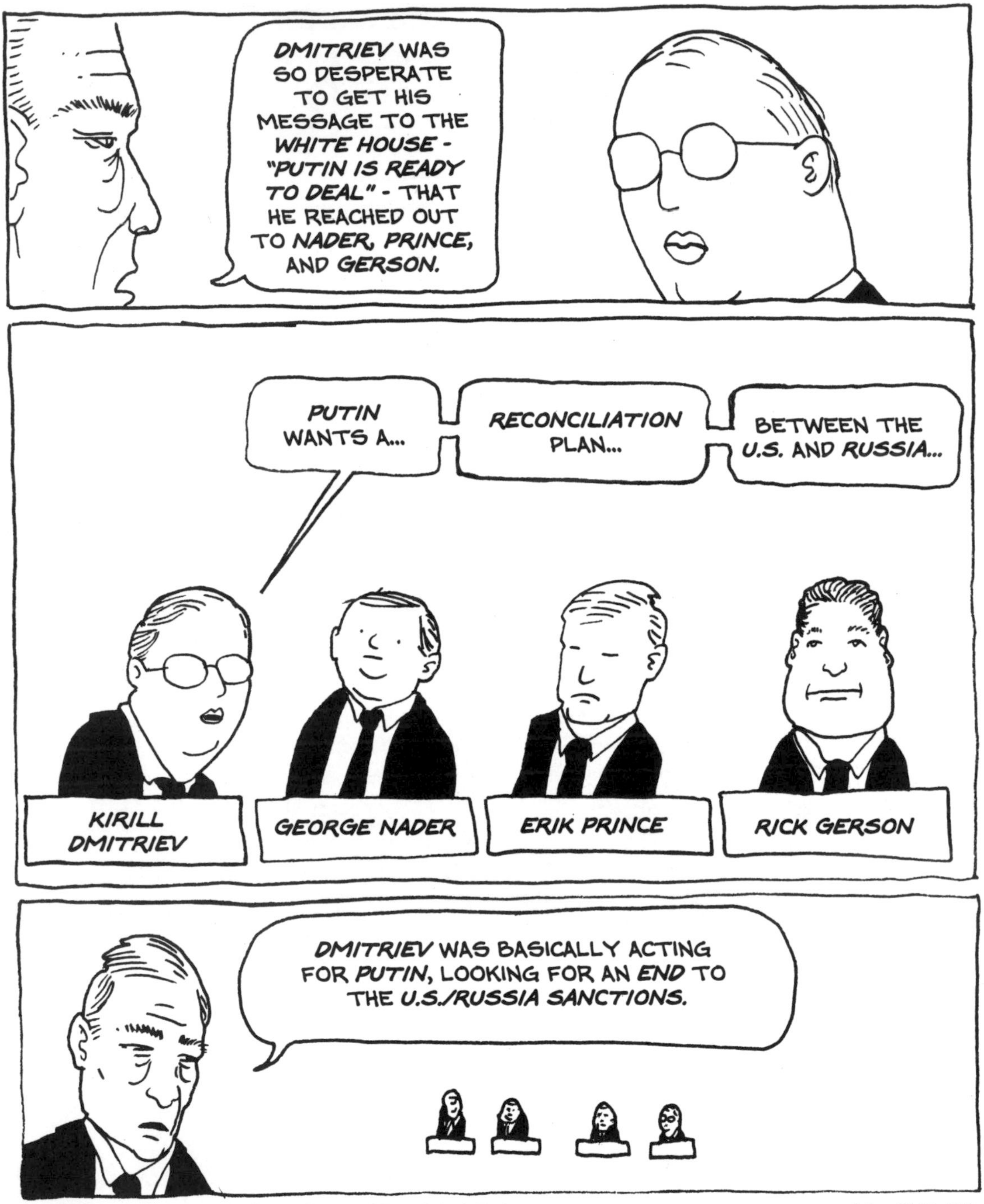
DMITRIEV WAS SO DESPERATE TO GET HIS MESSAGE TO THE WHITE HOUSE - "PUTIN IS READY TO DEAL" - THAT HE REACHED OUT TO NADER, PRINCE, AND GERSON.
PUTIN WANTS A...
RECONCILIATION PLAN...
BETWEEN THE U.S. AND RUSSIA...
KIRILL DMITRIEV
GEORGE NADER
ERIK PRINCE
RICK GERSON
DMITRIEV WAS BASICALLY ACTING FOR PUTIN, LOOKING FOR AN END TO THE U.S./RUSSIA SANCTIONS.

George Nader: Advisor to the Crown Prince of United Arab Emiates

Erik Prince: Former Navy SEAL and brother to Betsy Devos, Secretary of Education

Rick Gerson: Hedge-Fund manager and associate of Jared Kushner

vol 1, pg 147, 151

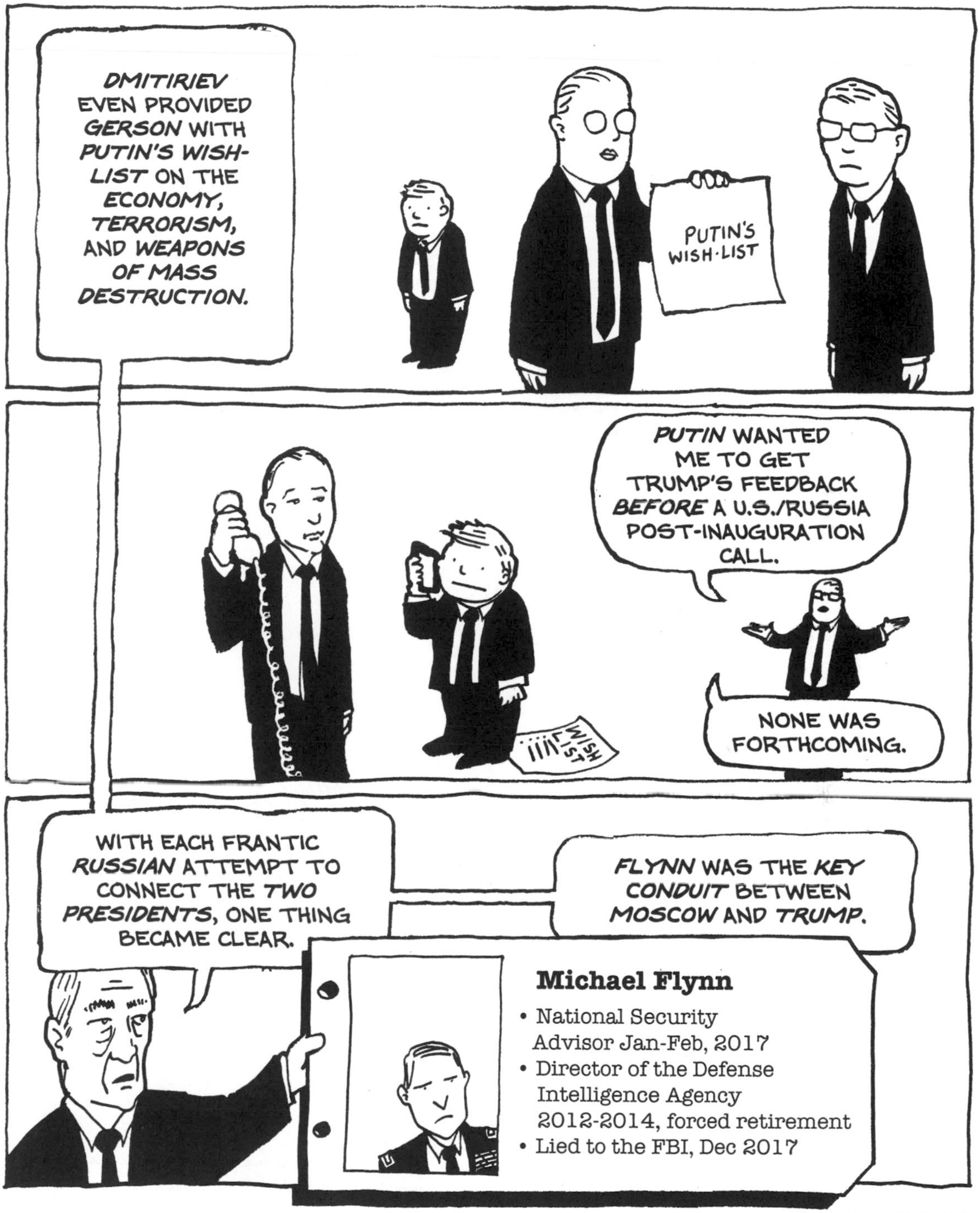
DMITIRIEV EVEN PROVIDED GERSON WITH PUTIN'S WISH-LIST ON THE ECONOMY, TERRORISM, AND WEAPONS OF MASS DESTRUCTION.
PUTIN'S WISH-LIST
PUTIN WANTED ME TO GET TRUMP'S FEEDBACK BEFORE A U.S./RUSSIA POST-INAUGURATION CALL.
WISH LIST
NONE WAS FORTHCOMING.
WITH EACH FRANTIC RUSSIAN ATTEMPT TO CONNECT THE TWO PRESIDENTS, ONE THING BECAME CLEAR.
FLYNN WAS THE KEY CONDUIT BETWEEN MOSCOW AND TRUMP.
Michael Flynn
• National Security Advisor Jan-Feb, 2017
• Director of the Defense Intelligence Agency 2012-2014, forced retirement
• Lied to the FBI, Dec 2017

vol 1, pg 158, 167

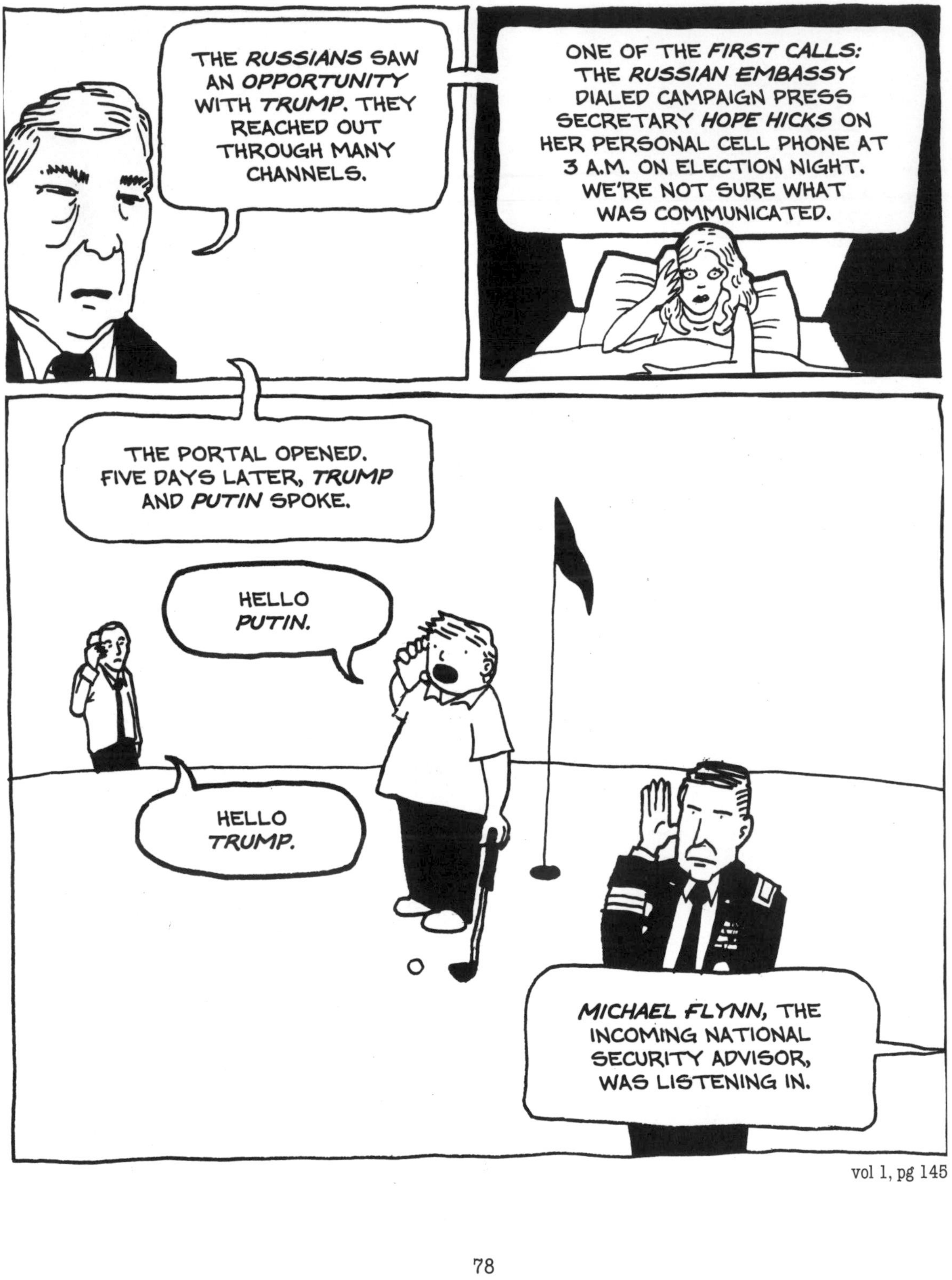
THE RUSSIANS SAW AN OPPORTUNITY WITH TRUMP. THEY REACHED OUT THROUGH MANY CHANNELS.
ONE OF THE FIRST CALLS: THE RUSSIAN EMBASSY DIALED CAMPAIGN PRESS SECRETARY HOPE HICKS ON HER PERSONAL CELL PHONE AT 3 A.M. ON ELECTION NIGHT. WE'RE NOT SURE WHAT WAS COMMUNICATED.
THE PORTAL OPENED. FIVE DAYS LATER, TRUMP AND PUTIN SPOKE.
HELLO PUTIN.
HELLO TRUMP.
MICHAEL FLYNN, THE INCOMING NATIONAL SECURITY ADVISOR, WAS LISTENING IN.

vol 1, pg 145

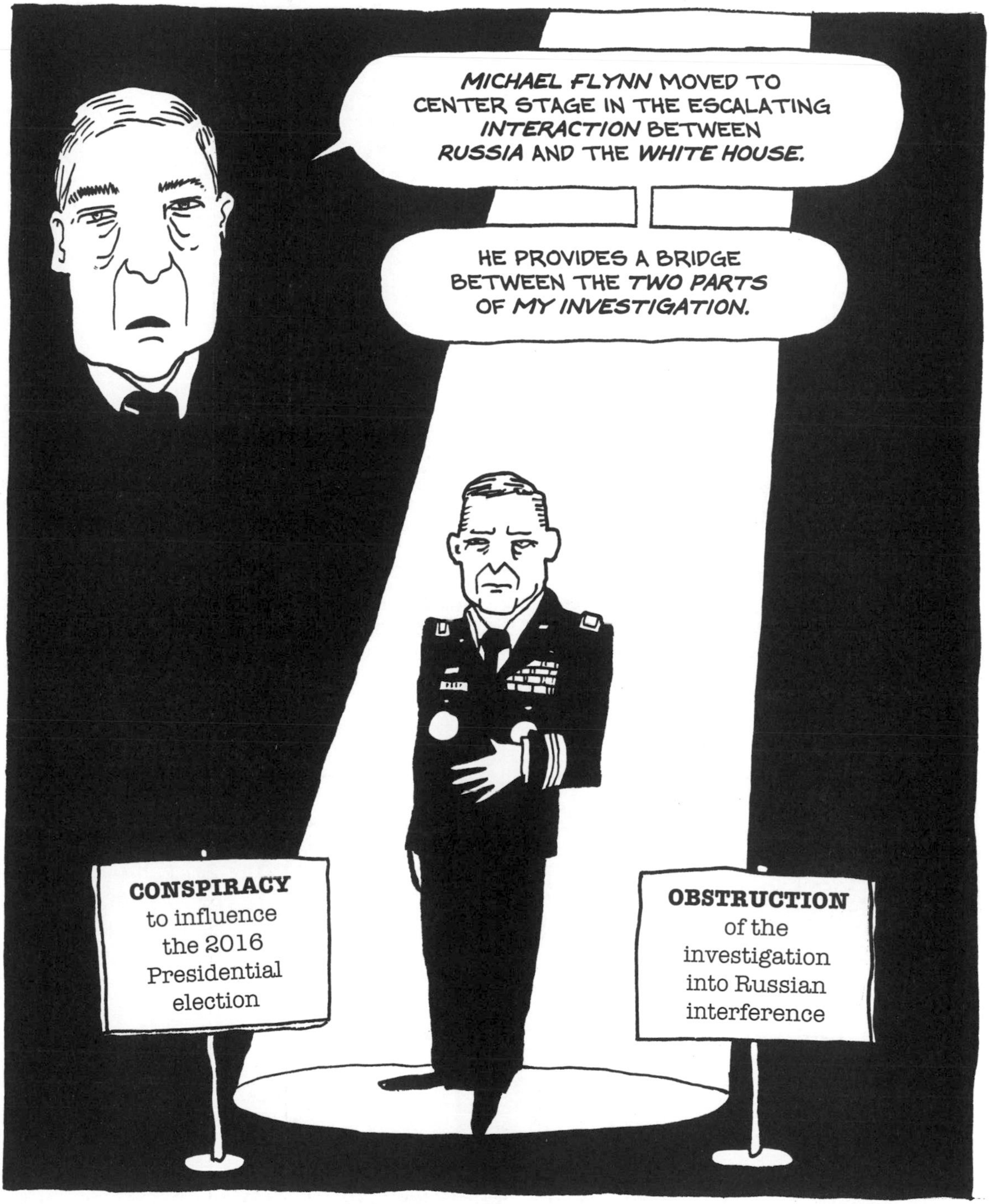
MICHAEL FLYNN MOVED TO CENTER STAGE IN THE ESCALATING INTERACTION BETWEEN RUSSIA AND THE WHITE HOUSE.
HE PROVIDES A BRIDGE BETWEEN THE TWO PARTS OF MY INVESTIGATION.
CONSPIRACY to influence the 2016 Presidential election
OBSTRUCTION of the investigation into Russian interference

vol 1, pg 167, 195

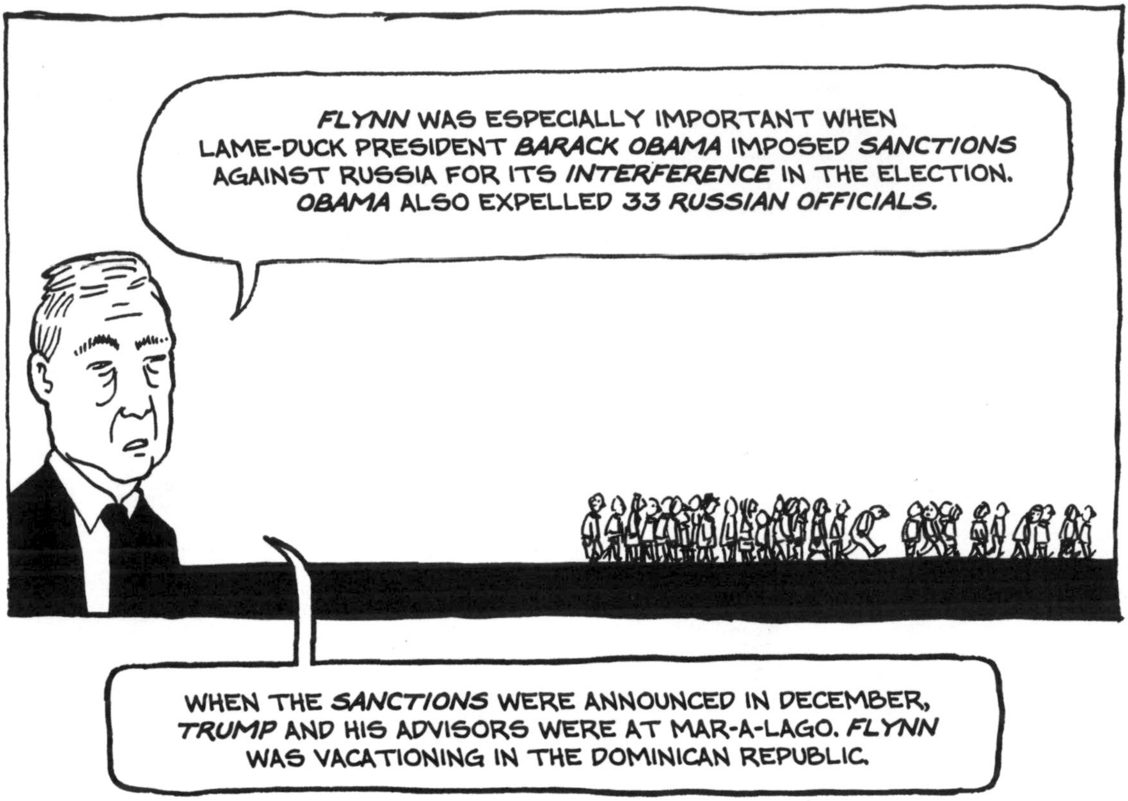
FLYNN WAS ESPECIALLY IMPORTANT WHEN LAME-DUCK PRESIDENT BARACK OBAMA IMPOSED SANCTIONS AGAINST RUSSIA FOR ITS INTERFERENCE IN THE ELECTION. OBAMA ALSO EXPELLED 33 RUSSIAN OFFICIALS.
WHEN THE SANCTIONS WERE ANNOUNCED IN DECEMBER, TRUMP AND HIS ADVISORS WERE AT MAR-A-LAGO. FLYNN WAS VACATIONING IN THE DOMINICAN REPUBLIC.

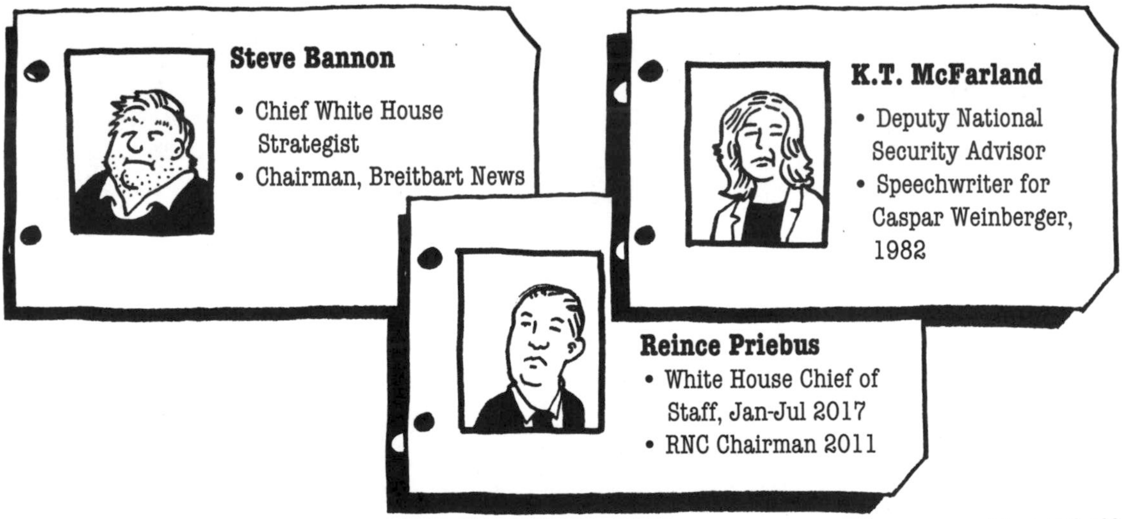
Steve Bannon
• Chief White House Strategist
• Chairman, Breitbart News
K.T. McFarland
• Deputy National Security Advisor
• Speechwriter for Caspar Weinberger, 1982
Reince Priebus
• White House Chief of Staff, Jan-Jul 2017
• RNC Chairman 2011

vol 1, pg 168-169

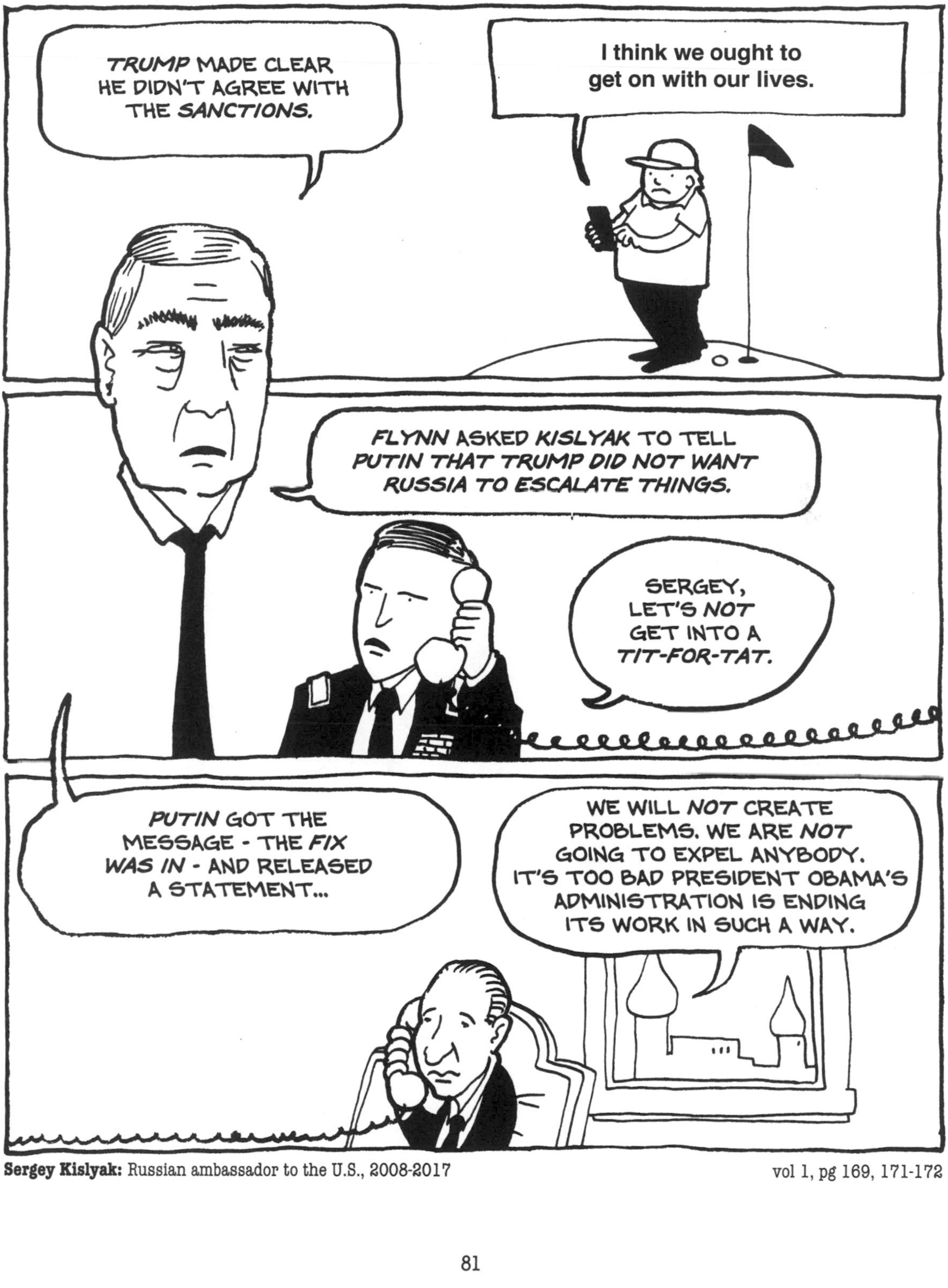
TRUMP MADE CLEAR HE DIDN'T AGREE WITH THE SANCTIONS.
I think we ought to get on with our lives.
FLYNN ASKED KISLYAK TO TELL PUTIN THAT TRUMP DID NOT WANT RUSSIA TO ESCALATE THINGS.
SERGEY, LET'S NOT GET INTO A TIT-FOR-TAT.
PUTIN GOT THE MESSAGE - THE FIX WAS IN - AND RELEASED A STATEMENT...
WE WILL NOT CREATE PROBLEMS. WE ARE NOT GOING TO EXPEL ANYBODY. IT'S TOO BAD PRESIDENT OBAMA'S ADMINISTRATION IS ENDING ITS WORK IN SUCH A WAY.

Sergey Kislyak: Russian ambassador to the U.S., 2008-2017

vol 1, pg 169, 171-172

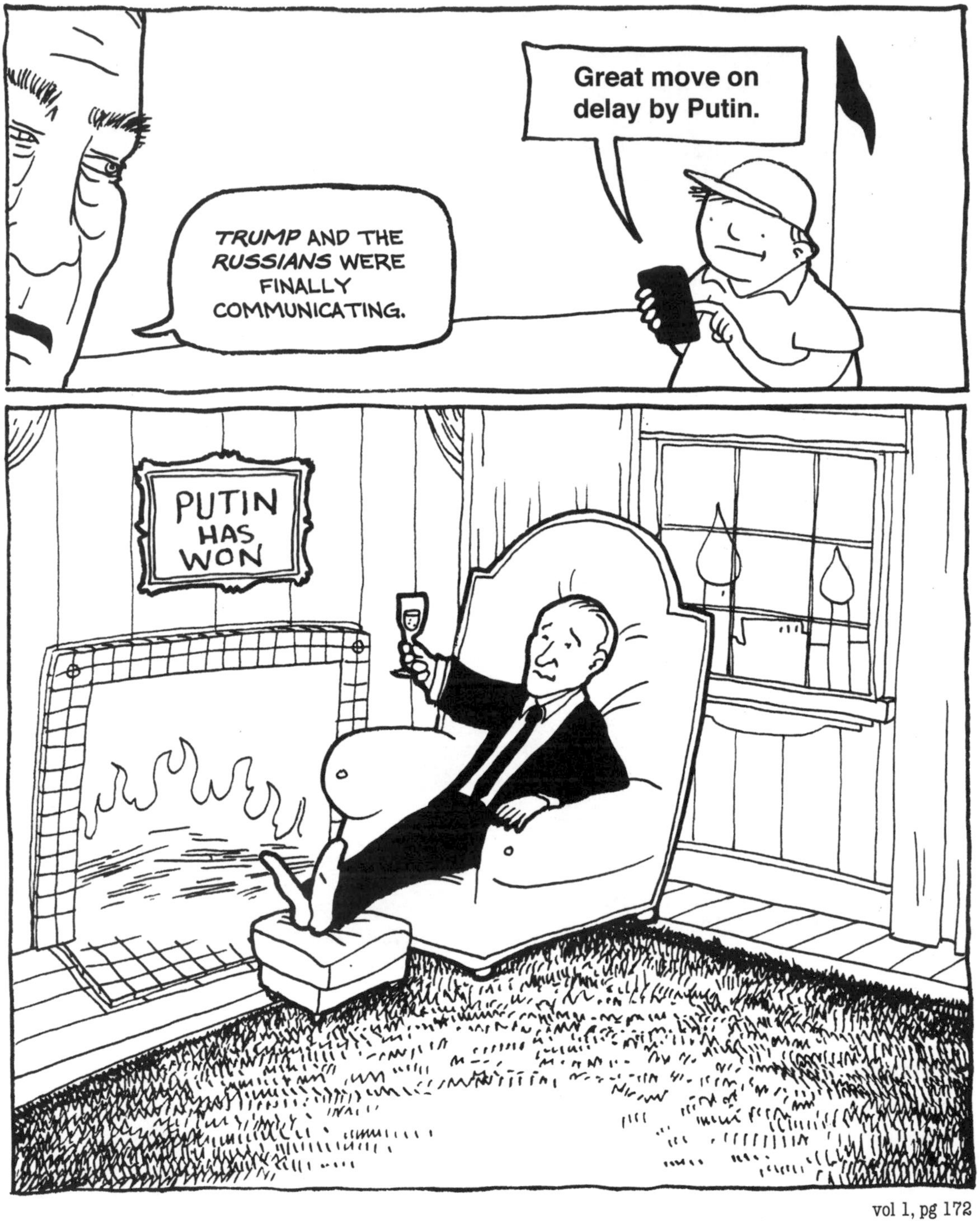
TRUMP AND THE *RUSSIANS* WERE FINALLY COMMUNICATING.
Great move on delay by Putin.
PUTIN HAS WON

vol 1, pg 172

CHAPTER 7

THE CASE FOR OBSTRUCTION

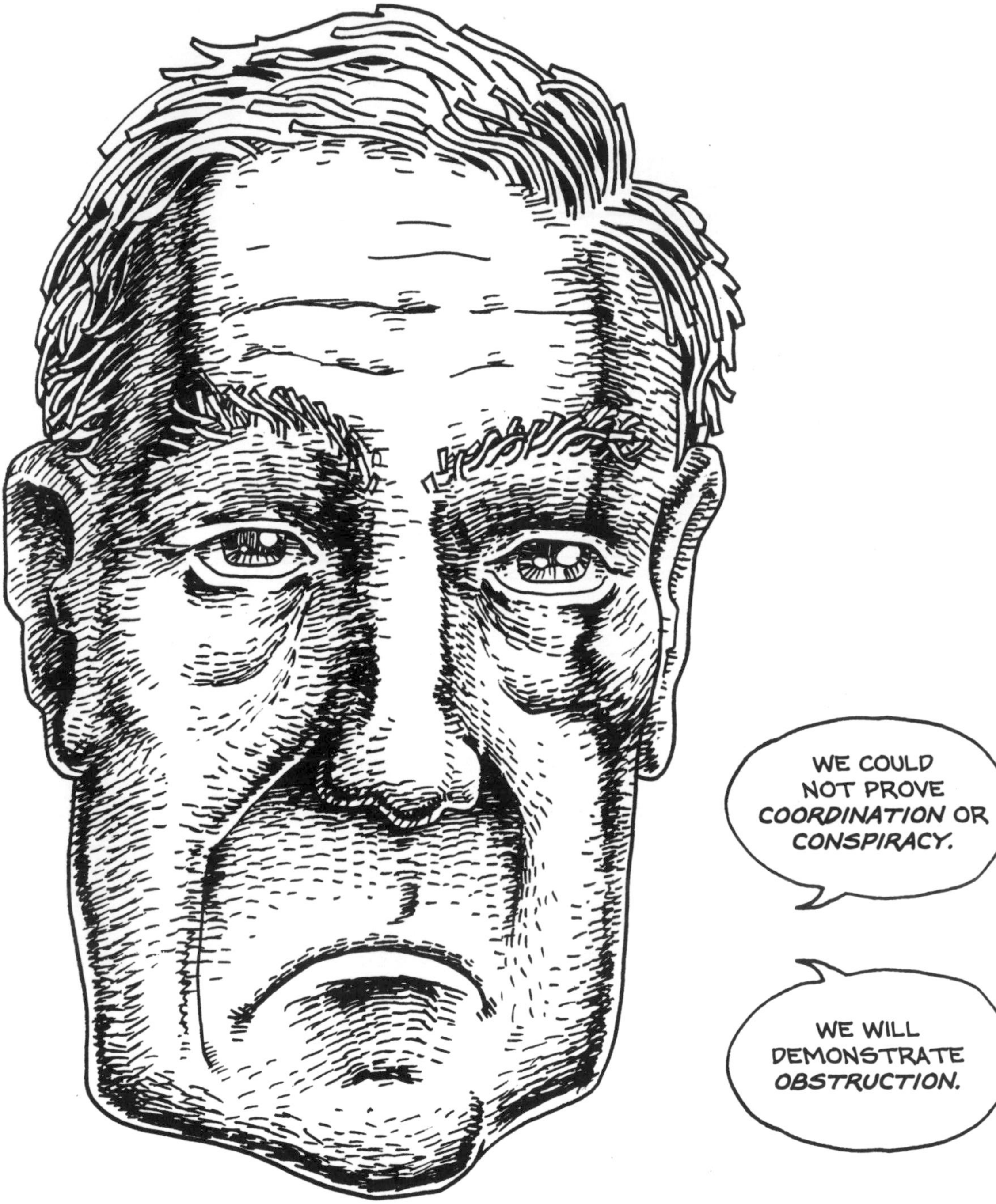
WE COULD NOT PROVE COORDINATION OR CONSPIRACY.
WE WILL DEMONSTRATE OBSTRUCTION.

vol 1, pg 173, 195

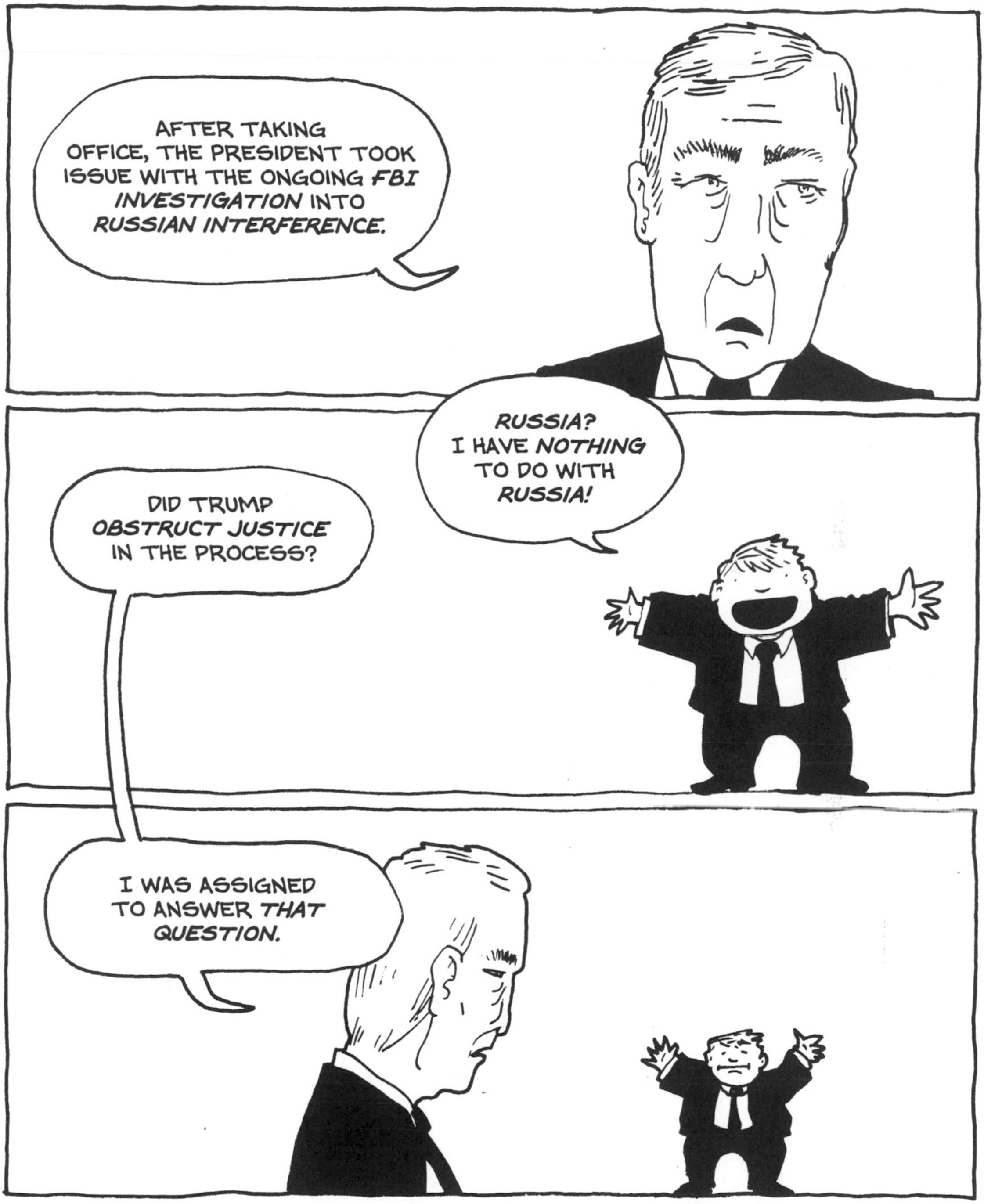
AFTER TAKING OFFICE, THE PRESIDENT TOOK ISSUE WITH THE ONGOING *FBI INVESTIGATION* INTO *RUSSIAN INTERFERENCE.*
RUSSIA? I HAVE *NOTHING* TO DO WITH *RUSSIA!*
DID TRUMP *OBSTRUCT JUSTICE* IN THE PROCESS?
I WAS ASSIGNED TO ANSWER *THAT QUESTION.*

vol 2, pg 1

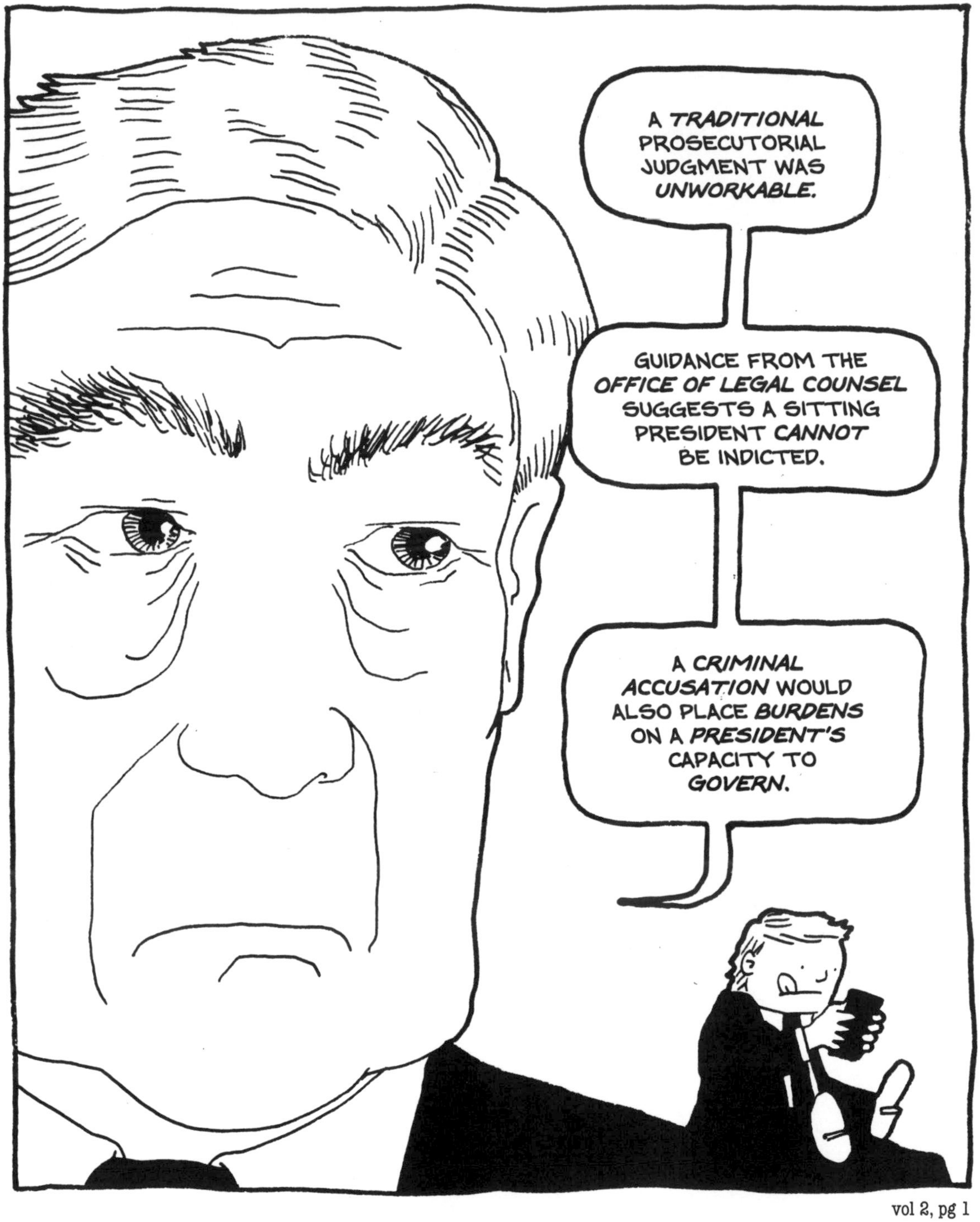
A TRADITIONAL PROSECUTORIAL JUDGMENT WAS UNWORKABLE.
GUIDANCE FROM THE OFFICE OF LEGAL COUNSEL SUGGESTS A SITTING PRESIDENT CANNOT BE INDICTED.
A CRIMINAL ACCUSATION WOULD ALSO PLACE BURDENS ON A PRESIDENT'S CAPACITY TO GOVERN.

vol 2, pg 1

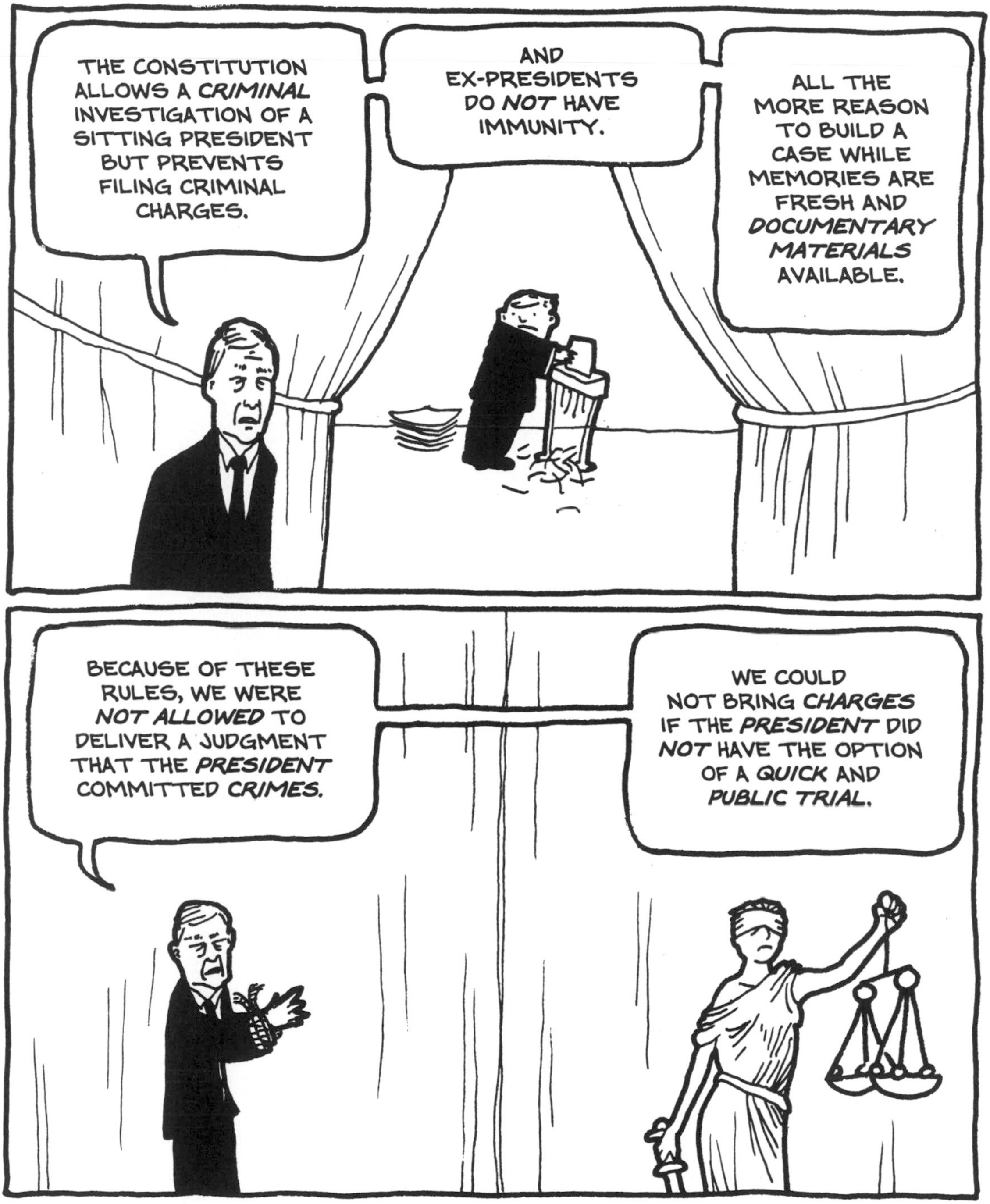
THE CONSTITUTION ALLOWS A CRIMINAL INVESTIGATION OF A SITTING PRESIDENT BUT PREVENTS FILING CRIMINAL CHARGES.
AND EX-PRESIDENTS DO NOT HAVE IMMUNITY.
ALL THE MORE REASON TO BUILD A CASE WHILE MEMORIES ARE FRESH AND DOCUMENTARY MATERIALS AVAILABLE.
BECAUSE OF THESE RULES, WE WERE NOT ALLOWED TO DELIVER A JUDGMENT THAT THE PRESIDENT COMMITTED CRIMES.
WE COULD NOT BRING CHARGES IF THE PRESIDENT DID NOT HAVE THE OPTION OF A QUICK AND PUBLIC TRIAL.

vol 2, pg 1-2

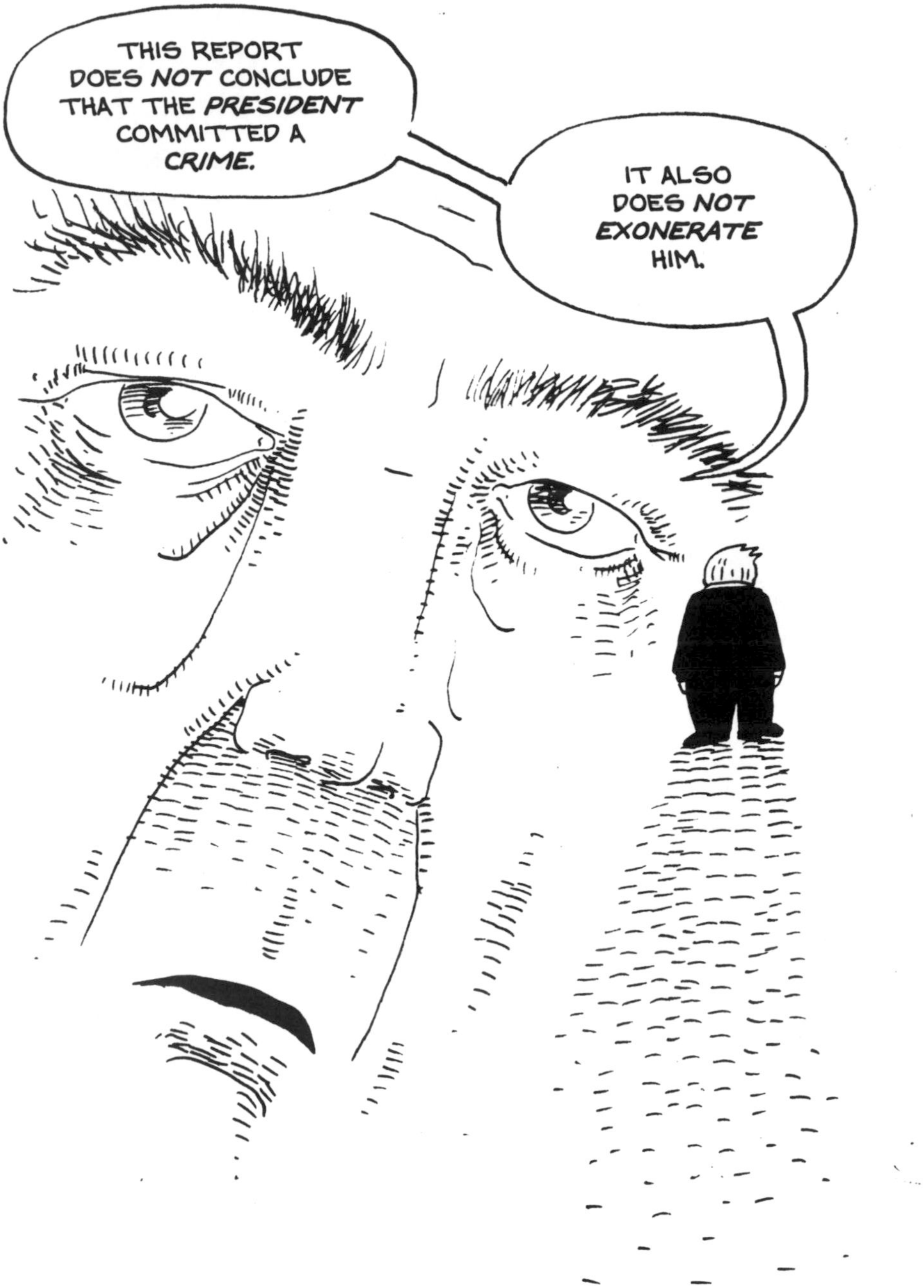
THIS REPORT DOES NOT CONCLUDE THAT THE PRESIDENT COMMITTED A CRIME.
IT ALSO DOES NOT EXONERATE HIM.

vol 2, pg 2

CHAPTER 8

FLYNN'S LIES AND THE LOYALTY PLEDGE

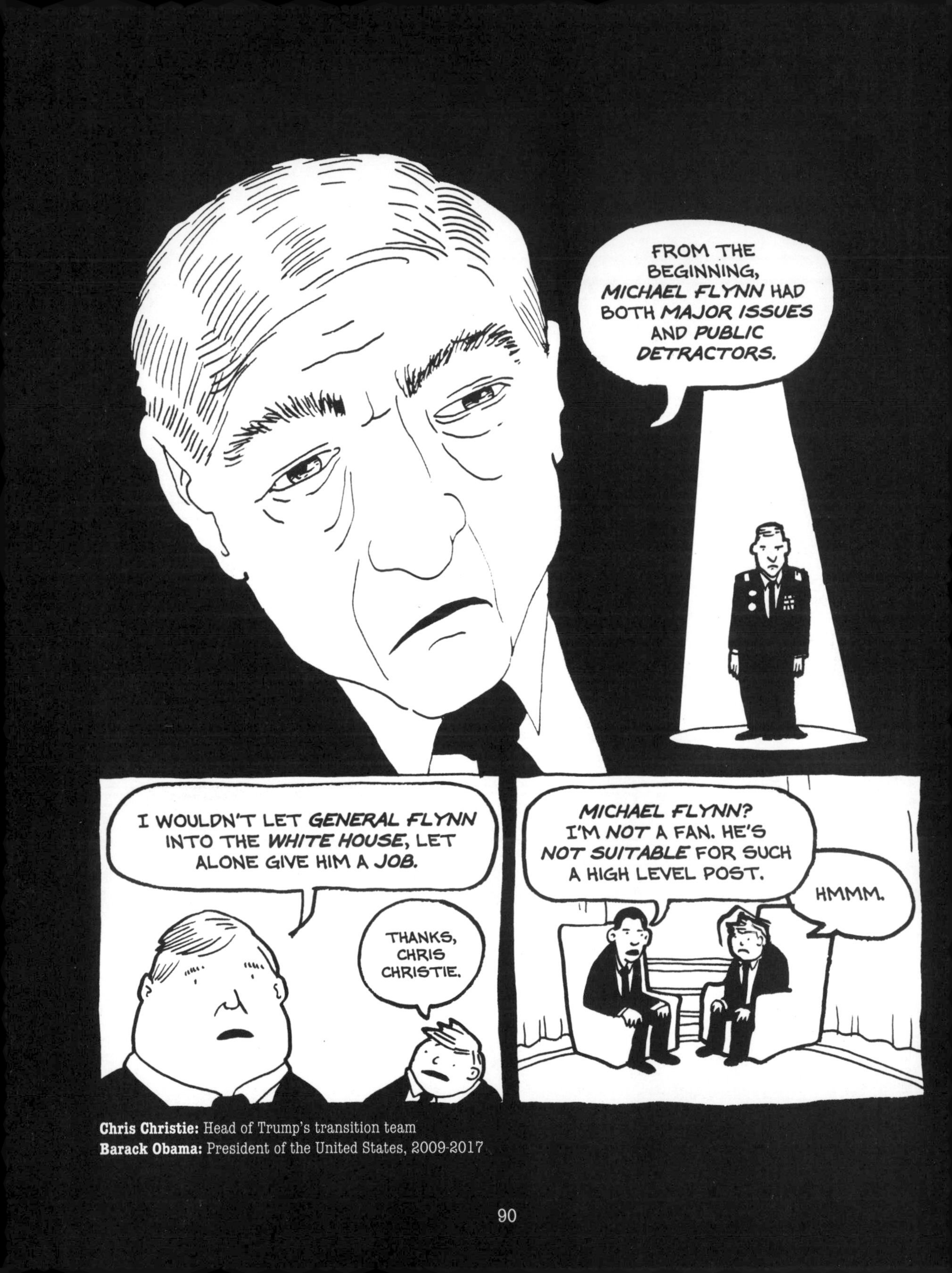
FROM THE BEGINNING, MICHAEL FLYNN HAD BOTH MAJOR ISSUES AND PUBLIC DETRACTORS.
I WOULDN'T LET GENERAL FLYNN INTO THE WHITE HOUSE, LET ALONE GIVE HIM A JOB.
THANKS, CHRIS CHRISTIE.
MICHAEL FLYNN? I'M NOT A FAN. HE'S NOT SUITABLE FOR SUCH A HIGH LEVEL POST.
HMMM.

Chris Christie: Head of Trump's transition team
Barack Obama: President of the United States, 2009-2017

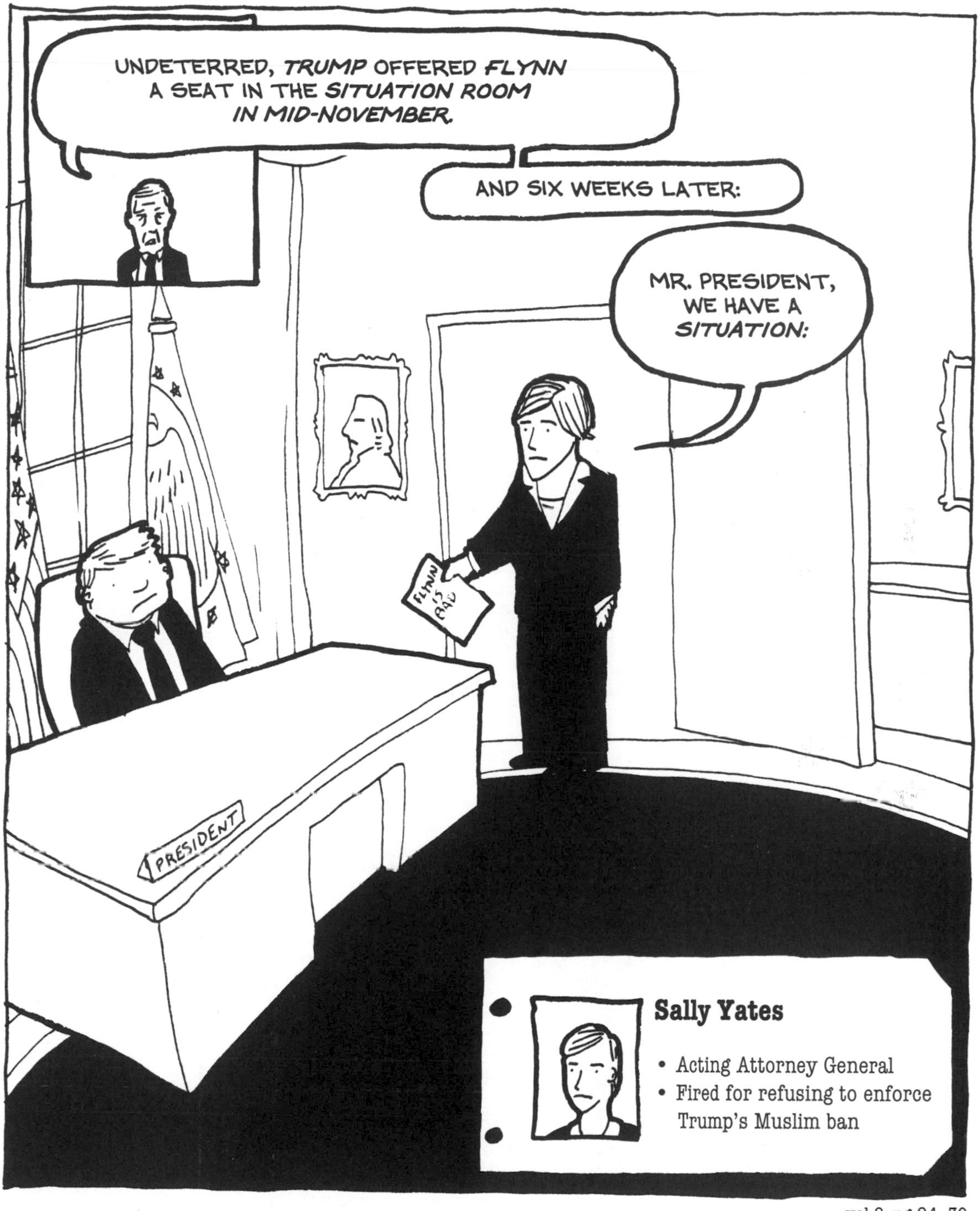
UNDETERRED, TRUMP OFFERED FLYNN A SEAT IN THE SITUATION ROOM IN MID-NOVEMBER.
AND SIX WEEKS LATER:
MR. PRESIDENT, WE HAVE A SITUATION:
FLYNN IS BAD
PRESIDENT
Sally Yates
• Acting Attorney General
• Fired for refusing to enforce Trump's Muslim ban

vol 2, pg 24, 30

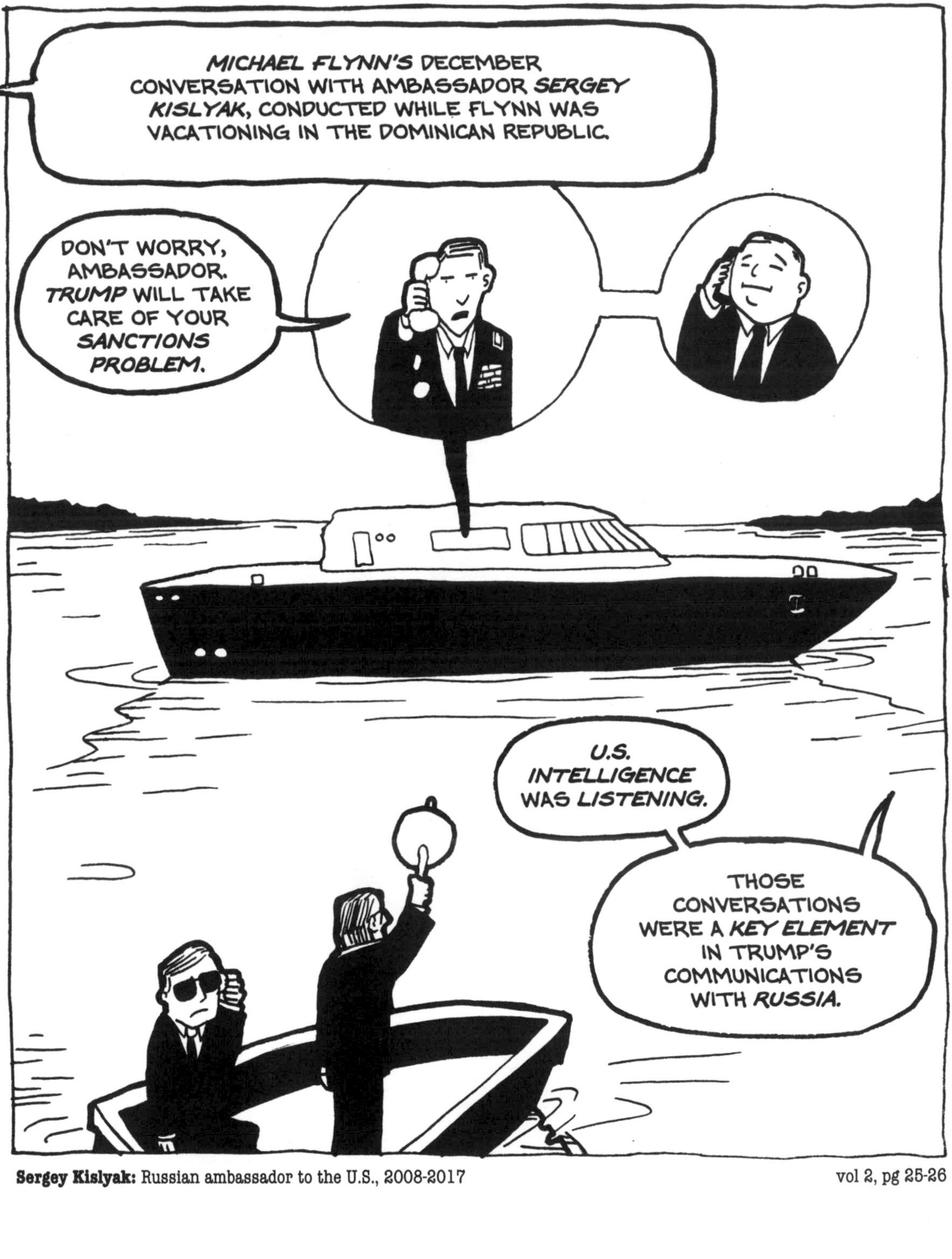
MICHAEL FLYNN'S DECEMBER CONVERSATION WITH AMBASSADOR SERGEY KISLYAK, CONDUCTED WHILE FLYNN WAS VACATIONING IN THE DOMINICAN REPUBLIC.
DON'T WORRY, AMBASSADOR. TRUMP WILL TAKE CARE OF YOUR SANCTIONS PROBLEM.
U.S. INTELLIGENCE WAS LISTENING.
THOSE CONVERSATIONS WERE A KEY ELEMENT IN TRUMP'S COMMUNICATIONS WITH RUSSIA.

Sergey Kislyak: Russian ambassador to the U.S., 2008-2017 vol 2, pg 25-26

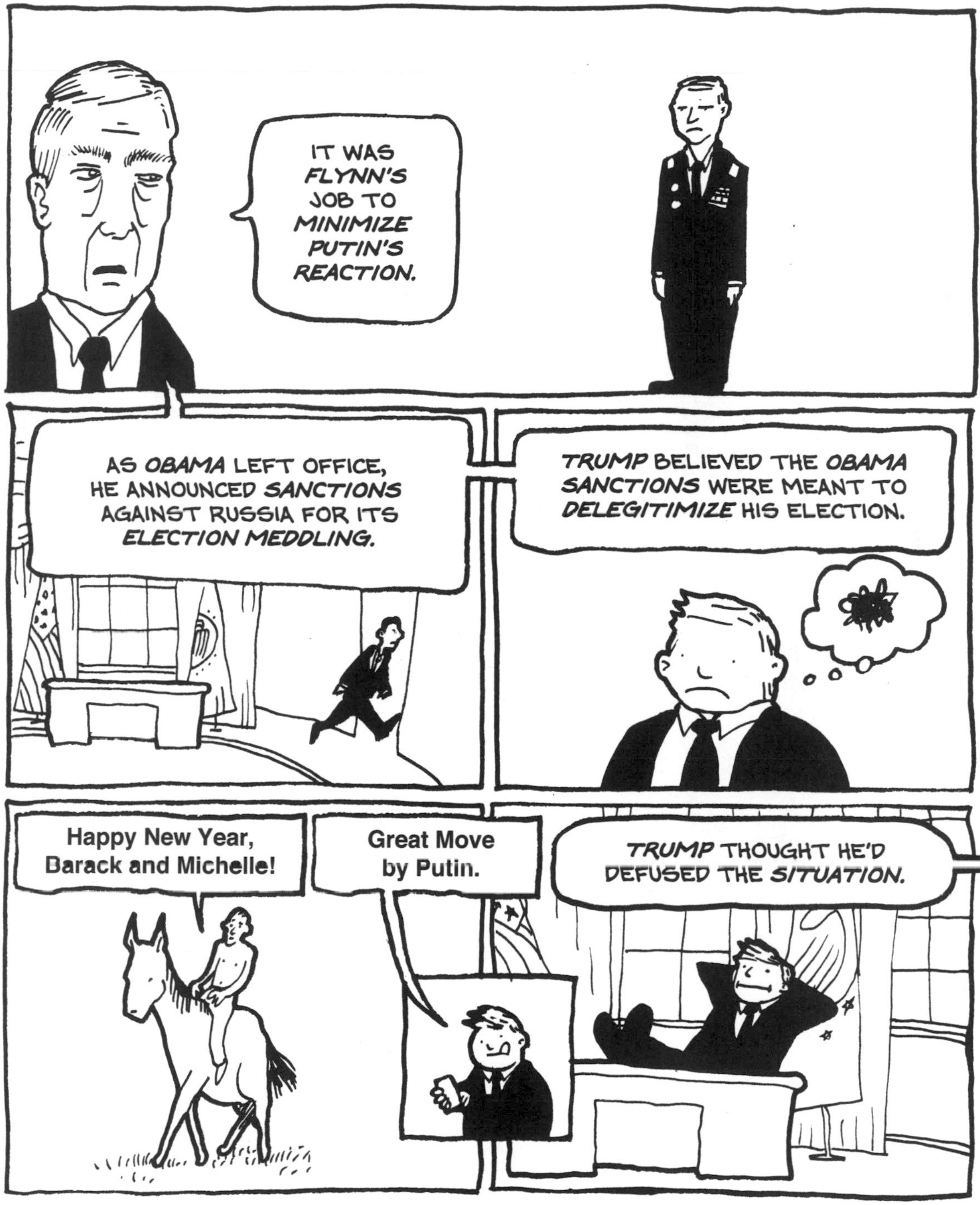
IT WAS FLYNN'S JOB TO MINIMIZE PUTIN'S REACTION.
AS OBAMA LEFT OFFICE, HE ANNOUNCED SANCTIONS AGAINST RUSSIA FOR ITS ELECTION MEDDLING.
TRUMP BELIEVED THE OBAMA SANCTIONS WERE MEANT TO DELEGITIMIZE HIS ELECTION.
Happy New Year, Barack and Michelle!
Great Move by Putin.
TRUMP THOUGHT HE'D DEFUSED THE SITUATION.

vol 2, pg 24-26

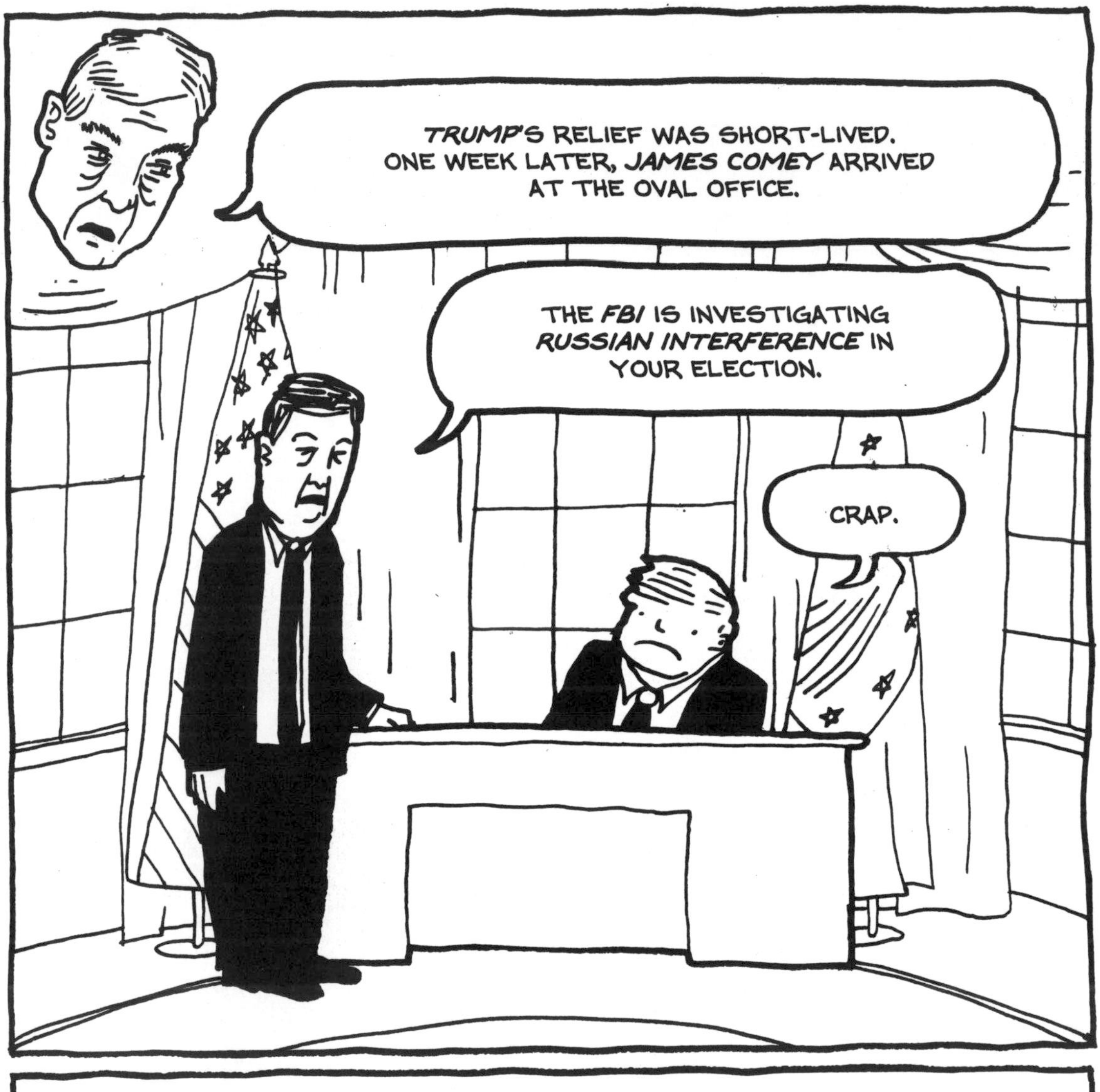
TRUMP'S RELIEF WAS SHORT-LIVED. ONE WEEK LATER, JAMES COMEY ARRIVED AT THE OVAL OFFICE.
THE FBI IS INVESTIGATING RUSSIAN INTERFERENCE IN YOUR ELECTION.
CRAP.

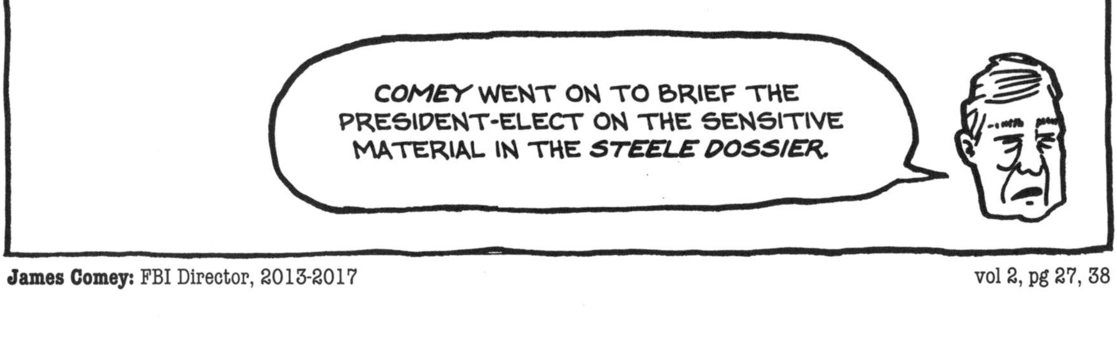
COMEY WENT ON TO BRIEF THE PRESIDENT-ELECT ON THE SENSITIVE MATERIAL IN THE STEELE DOSSIER.

James Comey: FBI Director, 2013-2017

vol 2, pg 27, 38

THE *STEELE DOSSIER* WAS AN EXTENSIVE REPORT DETAILING *MULTIPLE ALLEGATIONS* AGAINST *TRUMP*.

1. *FUSION GPS* WAS ORIGINALLY HIRED IN *2015* TO DO *OPPOSITION RESEARCH* ON *DONALD TRUMP* BY *THE WASHINGTON FREE BEACON,* A CONSERVATIVE WEBSITE. THE *FREE BEACON* WAS FUNDED BY *PAUL SINGER,* A MAJOR SUPPORTER OF *SEN. MARCO RUBIO* OF FLORIDA, *TRUMP'S* RIVAL FOR THE *GOP NOMINATION.*

2. THE *FREE BEACON'S* INVESTIGATION OF *TRUMP,* AND HIS TIES TO *RUSSIA,* ENDED IN APRIL 2016.

3. THE *DEMOCRATS* THEN HIRED *FUSION GPS* TO CONTINUE ITS RESEARCH ON BEHALF OF THE *CLINTON CAMPAIGN* AND THE *DEMOCRATIC NATIONAL COMMITTEE.*

4. FUSION HIRED *CHRISTOPHER STEELE,* A FORMER BRITISH INTELLIGENCE OFFICER, TO FLESH OUT TRUMP'S *CONNECTIONS* TO THE *RUSSIAN GOVERNMENT.*

5. *STEELE* RETURNED WITH SEVERAL *UNPROVEN* CONJECTURES, AMONG THEM THAT *TRUMP* HAD WORKED WITH *RUSSIAN INTELLIGENCE* FOR *YEARS.*

6. THE MOST *SALACIOUS* STEELE ANECDOTE INVOLVED TRUMP AND PROSTITUTES AT THE MOSCOW RITZ-CARLTON. IT WAS ONE MORE REASON STEELE BELIEVED TRUMP WOULD BE SUSCEPTIBLE TO *RUSSIAN BLACKMAIL.*

7. STEELE WAS SO *SHAKEN* BY THE INTEL, HE REPORTED HIS CONCLUSIONS TO THE *FBI,* HELPING TO TRIGGER ITS *INVESTIGATION.*

8. *BUZZFEED* PUBLISHED THE COMPLETE DOSSIER ON *JAN. 10, 2017.*

vol 2, pg 28

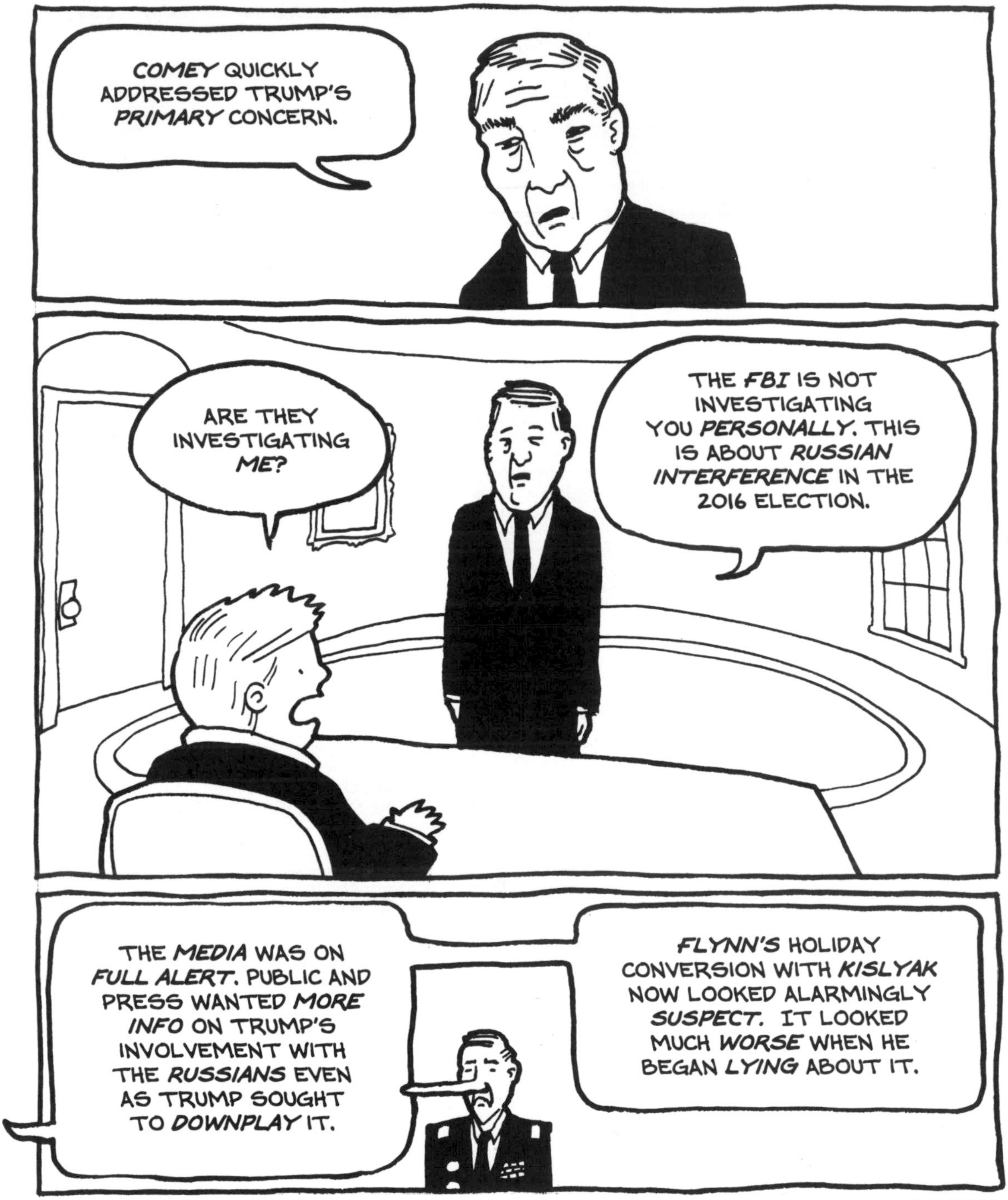
COMEY QUICKLY ADDRESSED TRUMP'S PRIMARY CONCERN.
ARE THEY INVESTIGATING ME?
THE FBI IS NOT INVESTIGATING YOU PERSONALLY. THIS IS ABOUT RUSSIAN INTERFERENCE IN THE 2016 ELECTION.
THE MEDIA WAS ON FULL ALERT. PUBLIC AND PRESS WANTED MORE INFO ON TRUMP'S INVOLVEMENT WITH THE RUSSIANS EVEN AS TRUMP SOUGHT TO DOWNPLAY IT.
FLYNN'S HOLIDAY CONVERSION WITH KISLYAK NOW LOOKED ALARMINGLY SUSPECT. IT LOOKED MUCH WORSE WHEN HE BEGAN LYING ABOUT IT.
vol 2, pg 28-29

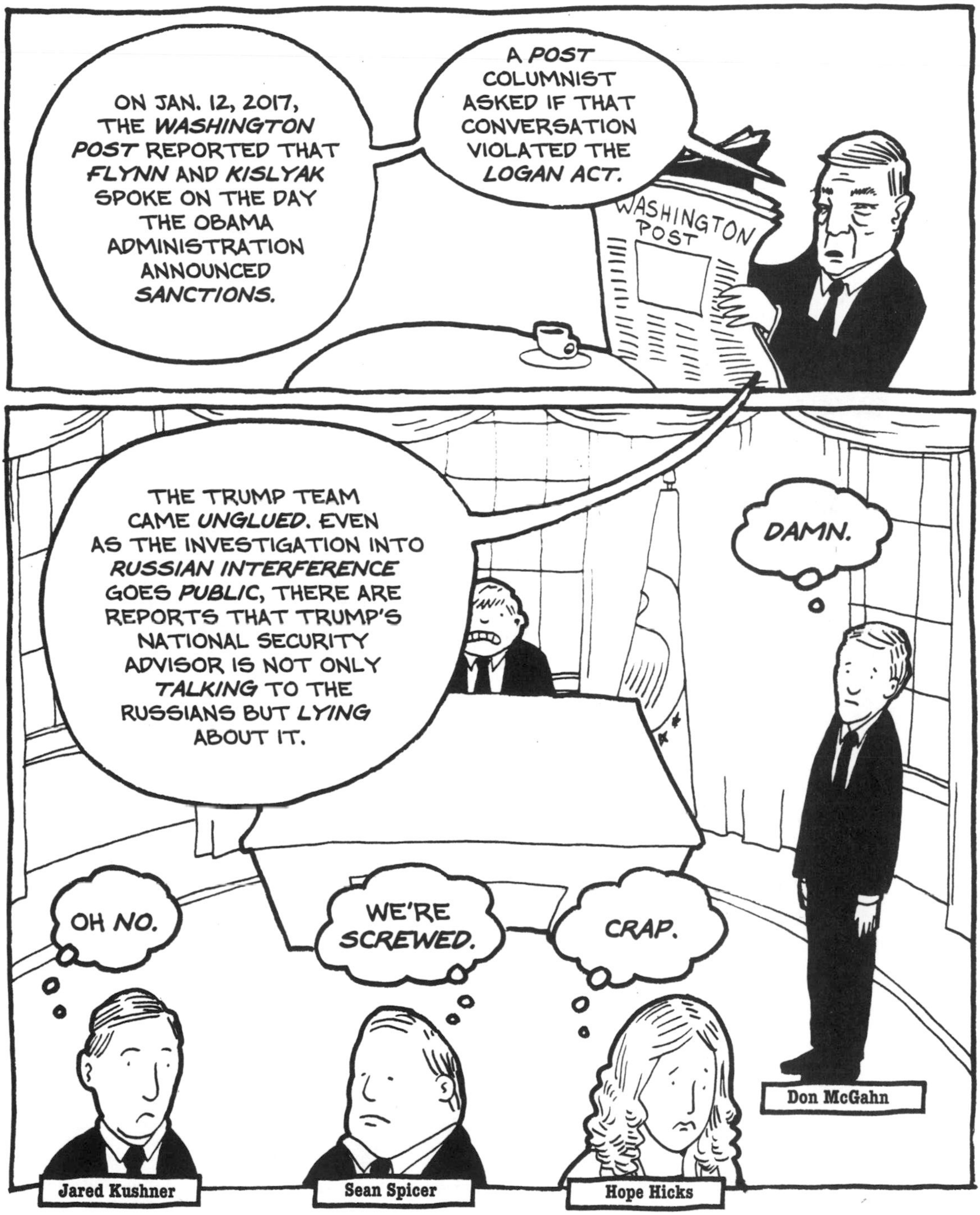
ON JAN. 12, 2017, THE *WASHINGTON POST* REPORTED THAT *FLYNN* AND *KISLYAK* SPOKE ON THE DAY THE OBAMA ADMINISTRATION ANNOUNCED *SANCTIONS*.
A *POST* COLUMNIST ASKED IF THAT CONVERSATION VIOLATED THE *LOGAN ACT*.
WASHINGTON POST
THE TRUMP TEAM CAME *UNGLUED*. EVEN AS THE INVESTIGATION INTO *RUSSIAN INTERFERENCE* GOES *PUBLIC*, THERE ARE REPORTS THAT TRUMP'S NATIONAL SECURITY ADVISOR IS NOT ONLY *TALKING* TO THE RUSSIANS BUT *LYING* ABOUT IT.
DAMN.
OH *NO.*
WE'RE *SCREWED.*
CRAP.
Don McGahn
Jared Kushner
Sean Spicer
Hope Hicks

Logan Act: Criminalizes unauthorized contact with foreign governments in dispute with the U.S. vol 2, pg 29

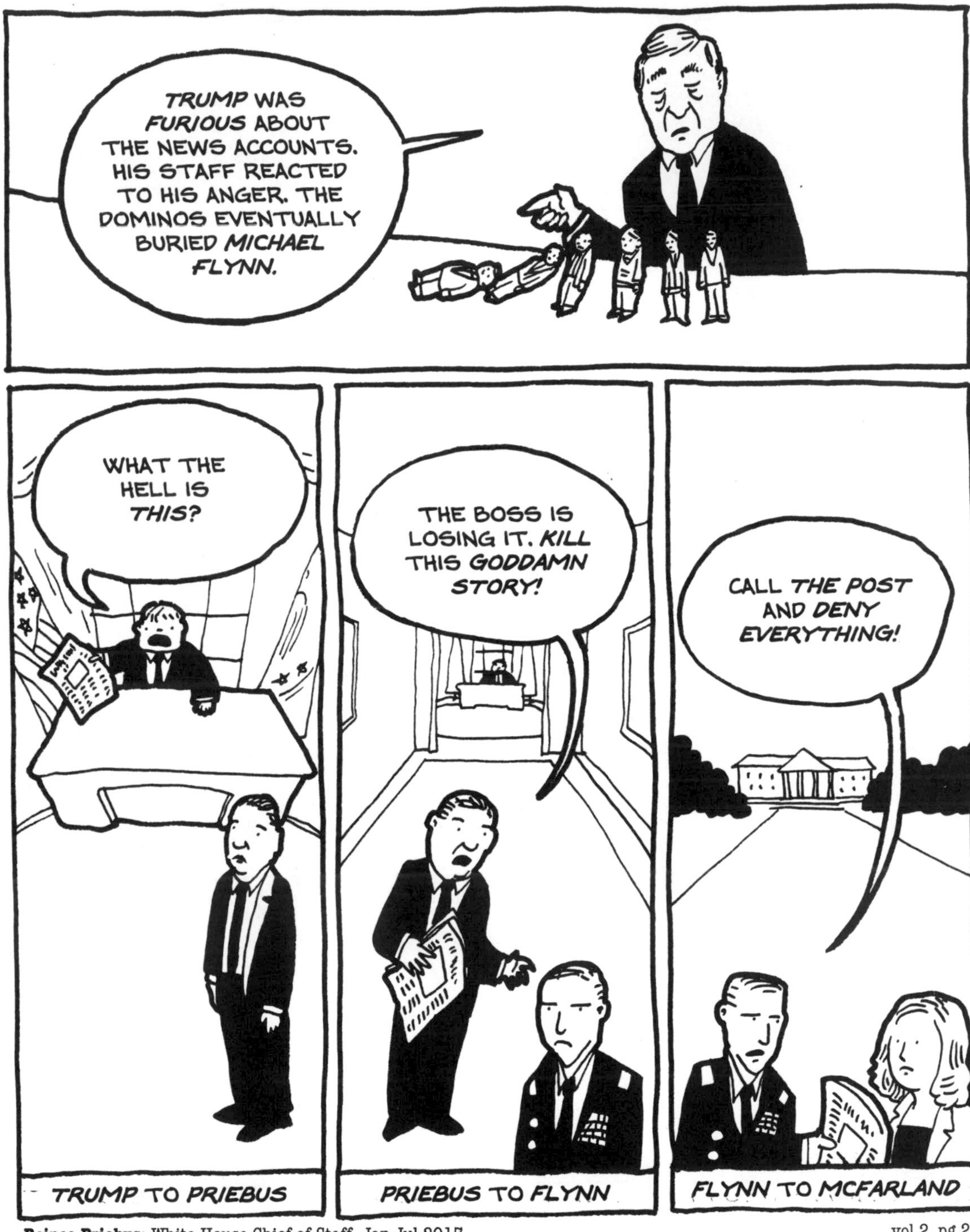
TRUMP WAS FURIOUS ABOUT THE NEWS ACCOUNTS. HIS STAFF REACTED TO HIS ANGER. THE DOMINOS EVENTUALLY BURIED MICHAEL FLYNN.
WHAT THE HELL IS THIS?
TRUMP TO PRIEBUS
THE BOSS IS LOSING IT. KILL THIS GODDAMN STORY!
PRIEBUS TO FLYNN
CALL THE POST AND DENY EVERYTHING!
FLYNN TO MCFARLAND

Reince Priebus: White House Chief of Staff, Jan-Jul 2017

K.T. McFarland: Deputy National Security Advisor, May 2017-Feb 2018

vol 2, pg 29

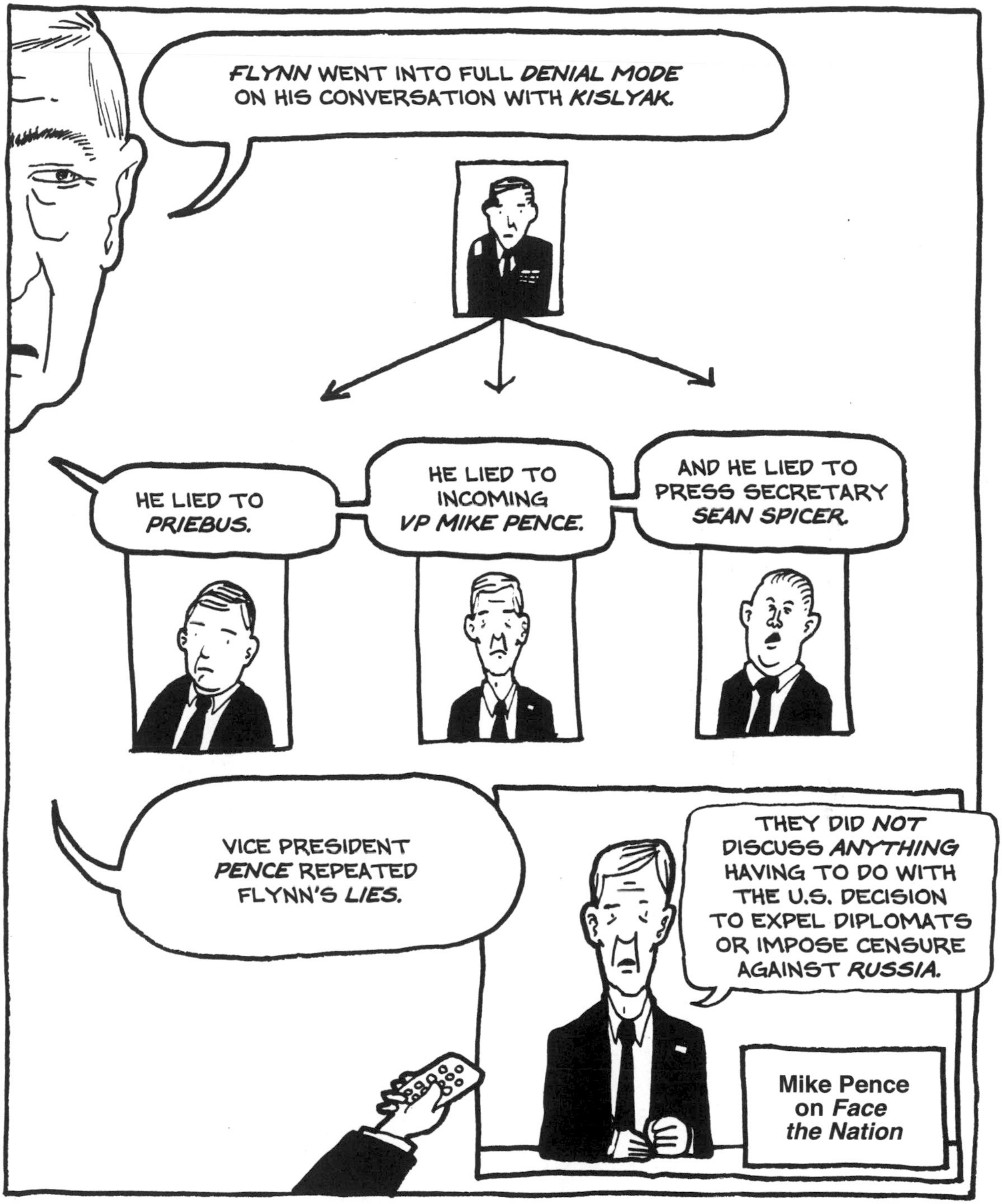
FLYNN WENT INTO FULL DENIAL MODE ON HIS CONVERSATION WITH KISLYAK.
HE LIED TO PRIEBUS.
HE LIED TO INCOMING VP MIKE PENCE.
AND HE LIED TO PRESS SECRETARY SEAN SPICER.
VICE PRESIDENT PENCE REPEATED FLYNN'S LIES.
THEY DID NOT DISCUSS ANYTHING HAVING TO DO WITH THE U.S. DECISION TO EXPEL DIPLOMATS OR IMPOSE CENSURE AGAINST RUSSIA.
Mike Pence on Face the Nation

vol 2, pg 29-30

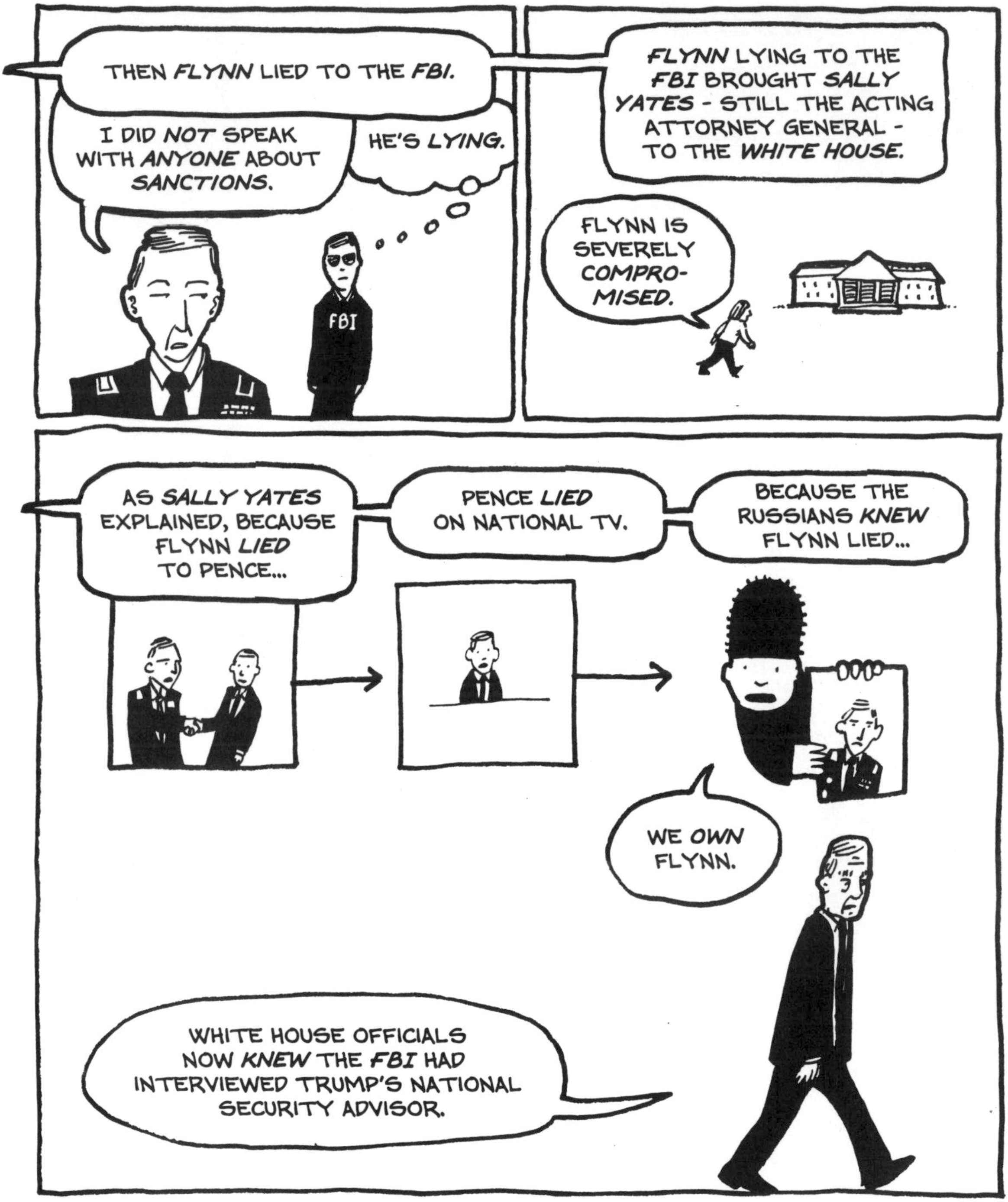
THEN FLYNN LIED TO THE FBI.
I DID NOT SPEAK WITH ANYONE ABOUT SANCTIONS.
HE'S LYING.
FBI
FLYNN LYING TO THE FBI BROUGHT SALLY YATES - STILL THE ACTING ATTORNEY GENERAL - TO THE WHITE HOUSE.
FLYNN IS SEVERELY COMPRO-MISED.
AS SALLY YATES EXPLAINED, BECAUSE FLYNN LIED TO PENCE...
PENCE LIED ON NATIONAL TV.
BECAUSE THE RUSSIANS KNEW FLYNN LIED...
WE OWN FLYNN.
WHITE HOUSE OFFICIALS NOW KNEW THE FBI HAD INTERVIEWED TRUMP'S NATIONAL SECURITY ADVISOR.

vol 2, pg 30-31

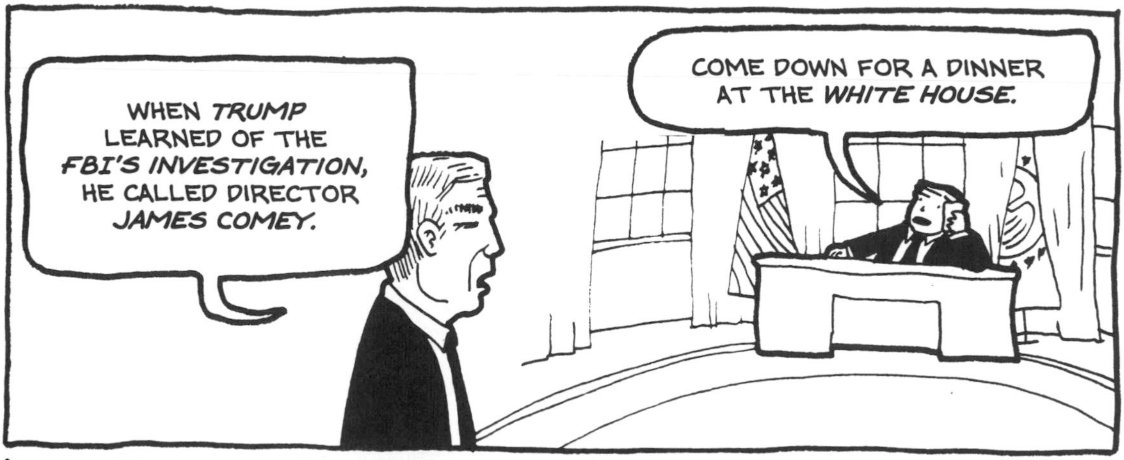
WHEN *TRUMP* LEARNED OF THE *FBI'S INVESTIGATION,* HE CALLED DIRECTOR *JAMES COMEY.*
COME DOWN FOR A DINNER AT THE *WHITE HOUSE.*

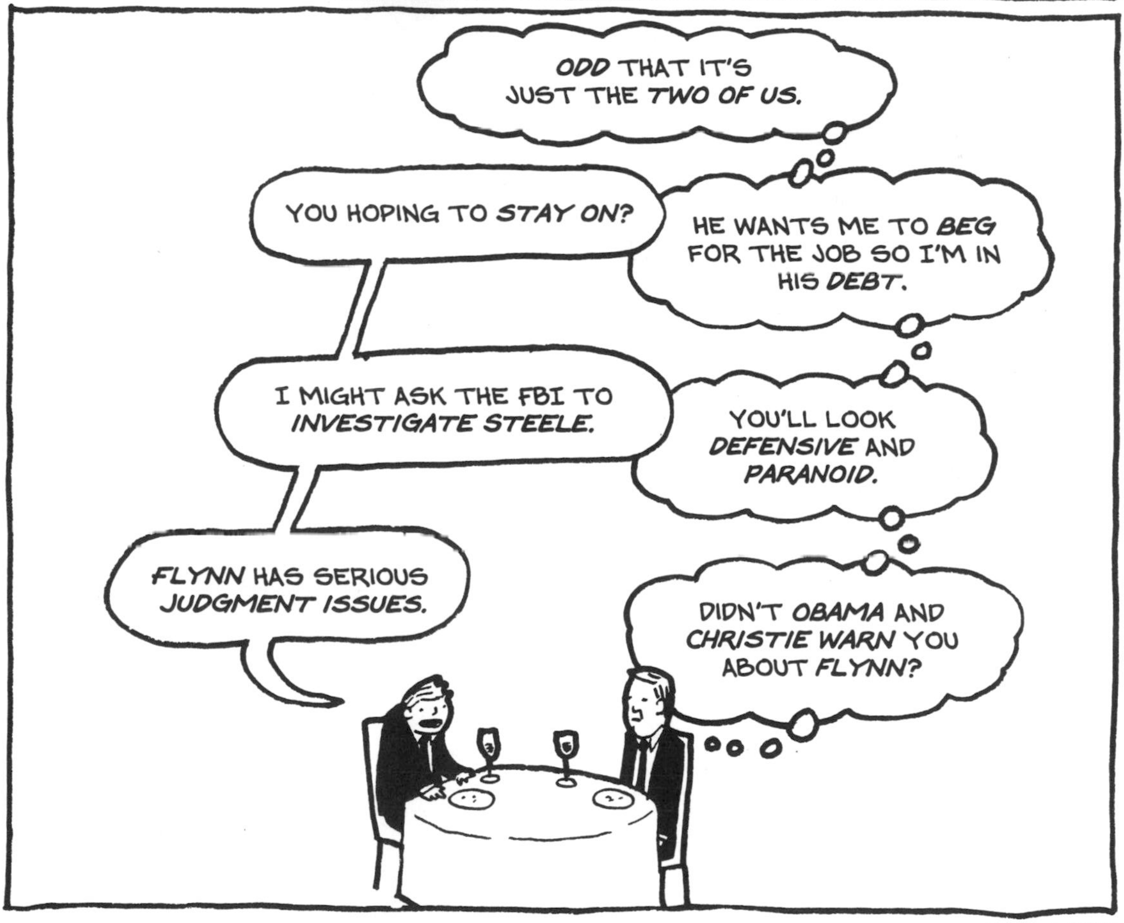
ODD THAT IT'S JUST THE *TWO OF US.*
YOU HOPING TO *STAY ON?*
HE WANTS ME TO *BEG* FOR THE JOB SO I'M IN HIS *DEBT.*
I MIGHT ASK THE FBI TO *INVESTIGATE STEELE.*
YOU'LL LOOK *DEFENSIVE* AND *PARANOID.*
FLYNN HAS SERIOUS *JUDGMENT ISSUES.*
DIDN'T *OBAMA* AND *CHRISTIE WARN* YOU ABOUT *FLYNN?*

vol 2, pg 33-34

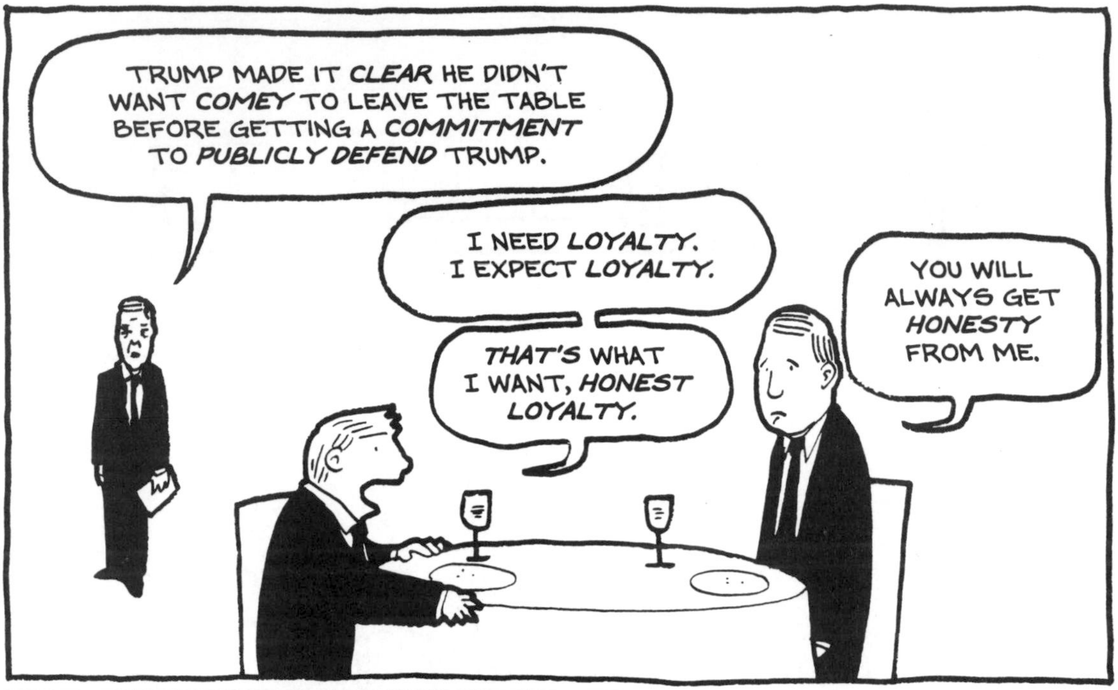
TRUMP MADE IT CLEAR HE DIDN'T WANT COMEY TO LEAVE THE TABLE BEFORE GETTING A COMMITMENT TO PUBLICLY DEFEND TRUMP.
I NEED LOYALTY. I EXPECT LOYALTY.
YOU WILL ALWAYS GET HONESTY FROM ME.
THAT'S WHAT I WANT, HONEST LOYALTY.

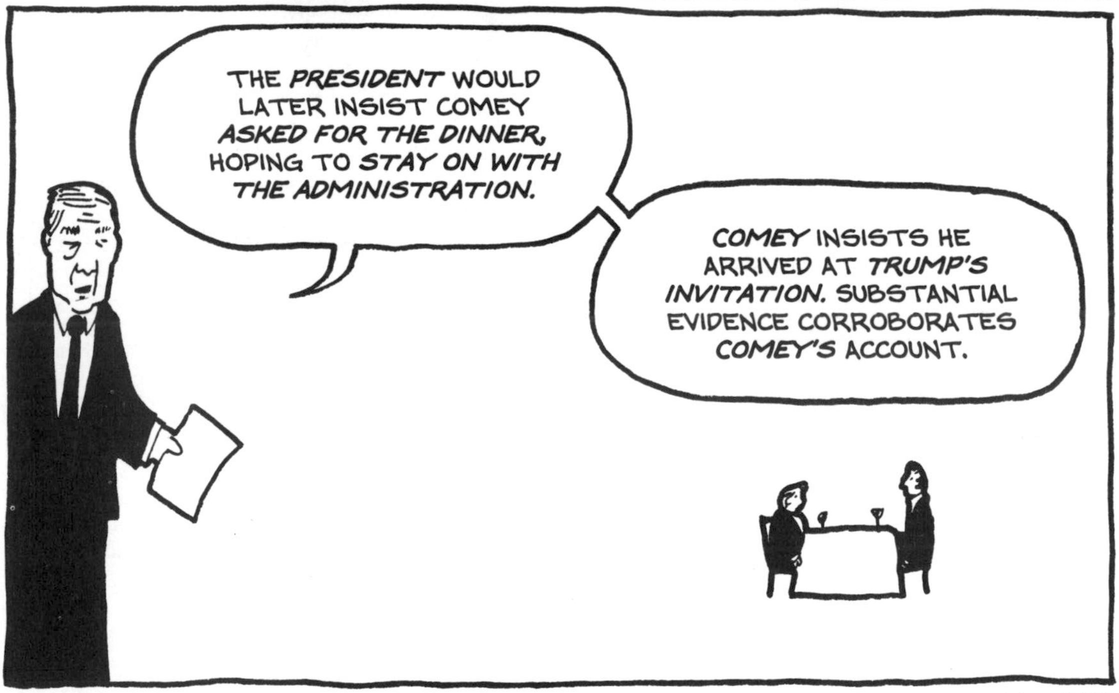
THE PRESIDENT WOULD LATER INSIST COMEY ASKED FOR THE DINNER, HOPING TO STAY ON WITH THE ADMINISTRATION.
COMEY INSISTS HE ARRIVED AT TRUMP'S INVITATION. SUBSTANTIAL EVIDENCE CORROBORATES COMEY'S ACCOUNT.

vol 2, pg 34-35

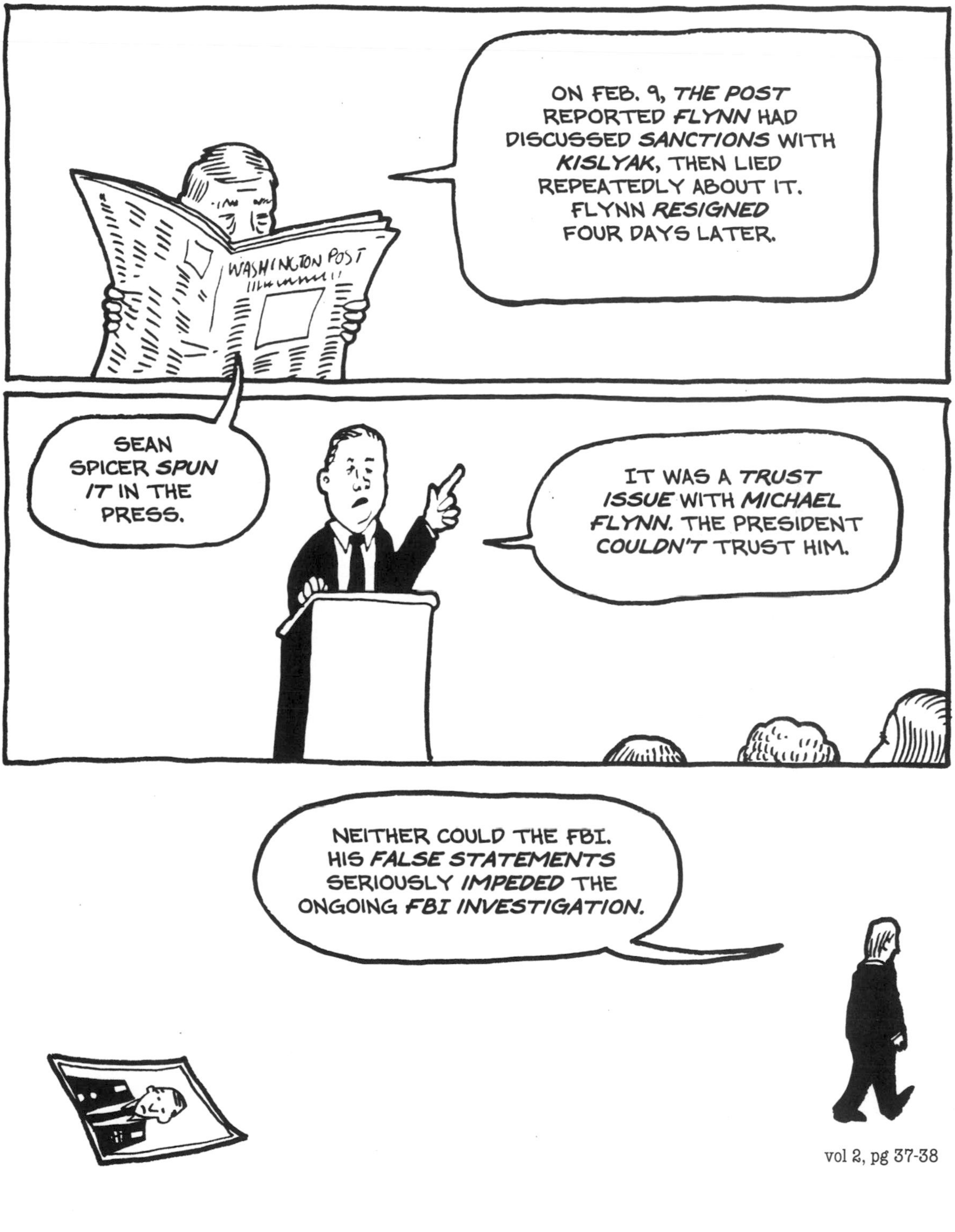
ON FEB. 9, THE POST REPORTED FLYNN HAD DISCUSSED SANCTIONS WITH KISLYAK, THEN LIED REPEATEDLY ABOUT IT. FLYNN RESIGNED FOUR DAYS LATER.
WASHINGTON POST
SEAN SPICER SPUN IT IN THE PRESS.
IT WAS A TRUST ISSUE WITH MICHAEL FLYNN. THE PRESIDENT COULDN'T TRUST HIM.
NEITHER COULD THE FBI. HIS FALSE STATEMENTS SERIOUSLY IMPEDED THE ONGOING FBI INVESTIGATION.

vol 2, pg 37-38

CHAPTER 9

VALENTINE'S DAY
WITH
CHRIS CHRISTIE

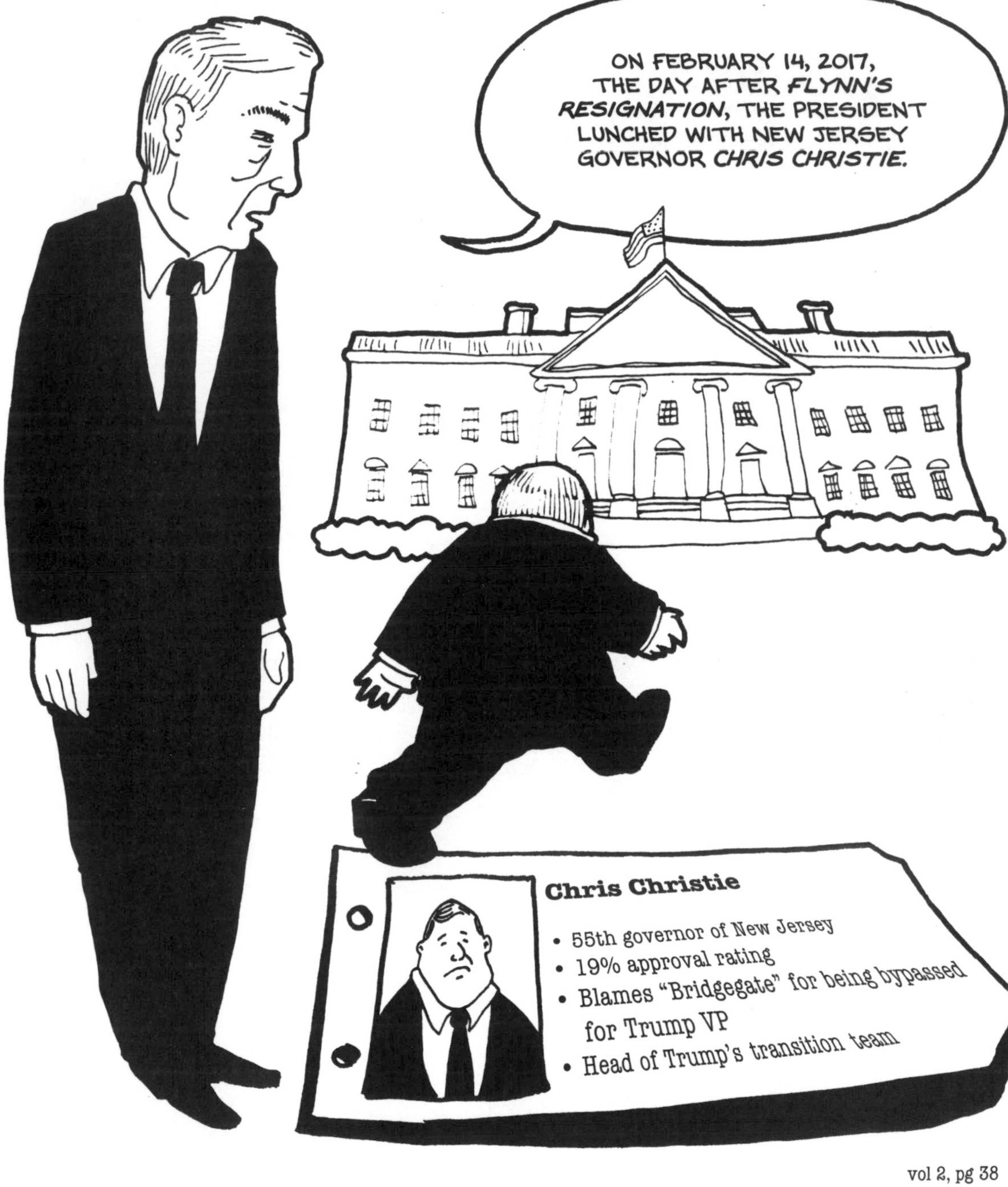

ON FEBRUARY 14, 2017, THE DAY AFTER *FLYNN'S RESIGNATION*, THE PRESIDENT LUNCHED WITH NEW JERSEY GOVERNOR *CHRIS CHRISTIE.*
Chris Christie
• 55th governor of New Jersey
• 19% approval rating
• Blames "Bridgegate" for being bypassed for Trump VP
• Head of Trump's transition team

vol 2, pg 38

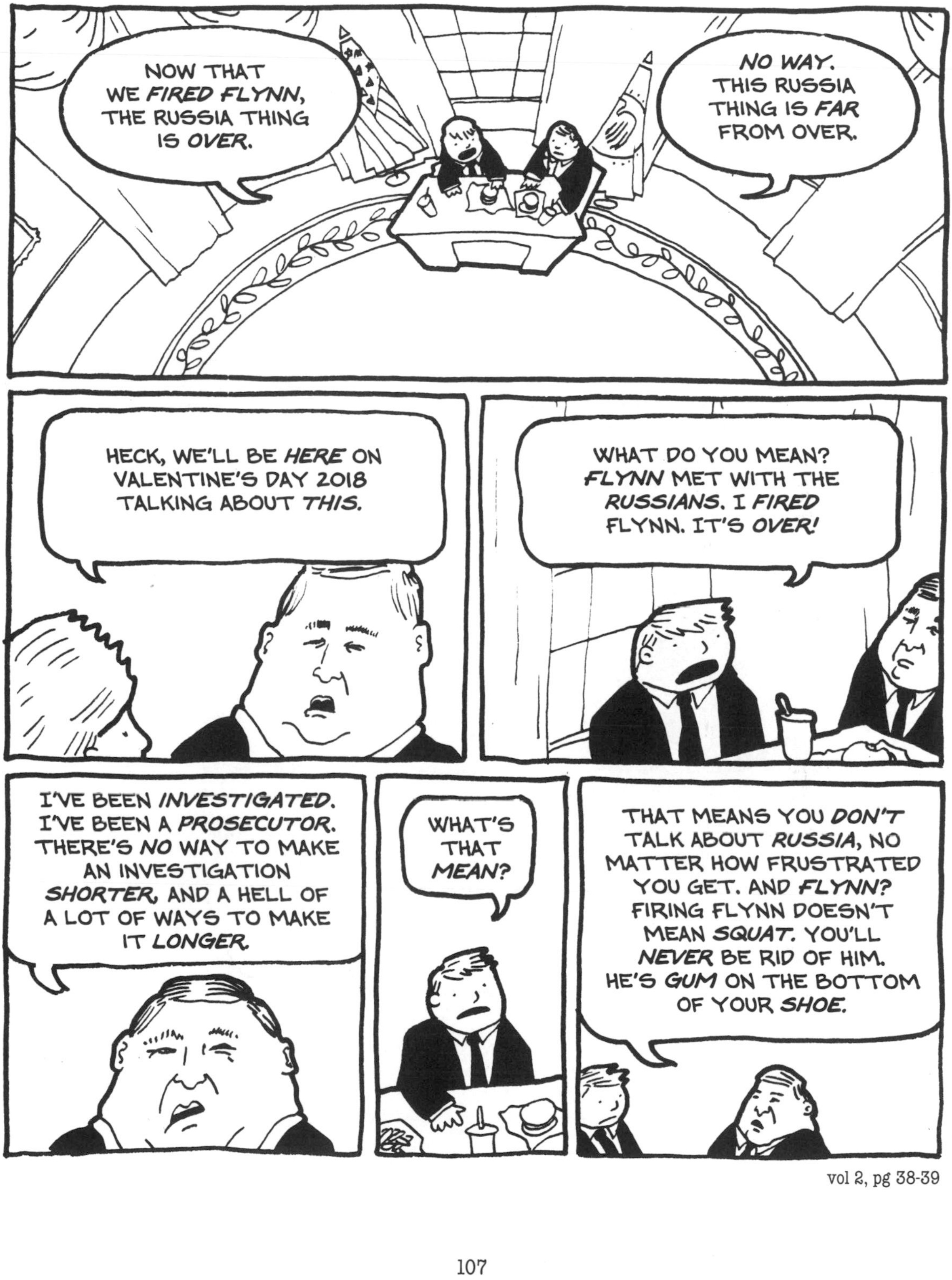
NOW THAT WE *FIRED FLYNN*, THE RUSSIA THING IS *OVER*.
NO WAY. THIS RUSSIA THING IS *FAR* FROM OVER.
HECK, WE'LL BE *HERE* ON VALENTINE'S DAY 2018 TALKING ABOUT *THIS*.
WHAT DO YOU MEAN? *FLYNN* MET WITH THE *RUSSIANS*. I *FIRED* FLYNN. IT'S *OVER!*
I'VE BEEN *INVESTIGATED*. I'VE BEEN A *PROSECUTOR*. THERE'S *NO* WAY TO MAKE AN INVESTIGATION *SHORTER*, AND A HELL OF A LOT OF WAYS TO MAKE IT *LONGER*.
WHAT'S THAT *MEAN?*
THAT MEANS YOU *DON'T* TALK ABOUT *RUSSIA*, NO MATTER HOW FRUSTRATED YOU GET. AND *FLYNN?* FIRING FLYNN DOESN'T MEAN *SQUAT*. YOU'LL *NEVER* BE RID OF HIM. HE'S *GUM* ON THE BOTTOM OF YOUR *SHOE*.

vol 2, pg 38-39

YOU STILL *FRIENDLY* WITH COMEY?

SURE.

CALL HIM. TELL HIM I REALLY *LIKE* HIM. TELL HIM HE'S PART OF THE *TEAM.*

SERIOUSLY. CALL HIM. *LOVE* THE GUY. PART OF THE *TEAM.*

CHRISTIE HAD *NO* INTENTION OF CALLING *COMEY.* HE THOUGHT TRUMP'S REQUEST WAS *NONSENSE.* BUT TRUMP WAS GETTING *IMPATIENT.*

vol 2, pg 39

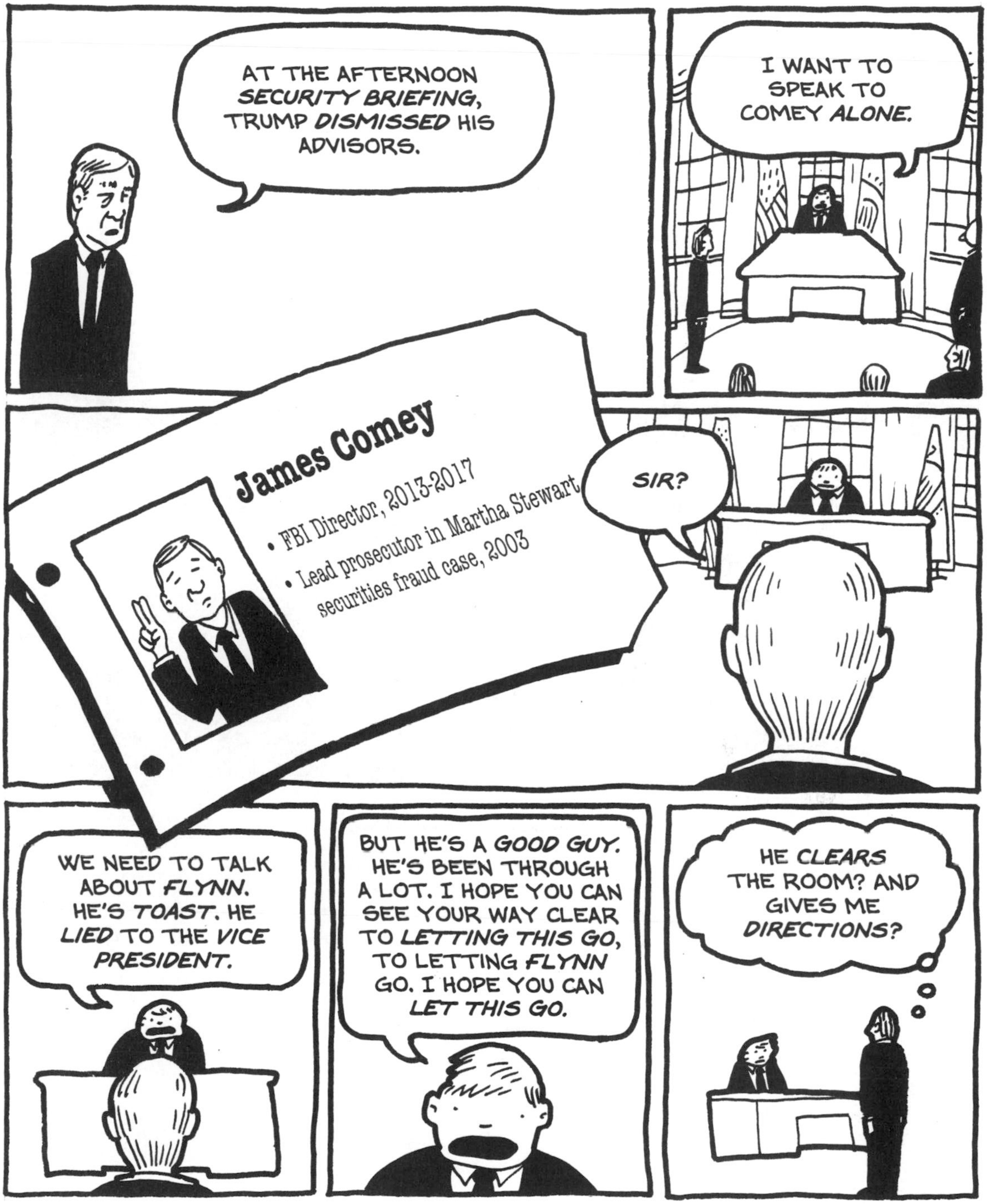
AT THE AFTERNOON SECURITY BRIEFING, TRUMP DISMISSED HIS ADVISORS.
I WANT TO SPEAK TO COMEY ALONE.
James Comey
• FBI Director, 2013-2017
• Lead prosecutor in Martha Stewart securities fraud case, 2003
SIR?
WE NEED TO TALK ABOUT FLYNN. HE'S TOAST. HE LIED TO THE VICE PRESIDENT.
BUT HE'S A GOOD GUY. HE'S BEEN THROUGH A LOT. I HOPE YOU CAN SEE YOUR WAY CLEAR TO LETTING THIS GO, TO LETTING FLYNN GO. I HOPE YOU CAN LET THIS GO.
HE CLEARS THE ROOM? AND GIVES ME DIRECTIONS?

vol 2, pg 39-40

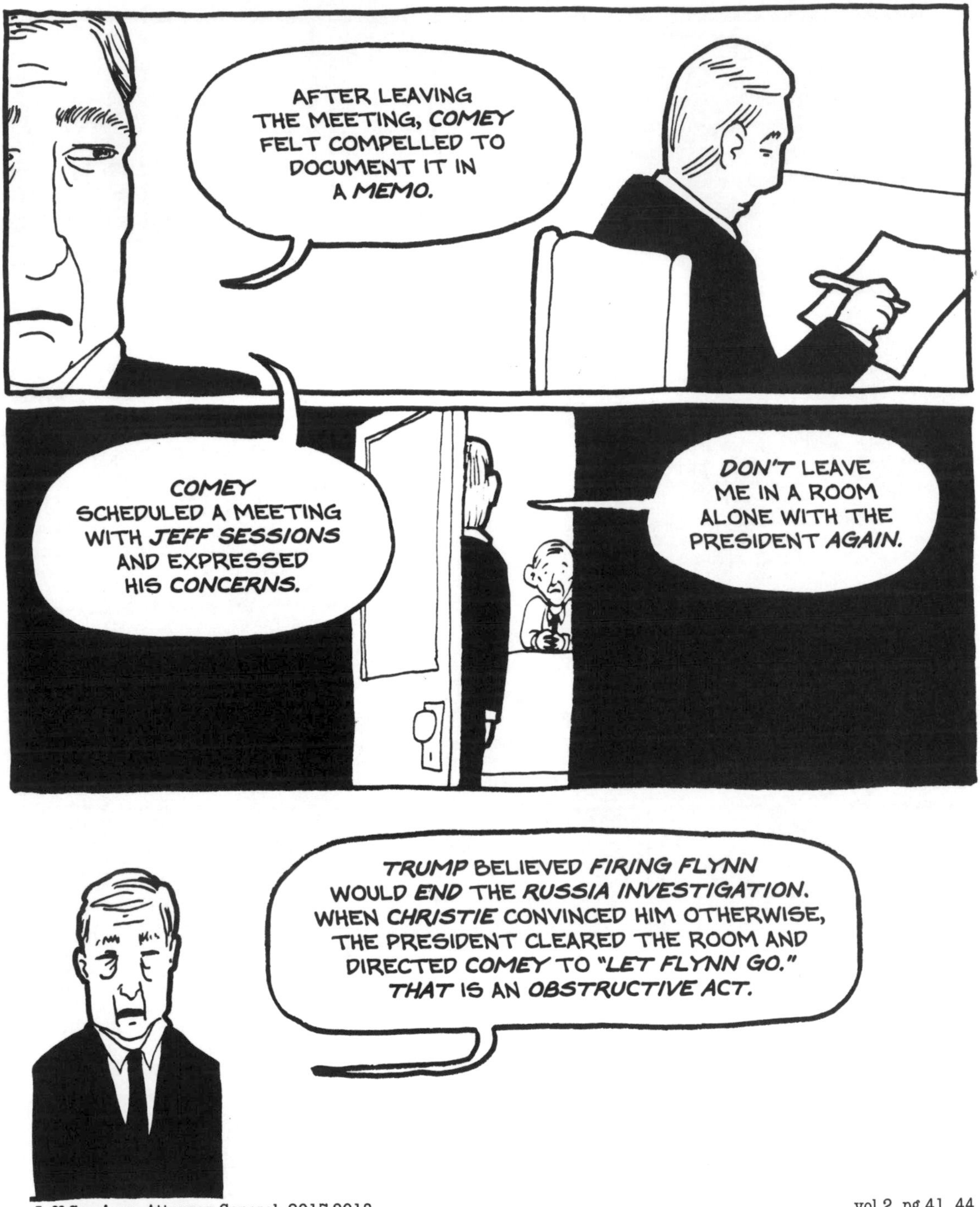
AFTER LEAVING THE MEETING, COMEY FELT COMPELLED TO DOCUMENT IT IN A MEMO.
COMEY SCHEDULED A MEETING WITH JEFF SESSIONS AND EXPRESSED HIS CONCERNS.
DON'T LEAVE ME IN A ROOM ALONE WITH THE PRESIDENT AGAIN.
TRUMP BELIEVED FIRING FLYNN WOULD END THE RUSSIA INVESTIGATION. WHEN CHRISTIE CONVINCED HIM OTHERWISE, THE PRESIDENT CLEARED THE ROOM AND DIRECTED COMEY TO "LET FLYNN GO." THAT IS AN OBSTRUCTIVE ACT.

Jeff Sessions: Attorney General, 2017-2018

vol 2, pg 41, 44

CHAPTER 10

THE JEFF SESSIONS RECUSAL

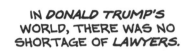

IN *DONALD TRUMP'S* WORLD, THERE WAS NO SHORTAGE OF *LAWYERS.*

WHETHER HE WAS DECLARING *BANKRUPTCY,* *SHORTING BUILDING CONTRACTORS,* OR *NEGOTIATING* WITH *PORN STARS,* LAWYERS HAD HIS BACK.

WHERE'S MY *ROY COHN?**

*ROY COHN WAS JOSEPH MCCARTHY'S LAWYER.

A ROTATING CAST OF *LAWYERS* INSULATED HIM UNTIL THE *RUSSIA INVESTIGATION.*

vol 2, pg 50, footnote 294

112

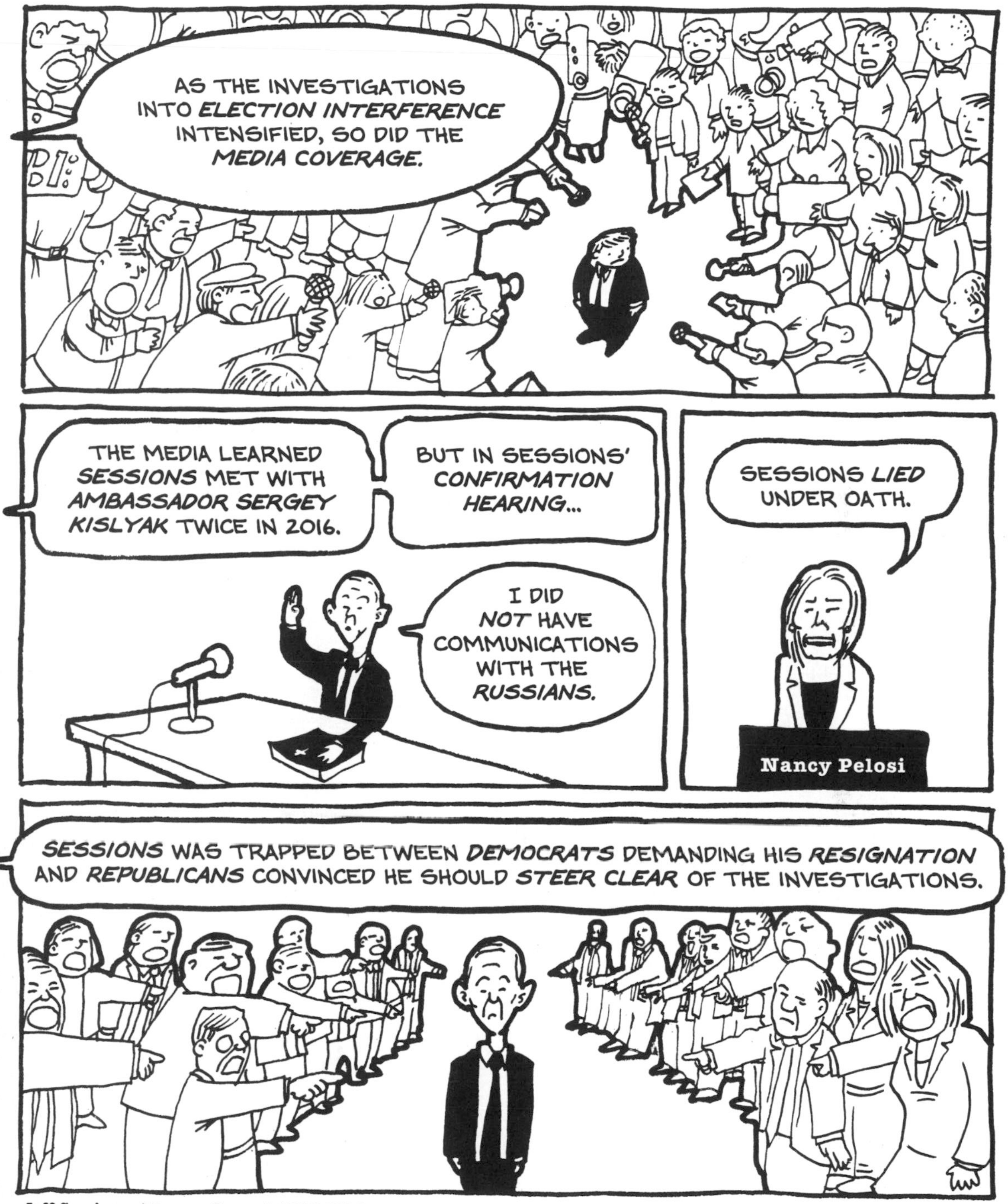
AS THE INVESTIGATIONS INTO ELECTION INTERFERENCE INTENSIFIED, SO DID THE MEDIA COVERAGE.
THE MEDIA LEARNED SESSIONS MET WITH AMBASSADOR SERGEY KISLYAK TWICE IN 2016.
BUT IN SESSIONS' CONFIRMATION HEARING...
I DID NOT HAVE COMMUNICATIONS WITH THE RUSSIANS.
SESSIONS LIED UNDER OATH.
Nancy Pelosi
SESSIONS WAS TRAPPED BETWEEN DEMOCRATS DEMANDING HIS RESIGNATION AND REPUBLICANS CONVINCED HE SHOULD STEER CLEAR OF THE INVESTIGATIONS.

Jeff Sessions: Attorney General, 2017-2018
Sergey Kislyak: Russian senior diplomat
Nancy Pelosi: Speaker of the House 2019-

vol 2, pg 48, Pelosi's Twitter, Mar 2, 2017, 5:52 am

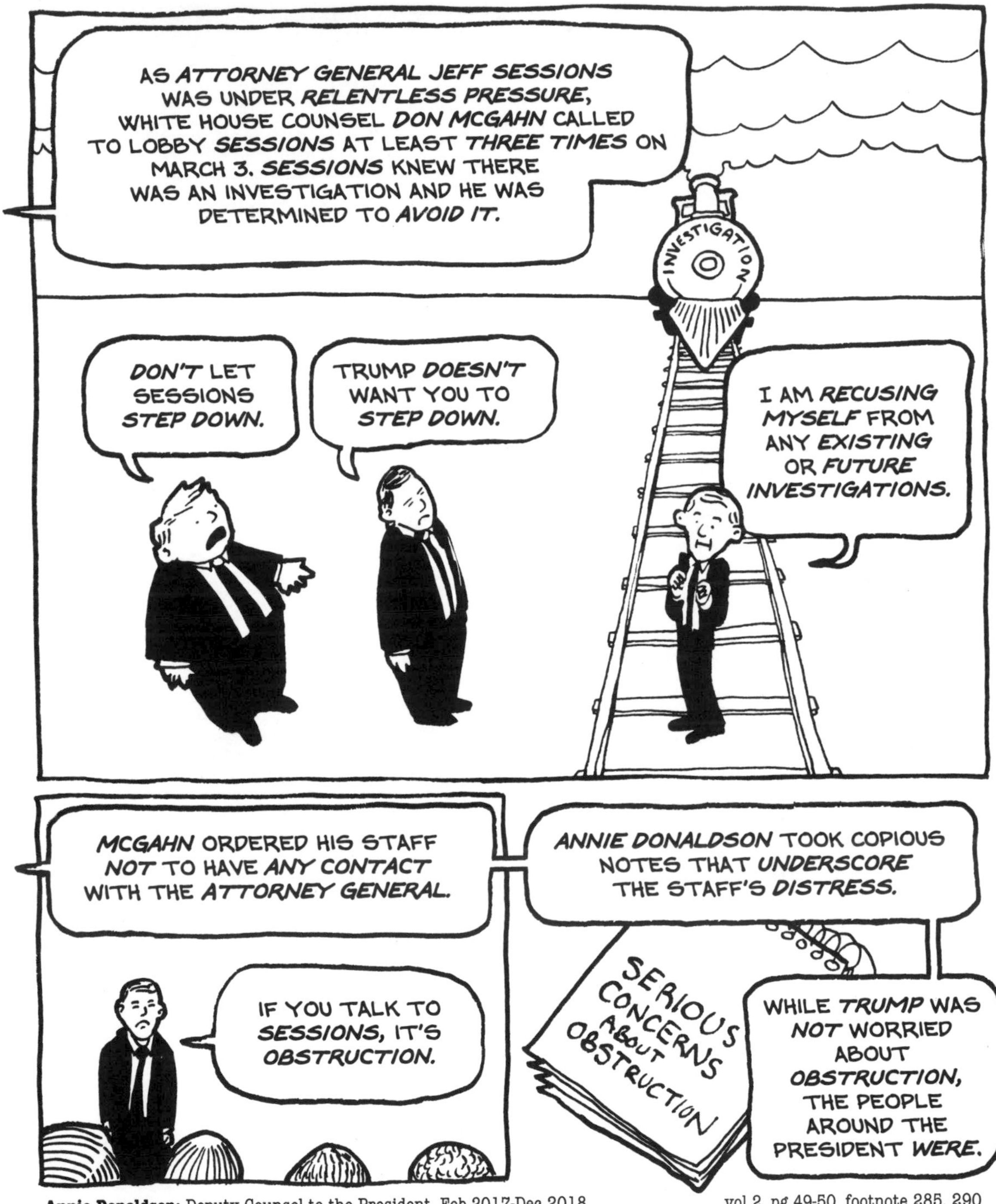
AS ATTORNEY GENERAL JEFF SESSIONS WAS UNDER RELENTLESS PRESSURE, WHITE HOUSE COUNSEL DON MCGAHN CALLED TO LOBBY SESSIONS AT LEAST THREE TIMES ON MARCH 3. SESSIONS KNEW THERE WAS AN INVESTIGATION AND HE WAS DETERMINED TO AVOID IT.
INVESTIGATION
DON'T LET SESSIONS STEP DOWN.
TRUMP DOESN'T WANT YOU TO STEP DOWN.
I AM RECUSING MYSELF FROM ANY EXISTING OR FUTURE INVESTIGATIONS.
MCGAHN ORDERED HIS STAFF NOT TO HAVE ANY CONTACT WITH THE ATTORNEY GENERAL.
IF YOU TALK TO SESSIONS, IT'S OBSTRUCTION.
ANNIE DONALDSON TOOK COPIOUS NOTES THAT UNDERSCORE THE STAFF'S DISTRESS.
SERIOUS CONCERNS ABOUT OBSTRUCTION
WHILE TRUMP WAS NOT WORRIED ABOUT OBSTRUCTION, THE PEOPLE AROUND THE PRESIDENT WERE.

Annie Donaldson: Deputy Counsel to the President, Feb 2017-Dec 2018
Don McGahn: White House Counsel, Jan 2017-Oct 2018

vol 2, pg 49-50, footnote 285, 290

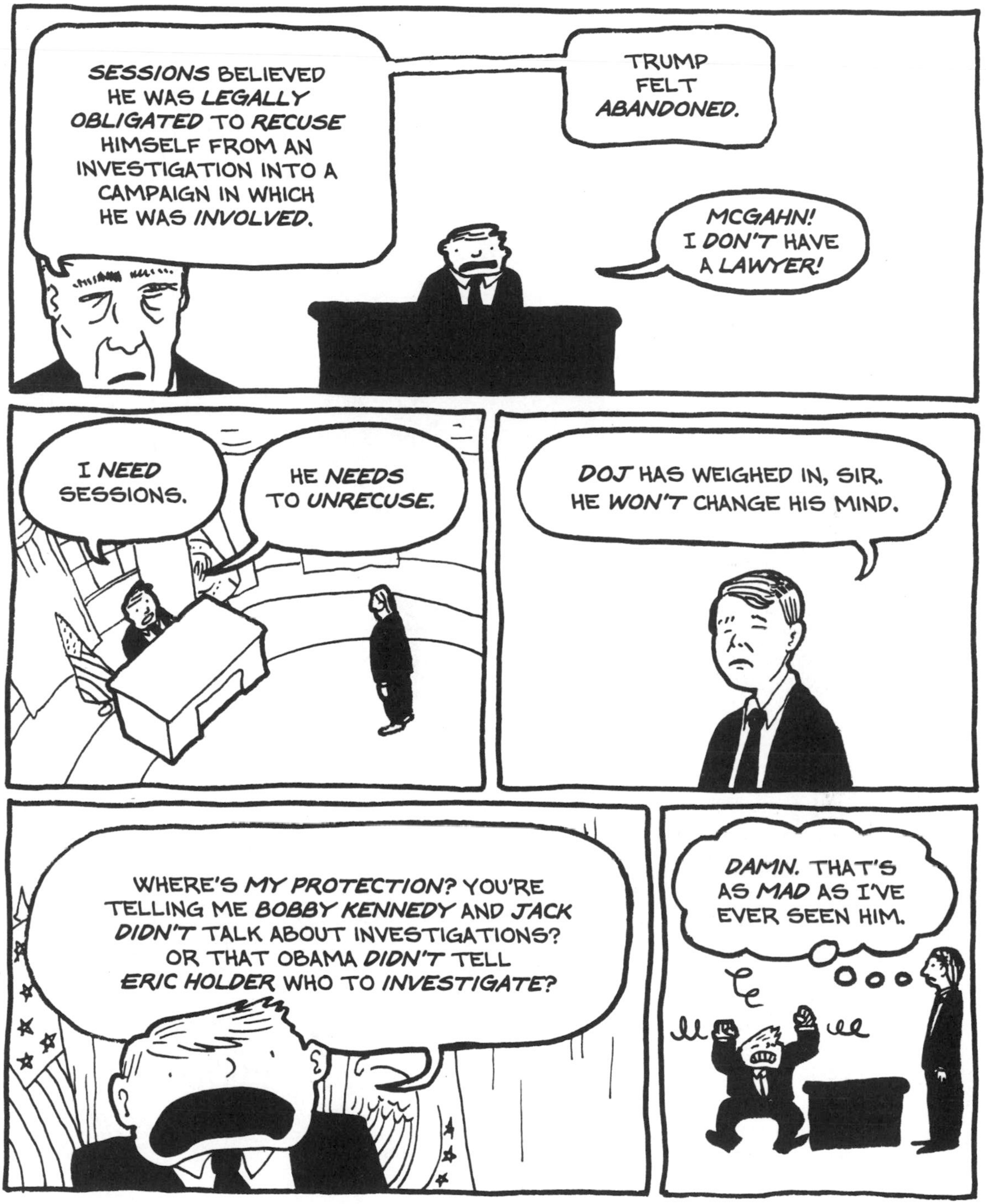
SESSIONS BELIEVED HE WAS LEGALLY OBLIGATED TO RECUSE HIMSELF FROM AN INVESTIGATION INTO A CAMPAIGN IN WHICH HE WAS INVOLVED.
TRUMP FELT ABANDONED.
MCGAHN! I DON'T HAVE A LAWYER!
I NEED SESSIONS.
HE NEEDS TO UNRECUSE.
DOJ HAS WEIGHED IN, SIR. HE WON'T CHANGE HIS MIND.
WHERE'S MY PROTECTION? YOU'RE TELLING ME BOBBY KENNEDY AND JACK DIDN'T TALK ABOUT INVESTIGATIONS? OR THAT OBAMA DIDN'T TELL ERIC HOLDER WHO TO INVESTIGATE?
DAMN. THAT'S AS MAD AS I'VE EVER SEEN HIM.

vol 2, pg 50-51

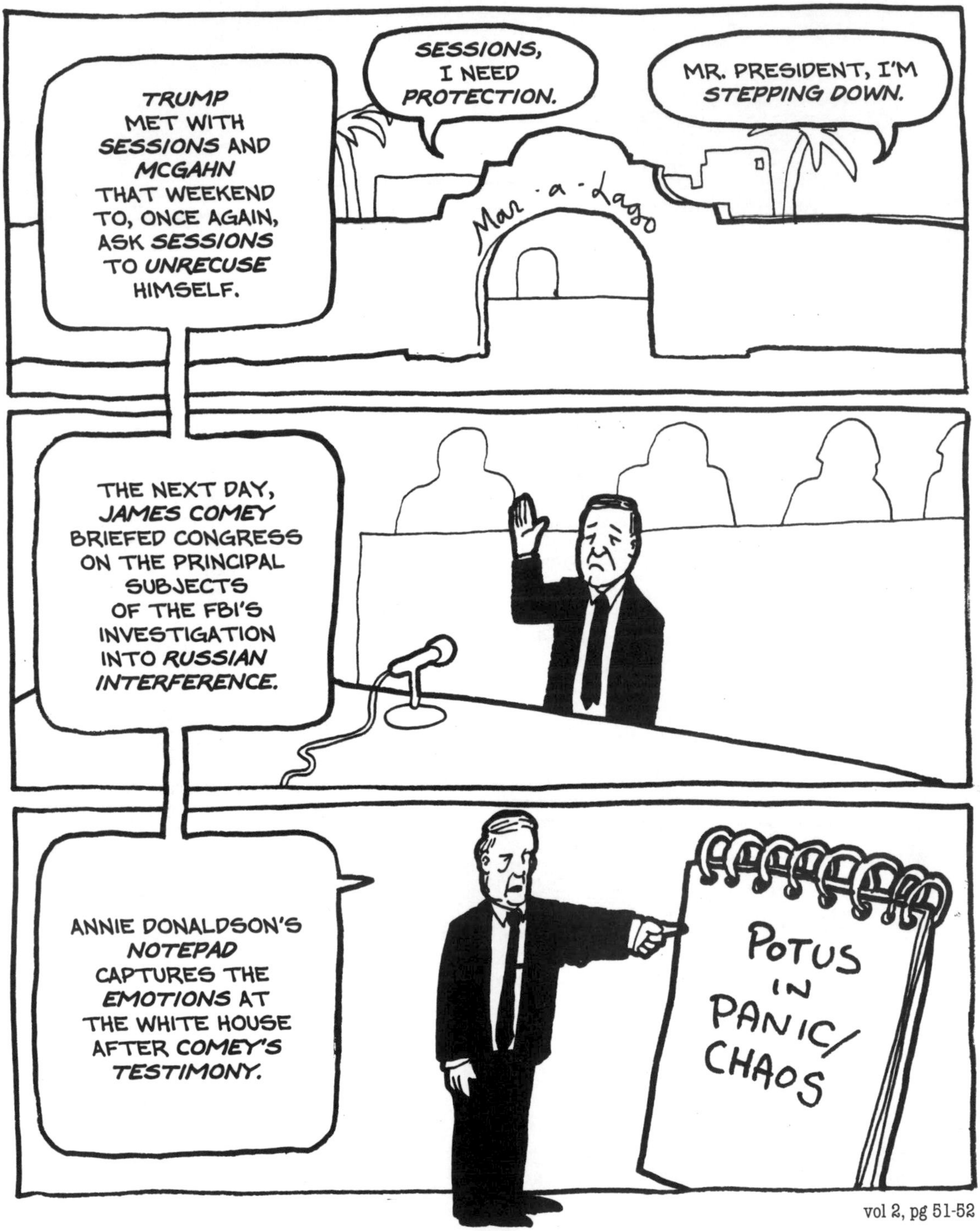
TRUMP MET WITH SESSIONS AND MCGAHN THAT WEEKEND TO, ONCE AGAIN, ASK SESSIONS TO UNRECUSE HIMSELF.
SESSIONS, I NEED PROTECTION.
MR. PRESIDENT, I'M STEPPING DOWN.
Mar-a-Lago
THE NEXT DAY, JAMES COMEY BRIEFED CONGRESS ON THE PRINCIPAL SUBJECTS OF THE FBI'S INVESTIGATION INTO RUSSIAN INTERFERENCE.
ANNIE DONALDSON'S NOTEPAD CAPTURES THE EMOTIONS AT THE WHITE HOUSE AFTER COMEY'S TESTIMONY.
POTUS IN PANIC/ CHAOS

vol 2, pg 51-52

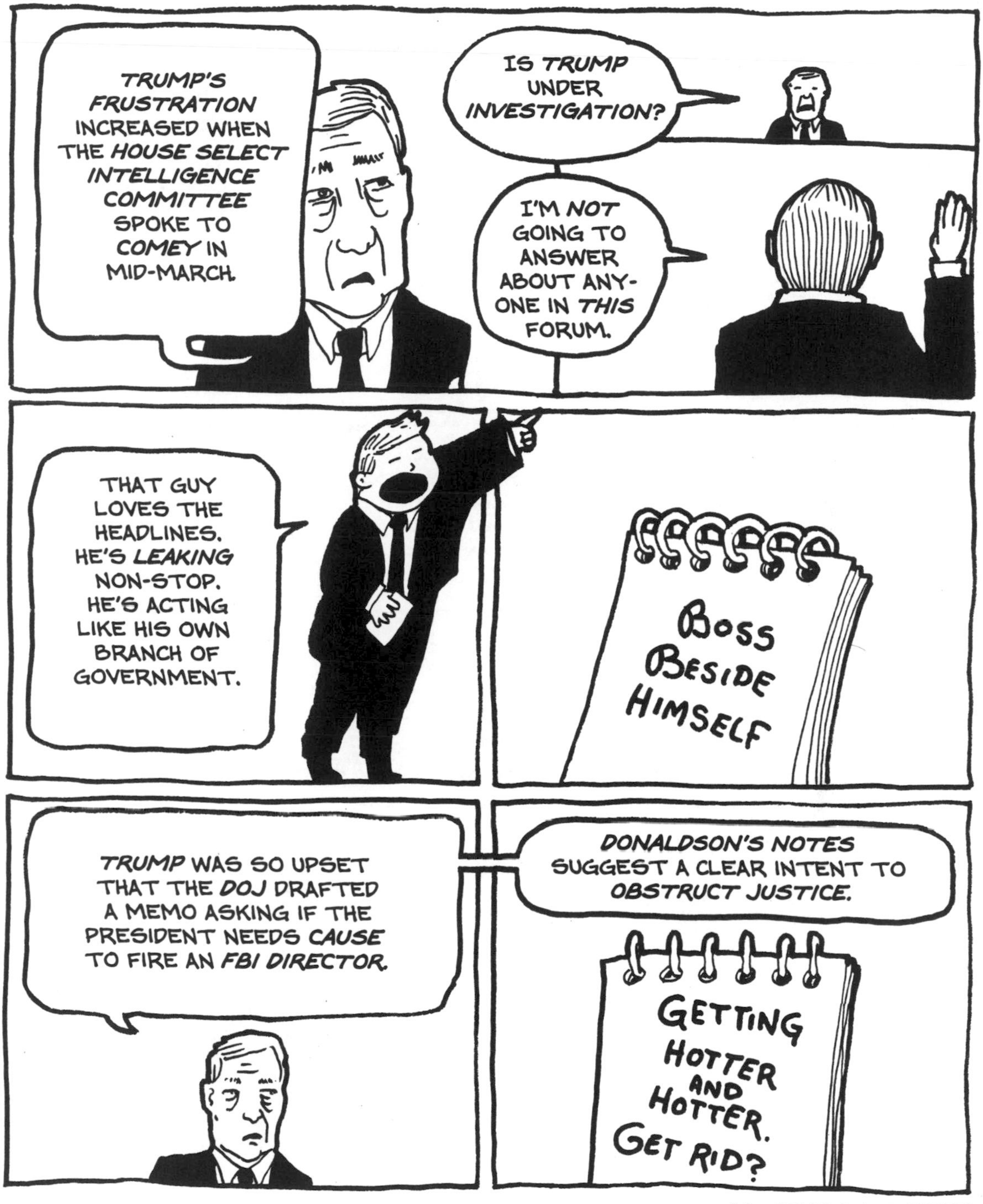
TRUMP'S FRUSTRATION INCREASED WHEN THE HOUSE SELECT INTELLIGENCE COMMITTEE SPOKE TO COMEY IN MID-MARCH.
IS TRUMP UNDER INVESTIGATION?
I'M NOT GOING TO ANSWER ABOUT ANY-ONE IN THIS FORUM.
THAT GUY LOVES THE HEADLINES. HE'S LEAKING NON-STOP. HE'S ACTING LIKE HIS OWN BRANCH OF GOVERNMENT.
BOSS BESIDE HIMSELF
TRUMP WAS SO UPSET THAT THE DOJ DRAFTED A MEMO ASKING IF THE PRESIDENT NEEDS CAUSE TO FIRE AN FBI DIRECTOR.
DONALDSON'S NOTES SUGGEST A CLEAR INTENT TO OBSTRUCT JUSTICE.
GETTING HOTTER AND HOTTER. GET RID?

vol 2, pg 52-54, footnote 323-325

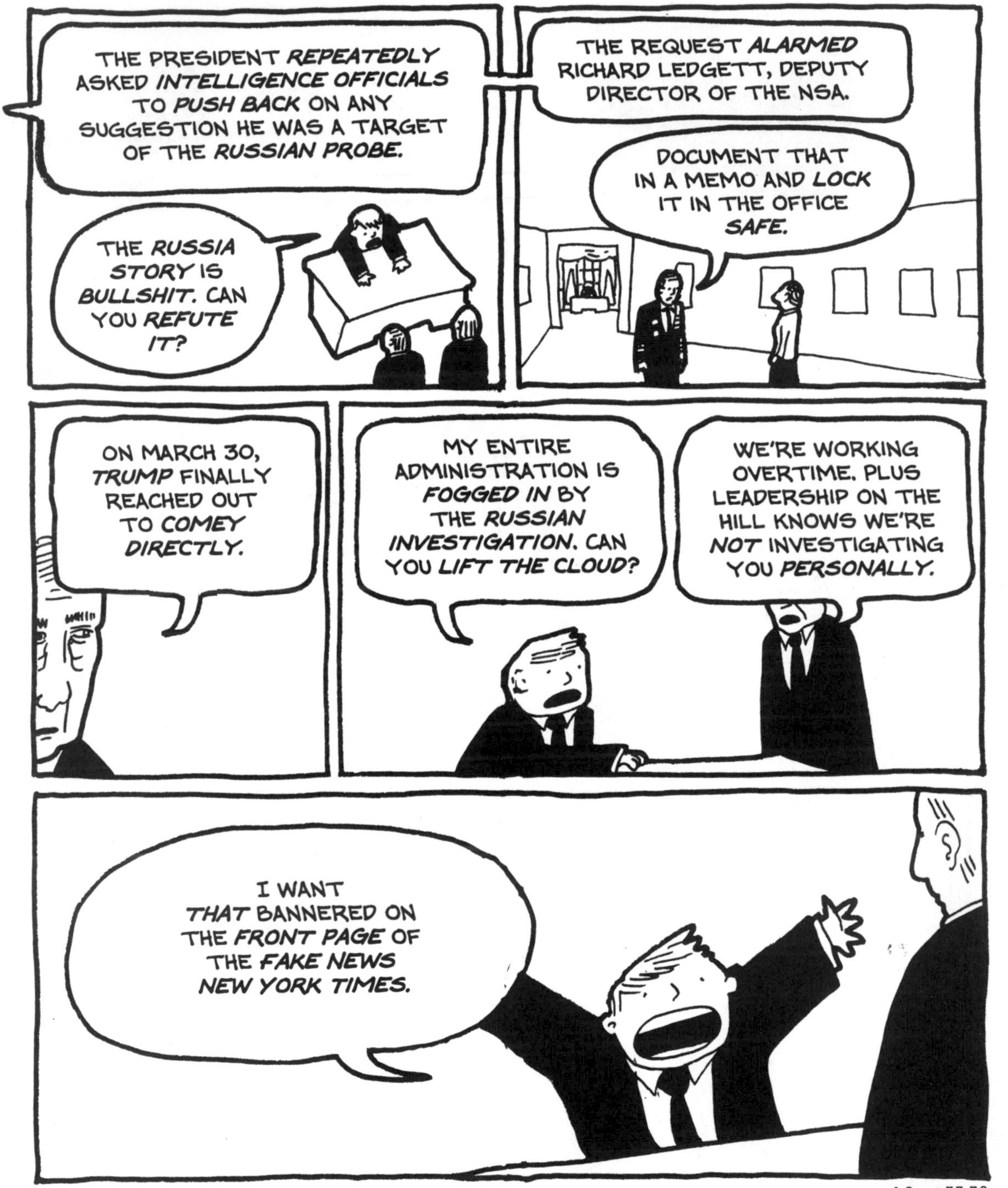
THE PRESIDENT REPEATEDLY ASKED INTELLIGENCE OFFICIALS TO PUSH BACK ON ANY SUGGESTION HE WAS A TARGET OF THE RUSSIAN PROBE.
THE RUSSIA STORY IS BULLSHIT. CAN YOU REFUTE IT?
THE REQUEST ALARMED RICHARD LEDGETT, DEPUTY DIRECTOR OF THE NSA.
DOCUMENT THAT IN A MEMO AND LOCK IT IN THE OFFICE SAFE.
ON MARCH 30, TRUMP FINALLY REACHED OUT TO COMEY DIRECTLY.
MY ENTIRE ADMINISTRATION IS FOGGED IN BY THE RUSSIAN INVESTIGATION. CAN YOU LIFT THE CLOUD?
WE'RE WORKING OVERTIME. PLUS LEADERSHIP ON THE HILL KNOWS WE'RE NOT INVESTIGATING YOU PERSONALLY.
I WANT THAT BANNERED ON THE FRONT PAGE OF THE FAKE NEWS NEW YORK TIMES.

vol 2, pg 55-58

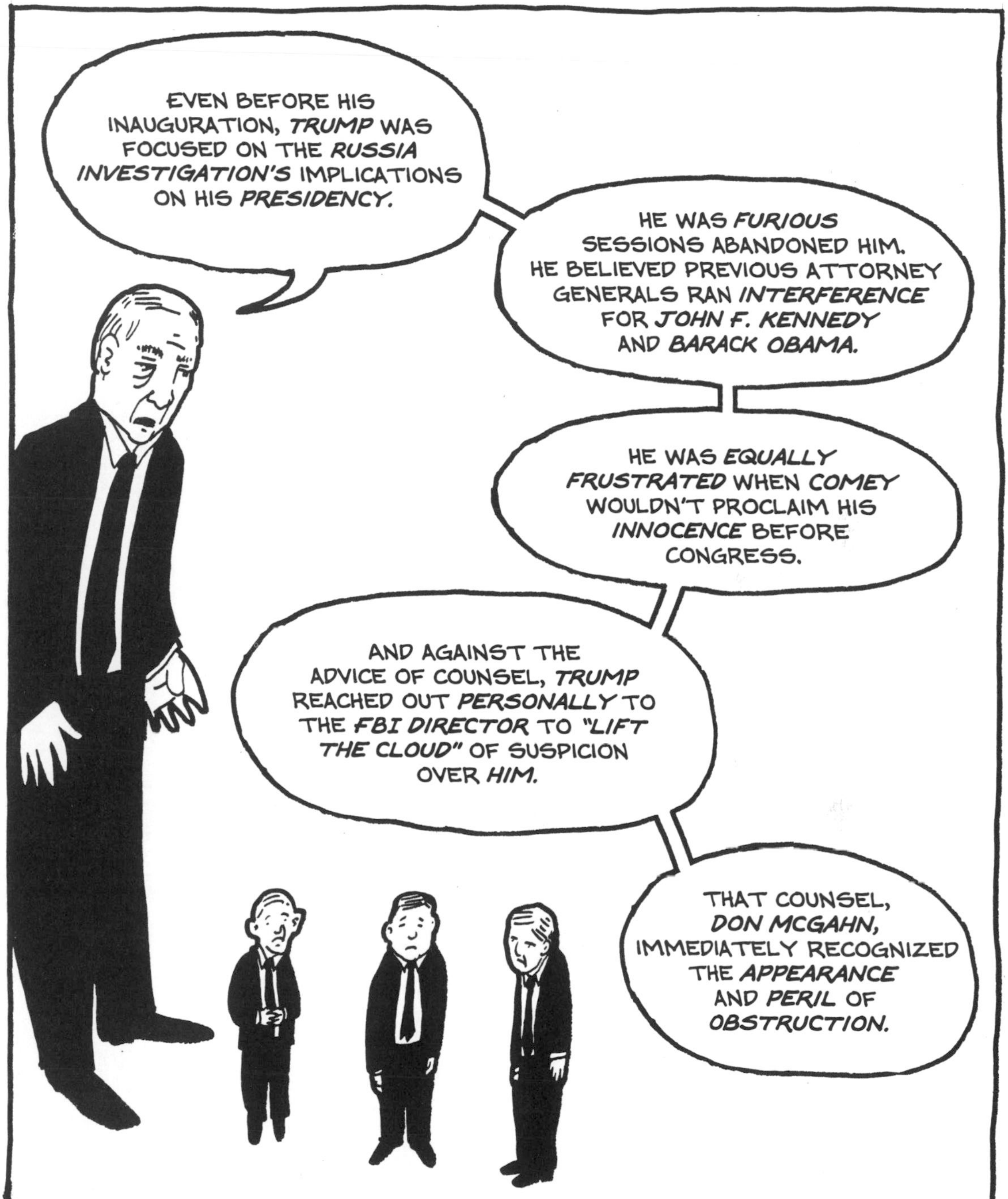
EVEN BEFORE HIS INAUGURATION, TRUMP WAS FOCUSED ON THE RUSSIA INVESTIGATION'S IMPLICATIONS ON HIS PRESIDENCY.
HE WAS FURIOUS SESSIONS ABANDONED HIM. HE BELIEVED PREVIOUS ATTORNEY GENERALS RAN INTERFERENCE FOR JOHN F. KENNEDY AND BARACK OBAMA.
HE WAS EQUALLY FRUSTRATED WHEN COMEY WOULDN'T PROCLAIM HIS INNOCENCE BEFORE CONGRESS.
AND AGAINST THE ADVICE OF COUNSEL, TRUMP REACHED OUT PERSONALLY TO THE FBI DIRECTOR TO "LIFT THE CLOUD" OF SUSPICION OVER HIM.
THAT COUNSEL, DON MCGAHN, IMMEDIATELY RECOGNIZED THE APPEARANCE AND PERIL OF OBSTRUCTION.

vol 2, pg 61

CHAPTER 11

TRUMP FIRES COMEY AND LIES ABOUT IT

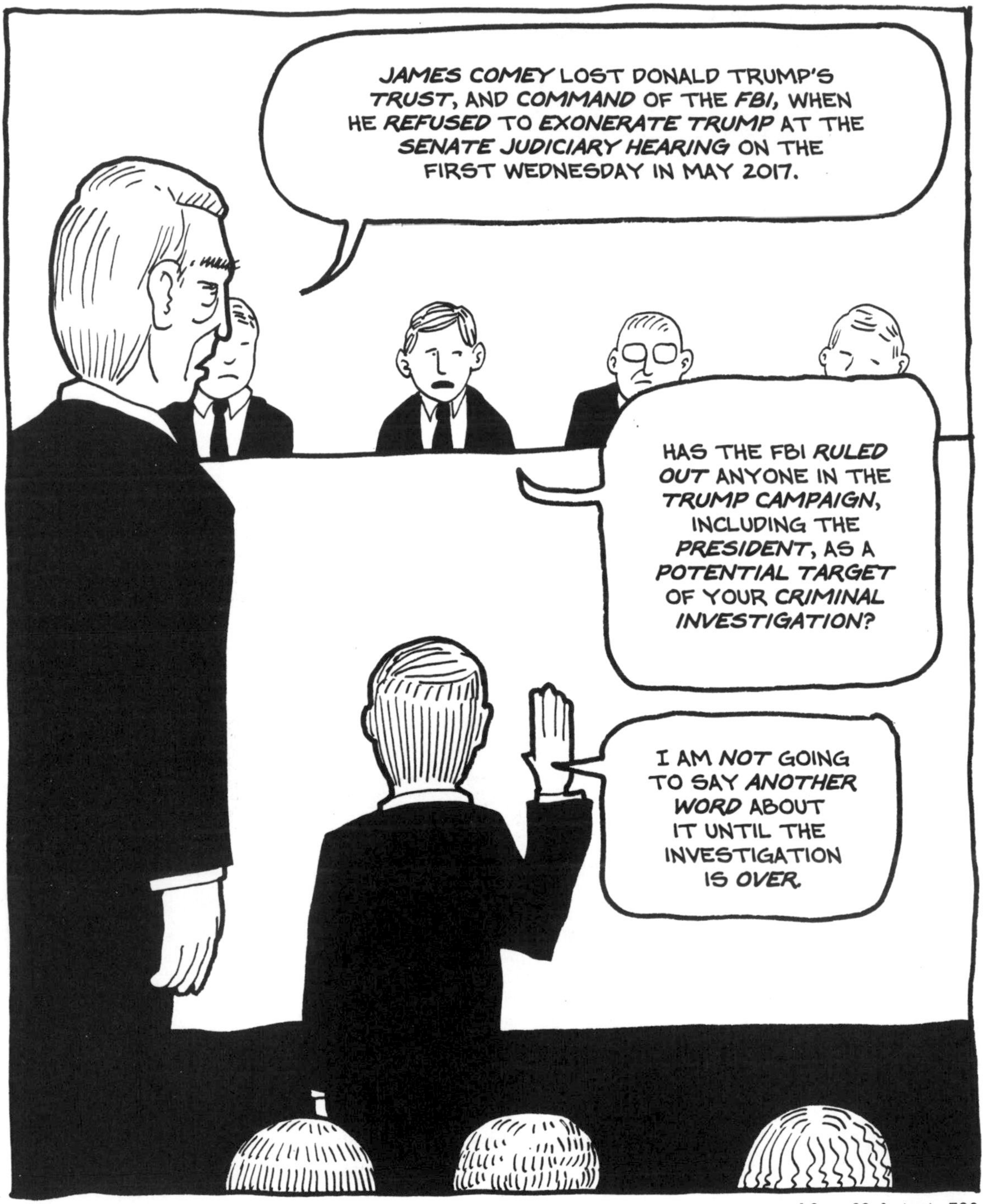

JAMES COMEY LOST DONALD TRUMP'S TRUST, AND COMMAND OF THE FBI, WHEN HE REFUSED TO EXONERATE TRUMP AT THE SENATE JUDICIARY HEARING ON THE FIRST WEDNESDAY IN MAY 2017.
HAS THE FBI RULED OUT ANYONE IN THE TRUMP CAMPAIGN, INCLUDING THE PRESIDENT, AS A POTENTIAL TARGET OF YOUR CRIMINAL INVESTIGATION?
I AM NOT GOING TO SAY ANOTHER WORD ABOUT IT UNTIL THE INVESTIGATION IS OVER.

vol 2, pg 62, footnote 386

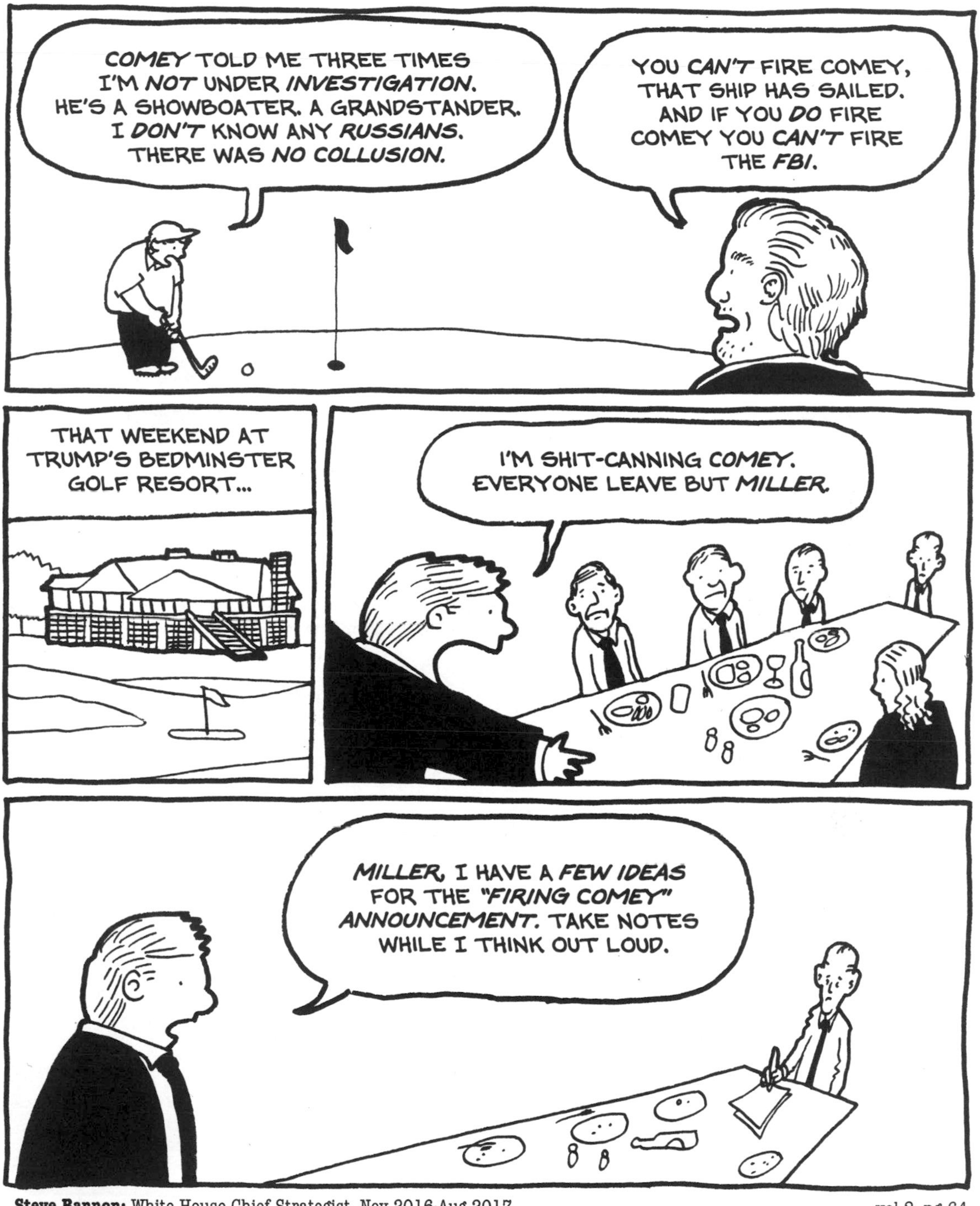
COMEY TOLD ME THREE TIMES I'M NOT UNDER INVESTIGATION. HE'S A SHOWBOATER. A GRANDSTANDER. I DON'T KNOW ANY RUSSIANS. THERE WAS NO COLLUSION.
YOU CAN'T FIRE COMEY, THAT SHIP HAS SAILED. AND IF YOU DO FIRE COMEY YOU CAN'T FIRE THE FBI.
THAT WEEKEND AT TRUMP'S BEDMINSTER GOLF RESORT...
I'M SHIT-CANNING COMEY. EVERYONE LEAVE BUT MILLER.
MILLER, I HAVE A FEW IDEAS FOR THE "FIRING COMEY" ANNOUNCEMENT. TAKE NOTES WHILE I THINK OUT LOUD.

Steve Bannon: White House Chief Strategist, Nov 2016-Aug 2017
Stephen Miller: Trump's senior policy advisor, Jan 2017-

vol 2, pg 64

TRUMP AND *MILLER* WORKED ON THE MEMO FOR MUCH OF THE WEEKEND. WORRIED ABOUT *LEAKS*, TRUMP TOLD *MILLER* TO KEEP WHITE HOUSE STAFF *IN THE DARK*.

DEAR DIRECTOR COMEY,
WHILE I GREATLY APPRECIATE YOUR INFORMING ME, ON *THREE SEPARATE OCCASIONS*, THAT I AM *NOT* UNDER INVESTIGATION CONCERNING THE *FABRICATED* AND *POLITICALLY-MOTIVATED ALLEGATIONS* OF A *TRUMP-RUSSIA RELATIONSHIP* WITH RESPECT TO THE 2016 PRESIDENTIAL *ELECTION*, PLEASE BE INFORMED THAT I, ALONG WITH MEMBERS OF *BOTH POLITICAL PARTIES* AND, MOST IMPORTANTLY, THE *AMERICAN PUBLIC*, HAVE *LOST FAITH* IN YOU AS THE DIRECTOR OF THE *FBI* AND YOU ARE HEREBY *TERMINATED*.

vol 2, pg 64-65, footnote 413

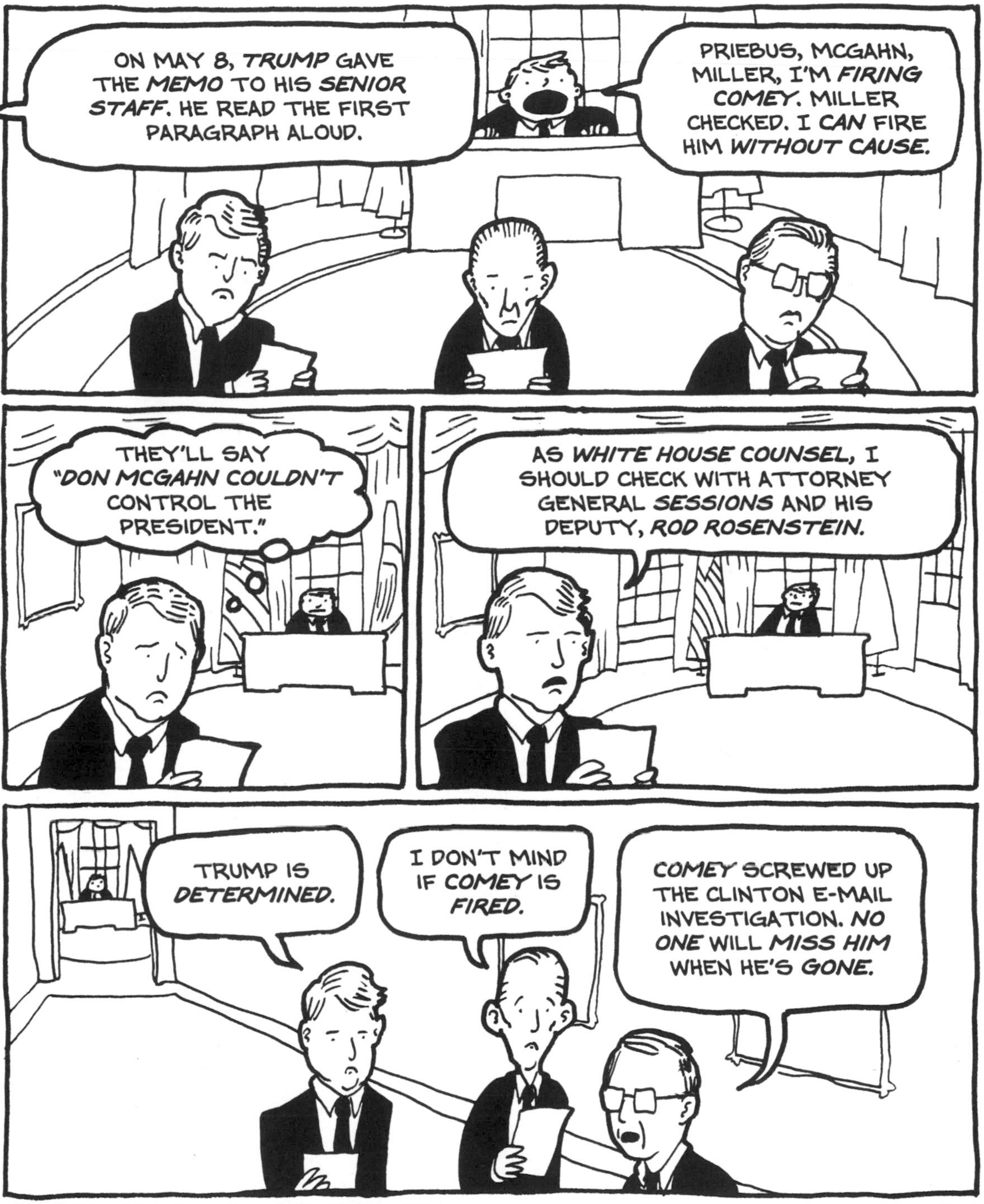
ON MAY 8, TRUMP GAVE THE MEMO TO HIS SENIOR STAFF. HE READ THE FIRST PARAGRAPH ALOUD.
PRIEBUS, MCGAHN, MILLER, I'M FIRING COMEY. MILLER CHECKED. I CAN FIRE HIM WITHOUT CAUSE.
THEY'LL SAY "DON MCGAHN COULDN'T CONTROL THE PRESIDENT."
AS WHITE HOUSE COUNSEL, I SHOULD CHECK WITH ATTORNEY GENERAL SESSIONS AND HIS DEPUTY, ROD ROSENSTEIN.
TRUMP IS DETERMINED.
I DON'T MIND IF COMEY IS FIRED.
COMEY SCREWED UP THE CLINTON E-MAIL INVESTIGATION. NO ONE WILL MISS HIM WHEN HE'S GONE.

Don McGahn: White House Counsel, Jan 2017-Oct 2018
Reince Priebus: White House Chief of Staff, Jan-Jul 2017
Rod Rosenstein: U.S. Deputy Attorney General, Apr 2017-May 2019

vol 2, pg 65-66

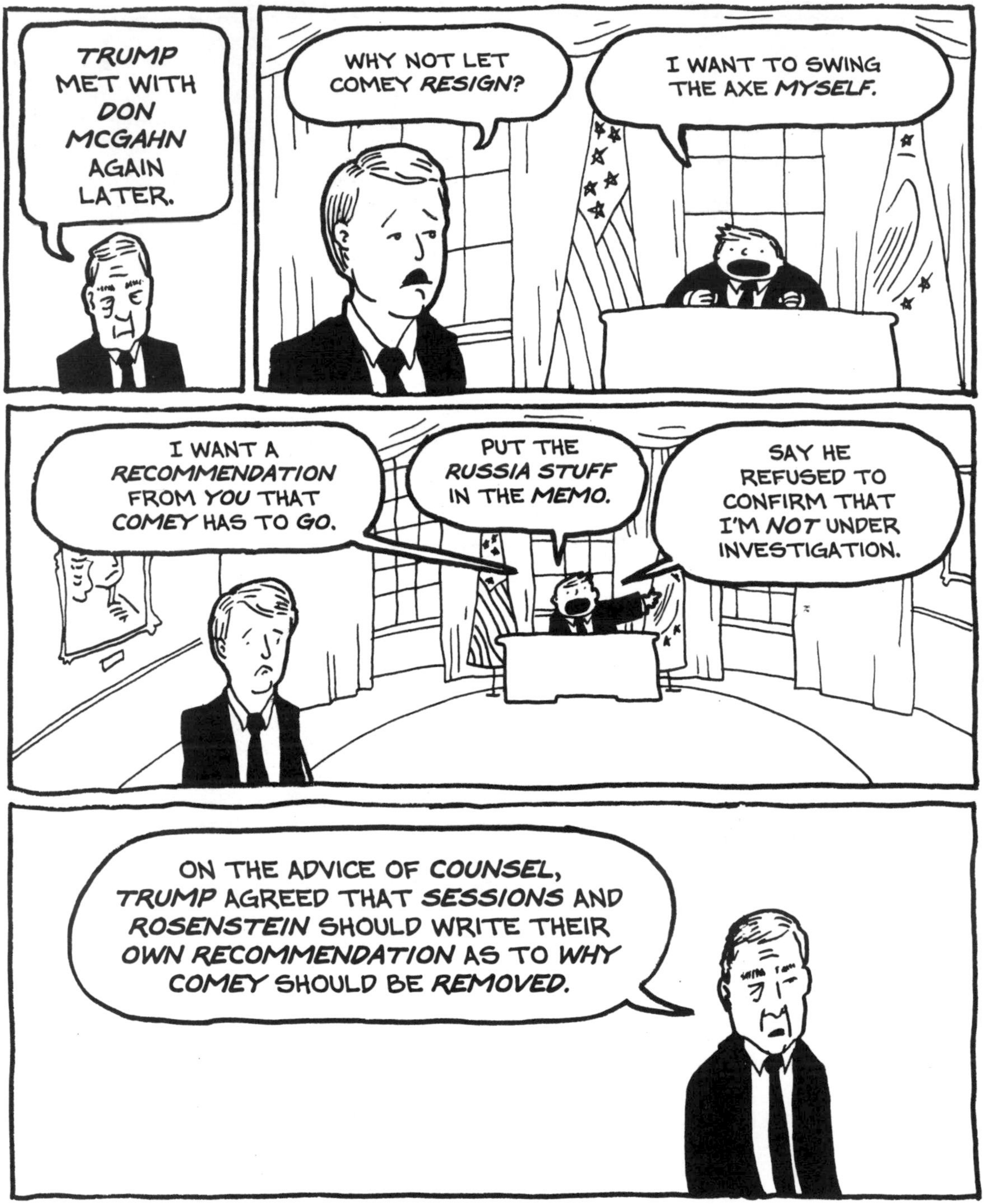

TRUMP MET WITH DON MCGAHN AGAIN LATER.
WHY NOT LET COMEY RESIGN?
I WANT TO SWING THE AXE MYSELF.
I WANT A RECOMMENDATION FROM YOU THAT COMEY HAS TO GO.
PUT THE RUSSIA STUFF IN THE MEMO.
SAY HE REFUSED TO CONFIRM THAT I'M NOT UNDER INVESTIGATION.
ON THE ADVICE OF COUNSEL, TRUMP AGREED THAT SESSIONS AND ROSENSTEIN SHOULD WRITE THEIR OWN RECOMMENDATION AS TO WHY COMEY SHOULD BE REMOVED.

vol 2, pg 67

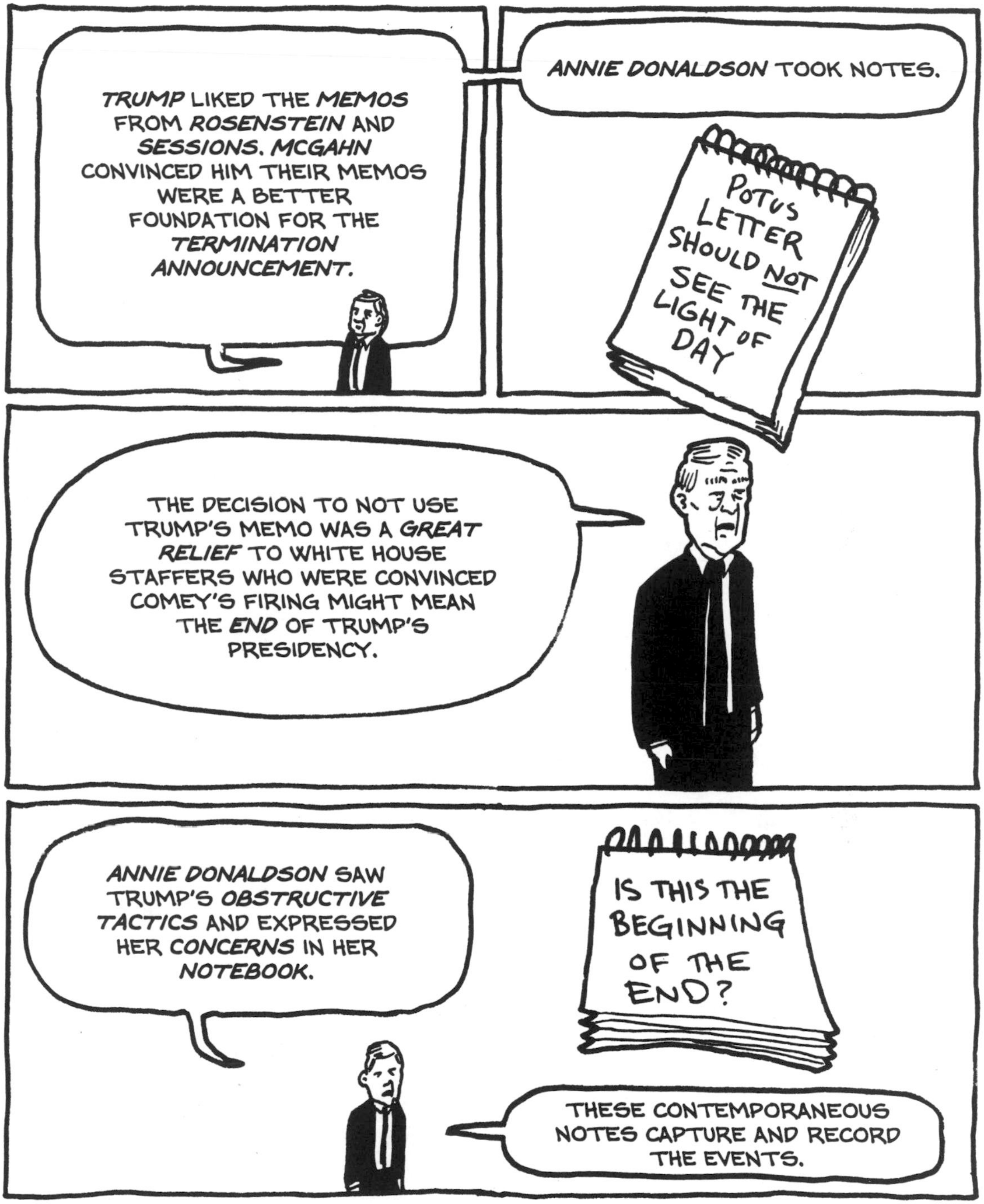
TRUMP LIKED THE MEMOS FROM ROSENSTEIN AND SESSIONS. MCGAHN CONVINCED HIM THEIR MEMOS WERE A BETTER FOUNDATION FOR THE TERMINATION ANNOUNCEMENT.
ANNIE DONALDSON TOOK NOTES.
POTUS LETTER SHOULD NOT SEE THE LIGHT OF DAY
THE DECISION TO NOT USE TRUMP'S MEMO WAS A GREAT RELIEF TO WHITE HOUSE STAFFERS WHO WERE CONVINCED COMEY'S FIRING MIGHT MEAN THE END OF TRUMP'S PRESIDENCY.
ANNIE DONALDSON SAW TRUMP'S OBSTRUCTIVE TACTICS AND EXPRESSED HER CONCERNS IN HER NOTEBOOK.
IS THIS THE BEGINNING OF THE END?
THESE CONTEMPORANEOUS NOTES CAPTURE AND RECORD THE EVENTS.

Annie Donaldson: Deputy Counsel to the President, Feb 2017-Dec 2018 vol 2, pg 68, footnote 441-442

AT THE NEXT PRESS CONFERENCE SEAN SPICER ANSWERED QUESTIONS.

TRUMP *FIRED* COMEY. ANY QUESTIONS?

HEY CHRISTIE, *FAKE NEWS* IS KILLING ME. WHAT THE HELL SHOULD I *DO*?

DID YOU FIRE COMEY BECAUSE OF *ROSENSTEIN'S MEMO*? THEN GET *ROSENSTEIN* TO *DEFEND* YOU.

TRUMP RECOGNIZED THE OPPORTUNITY TO *DEFLECT* ONTO ROSENSTEIN.

ROSENSTEIN, YOU NEED TO TALK TO THE PRESS AND SAY *FIRING COMEY* WAS *YOUR IDEA*.

FIRING COMEY *WASN'T* MY IDEA. YOU DROP ME IN A ROOM WITH REPORTERS, AND *THAT'S* WHAT I'LL TELL THEM.

SHORTLY

ROSENSTEIN FIRED COMEY. THE WHITE HOUSE *WASN'T* INVOLVED. IT WAS A *DOJ DECISION*.

Chris Christie: Head of Trump's transition planning team, 2017-2018
Rod Rosenstein: U.S. Deputy Attorney General, Apr 2017-May 2019

vol 2, pg 69-70

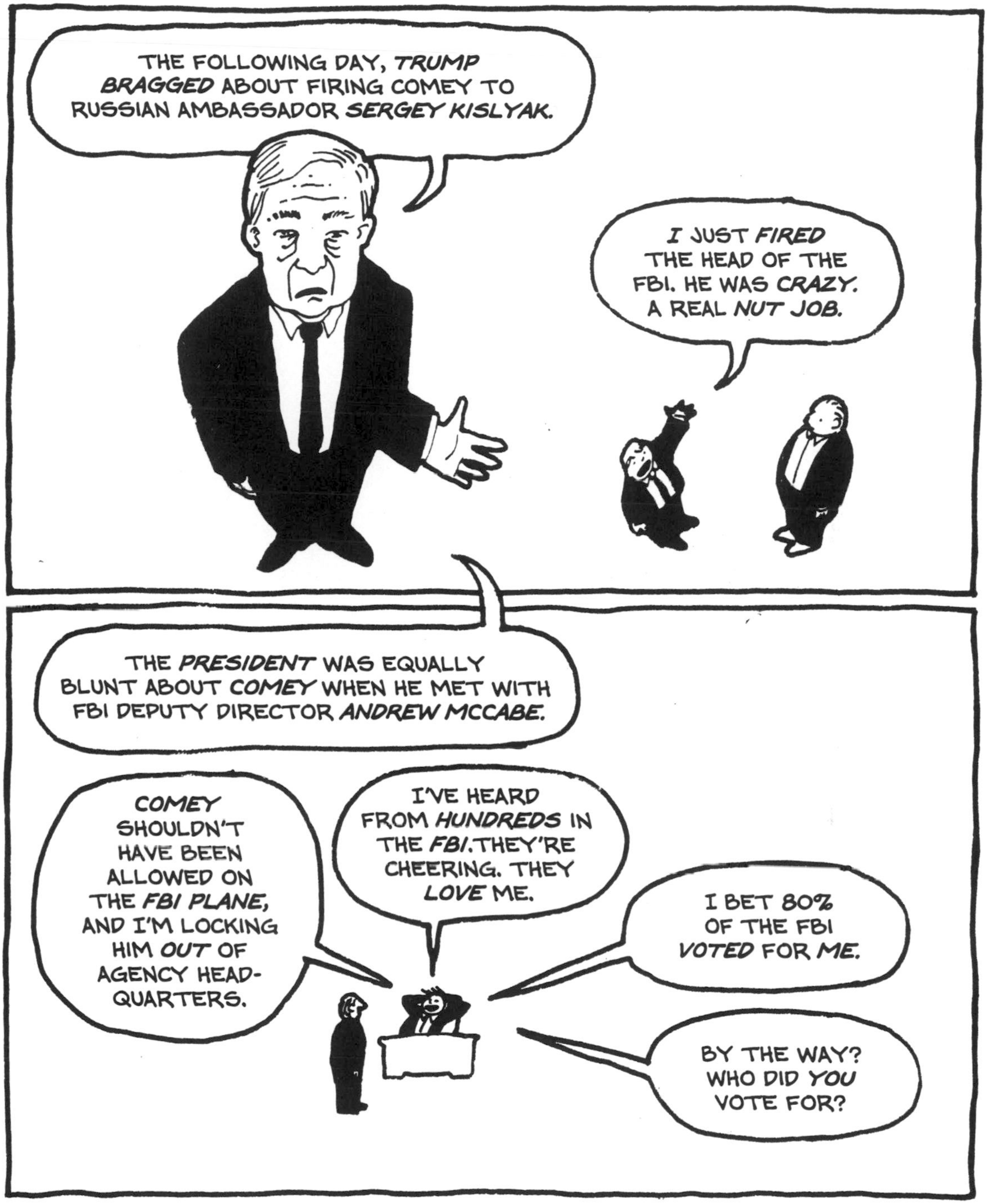
THE FOLLOWING DAY, TRUMP BRAGGED ABOUT FIRING COMEY TO RUSSIAN AMBASSADOR SERGEY KISLYAK.
I JUST FIRED THE HEAD OF THE FBI. HE WAS CRAZY. A REAL NUT JOB.
THE PRESIDENT WAS EQUALLY BLUNT ABOUT COMEY WHEN HE MET WITH FBI DEPUTY DIRECTOR ANDREW MCCABE.
COMEY SHOULDN'T HAVE BEEN ALLOWED ON THE FBI PLANE, AND I'M LOCKING HIM OUT OF AGENCY HEAD-QUARTERS.
I'VE HEARD FROM HUNDREDS IN THE FBI. THEY'RE CHEERING. THEY LOVE ME.
I BET 80% OF THE FBI VOTED FOR ME.
BY THE WAY? WHO DID YOU VOTE FOR?

Andrew McCabe: FBI Deputy Director, Feb 2016-Jan 2018

vol 2, pg 71-72

CHAPTER 12

THE SARAH SANDERS PRESS CONFERENCE

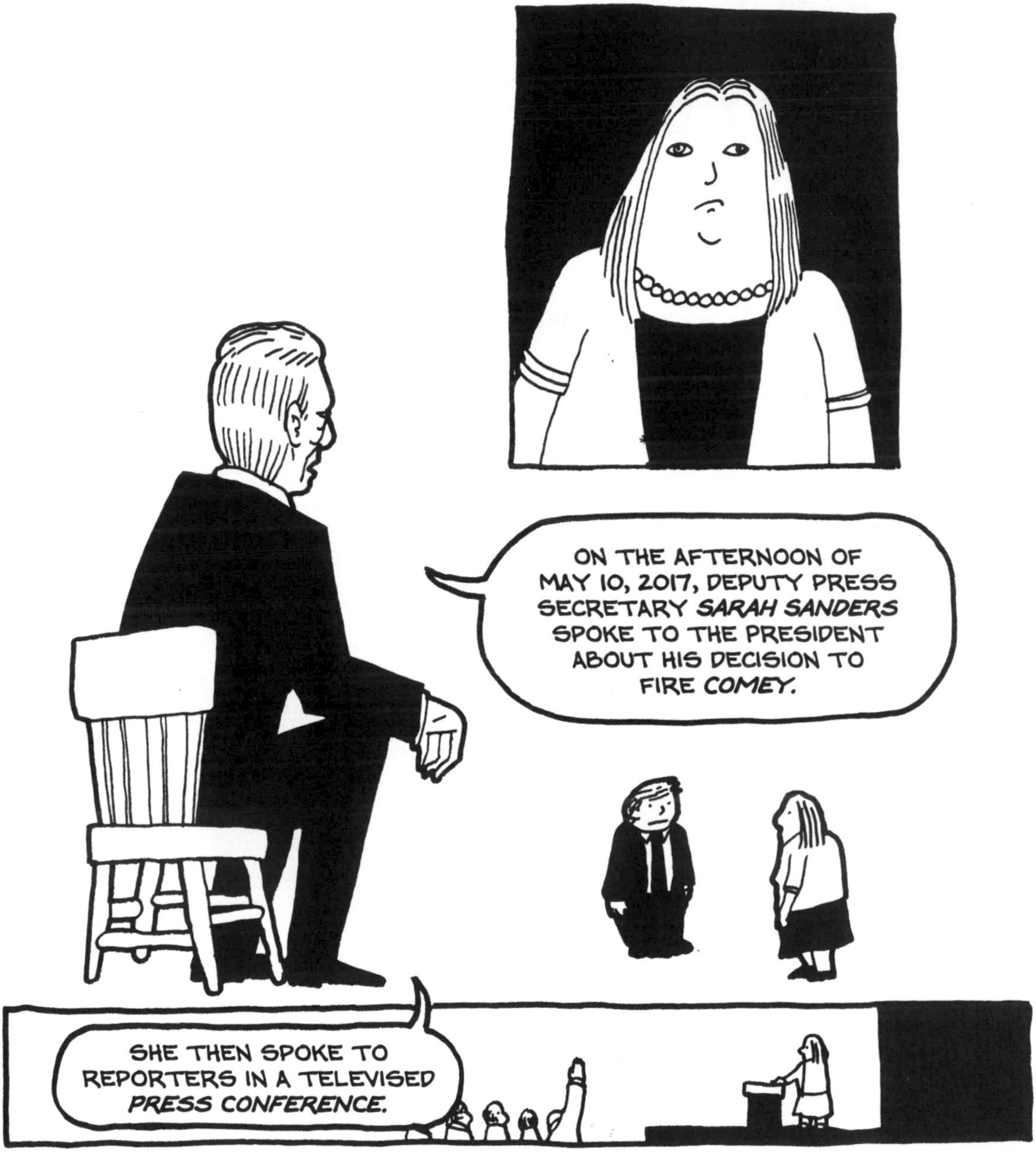
ON THE AFTERNOON OF MAY 10, 2017, DEPUTY PRESS SECRETARY *SARAH SANDERS* SPOKE TO THE PRESIDENT ABOUT HIS DECISION TO FIRE *COMEY*.
SHE THEN SPOKE TO REPORTERS IN A TELEVISED *PRESS CONFERENCE*.

Sarah Sanders: Press Secretary, May 2017-Jun 2019 vol 2, pg 72

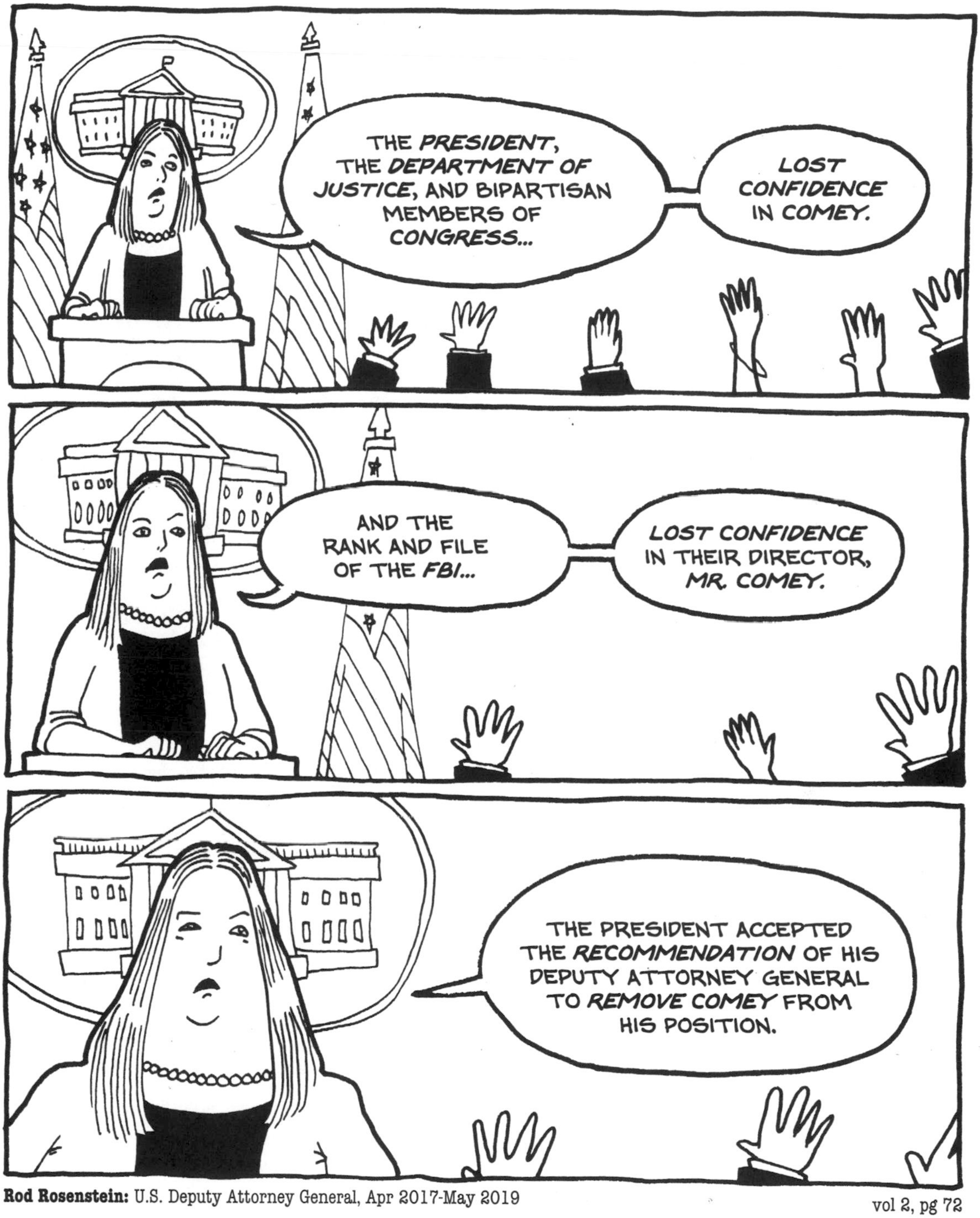
THE PRESIDENT, THE DEPARTMENT OF JUSTICE, AND BIPARTISAN MEMBERS OF CONGRESS...
LOST CONFIDENCE IN COMEY.
AND THE RANK AND FILE OF THE FBI...
LOST CONFIDENCE IN THEIR DIRECTOR, MR. COMEY.
THE PRESIDENT ACCEPTED THE RECOMMENDATION OF HIS DEPUTY ATTORNEY GENERAL TO REMOVE COMEY FROM HIS POSITION.

Rod Rosenstein: U.S. Deputy Attorney General, Apr 2017-May 2019

vol 2, pg 72

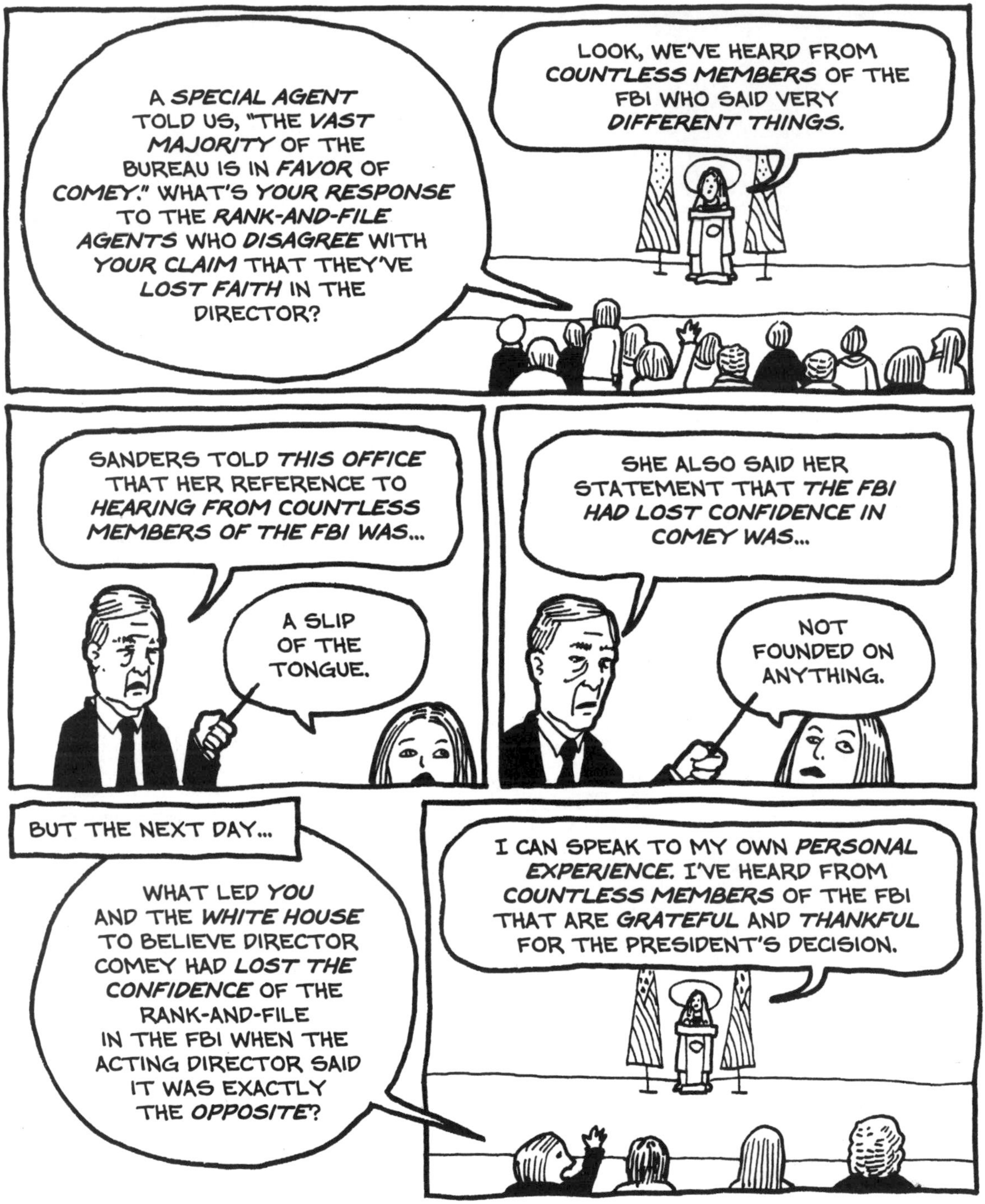
A SPECIAL AGENT TOLD US, "THE VAST MAJORITY OF THE BUREAU IS IN FAVOR OF COMEY." WHAT'S YOUR RESPONSE TO THE RANK-AND-FILE AGENTS WHO DISAGREE WITH YOUR CLAIM THAT THEY'VE LOST FAITH IN THE DIRECTOR?
LOOK, WE'VE HEARD FROM COUNTLESS MEMBERS OF THE FBI WHO SAID VERY DIFFERENT THINGS.
SANDERS TOLD THIS OFFICE THAT HER REFERENCE TO HEARING FROM COUNTLESS MEMBERS OF THE FBI WAS...
A SLIP OF THE TONGUE.
SHE ALSO SAID HER STATEMENT THAT THE FBI HAD LOST CONFIDENCE IN COMEY WAS...
NOT FOUNDED ON ANYTHING.
BUT THE NEXT DAY...
WHAT LED YOU AND THE WHITE HOUSE TO BELIEVE DIRECTOR COMEY HAD LOST THE CONFIDENCE OF THE RANK-AND-FILE IN THE FBI WHEN THE ACTING DIRECTOR SAID IT WAS EXACTLY THE OPPOSITE?
I CAN SPEAK TO MY OWN PERSONAL EXPERIENCE. I'VE HEARD FROM COUNTLESS MEMBERS OF THE FBI THAT ARE GRATEFUL AND THANKFUL FOR THE PRESIDENT'S DECISION.

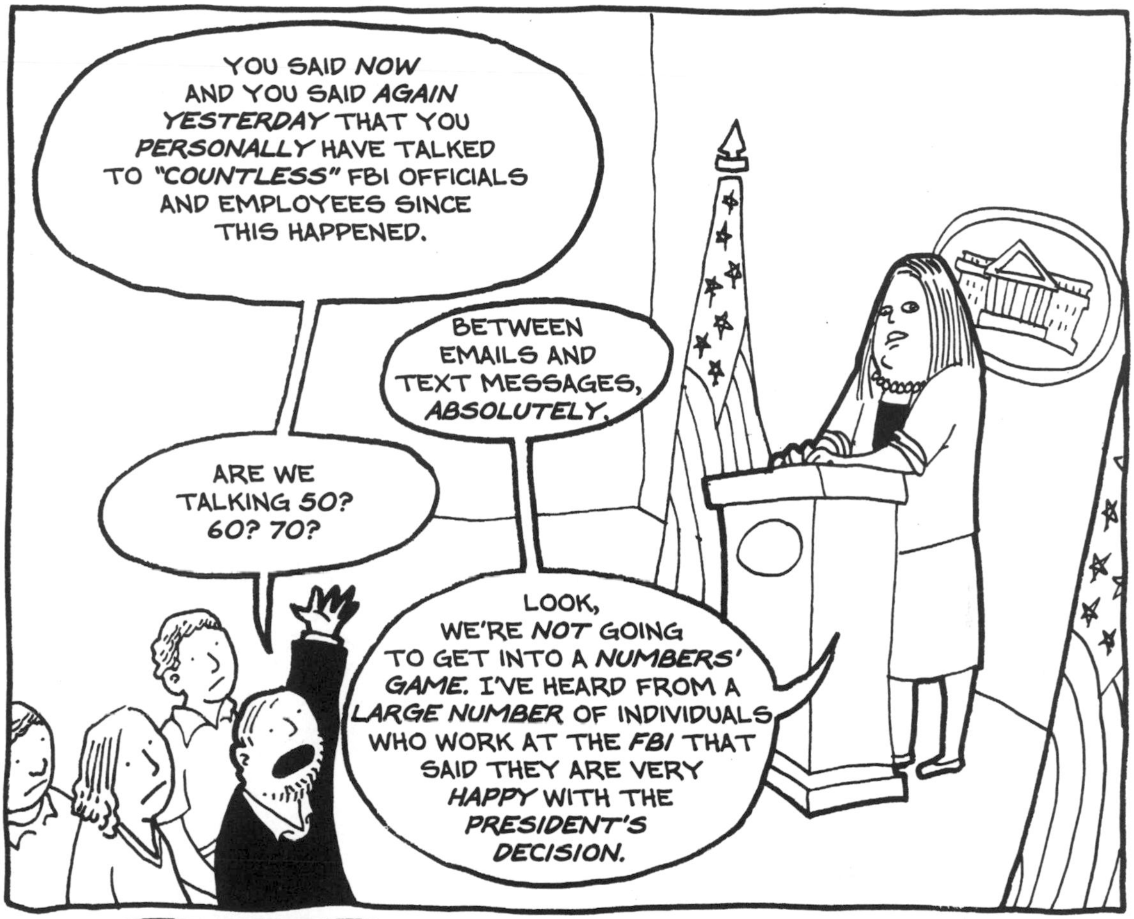
YOU SAID NOW AND YOU SAID AGAIN YESTERDAY THAT YOU PERSONALLY HAVE TALKED TO "COUNTLESS" FBI OFFICIALS AND EMPLOYEES SINCE THIS HAPPENED.
BETWEEN EMAILS AND TEXT MESSAGES, ABSOLUTELY.
ARE WE TALKING 50? 60? 70?
LOOK, WE'RE NOT GOING TO GET INTO A NUMBERS' GAME. I'VE HEARD FROM A LARGE NUMBER OF INDIVIDUALS WHO WORK AT THE FBI THAT SAID THEY ARE VERY HAPPY WITH THE PRESIDENT'S DECISION.

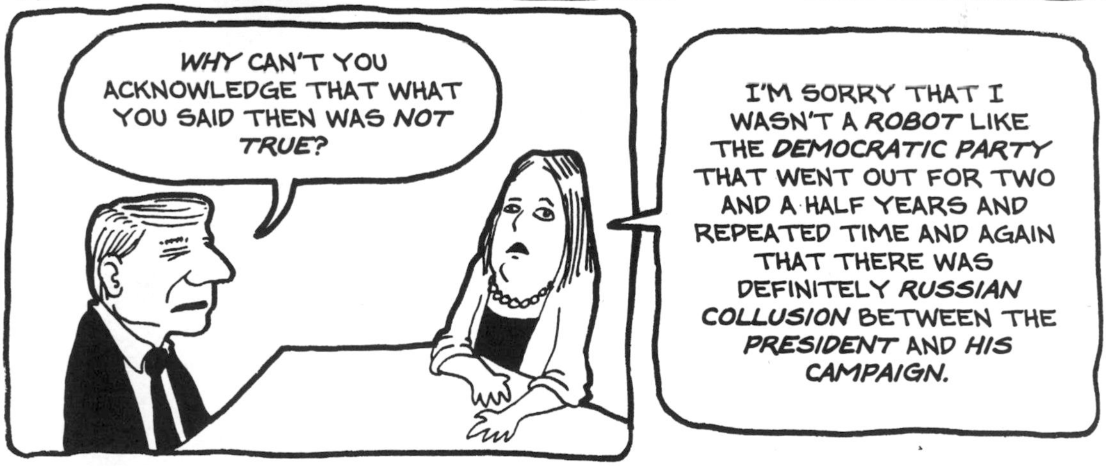
WHY CAN'T YOU ACKNOWLEDGE THAT WHAT YOU SAID THEN WAS NOT TRUE?
I'M SORRY THAT I WASN'T A ROBOT LIKE THE DEMOCRATIC PARTY THAT WENT OUT FOR TWO AND A HALF YEARS AND REPEATED TIME AND AGAIN THAT THERE WAS DEFINITELY RUSSIAN COLLUSION BETWEEN THE PRESIDENT AND HIS CAMPAIGN.

Good Morning America with **George Stephanopoulos**

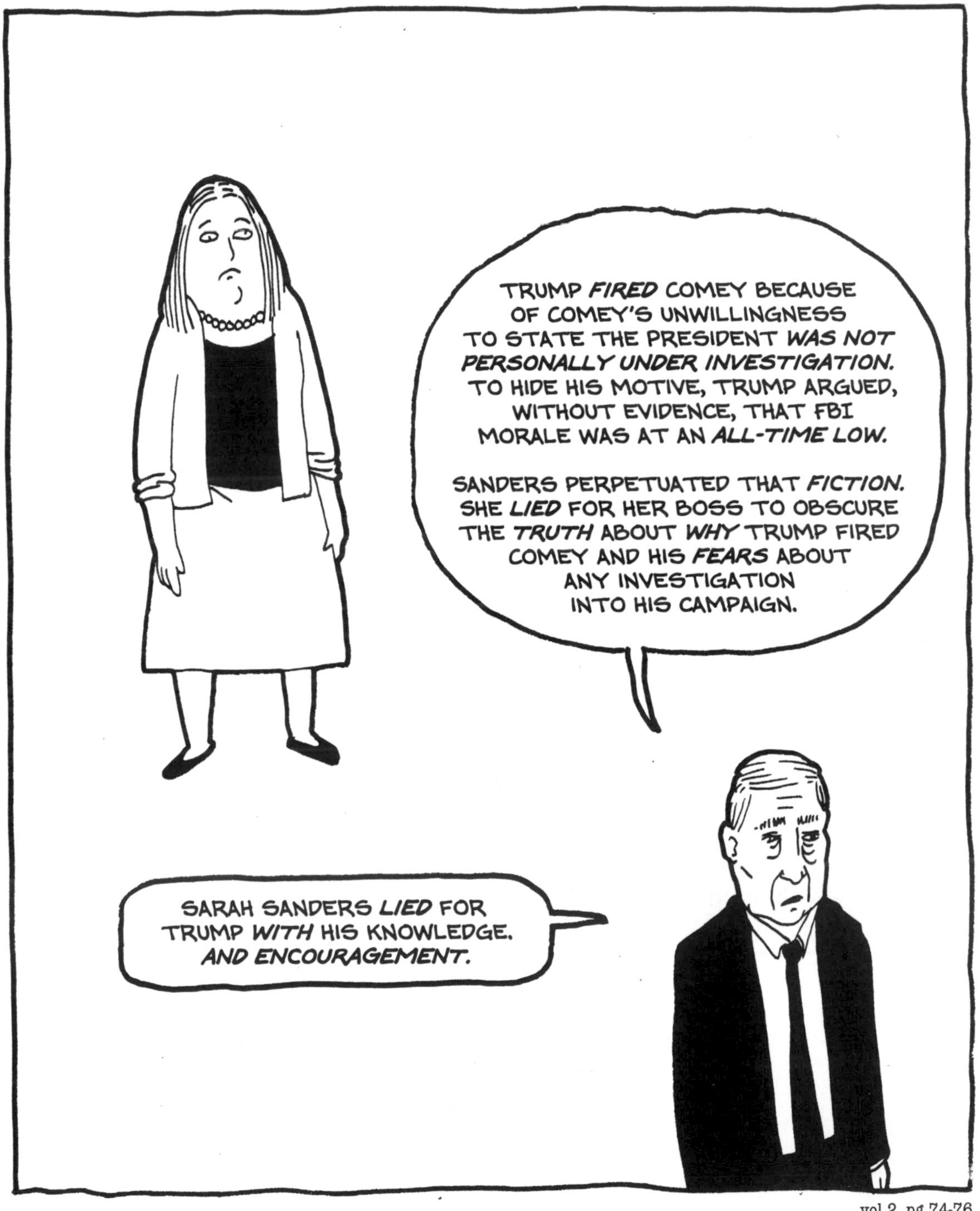
TRUMP *FIRED* COMEY BECAUSE OF COMEY'S UNWILLINGNESS TO STATE THE PRESIDENT *WAS NOT PERSONALLY UNDER INVESTIGATION.* TO HIDE HIS MOTIVE, TRUMP ARGUED, WITHOUT EVIDENCE, THAT FBI MORALE WAS AT AN *ALL-TIME LOW.*
SANDERS PERPETUATED THAT *FICTION.* SHE *LIED* FOR HER BOSS TO OBSCURE THE *TRUTH* ABOUT *WHY* TRUMP FIRED COMEY AND HIS *FEARS* ABOUT ANY INVESTIGATION INTO HIS CAMPAIGN.
SARAH SANDERS *LIED* FOR TRUMP *WITH* HIS KNOWLEDGE. *AND ENCOURAGEMENT.*

vol 2, pg 74-76

CHAPTER 13

DON MCGAHN
PUSHED TO LIE

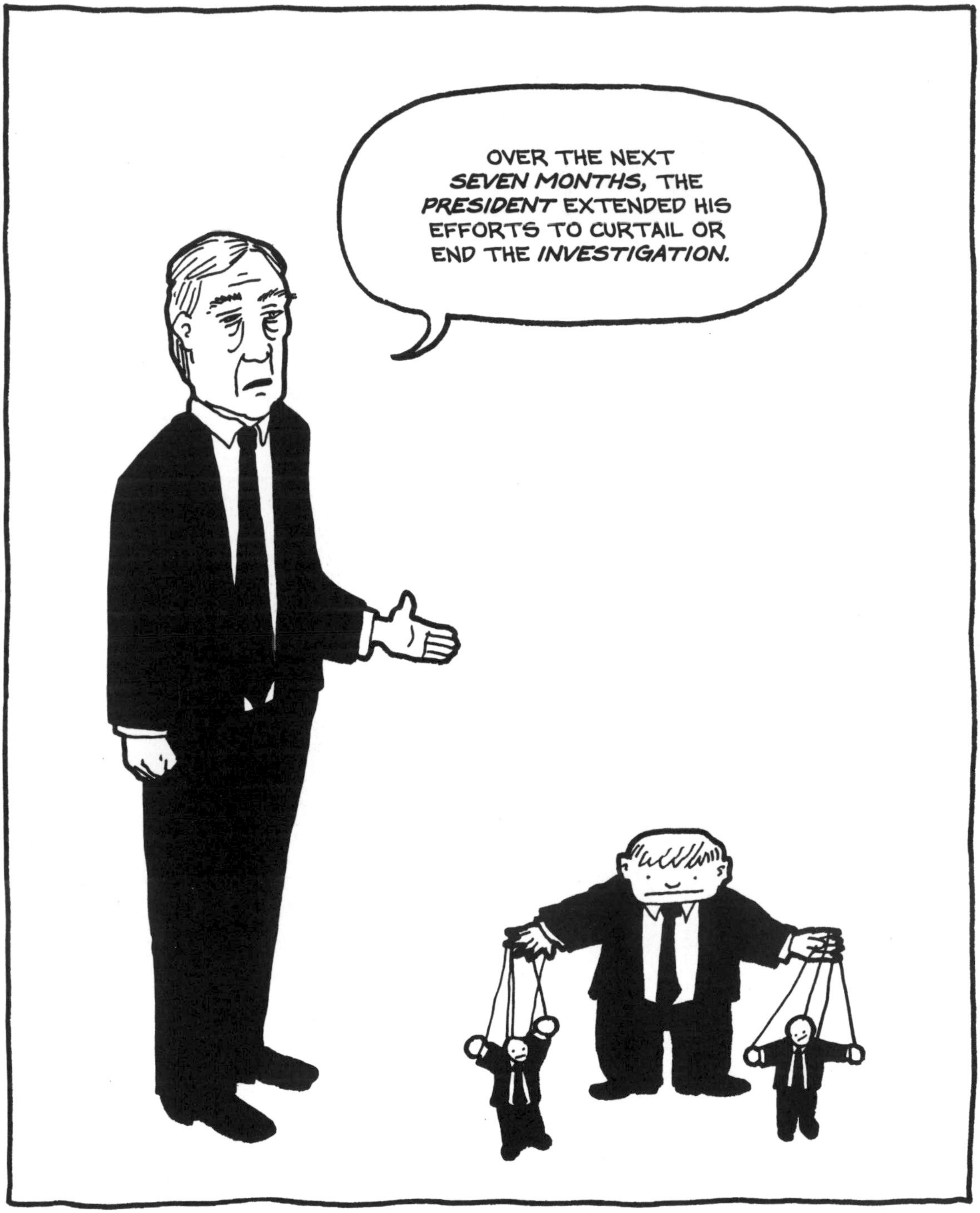
OVER THE NEXT *SEVEN MONTHS,* THE *PRESIDENT* EXTENDED HIS EFFORTS TO CURTAIL OR END THE *INVESTIGATION.*

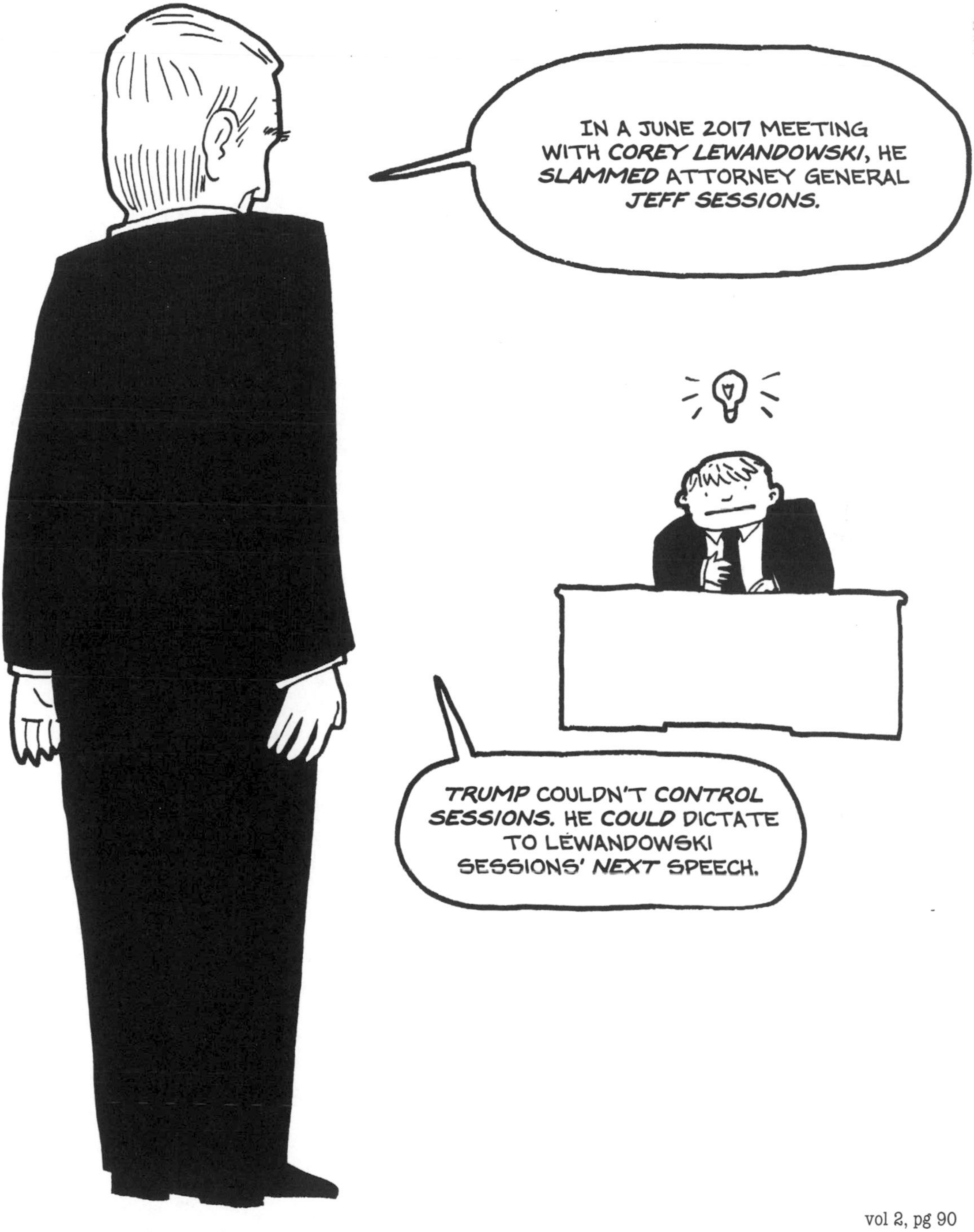
IN A JUNE 2017 MEETING WITH COREY LEWANDOWSKI, HE SLAMMED ATTORNEY GENERAL JEFF SESSIONS.
TRUMP COULDN'T CONTROL SESSIONS. HE COULD DICTATE TO LEWANDOWSKI SESSIONS' NEXT SPEECH.

vol 2, pg 90

Corey Lewandowski: Trump's campaign manager, Jan 2015-Jun 2016

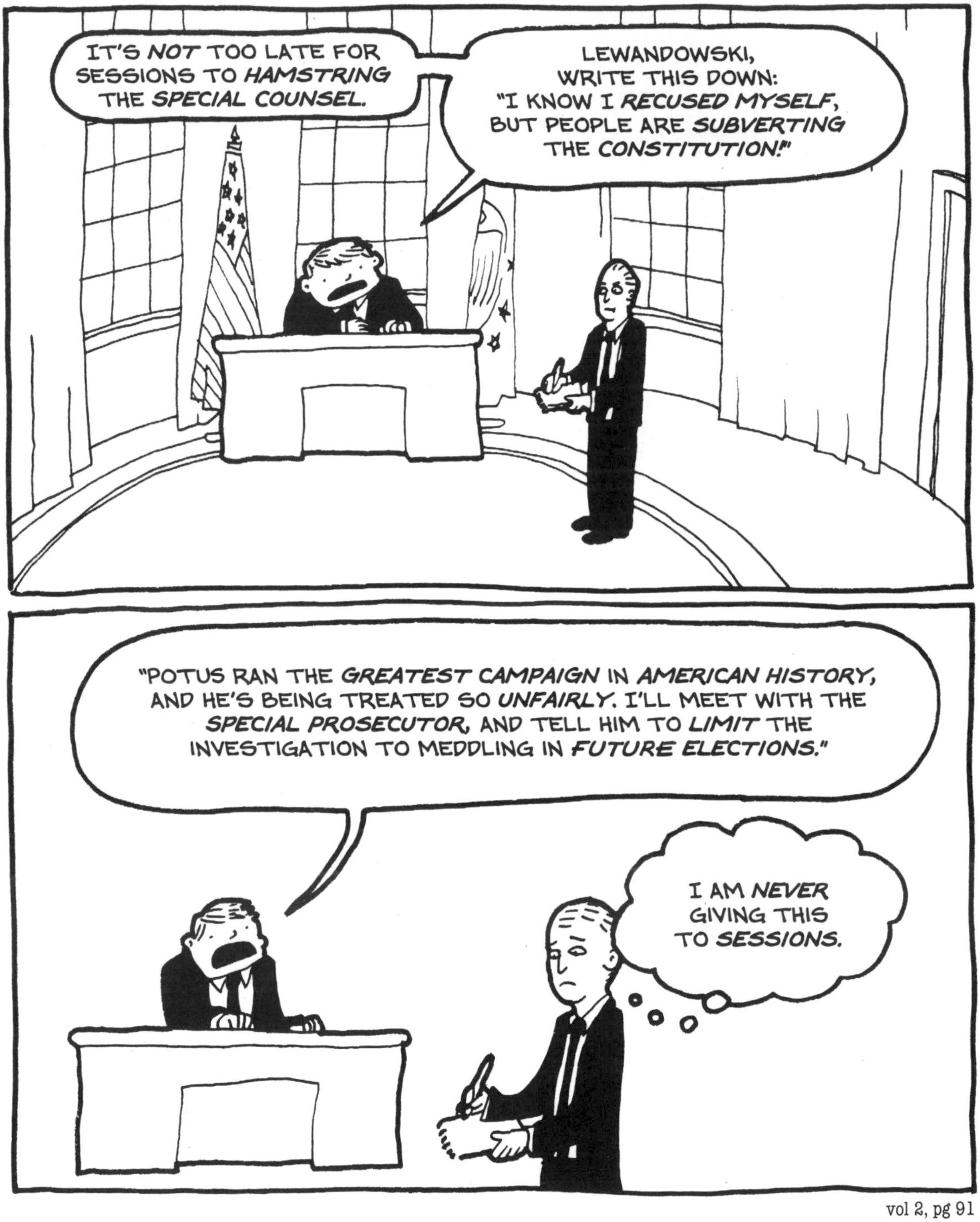
IT'S NOT TOO LATE FOR SESSIONS TO HAMSTRING THE SPECIAL COUNSEL.
LEWANDOWSKI, WRITE THIS DOWN: "I KNOW I RECUSED MYSELF, BUT PEOPLE ARE SUBVERTING THE CONSTITUTION!"
"POTUS RAN THE GREATEST CAMPAIGN IN AMERICAN HISTORY, AND HE'S BEING TREATED SO UNFAIRLY. I'LL MEET WITH THE SPECIAL PROSECUTOR, AND TELL HIM TO LIMIT THE INVESTIGATION TO MEDDLING IN FUTURE ELECTIONS."
I AM NEVER GIVING THIS TO SESSIONS.

vol 2, pg 91

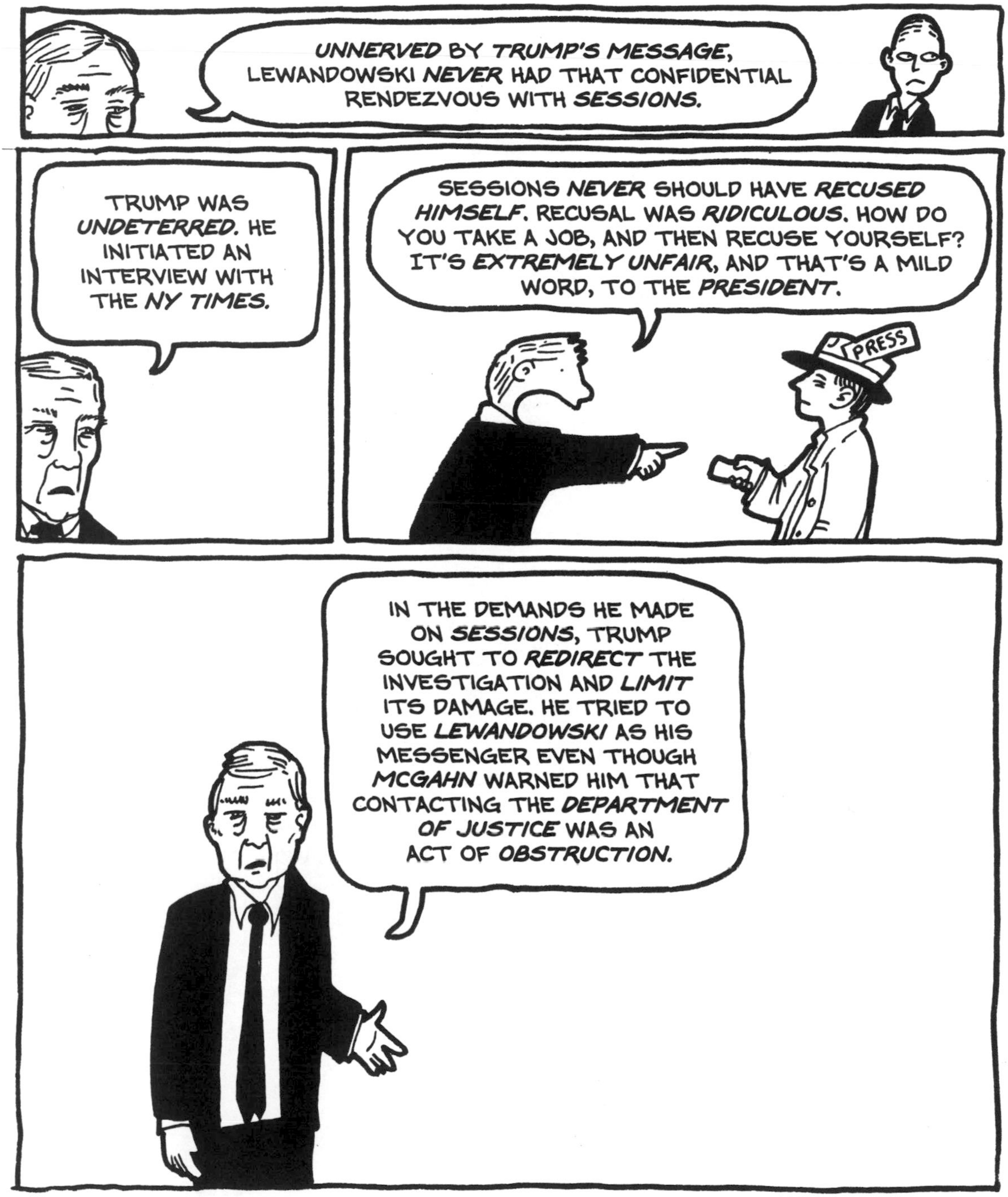
UNNERVED BY TRUMP'S MESSAGE, LEWANDOWSKI NEVER HAD THAT CONFIDENTIAL RENDEZVOUS WITH SESSIONS.
TRUMP WAS UNDETERRED. HE INITIATED AN INTERVIEW WITH THE NY TIMES.
SESSIONS NEVER SHOULD HAVE RECUSED HIMSELF. RECUSAL WAS RIDICULOUS. HOW DO YOU TAKE A JOB, AND THEN RECUSE YOURSELF? IT'S EXTREMELY UNFAIR, AND THAT'S A MILD WORD, TO THE PRESIDENT.
PRESS
IN THE DEMANDS HE MADE ON SESSIONS, TRUMP SOUGHT TO REDIRECT THE INVESTIGATION AND LIMIT ITS DAMAGE. HE TRIED TO USE LEWANDOWSKI AS HIS MESSENGER EVEN THOUGH MCGAHN WARNED HIM THAT CONTACTING THE DEPARTMENT OF JUSTICE WAS AN ACT OF OBSTRUCTION.

vol 2, pg 93-94, 97-98

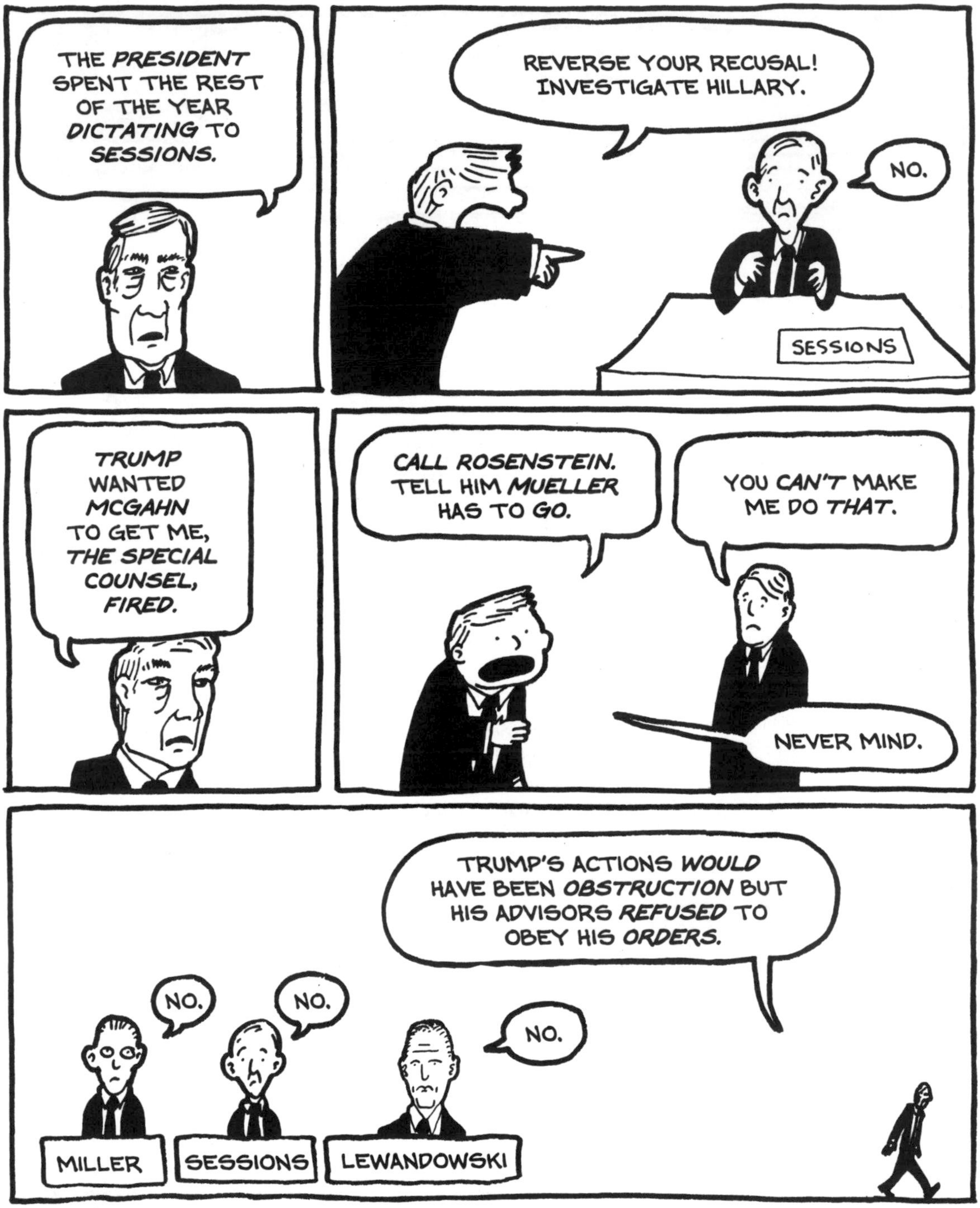
THE *PRESIDENT* SPENT THE REST OF THE YEAR *DICTATING* TO *SESSIONS*.
REVERSE YOUR RECUSAL! INVESTIGATE HILLARY.
NO.
SESSIONS
TRUMP WANTED *MCGAHN* TO GET ME, *THE SPECIAL COUNSEL, FIRED*.
CALL ROSENSTEIN. TELL HIM *MUELLER* HAS TO *GO*.
YOU *CAN'T* MAKE ME DO *THAT*.
NEVER MIND.
TRUMP'S ACTIONS *WOULD* HAVE BEEN *OBSTRUCTION* BUT HIS ADVISORS *REFUSED* TO OBEY HIS *ORDERS*.
NO.
NO.
NO.
MILLER
SESSIONS
LEWANDOWSKI

Stephen Miller: Trump's senior policy advisor, Jan 2017-
Jeff Sessions: Attorney General, 2017-2018

vol 2, pg 112-113

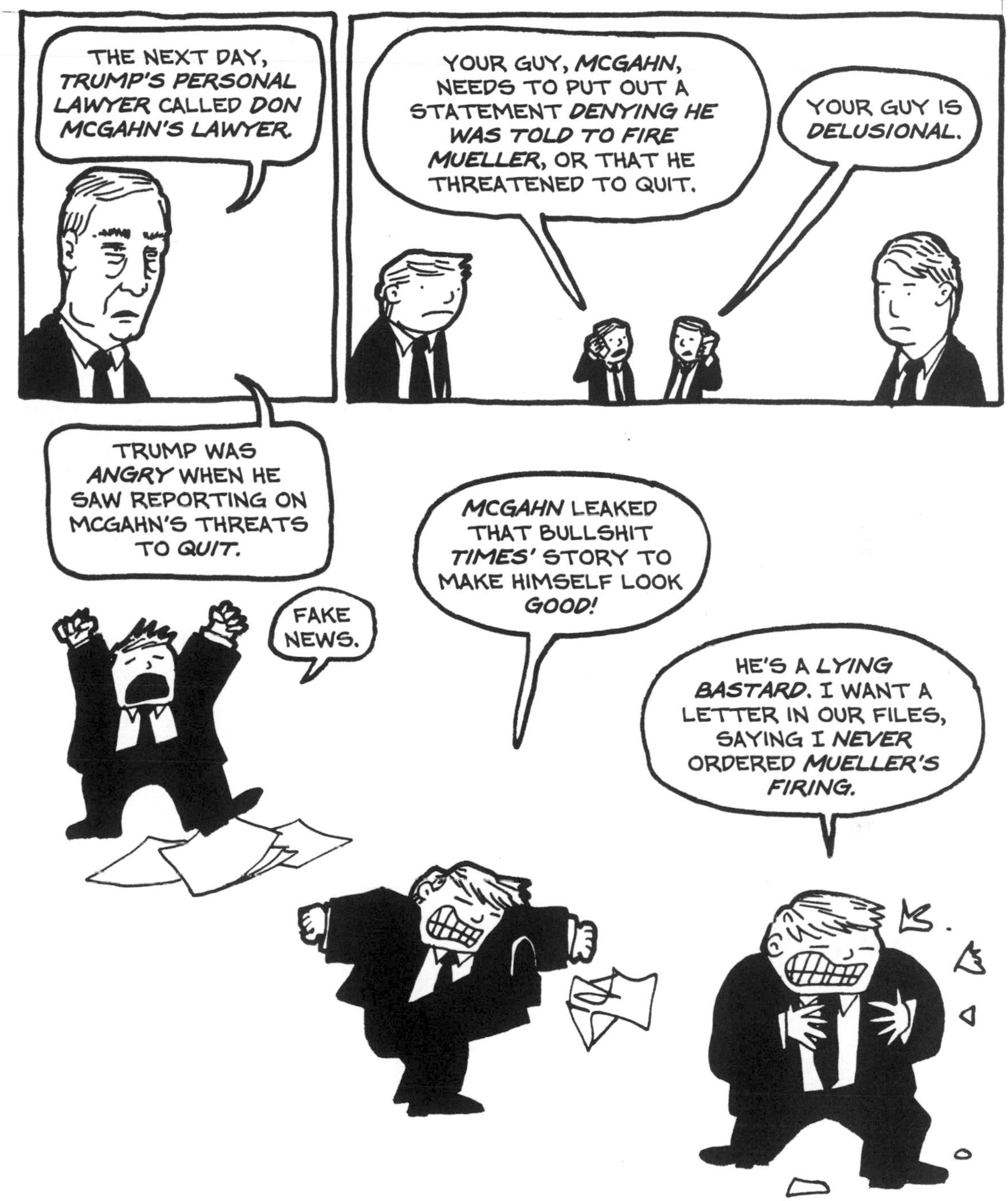
THE NEXT DAY, TRUMP'S PERSONAL LAWYER CALLED DON MCGAHN'S LAWYER.
YOUR GUY, MCGAHN, NEEDS TO PUT OUT A STATEMENT DENYING HE WAS TOLD TO FIRE MUELLER, OR THAT HE THREATENED TO QUIT.
YOUR GUY IS DELUSIONAL.
TRUMP WAS ANGRY WHEN HE SAW REPORTING ON MCGAHN'S THREATS TO QUIT.
FAKE NEWS.
MCGAHN LEAKED THAT BULLSHIT TIMES' STORY TO MAKE HIMSELF LOOK GOOD!
HE'S A LYING BASTARD. I WANT A LETTER IN OUR FILES, SAYING I NEVER ORDERED MUELLER'S FIRING.

vol 2, pg 113-115

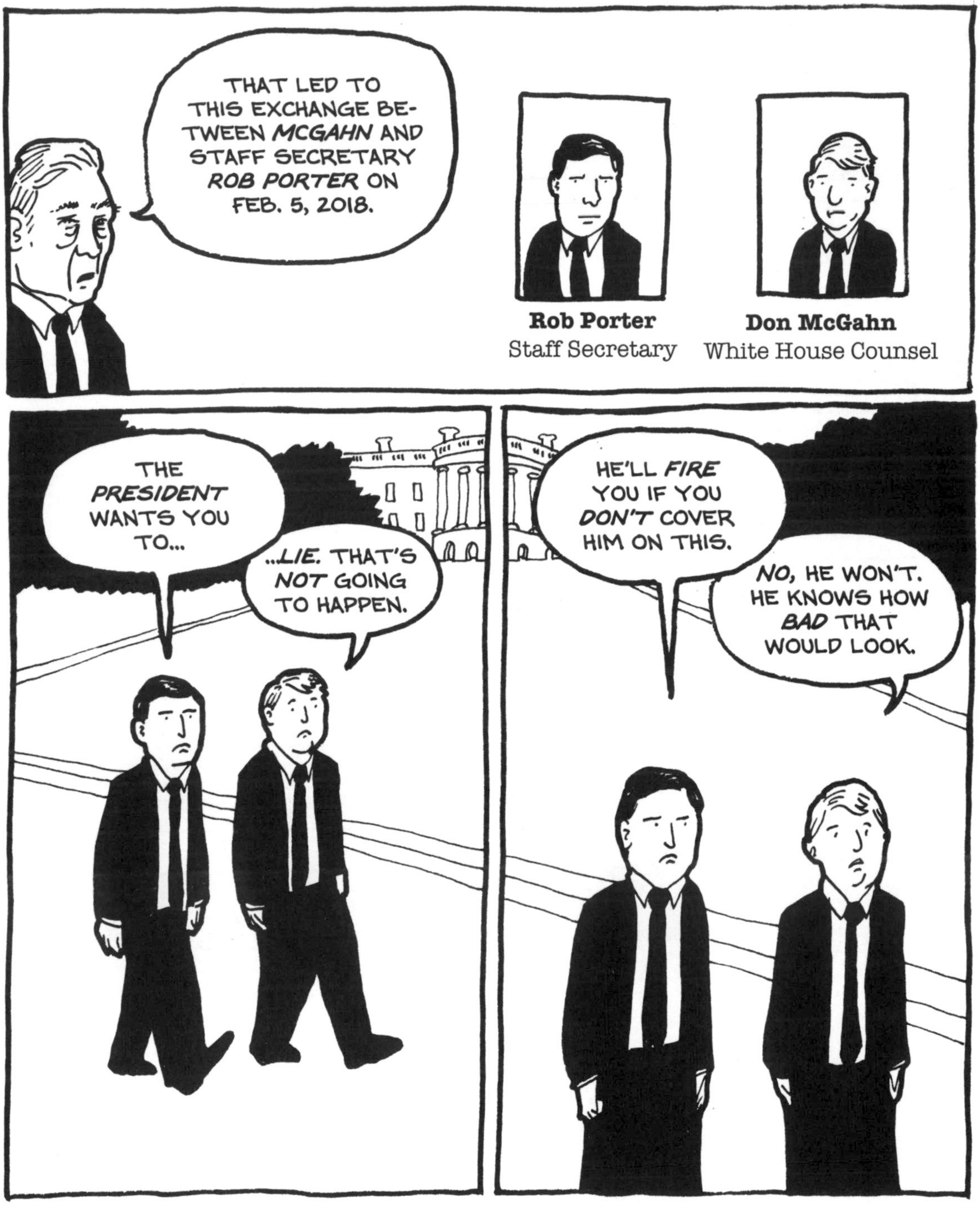
THAT LED TO THIS EXCHANGE BE- TWEEN MCGAHN AND STAFF SECRETARY ROB PORTER ON FEB. 5, 2018.
Rob Porter
Staff Secretary
Don McGahn
White House Counsel
THE PRESIDENT WANTS YOU TO...
...LIE. THAT'S NOT GOING TO HAPPEN.
HE'LL FIRE YOU IF YOU DON'T COVER HIM ON THIS.
NO, HE WON'T. HE KNOWS HOW BAD THAT WOULD LOOK.

Rob Porter: Trump's Staff Secretary, Jan 2017-Feb 2018

vol 2, pg 115-116

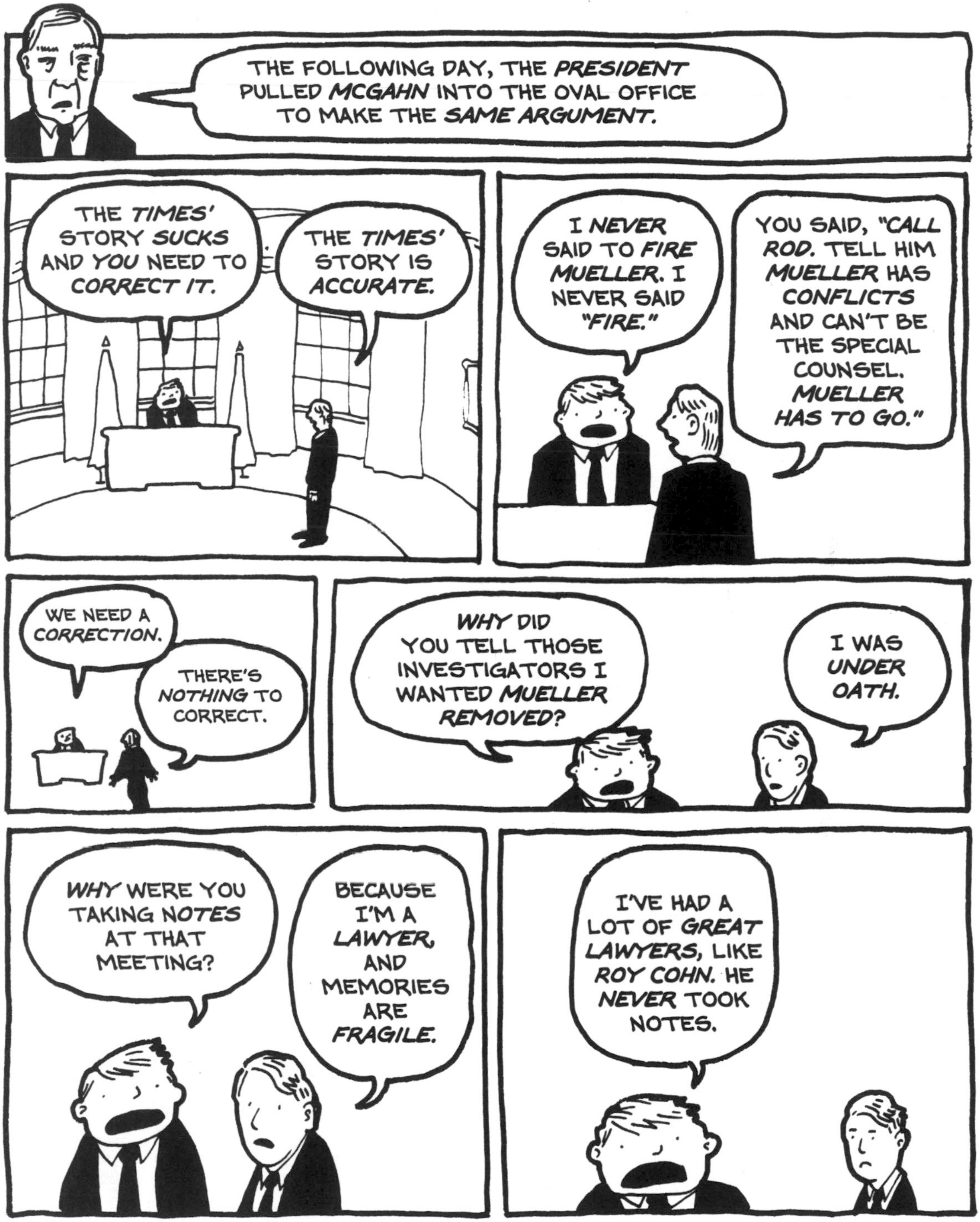
THE FOLLOWING DAY, THE PRESIDENT PULLED MCGAHN INTO THE OVAL OFFICE TO MAKE THE SAME ARGUMENT.
THE TIMES' STORY SUCKS AND YOU NEED TO CORRECT IT.
THE TIMES' STORY IS ACCURATE.
I NEVER SAID TO FIRE MUELLER. I NEVER SAID "FIRE."
YOU SAID, "CALL ROD. TELL HIM MUELLER HAS CONFLICTS AND CAN'T BE THE SPECIAL COUNSEL. MUELLER HAS TO GO."
WE NEED A CORRECTION.
THERE'S NOTHING TO CORRECT.
WHY DID YOU TELL THOSE INVESTIGATORS I WANTED MUELLER REMOVED?
I WAS UNDER OATH.
WHY WERE YOU TAKING NOTES AT THAT MEETING?
BECAUSE I'M A LAWYER, AND MEMORIES ARE FRAGILE.
I'VE HAD A LOT OF GREAT LAWYERS, LIKE ROY COHN. HE NEVER TOOK NOTES.

vol 2, pg 116-117

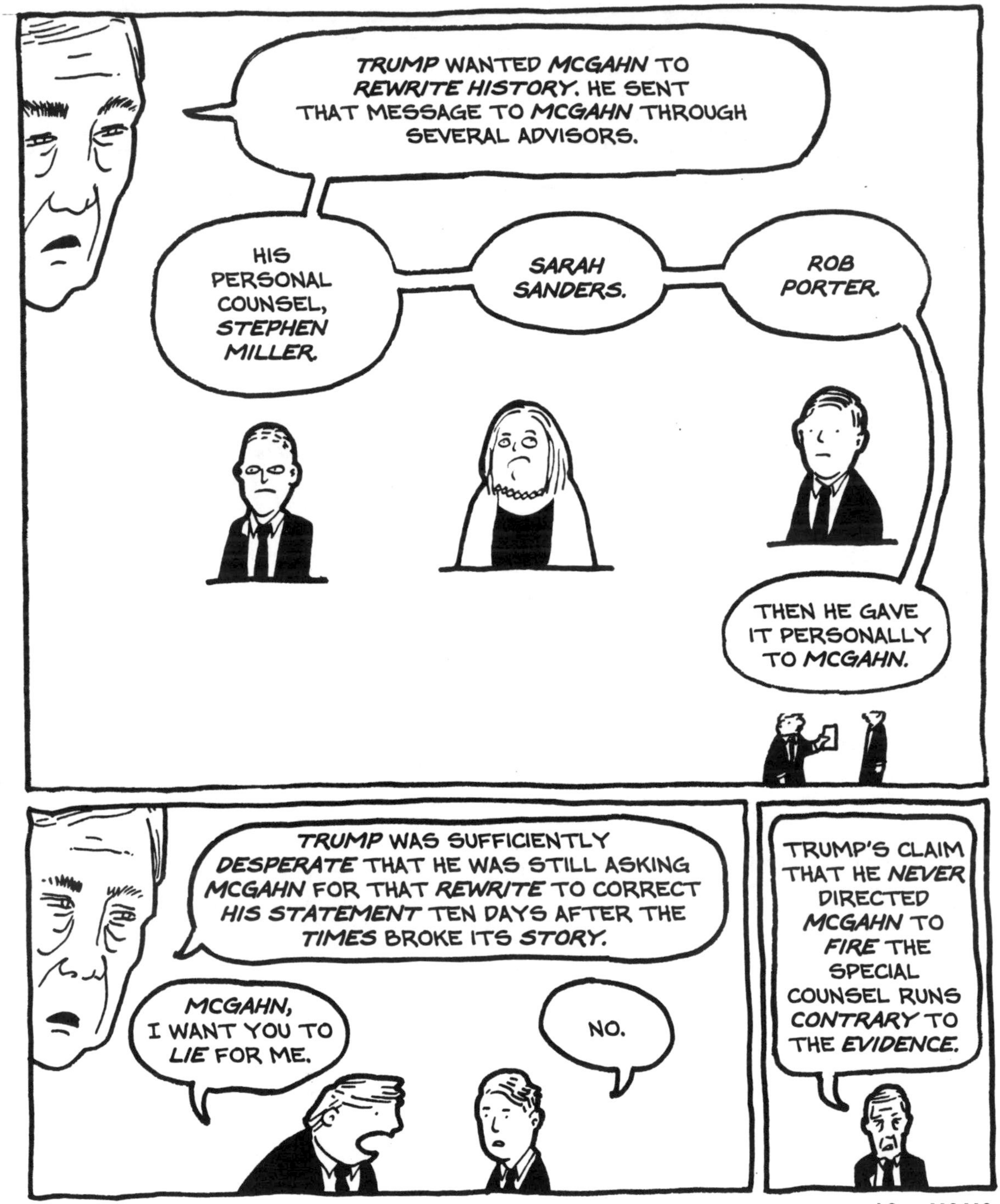
TRUMP WANTED MCGAHN TO REWRITE HISTORY. HE SENT THAT MESSAGE TO MCGAHN THROUGH SEVERAL ADVISORS.
HIS PERSONAL COUNSEL, STEPHEN MILLER.
SARAH SANDERS.
ROB PORTER.
THEN HE GAVE IT PERSONALLY TO MCGAHN.
TRUMP WAS SUFFICIENTLY DESPERATE THAT HE WAS STILL ASKING MCGAHN FOR THAT REWRITE TO CORRECT HIS STATEMENT TEN DAYS AFTER THE TIMES BROKE ITS STORY.
MCGAHN, I WANT YOU TO LIE FOR ME.
NO.
TRUMP'S CLAIM THAT HE NEVER DIRECTED MCGAHN TO FIRE THE SPECIAL COUNSEL RUNS CONTRARY TO THE EVIDENCE.

vol 2, pg 118-119

CHAPTER 14

MICHAEL
COHEN

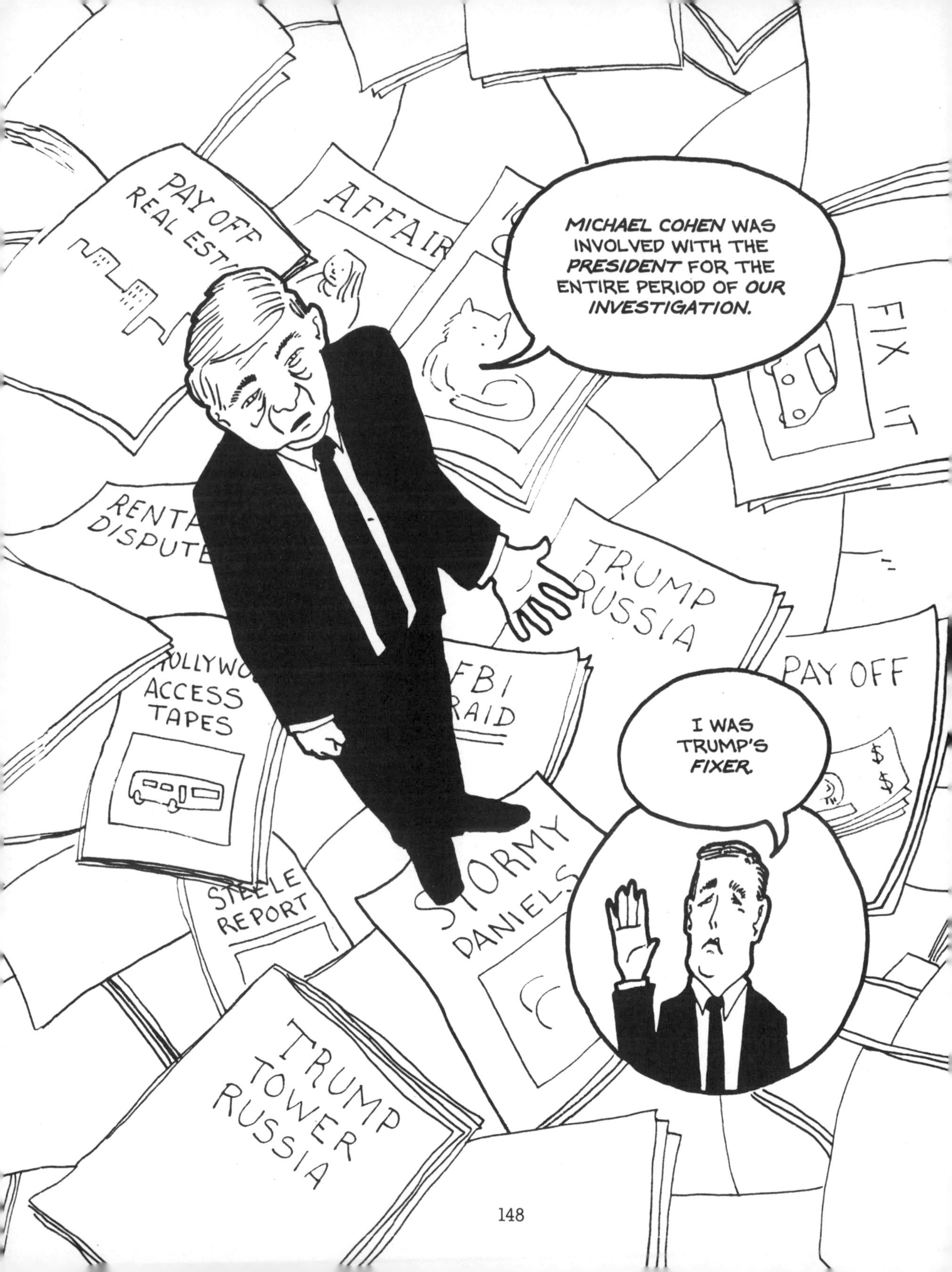
MICHAEL COHEN WAS INVOLVED WITH THE PRESIDENT FOR THE ENTIRE PERIOD OF OUR INVESTIGATION.
I WAS TRUMP'S FIXER.
PAY OFF
AFFAIR
FIX IT
TRUMP RUSSIA
FBI RAID
PAY OFF
ACCESS TAPES
STEELE REPORT
STORMY DANIELS
TRUMP TOWER RUSSIA

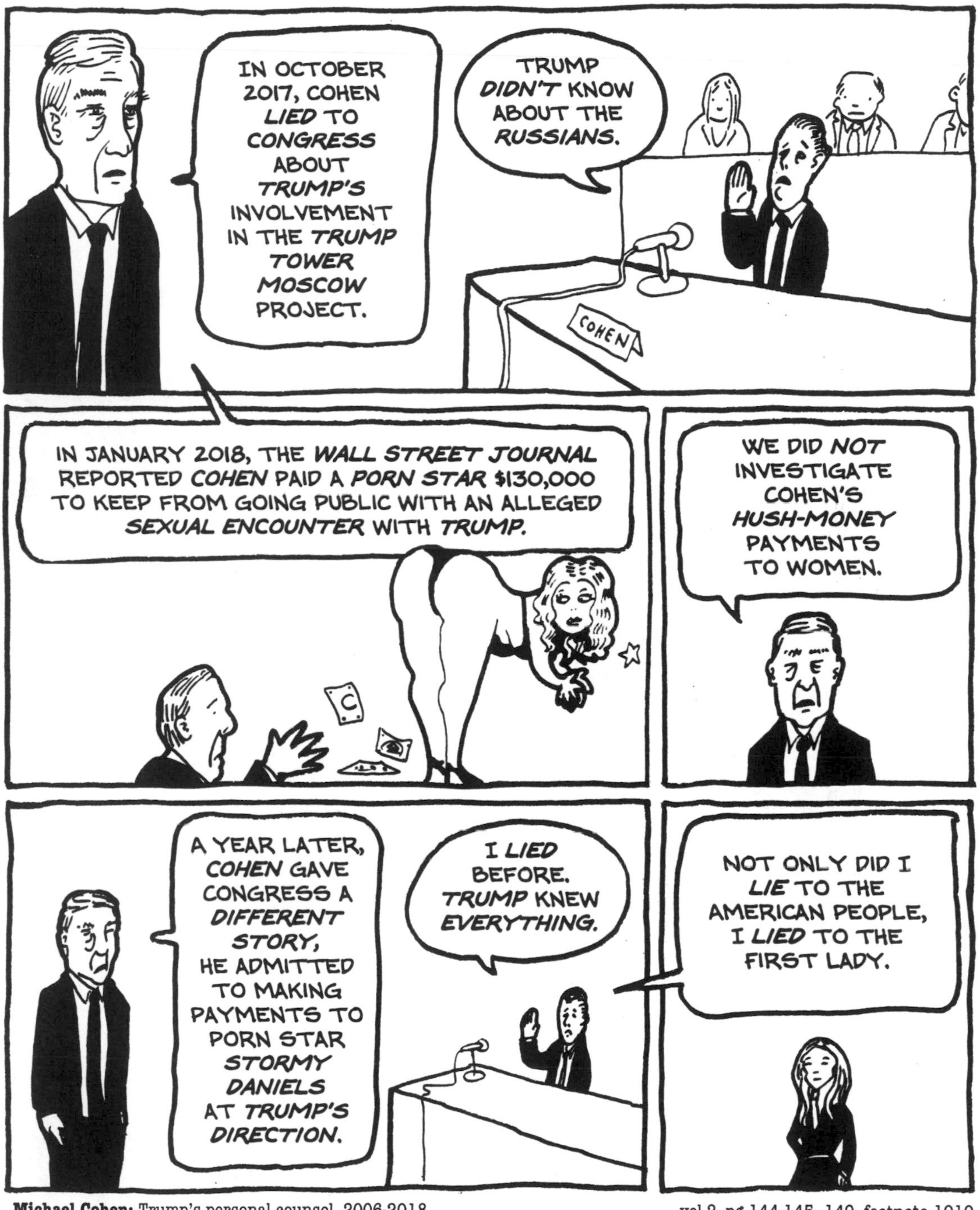

IN OCTOBER 2017, COHEN LIED TO CONGRESS ABOUT TRUMP'S INVOLVEMENT IN THE TRUMP TOWER MOSCOW PROJECT.
TRUMP DIDN'T KNOW ABOUT THE RUSSIANS.
COHEN
IN JANUARY 2018, THE WALL STREET JOURNAL REPORTED COHEN PAID A PORN STAR $130,000 TO KEEP FROM GOING PUBLIC WITH AN ALLEGED SEXUAL ENCOUNTER WITH TRUMP.
WE DID NOT INVESTIGATE COHEN'S HUSH-MONEY PAYMENTS TO WOMEN.
A YEAR LATER, COHEN GAVE CONGRESS A DIFFERENT STORY, HE ADMITTED TO MAKING PAYMENTS TO PORN STAR STORMY DANIELS AT TRUMP'S DIRECTION.
I LIED BEFORE. TRUMP KNEW EVERYTHING.
NOT ONLY DID I LIE TO THE AMERICAN PEOPLE, I LIED TO THE FIRST LADY.

Michael Cohen: Trump's personal counsel, 2006-2018
Stormy Daniels: Adult film star and director

vol 2, pg 144-145, 149, footnote 1010

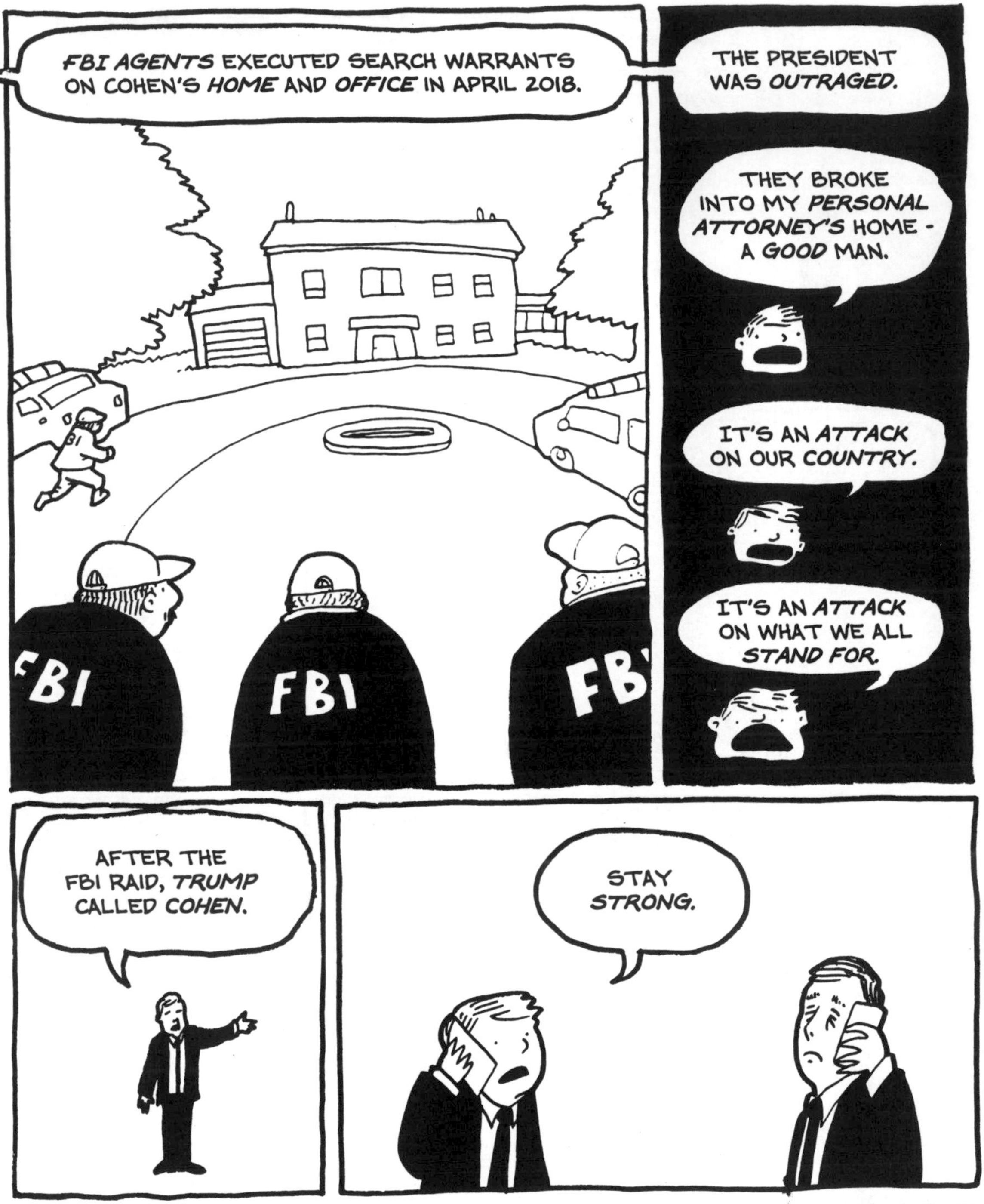
FBI AGENTS EXECUTED SEARCH WARRANTS ON COHEN'S HOME AND OFFICE IN APRIL 2018.
FBI
FBI
FB
THE PRESIDENT WAS OUTRAGED.
THEY BROKE INTO MY PERSONAL ATTORNEY'S HOME - A GOOD MAN.
IT'S AN ATTACK ON OUR COUNTRY.
IT'S AN ATTACK ON WHAT WE ALL STAND FOR.
AFTER THE FBI RAID, TRUMP CALLED COHEN.
STAY STRONG.

vol 2, pg 145-146

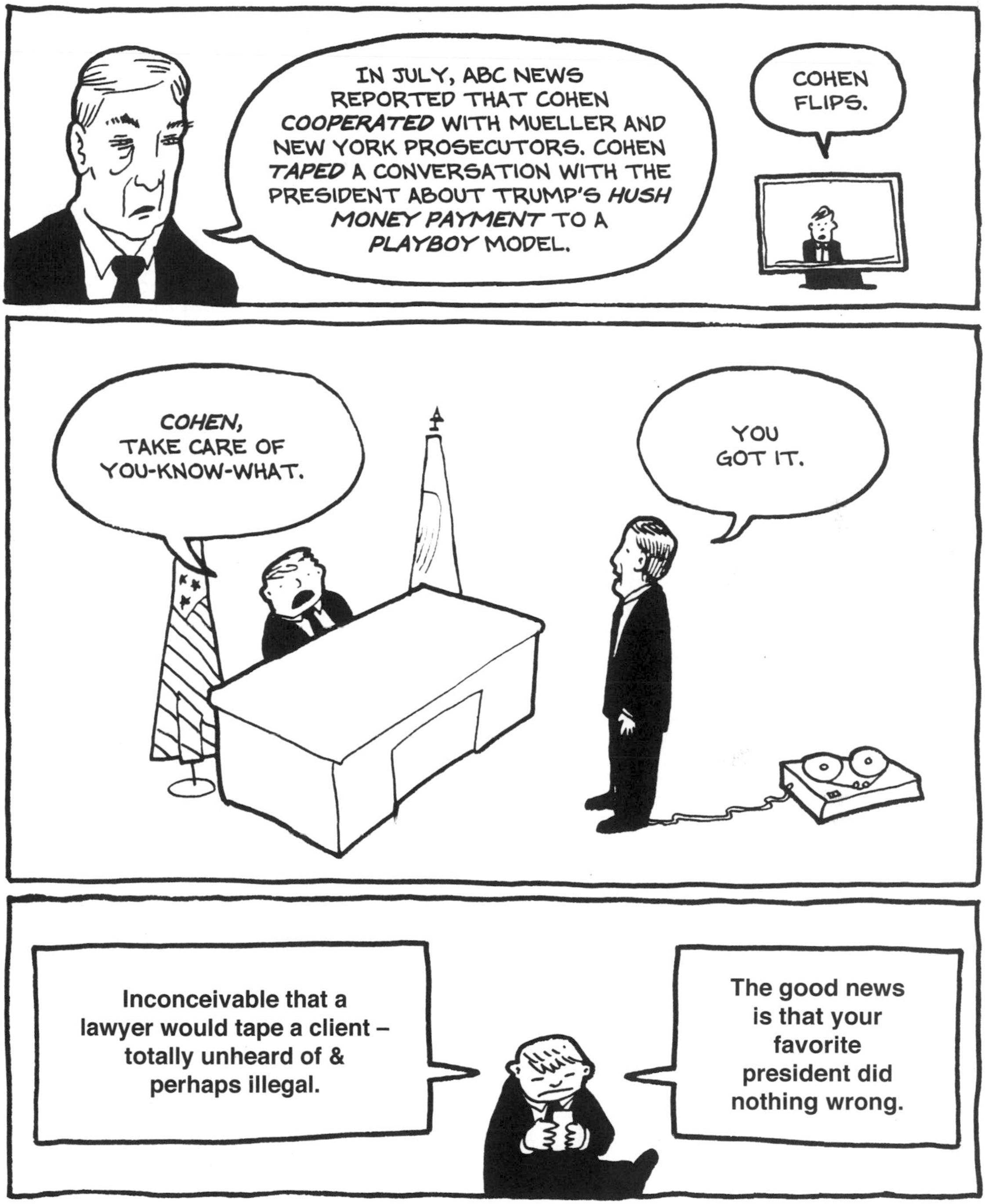
IN JULY, ABC NEWS REPORTED THAT COHEN *COOPERATED* WITH MUELLER AND NEW YORK PROSECUTORS. COHEN *TAPED* A CONVERSATION WITH THE PRESIDENT ABOUT TRUMP'S *HUSH MONEY PAYMENT* TO A *PLAYBOY* MODEL.
COHEN FLIPS.
COHEN, TAKE CARE OF YOU-KNOW-WHAT.
YOU GOT IT.
Inconceivable that a lawyer would tape a client – totally unheard of & perhaps illegal.
The good news is that your favorite president did nothing wrong.

vol 2, pg 148

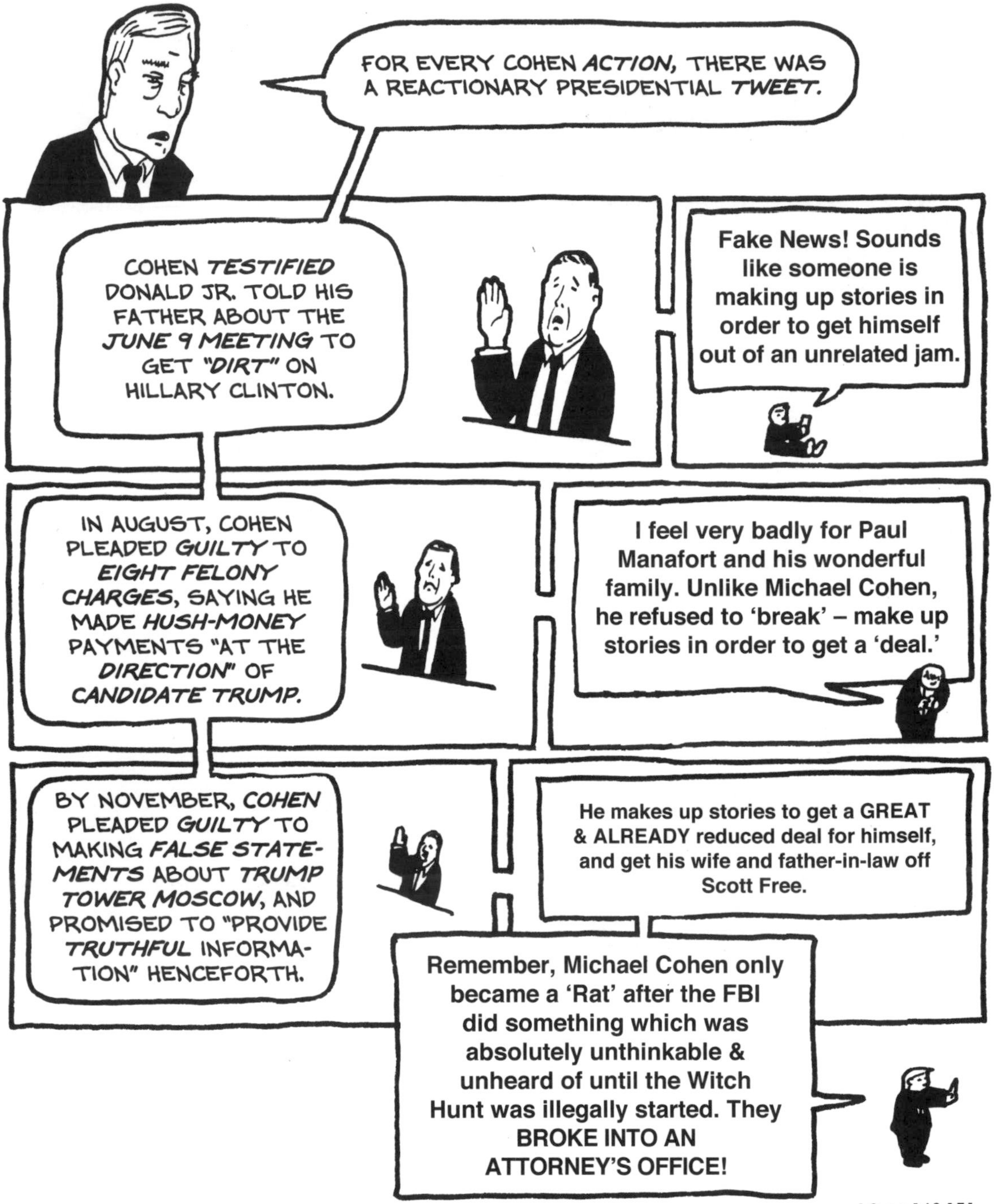
FOR EVERY COHEN ACTION, THERE WAS A REACTIONARY PRESIDENTIAL TWEET.
COHEN TESTIFIED DONALD JR. TOLD HIS FATHER ABOUT THE JUNE 9 MEETING TO GET "DIRT" ON HILLARY CLINTON.
Fake News! Sounds like someone is making up stories in order to get himself out of an unrelated jam.
IN AUGUST, COHEN PLEADED GUILTY TO EIGHT FELONY CHARGES, SAYING HE MADE HUSH-MONEY PAYMENTS "AT THE DIRECTION" OF CANDIDATE TRUMP.
I feel very badly for Paul Manafort and his wonderful family. Unlike Michael Cohen, he refused to 'break' – make up stories in order to get a 'deal.'
BY NOVEMBER, COHEN PLEADED GUILTY TO MAKING FALSE STATEMENTS ABOUT TRUMP TOWER MOSCOW, AND PROMISED TO "PROVIDE TRUTHFUL INFORMATION" HENCEFORTH.
He makes up stories to get a GREAT & ALREADY reduced deal for himself, and get his wife and father-in-law off Scott Free.
Remember, Michael Cohen only became a 'Rat' after the FBI did something which was absolutely unthinkable & unheard of until the Witch Hunt was illegally started. They BROKE INTO AN ATTORNEY'S OFFICE!

vol 2, pg 148-151

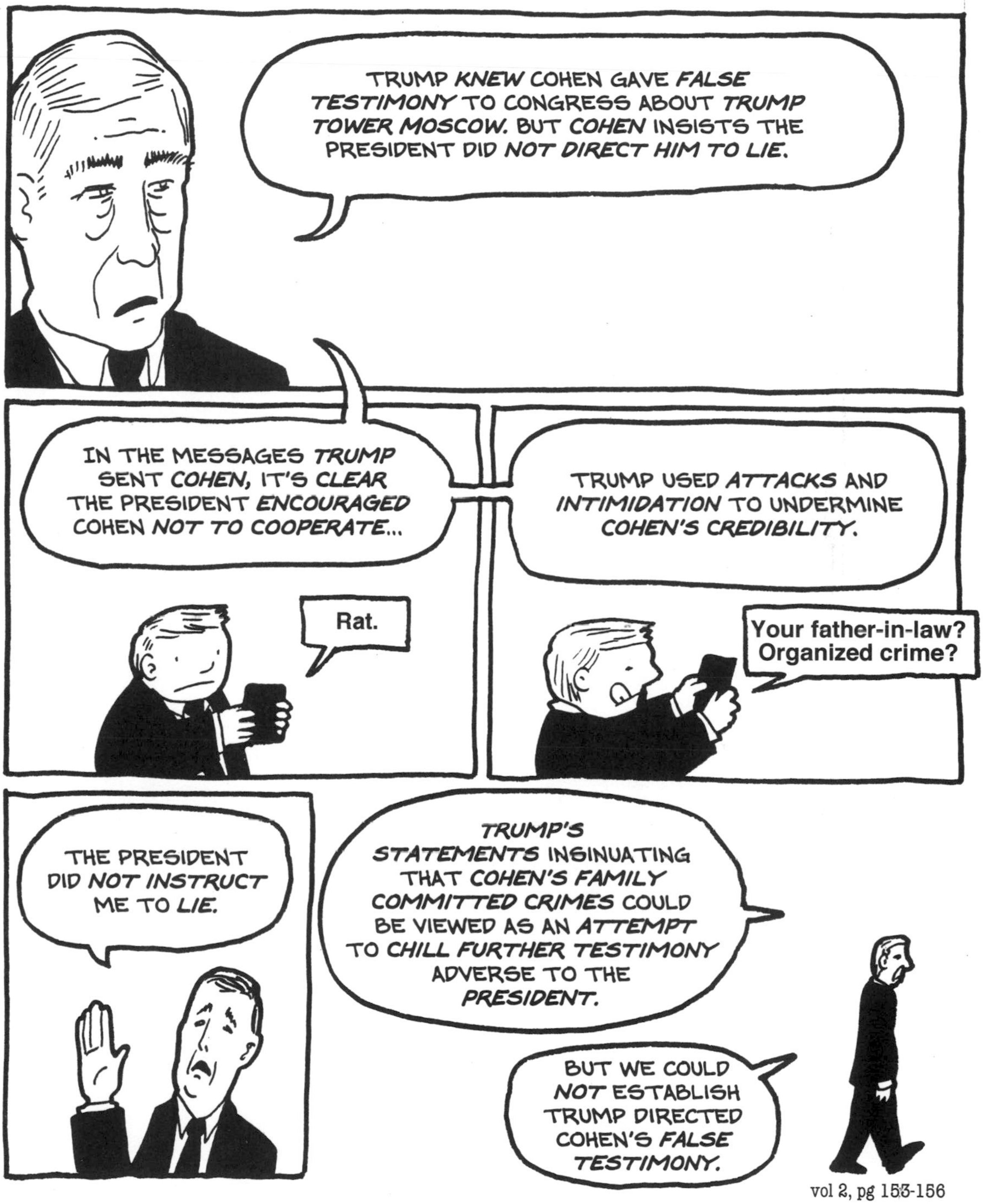
TRUMP KNEW COHEN GAVE FALSE TESTIMONY TO CONGRESS ABOUT TRUMP TOWER MOSCOW. BUT COHEN INSISTS THE PRESIDENT DID NOT DIRECT HIM TO LIE.
IN THE MESSAGES TRUMP SENT COHEN, IT'S CLEAR THE PRESIDENT ENCOURAGED COHEN NOT TO COOPERATE...
Rat.
TRUMP USED ATTACKS AND INTIMIDATION TO UNDERMINE COHEN'S CREDIBILITY.
Your father-in-law? Organized crime?
THE PRESIDENT DID NOT INSTRUCT ME TO LIE.
TRUMP'S STATEMENTS INSINUATING THAT COHEN'S FAMILY COMMITTED CRIMES COULD BE VIEWED AS AN ATTEMPT TO CHILL FURTHER TESTIMONY ADVERSE TO THE PRESIDENT.
BUT WE COULD NOT ESTABLISH TRUMP DIRECTED COHEN'S FALSE TESTIMONY.

vol 2, pg 153-156

CHAPTER 15

TRUMP THREATENS THE SPECIAL COUNSEL

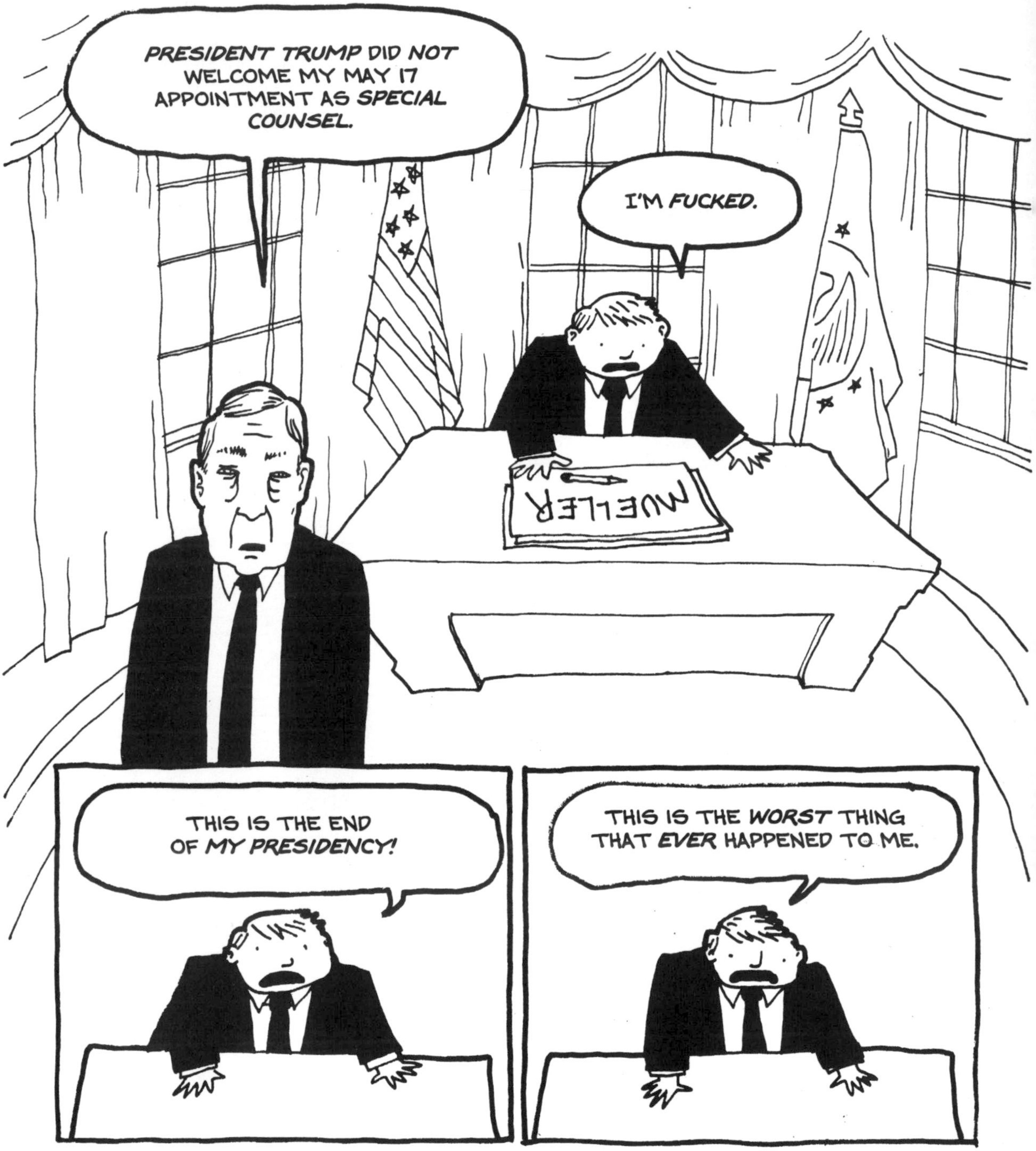
PRESIDENT TRUMP DID NOT WELCOME MY MAY 17 APPOINTMENT AS SPECIAL COUNSEL.
I'M FUCKED.
MUELLER
THIS IS THE END OF MY PRESIDENCY!
THIS IS THE WORST THING THAT EVER HAPPENED TO ME.

vol 2, pg 78

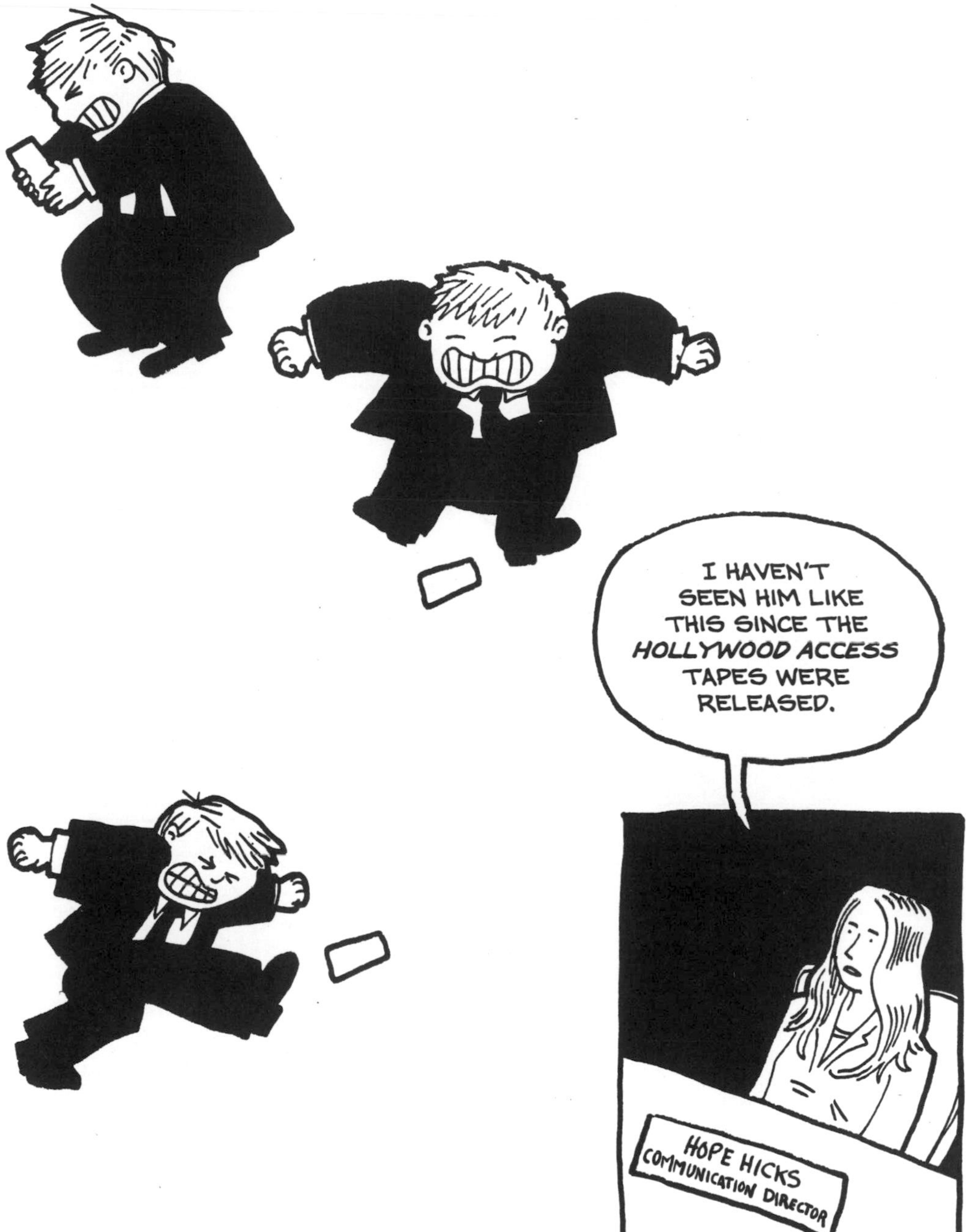
I HAVEN'T SEEN HIM LIKE THIS SINCE THE *HOLLYWOOD ACCESS* TAPES WERE RELEASED.
HOPE HICKS
COMMUNICATION DIRECTOR

vol 2, pg 79, footnote 512

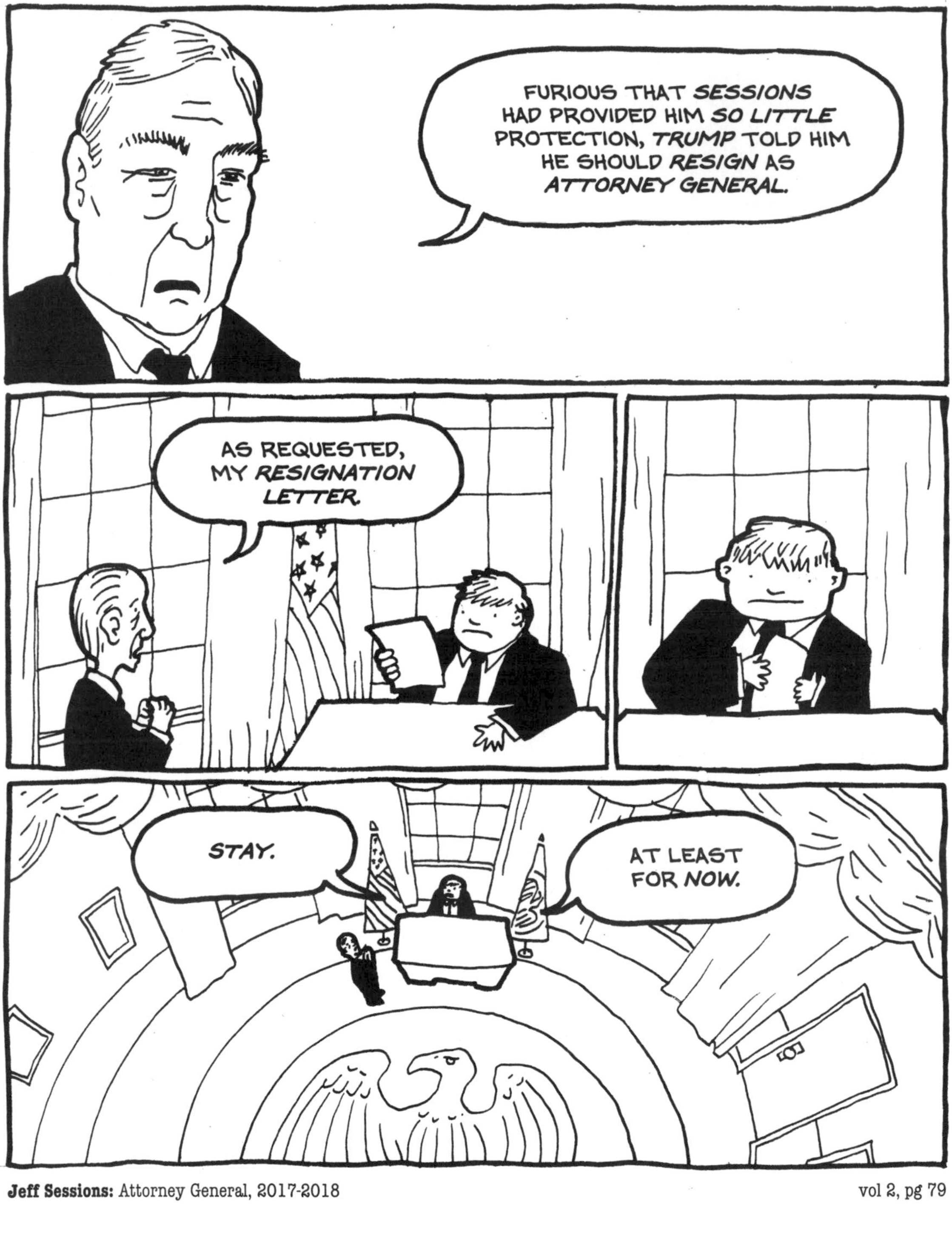
FURIOUS THAT SESSIONS HAD PROVIDED HIM SO LITTLE PROTECTION, TRUMP TOLD HIM HE SHOULD RESIGN AS ATTORNEY GENERAL.
AS REQUESTED, MY RESIGNATION LETTER.
STAY.
AT LEAST FOR NOW.

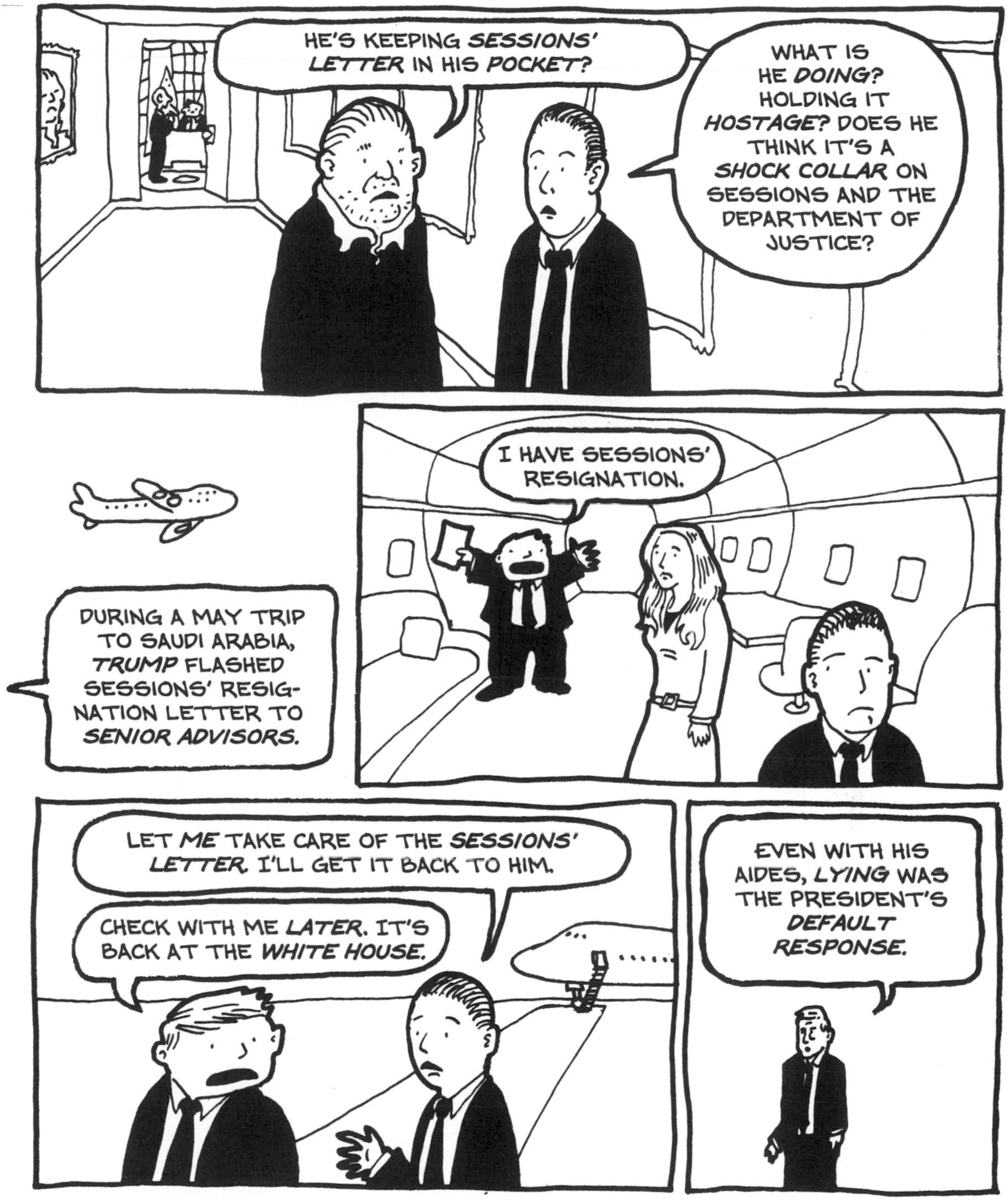
HE'S KEEPING SESSIONS' LETTER IN HIS POCKET?
WHAT IS HE DOING? HOLDING IT HOSTAGE? DOES HE THINK IT'S A SHOCK COLLAR ON SESSIONS AND THE DEPARTMENT OF JUSTICE?
DURING A MAY TRIP TO SAUDI ARABIA, TRUMP FLASHED SESSIONS' RESIGNATION LETTER TO SENIOR ADVISORS.
I HAVE SESSIONS' RESIGNATION.
LET ME TAKE CARE OF THE SESSIONS' LETTER. I'LL GET IT BACK TO HIM.
CHECK WITH ME LATER. IT'S BACK AT THE WHITE HOUSE.
EVEN WITH HIS AIDES, LYING WAS THE PRESIDENT'S DEFAULT RESPONSE.

Steve Bannon: White House Chief Strategist, Nov 2016-Aug 2017
Reince Priebus: White House Chief of Staff, Jan 2017-Jul 2017

vol 2, pg 79-80, footnote 526

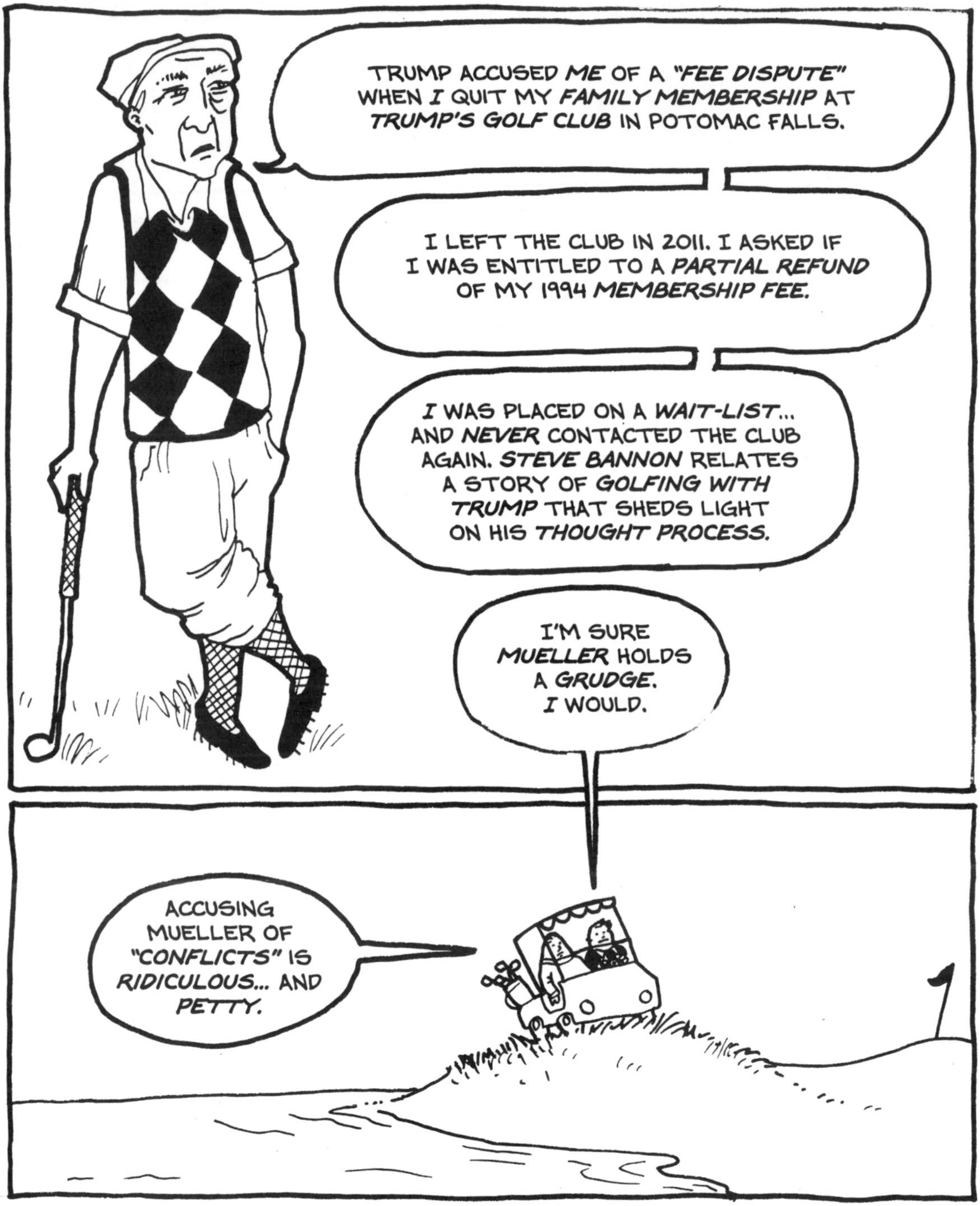
TRUMP ACCUSED *ME* OF A *"FEE DISPUTE"* WHEN *I* QUIT MY *FAMILY MEMBERSHIP* AT *TRUMP'S GOLF CLUB* IN POTOMAC FALLS.
I LEFT THE CLUB IN 2011. I ASKED IF I WAS ENTITLED TO A *PARTIAL REFUND* OF MY 1994 *MEMBERSHIP FEE.*
I WAS PLACED ON A *WAIT-LIST*... AND *NEVER* CONTACTED THE CLUB AGAIN. *STEVE BANNON* RELATES A STORY OF *GOLFING WITH TRUMP* THAT SHEDS LIGHT ON HIS *THOUGHT PROCESS.*
I'M SURE *MUELLER* HOLDS A *GRUDGE.* *I* WOULD.
ACCUSING MUELLER OF *"CONFLICTS"* IS *RIDICULOUS*... AND *PETTY.*

vol 2, pg 80-81

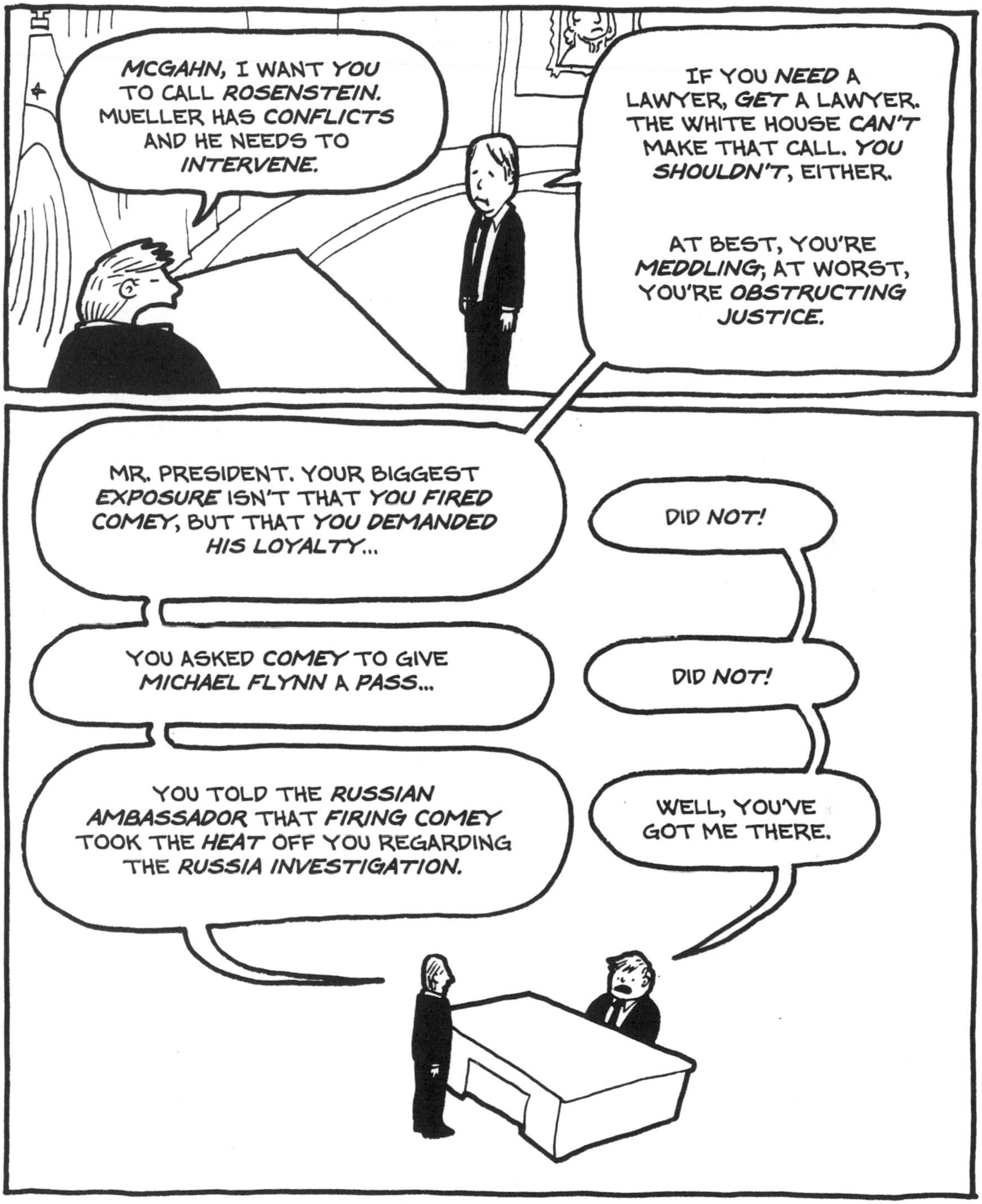
MCGAHN, I WANT YOU TO CALL ROSENSTEIN. MUELLER HAS CONFLICTS AND HE NEEDS TO INTERVENE.
IF YOU NEED A LAWYER, GET A LAWYER. THE WHITE HOUSE CAN'T MAKE THAT CALL. YOU SHOULDN'T, EITHER.
AT BEST, YOU'RE MEDDLING; AT WORST, YOU'RE OBSTRUCTING JUSTICE.
MR. PRESIDENT. YOUR BIGGEST EXPOSURE ISN'T THAT YOU FIRED COMEY, BUT THAT YOU DEMANDED HIS LOYALTY...
DID NOT!
YOU ASKED COMEY TO GIVE MICHAEL FLYNN A PASS...
DID NOT!
YOU TOLD THE RUSSIAN AMBASSADOR THAT FIRING COMEY TOOK THE HEAT OFF YOU REGARDING THE RUSSIA INVESTIGATION.
WELL, YOU'VE GOT ME THERE.

Don McGahn: White House Counsel, Jan 2017-Oct 2018
Rod Rosenstein: U.S. Deputy Attorney General, Apr 2017-May 2019

vol 2, pg 71

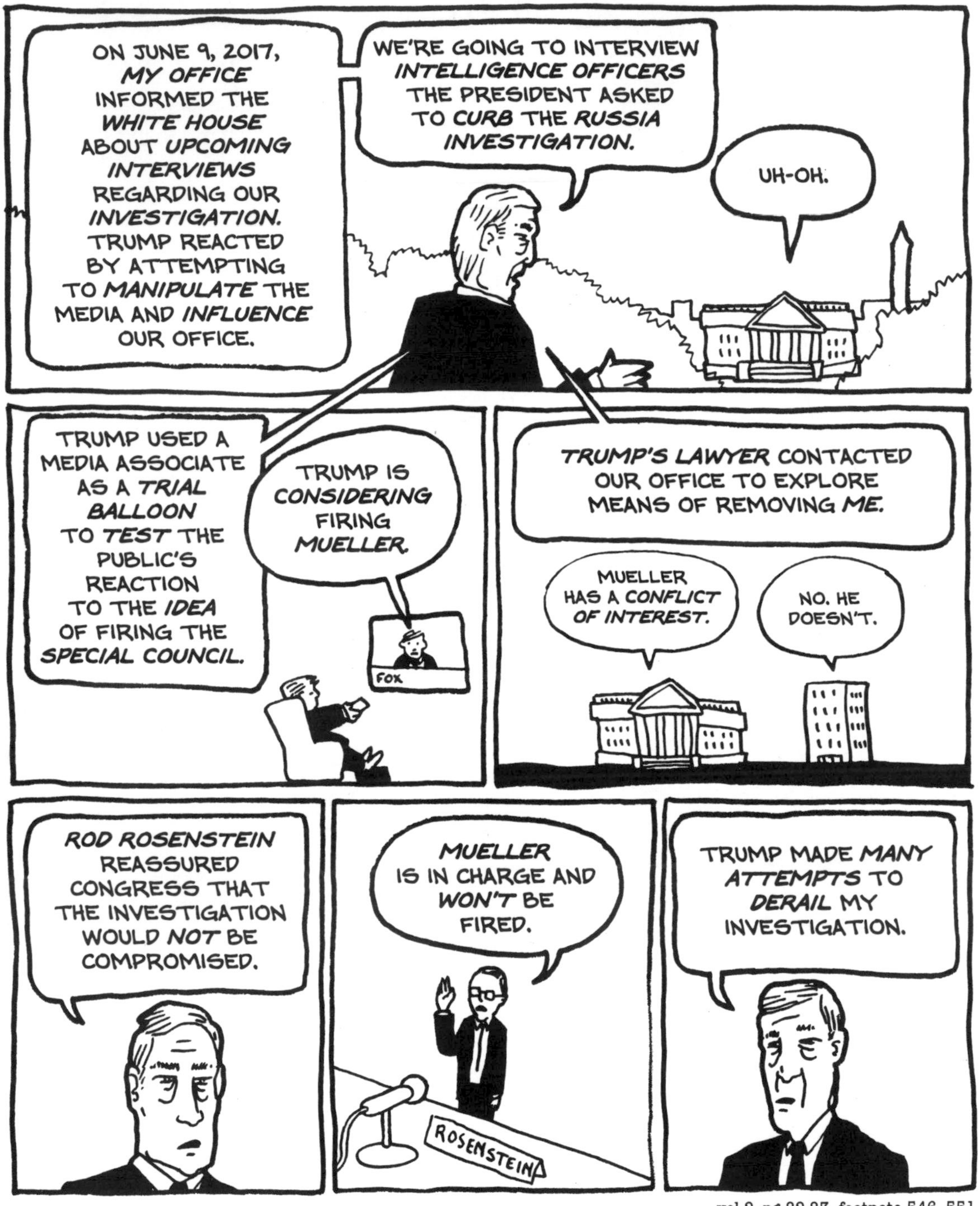

ON JUNE 9, 2017, MY OFFICE INFORMED THE WHITE HOUSE ABOUT UPCOMING INTERVIEWS REGARDING OUR INVESTIGATION. TRUMP REACTED BY ATTEMPTING TO MANIPULATE THE MEDIA AND INFLUENCE OUR OFFICE.
WE'RE GOING TO INTERVIEW INTELLIGENCE OFFICERS THE PRESIDENT ASKED TO CURB THE RUSSIA INVESTIGATION.
UH-OH.
TRUMP USED A MEDIA ASSOCIATE AS A TRIAL BALLOON TO TEST THE PUBLIC'S REACTION TO THE IDEA OF FIRING THE SPECIAL COUNCIL.
TRUMP IS CONSIDERING FIRING MUELLER.
FOX
TRUMP'S LAWYER CONTACTED OUR OFFICE TO EXPLORE MEANS OF REMOVING ME.
MUELLER HAS A CONFLICT OF INTEREST.
NO. HE DOESN'T.
ROD ROSENSTEIN REASSURED CONGRESS THAT THE INVESTIGATION WOULD NOT BE COMPROMISED.
MUELLER IS IN CHARGE AND WON'T BE FIRED.
ROSENSTEIN
TRUMP MADE MANY ATTEMPTS TO DERAIL MY INVESTIGATION.

vol 2, pg 82-83, footnote 546, 551

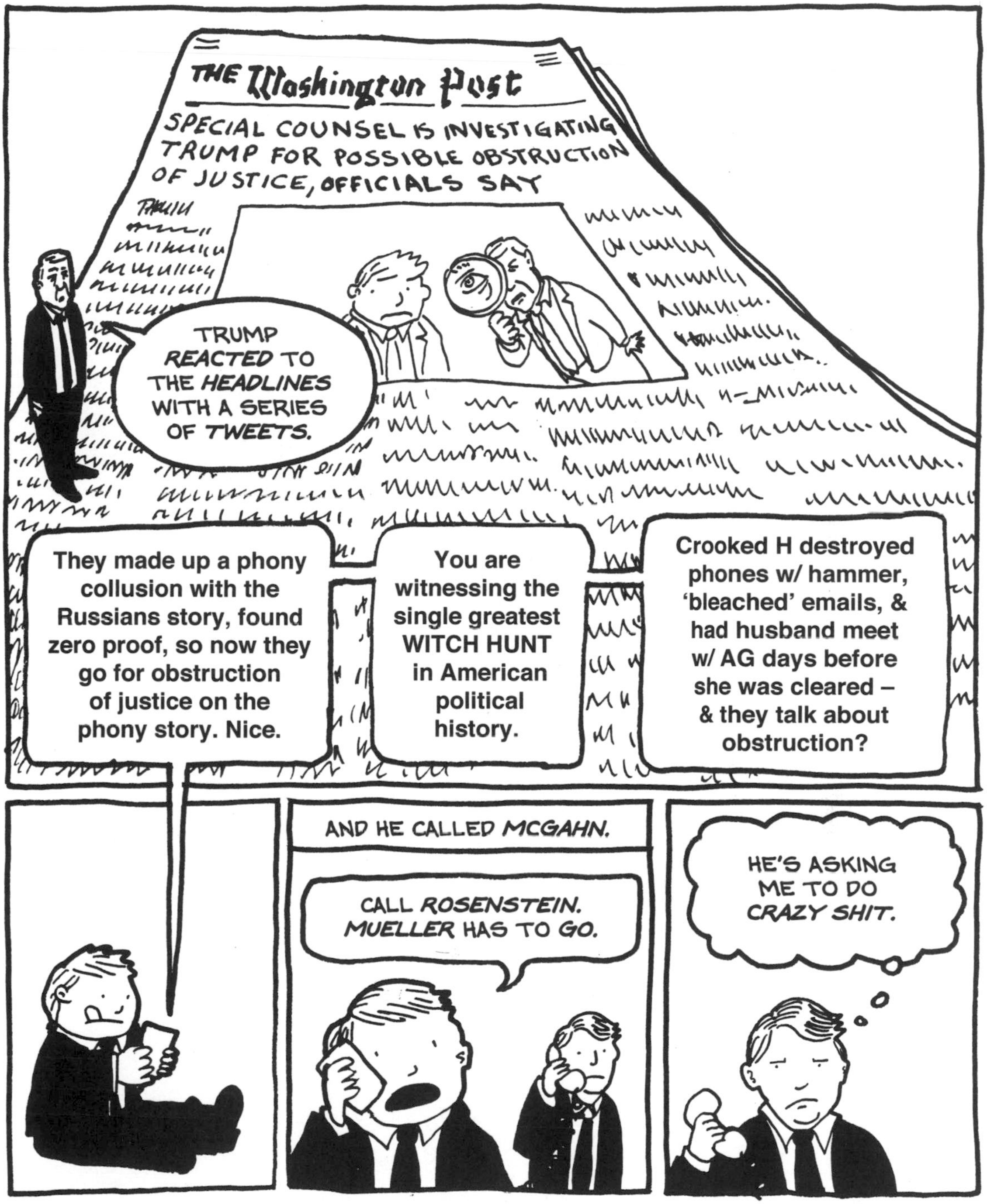

THE Washington Post
SPECIAL COUNSEL IS INVESTIGATING TRUMP FOR POSSIBLE OBSTRUCTION OF JUSTICE, OFFICIALS SAY
TRUMP REACTED TO THE HEADLINES WITH A SERIES OF TWEETS.
They made up a phony collusion with the Russians story, found zero proof, so now they go for obstruction of justice on the phony story. Nice.
You are witnessing the single greatest WITCH HUNT in American political history.
Crooked H destroyed phones w/ hammer, 'bleached' emails, & had husband meet w/ AG days before she was cleared – & they talk about obstruction?
AND HE CALLED MCGAHN.
CALL ROSENSTEIN. MUELLER HAS TO GO.
HE'S ASKING ME TO DO CRAZY SHIT.

vol 2, pg 84-87, footnote 573

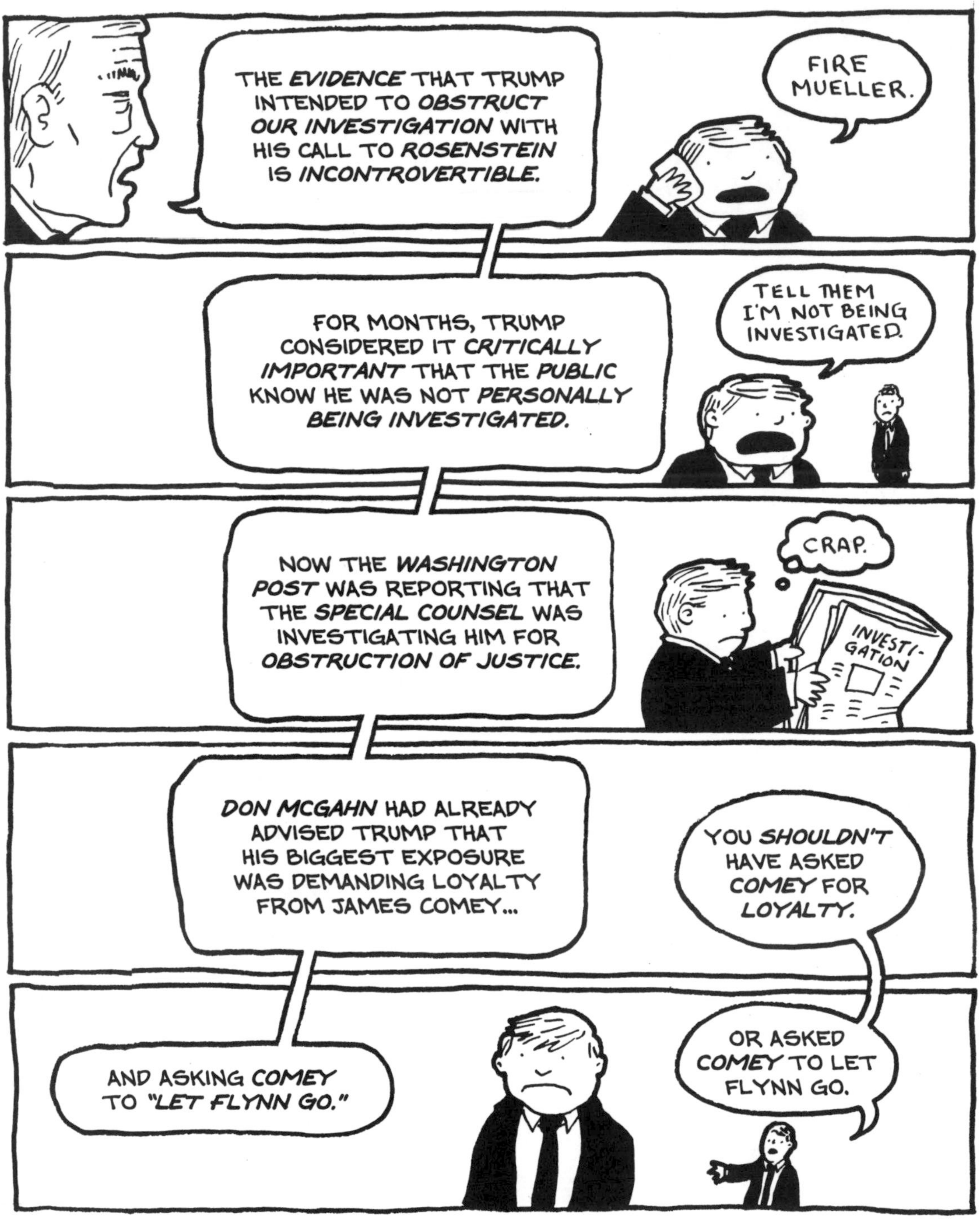
THE EVIDENCE THAT TRUMP INTENDED TO OBSTRUCT OUR INVESTIGATION WITH HIS CALL TO ROSENSTEIN IS INCONTROVERTIBLE.
FIRE MUELLER.
FOR MONTHS, TRUMP CONSIDERED IT CRITICALLY IMPORTANT THAT THE PUBLIC KNOW HE WAS NOT PERSONALLY BEING INVESTIGATED.
TELL THEM I'M NOT BEING INVESTIGATED.
NOW THE WASHINGTON POST WAS REPORTING THAT THE SPECIAL COUNSEL WAS INVESTIGATING HIM FOR OBSTRUCTION OF JUSTICE.
CRAP.
INVESTI-GATION
DON MCGAHN HAD ALREADY ADVISED TRUMP THAT HIS BIGGEST EXPOSURE WAS DEMANDING LOYALTY FROM JAMES COMEY...
YOU SHOULDN'T HAVE ASKED COMEY FOR LOYALTY.
AND ASKING COMEY TO "LET FLYNN GO."
OR ASKED COMEY TO LET FLYNN GO.

FIRE THE SPECIAL COUNSEL!

TRUMP KNEW THE *SPECIAL COUNSEL* WAS CONDUCTING THE *MICHAEL FLYNN INQUIRY.* TRUMP WANTED THE SPECIAL COUNSEL *GONE.*

IT WAS *WHIMSY* TO BOAST TO *CHRIS CHRISTIE* ABOUT FIRING ME. IT WAS A *CRIME* TO CALL THE *WHITE HOUSE COUNSEL* AND MAKE *DEMANDS...*

DON'T FIRE THE SPECIAL COUNSEL.

ESPECIALLY WHEN *MCGAHN* HAD ADVISED HIM *THE WHITE HOUSE COUNSEL'S OFFICE* COULD *NOT* BE INVOLVED IN OBJECTING TO *MY APPOINTMENT.*

MCGAHN KNEW HE COULD NOT *LEGALLY FOLLOW* TRUMP'S ORDERS. HE DROVE TO THE WHITE HOUSE, PACKED HIS OFFICE AND DRAFTED A *RESIGNATION LETTER.*

I'M QUITING.

ME TOO.

WHEN *MCGAHN* SHARED HIS RESIGNATION PLANS WITH *ANNIE DONALDSON,* HIS CHIEF OF STAFF, SHE PREPARED TO *RESIGN* ALONGSIDE HIM.

Michael Flynn: Trump's National Security Advisor, Jan-Feb 2017
Annie Donaldson: Deputy Counsel to the President Feb 2017-Dec 2018

vol 2, pg 85-87

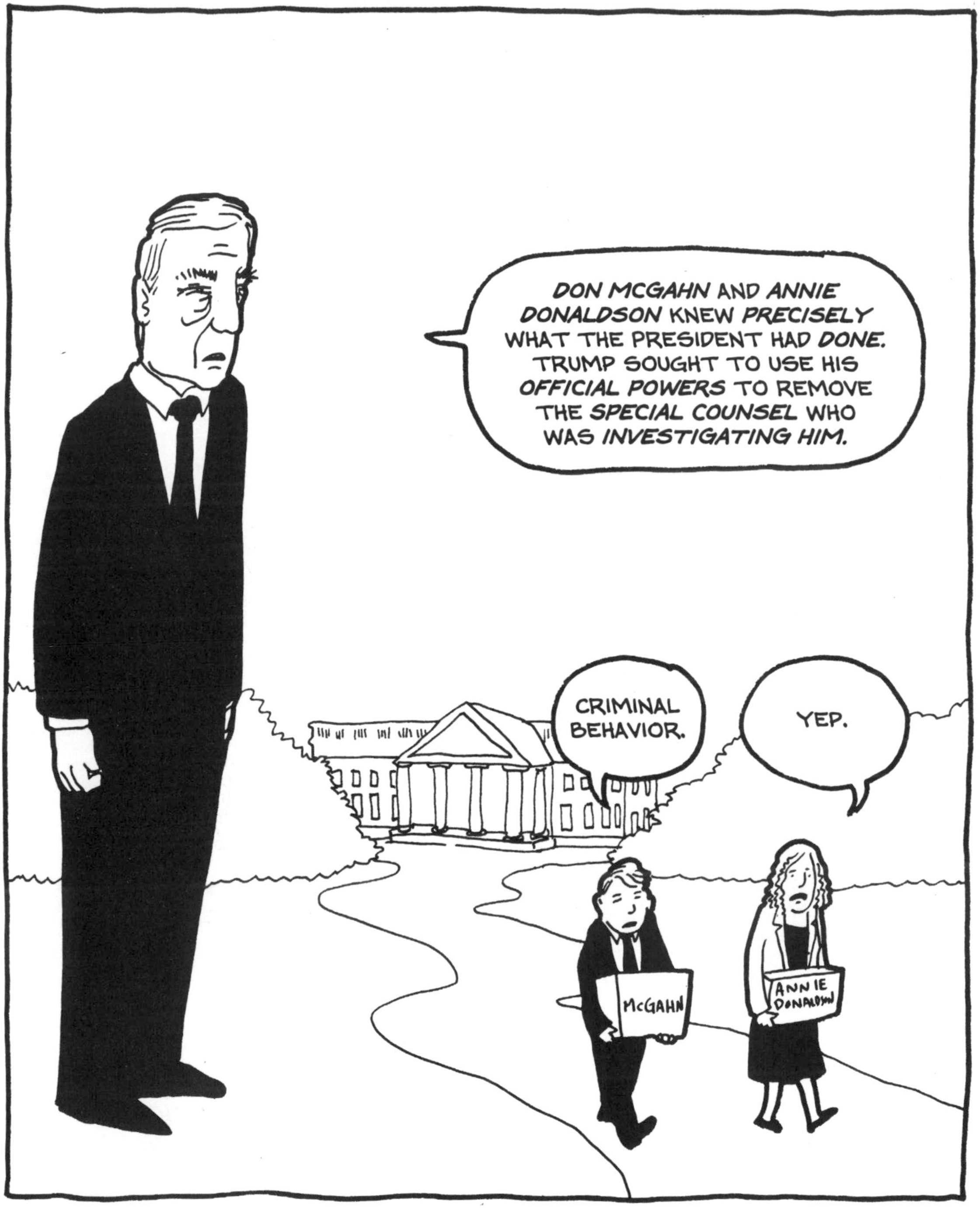
DON MCGAHN AND ANNIE DONALDSON KNEW PRECISELY WHAT THE PRESIDENT HAD DONE. TRUMP SOUGHT TO USE HIS OFFICIAL POWERS TO REMOVE THE SPECIAL COUNSEL WHO WAS INVESTIGATING HIM.
CRIMINAL BEHAVIOR.
YEP.
McGAHN
ANNIE DONALDSON

CHAPTER 16

QUESTIONS
FOR TRUMP

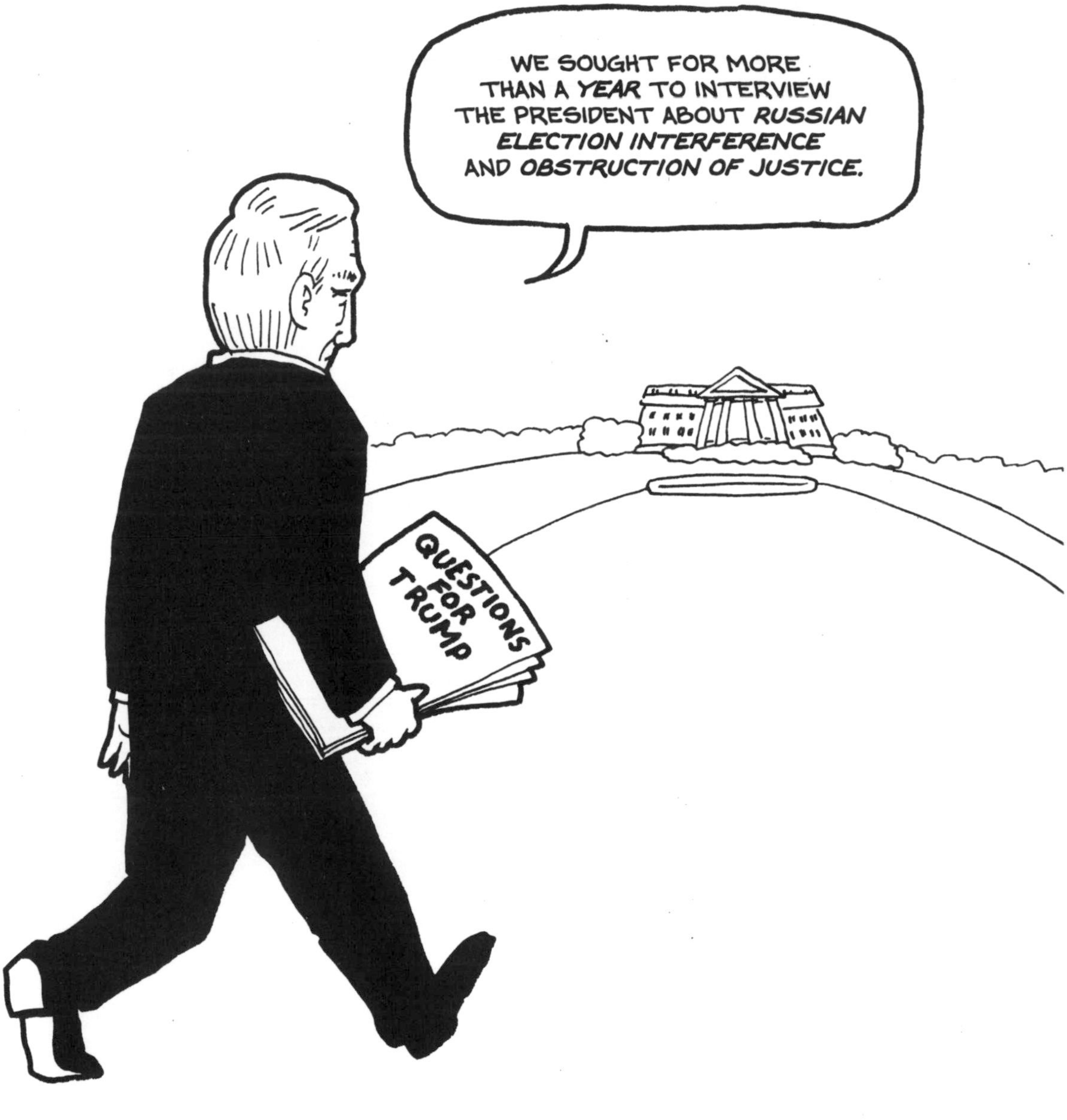
WE SOUGHT FOR MORE THAN A *YEAR* TO INTERVIEW THE PRESIDENT ABOUT *RUSSIAN ELECTION INTERFERENCE* AND *OBSTRUCTION OF JUSTICE.*
QUESTIONS FOR TRUMP

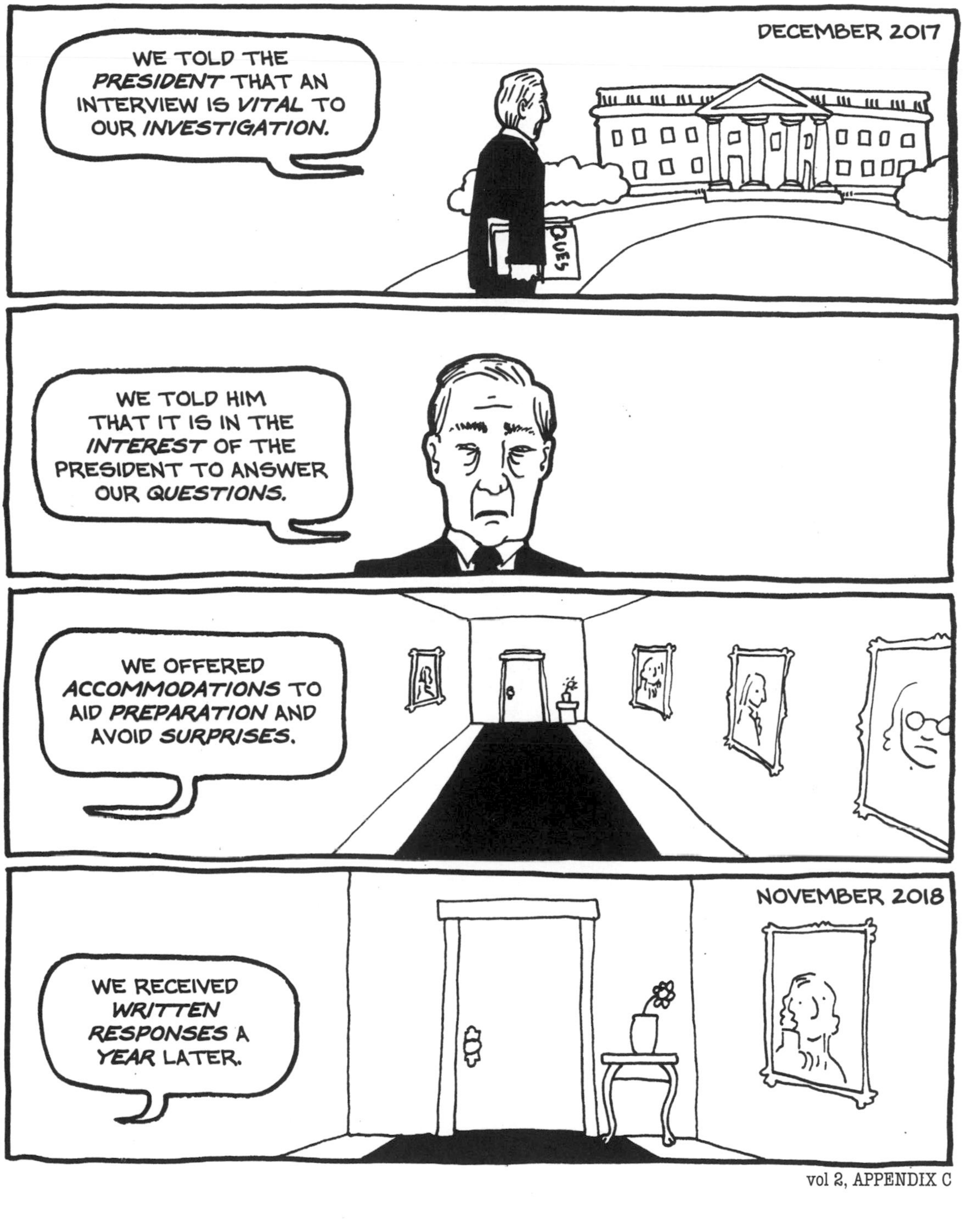
DECEMBER 2017
WE TOLD THE PRESIDENT THAT AN INTERVIEW IS VITAL TO OUR INVESTIGATION.
QUES
WE TOLD HIM THAT IT IS IN THE INTEREST OF THE PRESIDENT TO ANSWER OUR QUESTIONS.
WE OFFERED ACCOMMODATIONS TO AID PREPARATION AND AVOID SURPRISES.
NOVEMBER 2018
WE RECEIVED WRITTEN RESPONSES A YEAR LATER.

vol 2, APPENDIX C

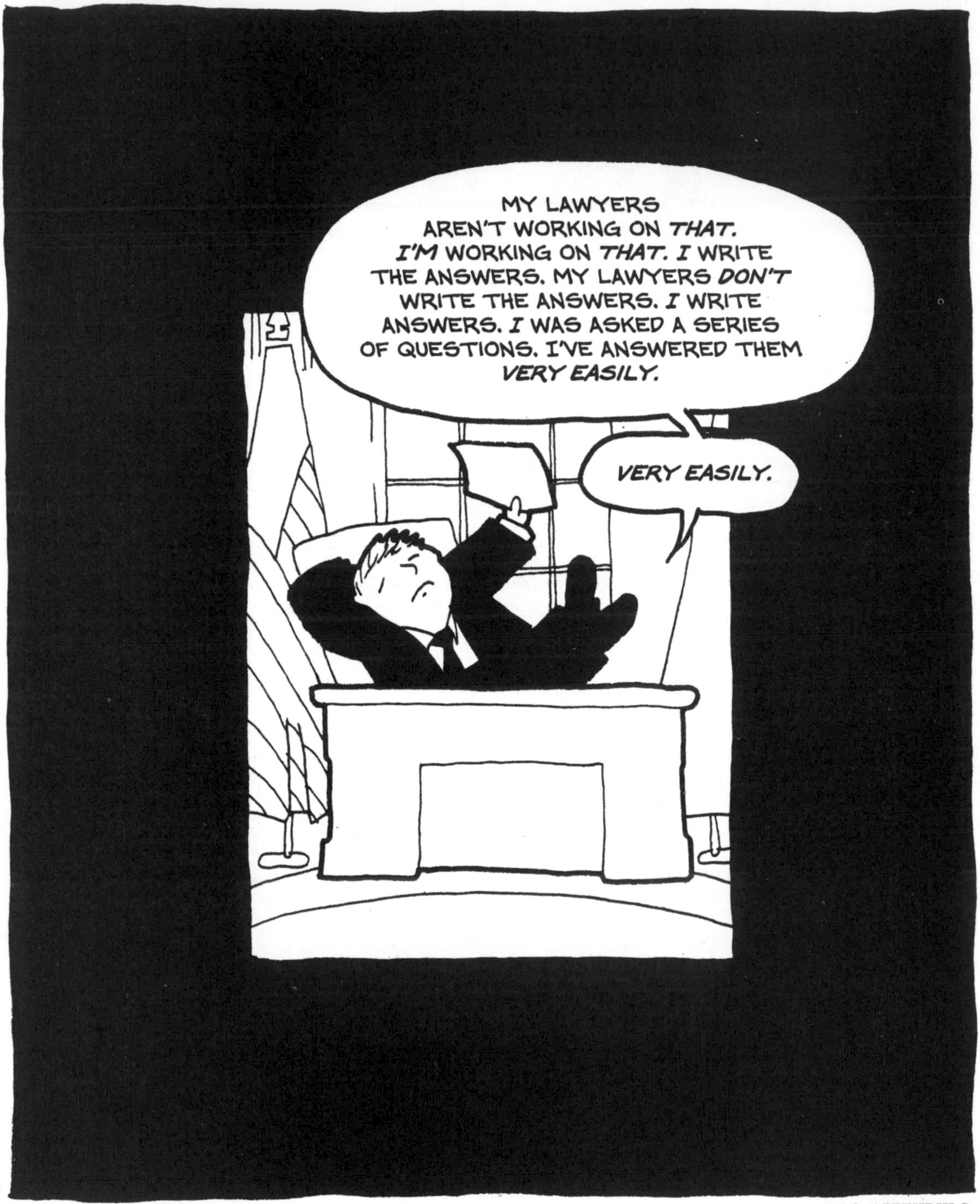
MY LAWYERS AREN'T WORKING ON *THAT*. *I'M* WORKING ON *THAT*. *I* WRITE THE ANSWERS. MY LAWYERS *DON'T* WRITE THE ANSWERS. *I* WRITE ANSWERS. *I* WAS ASKED A SERIES OF QUESTIONS. I'VE ANSWERED THEM *VERY EASILY*.
VERY EASILY.

vol 2, APPENDIX C

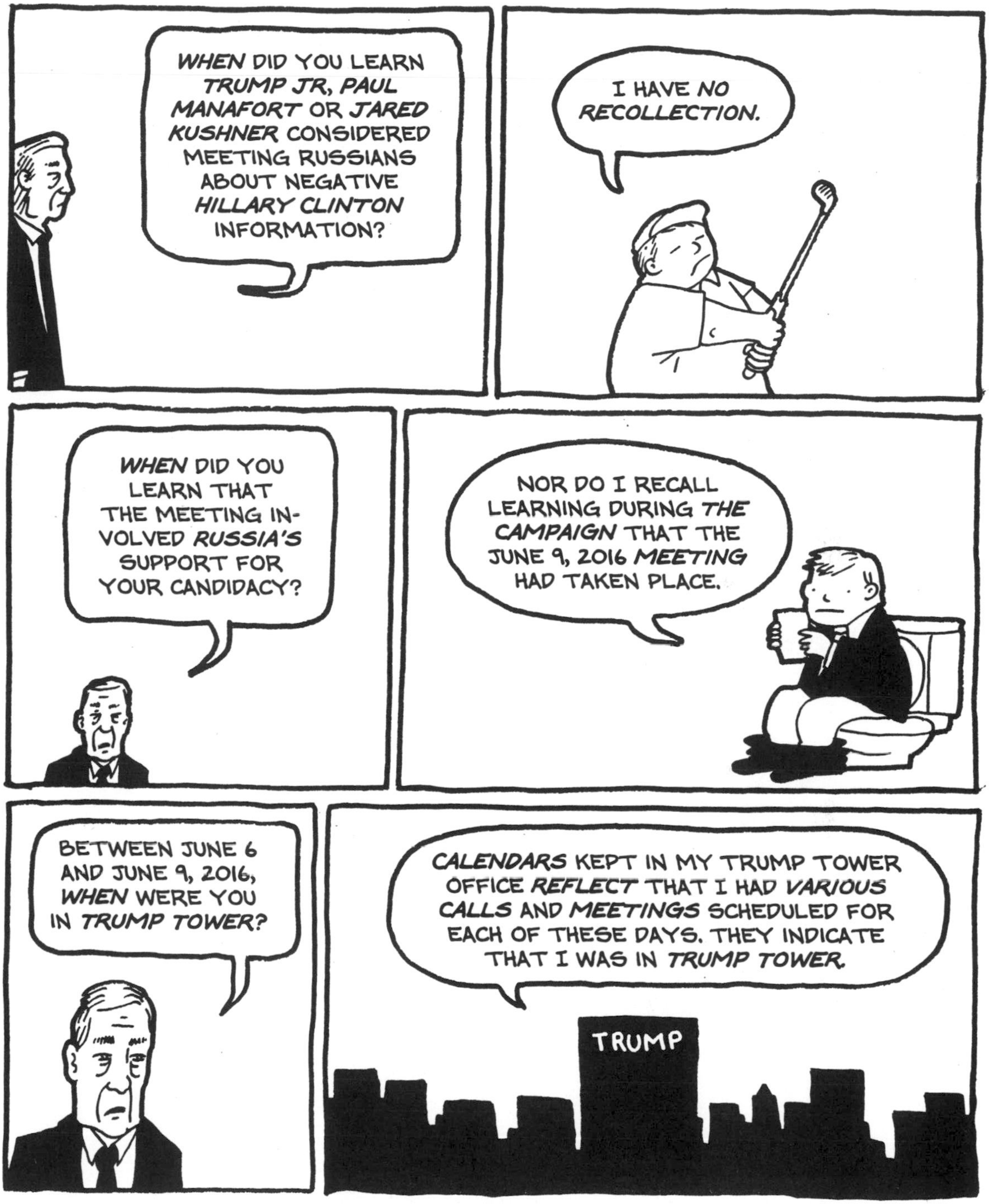
WHEN DID YOU LEARN TRUMP JR, PAUL MANAFORT OR JARED KUSHNER CONSIDERED MEETING RUSSIANS ABOUT NEGATIVE HILLARY CLINTON INFORMATION?
I HAVE NO RECOLLECTION.
WHEN DID YOU LEARN THAT THE MEETING IN-VOLVED RUSSIA'S SUPPORT FOR YOUR CANDIDACY?
NOR DO I RECALL LEARNING DURING THE CAMPAIGN THAT THE JUNE 9, 2016 MEETING HAD TAKEN PLACE.
BETWEEN JUNE 6 AND JUNE 9, 2016, WHEN WERE YOU IN TRUMP TOWER?
CALENDARS KEPT IN MY TRUMP TOWER OFFICE REFLECT THAT I HAD VARIOUS CALLS AND MEETINGS SCHEDULED FOR EACH OF THESE DAYS. THEY INDICATE THAT I WAS IN TRUMP TOWER.
TRUMP

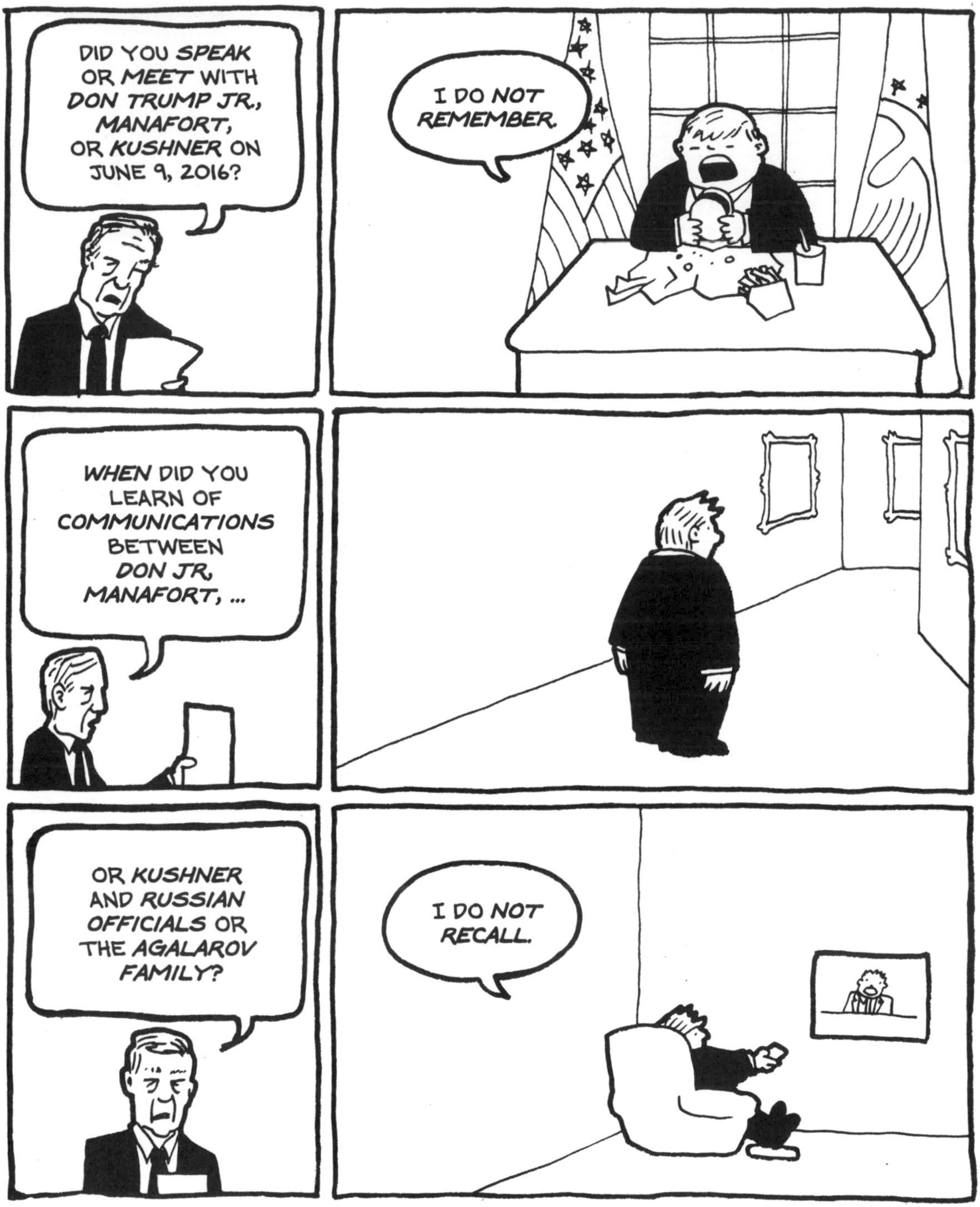
DID YOU SPEAK OR MEET WITH DON TRUMP JR., MANAFORT, OR KUSHNER ON JUNE 9, 2016?
I DO NOT REMEMBER.
WHEN DID YOU LEARN OF COMMUNICATIONS BETWEEN DON JR, MANAFORT, ...
OR KUSHNER AND RUSSIAN OFFICIALS OR THE AGALAROV FAMILY?
I DO NOT RECALL.

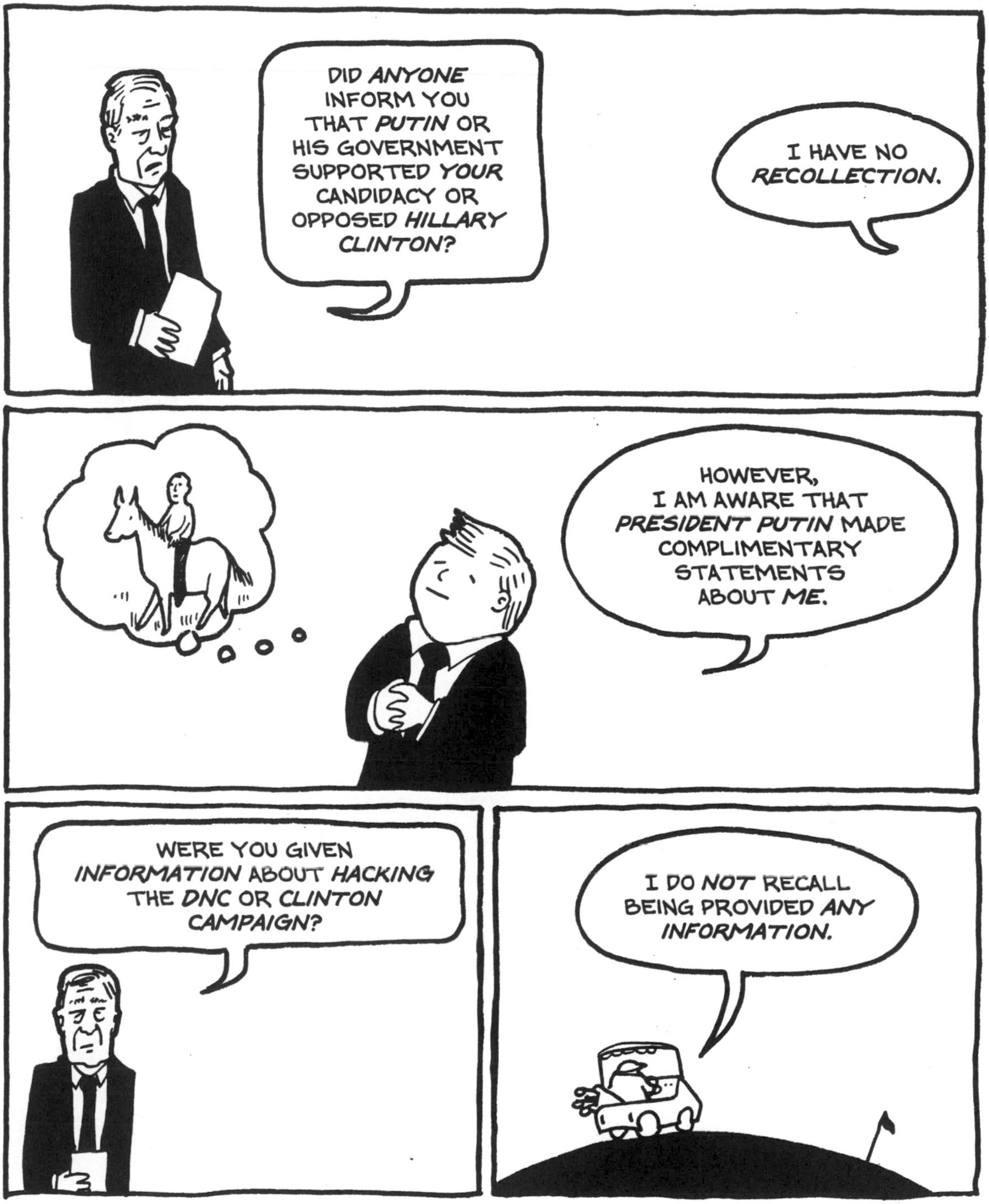
DID ANYONE INFORM YOU THAT PUTIN OR HIS GOVERNMENT SUPPORTED YOUR CANDIDACY OR OPPOSED HILLARY CLINTON?
I HAVE NO RECOLLECTION.
HOWEVER, I AM AWARE THAT PRESIDENT PUTIN MADE COMPLIMENTARY STATEMENTS ABOUT ME.
WERE YOU GIVEN INFORMATION ABOUT HACKING THE DNC OR CLINTON CAMPAIGN?
I DO NOT RECALL BEING PROVIDED ANY INFORMATION.

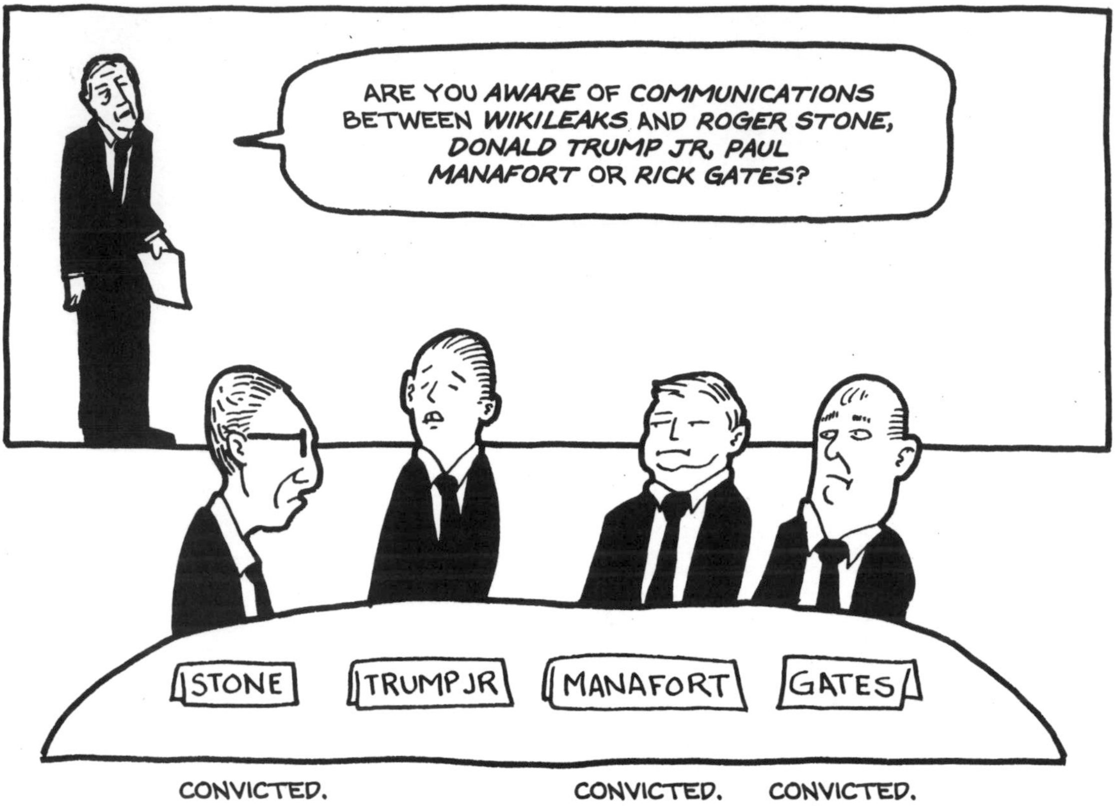
ARE YOU AWARE OF COMMUNICATIONS BETWEEN WIKILEAKS AND ROGER STONE, DONALD TRUMP JR, PAUL MANAFORT OR RICK GATES?
STONE
TRUMP JR
MANAFORT
GATES
CONVICTED.
CONVICTED.
CONVICTED.

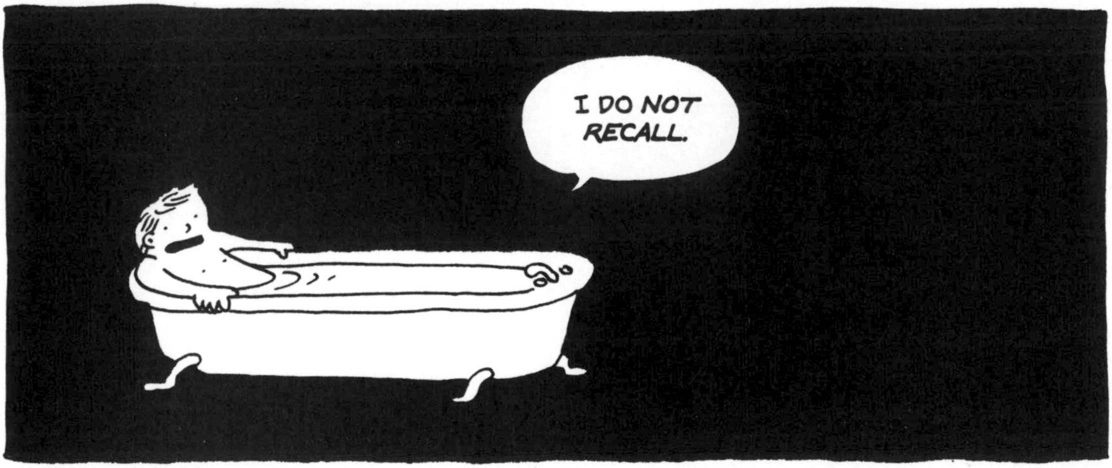
I DO NOT RECALL.

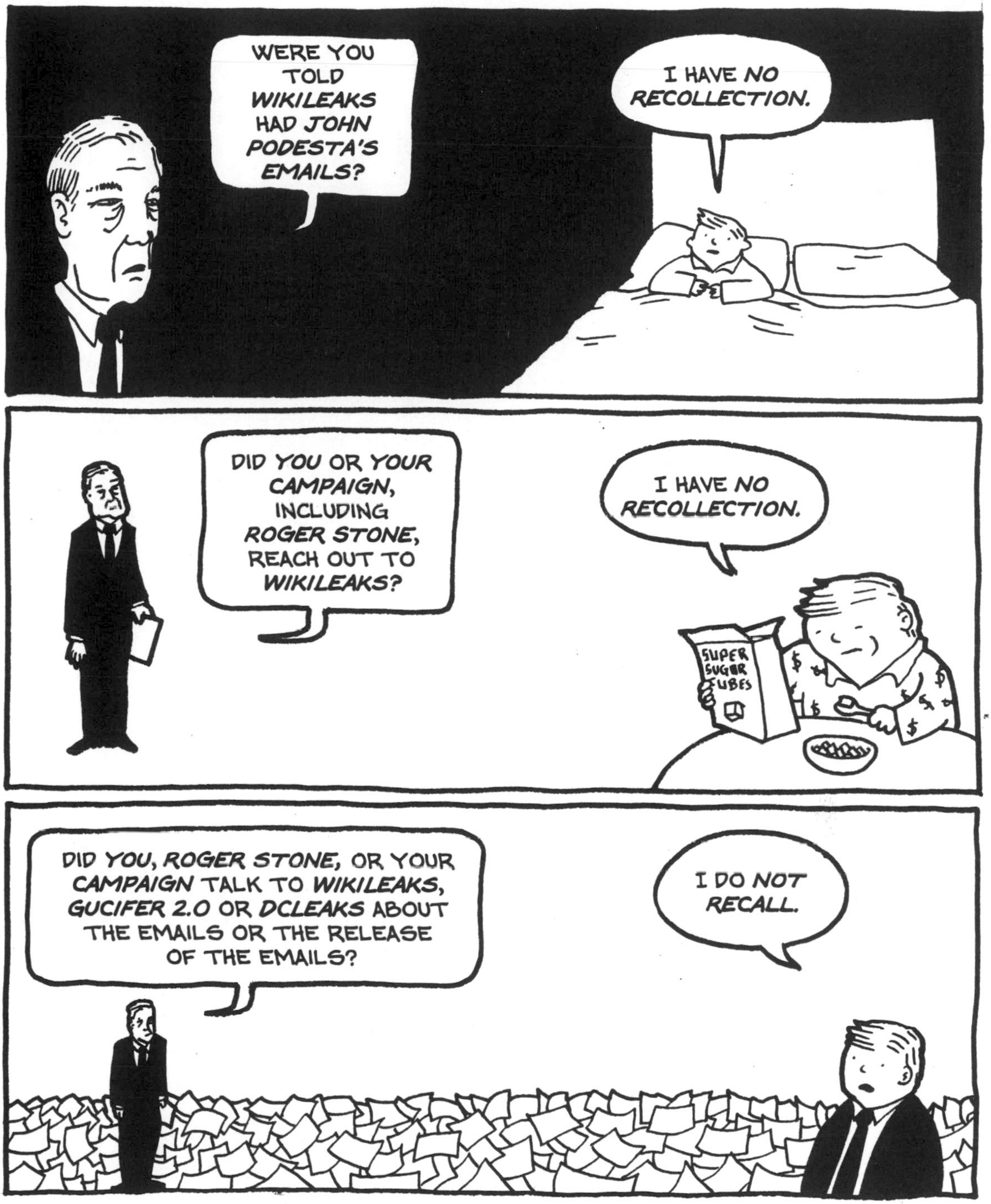
WERE YOU TOLD WIKILEAKS HAD JOHN PODESTA'S EMAILS?
I HAVE NO RECOLLECTION.
DID YOU OR YOUR CAMPAIGN, INCLUDING ROGER STONE, REACH OUT TO WIKILEAKS?
I HAVE NO RECOLLECTION.
SUPER SUGAR CUBES
DID YOU, ROGER STONE, OR YOUR CAMPAIGN TALK TO WIKILEAKS, GUCIFER 2.0 OR DCLEAKS ABOUT THE EMAILS OR THE RELEASE OF THE EMAILS?
I DO NOT RECALL.

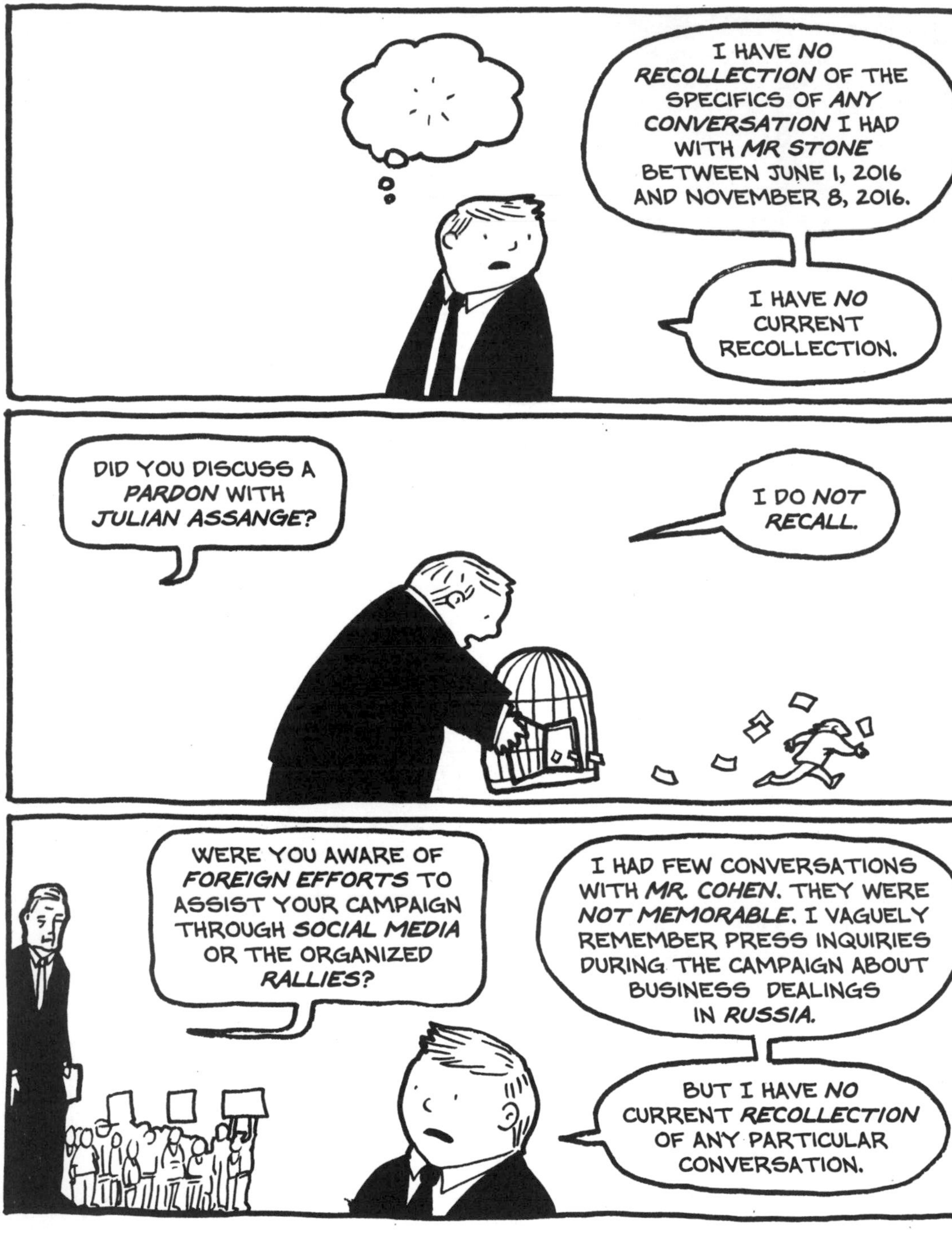

I HAVE *NO RECOLLECTION* OF THE SPECIFICS OF *ANY CONVERSATION* I HAD WITH *MR STONE* BETWEEN JUNE 1, 2016 AND NOVEMBER 8, 2016.
I HAVE *NO* CURRENT RECOLLECTION.
DID YOU DISCUSS A *PARDON* WITH *JULIAN ASSANGE?*
I DO *NOT RECALL.*
WERE YOU AWARE OF *FOREIGN EFFORTS* TO ASSIST YOUR CAMPAIGN THROUGH *SOCIAL MEDIA* OR THE ORGANIZED *RALLIES?*
I HAD FEW CONVERSATIONS WITH *MR. COHEN*. THEY WERE *NOT MEMORABLE*. I VAGUELY REMEMBER PRESS INQUIRIES DURING THE CAMPAIGN ABOUT BUSINESS DEALINGS IN *RUSSIA*.
BUT I HAVE *NO* CURRENT *RECOLLECTION* OF ANY PARTICULAR CONVERSATION.

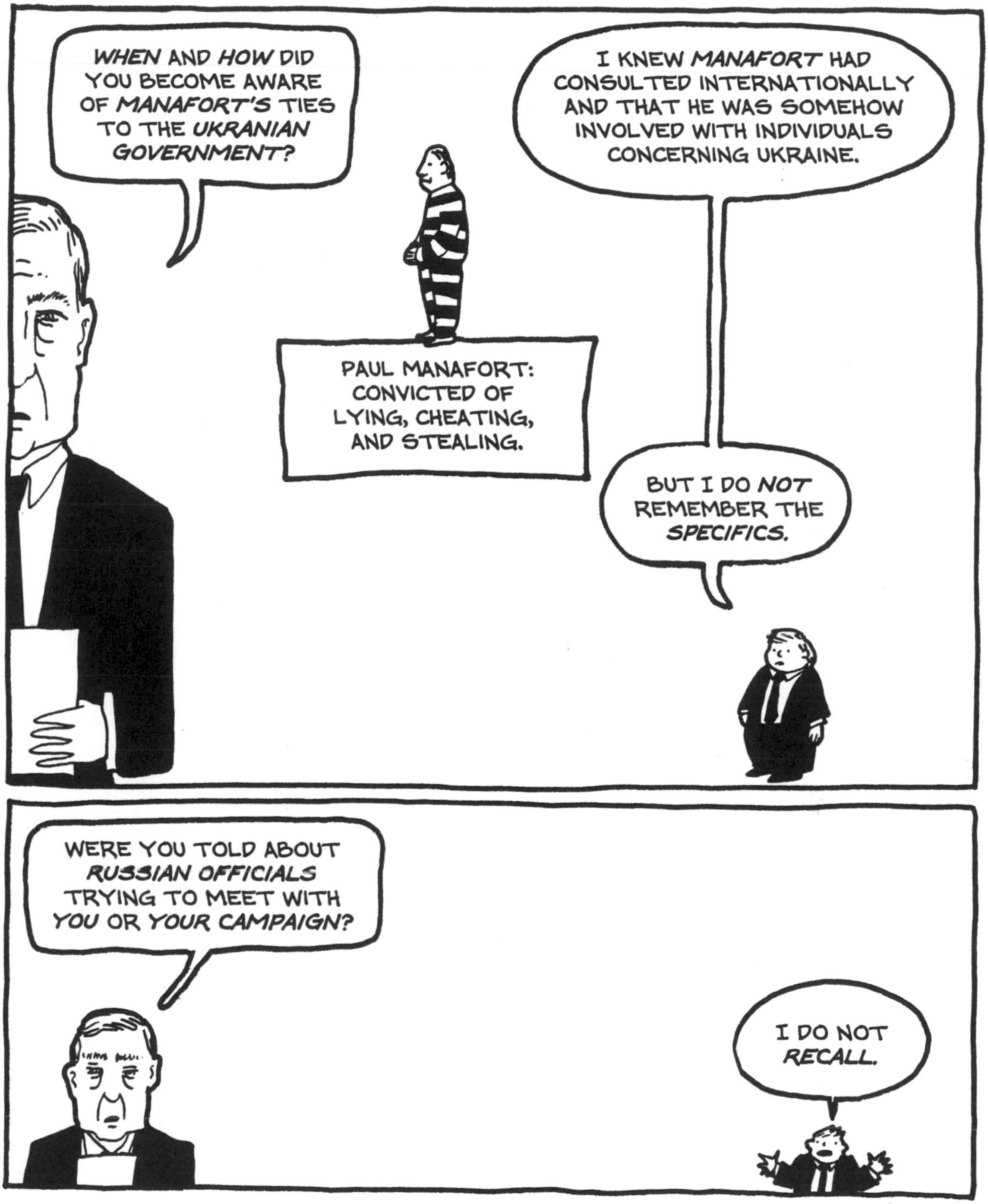
WHEN AND HOW DID YOU BECOME AWARE OF MANAFORT'S TIES TO THE UKRANIAN GOVERNMENT?
PAUL MANAFORT: CONVICTED OF LYING, CHEATING, AND STEALING.
I KNEW MANAFORT HAD CONSULTED INTERNATIONALLY AND THAT HE WAS SOMEHOW INVOLVED WITH INDIVIDUALS CONCERNING UKRAINE.
BUT I DO NOT REMEMBER THE SPECIFICS.
WERE YOU TOLD ABOUT RUSSIAN OFFICIALS TRYING TO MEET WITH YOU OR YOUR CAMPAIGN?
I DO NOT RECALL.

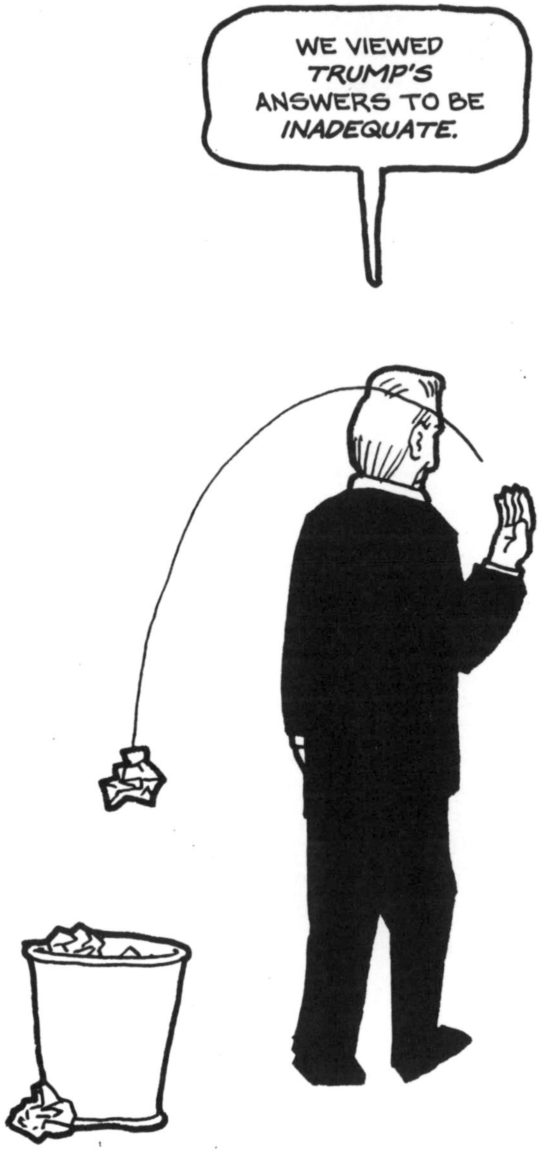
WE VIEWED *TRUMP'S* ANSWERS TO BE *INADEQUATE.*

CHAPTER 17

THE RUSSIANS
ARE JUST GETTING
STARTED

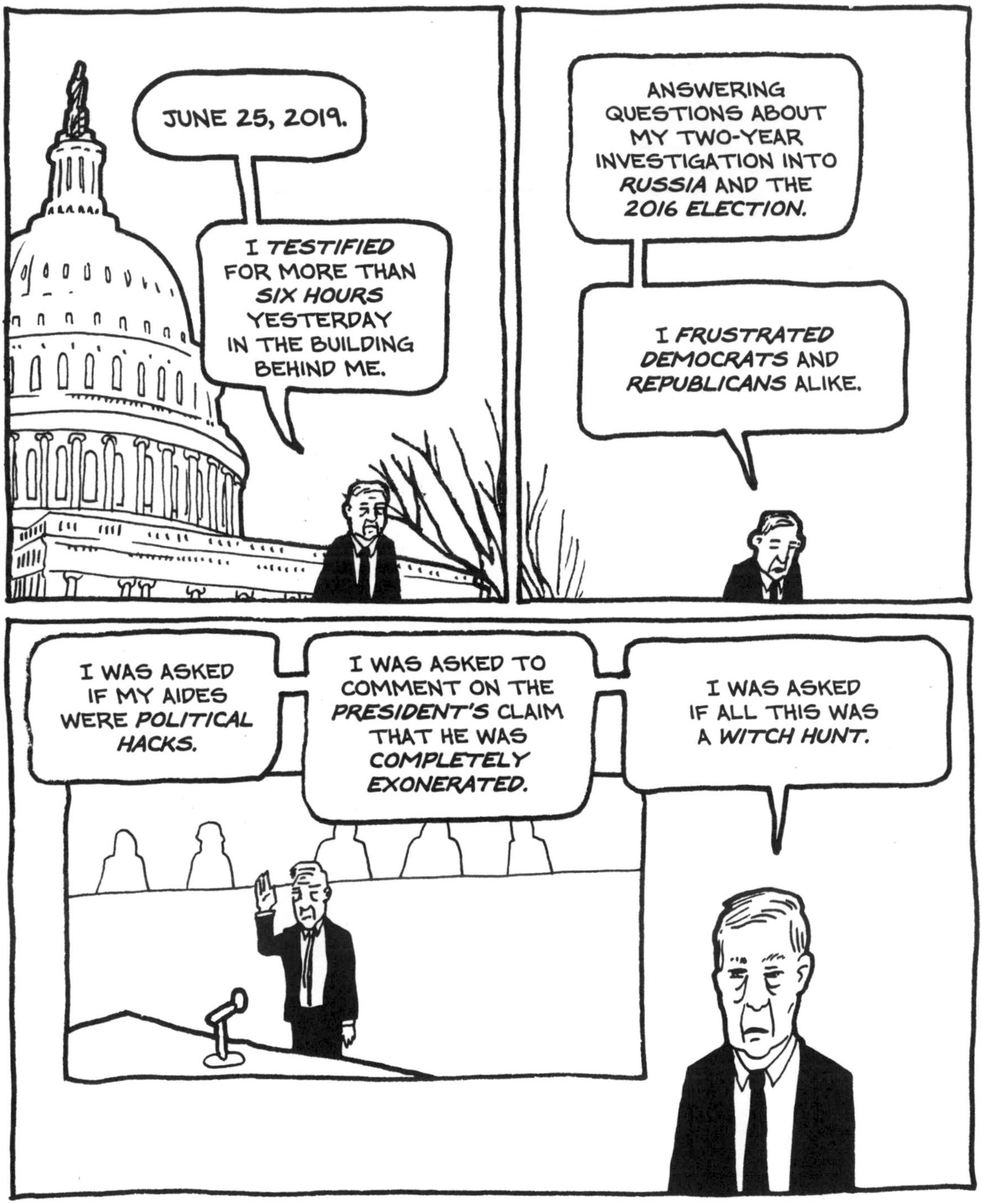
JUNE 25, 2019.
I TESTIFIED FOR MORE THAN SIX HOURS YESTERDAY IN THE BUILDING BEHIND ME.
ANSWERING QUESTIONS ABOUT MY TWO-YEAR INVESTIGATION INTO RUSSIA AND THE 2016 ELECTION.
I FRUSTRATED DEMOCRATS AND REPUBLICANS ALIKE.
I WAS ASKED IF MY AIDES WERE POLITICAL HACKS.
I WAS ASKED TO COMMENT ON THE PRESIDENT'S CLAIM THAT HE WAS COMPLETELY EXONERATED.
I WAS ASKED IF ALL THIS WAS A WITCH HUNT.

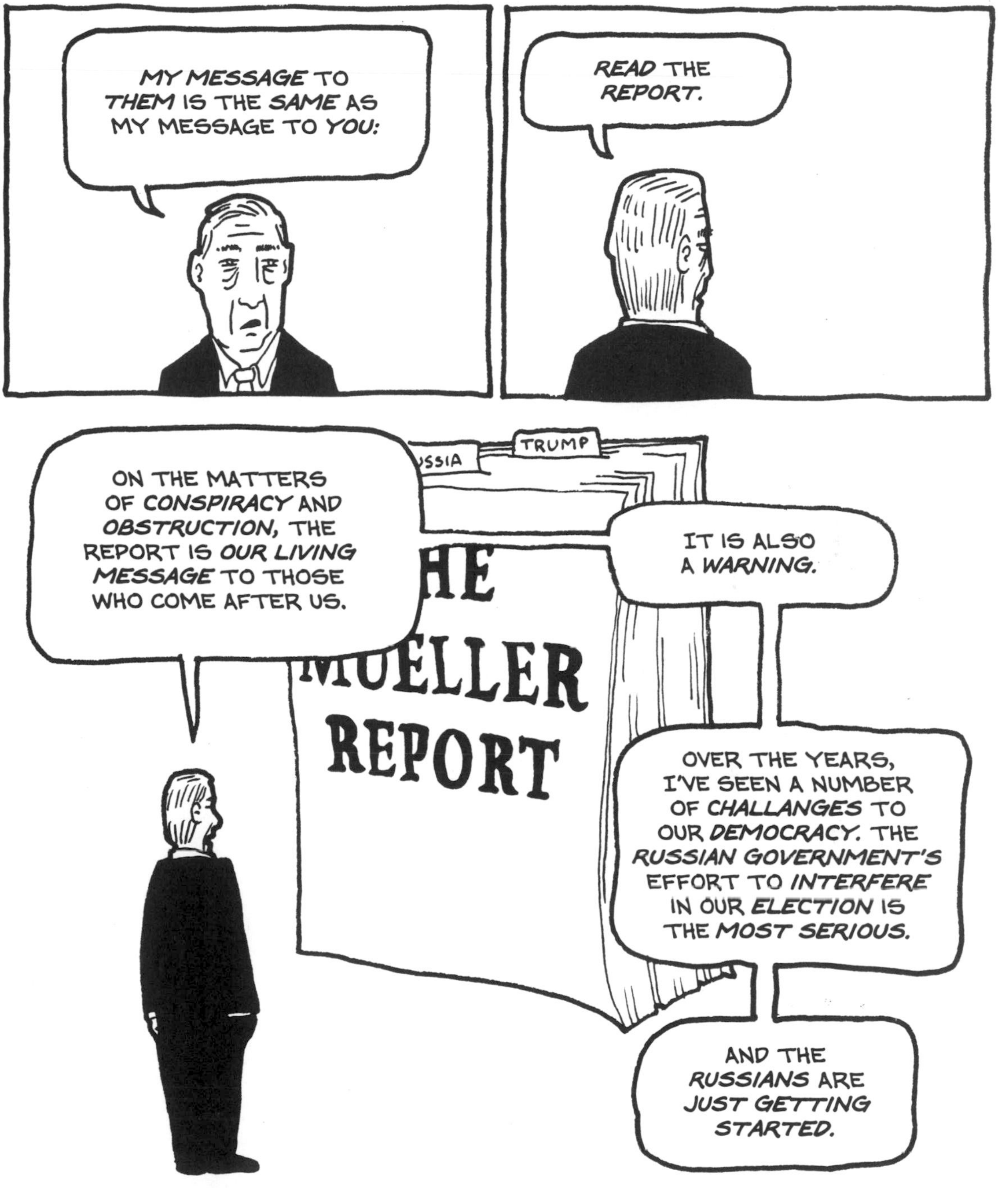
MY MESSAGE TO THEM IS THE SAME AS MY MESSAGE TO YOU:
READ THE REPORT.
TRUMP
SSIA
ON THE MATTERS OF CONSPIRACY AND OBSTRUCTION, THE REPORT IS OUR LIVING MESSAGE TO THOSE WHO COME AFTER US.
HE
MUELLER
REPORT
IT IS ALSO A WARNING.
OVER THE YEARS, I'VE SEEN A NUMBER OF CHALLANGES TO OUR DEMOCRACY. THE RUSSIAN GOVERNMENT'S EFFORT TO INTERFERE IN OUR ELECTION IS THE MOST SERIOUS.
AND THE RUSSIANS ARE JUST GETTING STARTED.

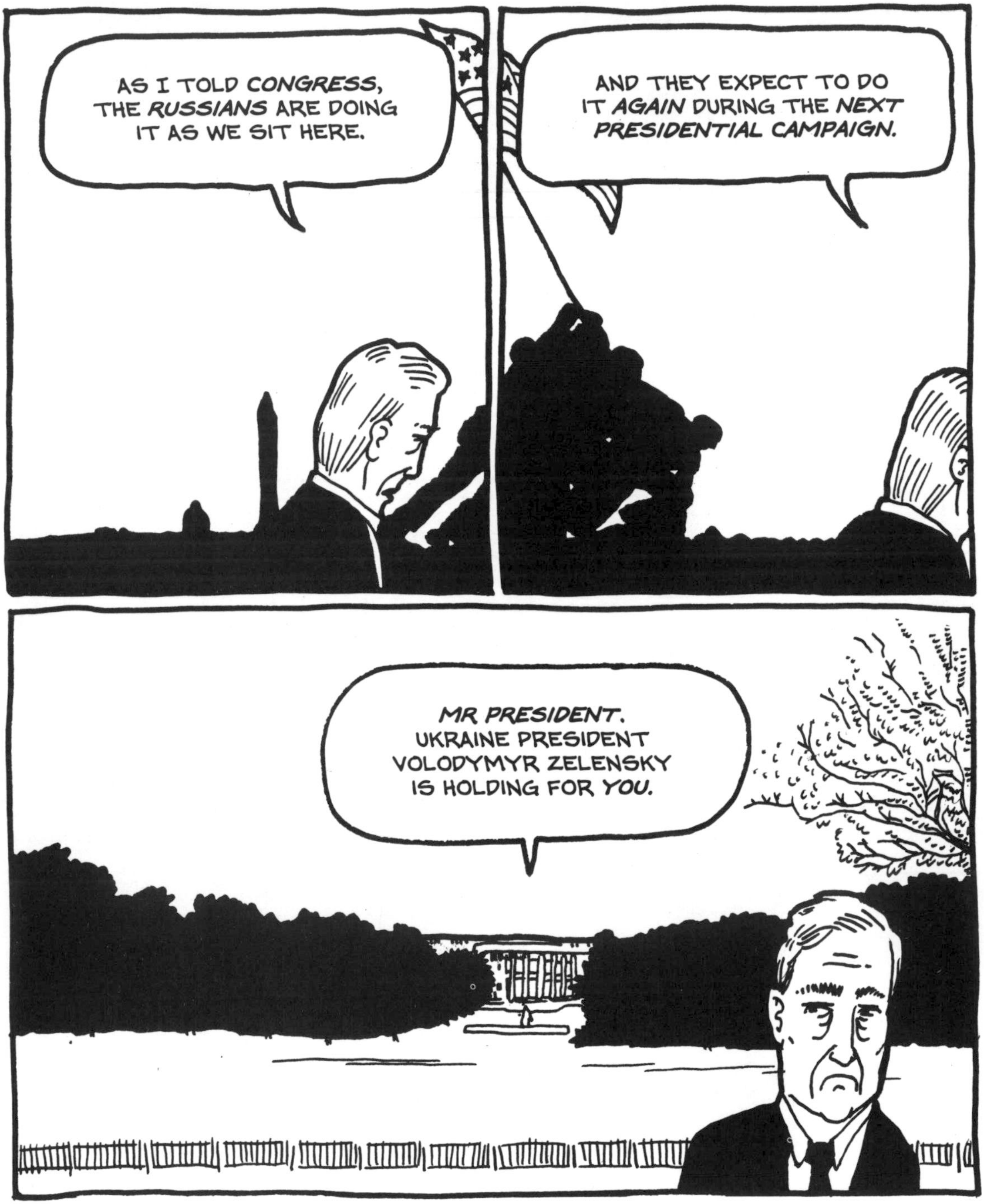
AS I TOLD *CONGRESS*, THE *RUSSIANS* ARE DOING IT AS WE SIT HERE.
AND THEY EXPECT TO DO IT *AGAIN* DURING THE *NEXT PRESIDENTIAL CAMPAIGN.*
MR PRESIDENT. UKRAINE PRESIDENT VOLODYMYR ZELENSKY IS HOLDING FOR *YOU.*

TIMELINE

2015 JUN 16

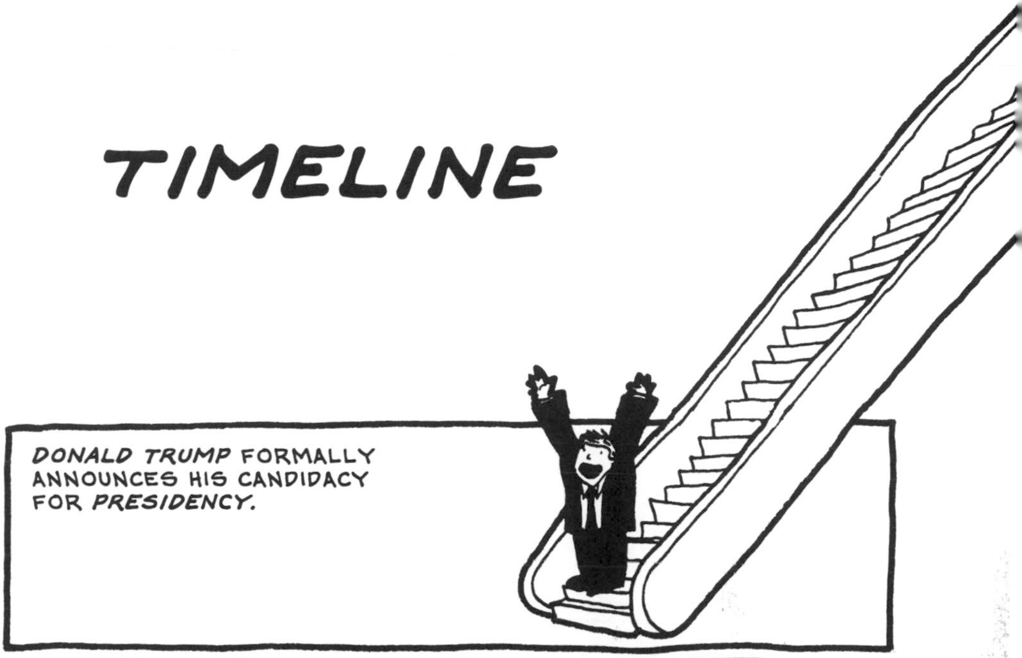

DONALD TRUMP FORMALLY ANNOUNCES HIS CANDIDACY FOR PRESIDENCY.

2016 FEB

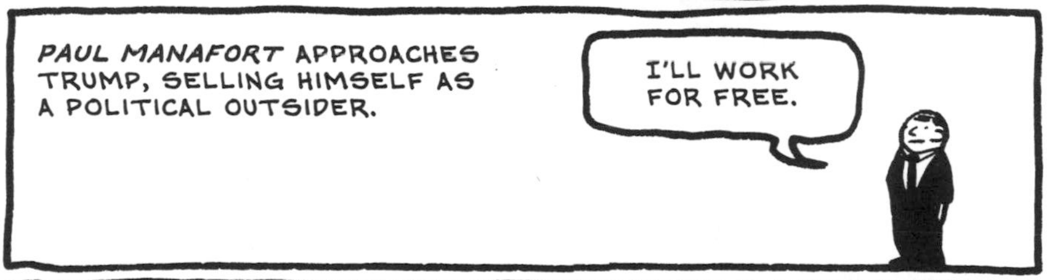

PAUL MANAFORT APPROACHES TRUMP, SELLING HIMSELF AS A POLITICAL OUTSIDER.
I'LL WORK FOR FREE.

MAR 6

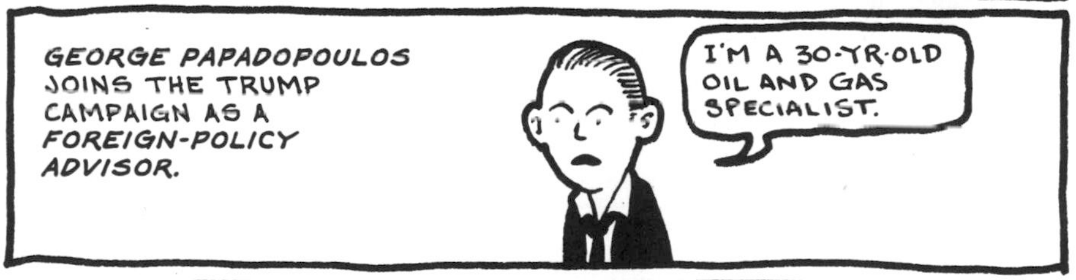

GEORGE PAPADOPOULOS JOINS THE TRUMP CAMPAIGN AS A FOREIGN-POLICY ADVISOR.
I'M A 30-YR-OLD OIL AND GAS SPECIALIST.

APR 26

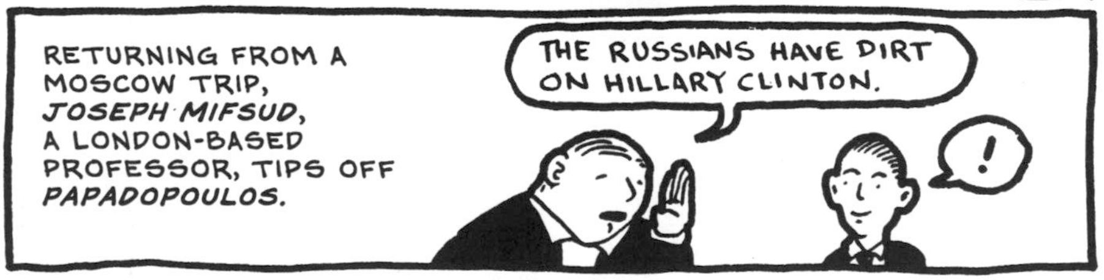

RETURNING FROM A MOSCOW TRIP, JOSEPH MIFSUD, A LONDON-BASED PROFESSOR, TIPS OFF PAPADOPOULOS.
THE RUSSIANS HAVE DIRT ON HILLARY CLINTON.
!

Joseph Mifsud: Academic accused of linking Trump's campaign and Russia

MAY 6

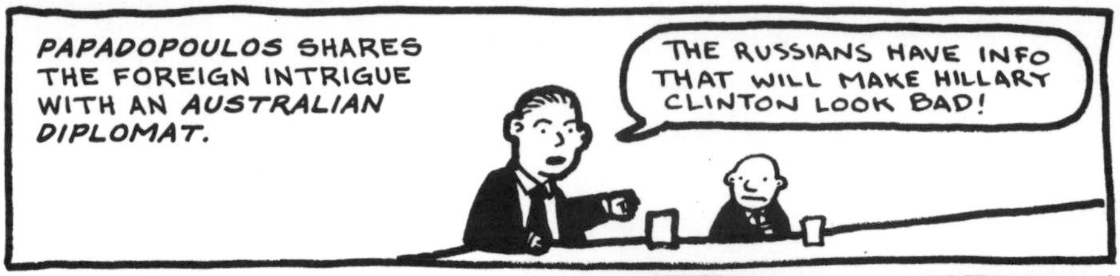
PAPADOPOULOS SHARES THE FOREIGN INTRIGUE WITH AN AUSTRALIAN DIPLOMAT.
THE RUSSIANS HAVE INFO THAT WILL MAKE HILLARY CLINTON LOOK BAD!

JUNE 3

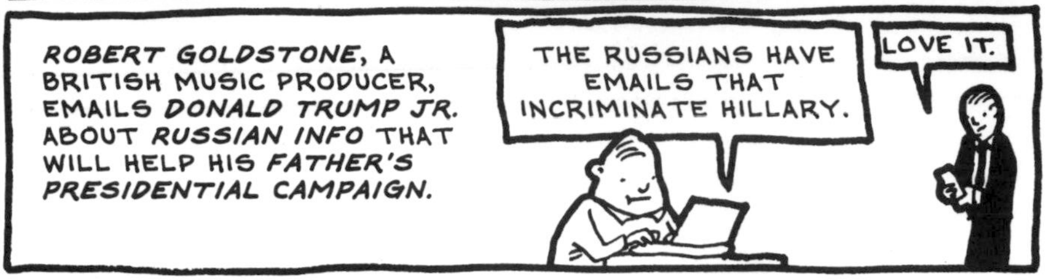
ROBERT GOLDSTONE, A BRITISH MUSIC PRODUCER, EMAILS DONALD TRUMP JR. ABOUT RUSSIAN INFO THAT WILL HELP HIS FATHER'S PRESIDENTIAL CAMPAIGN.
THE RUSSIANS HAVE EMAILS THAT INCRIMINATE HILLARY.
LOVE IT.

JUNE 9

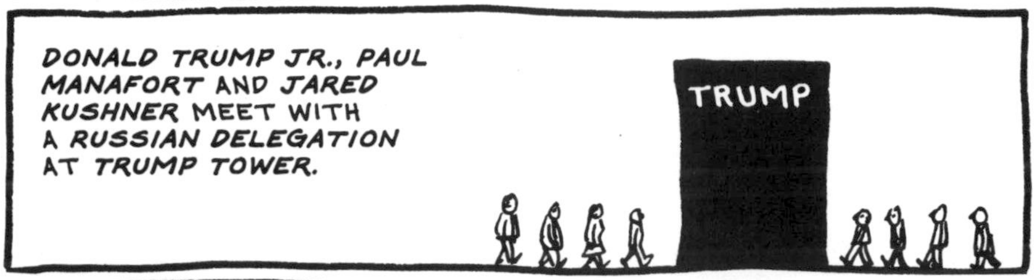
DONALD TRUMP JR., PAUL MANAFORT AND JARED KUSHNER MEET WITH A RUSSIAN DELEGATION AT TRUMP TOWER.
TRUMP

JULY 22

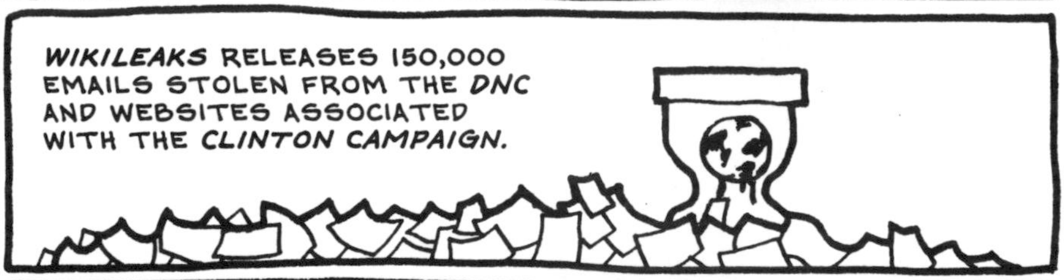
WIKILEAKS RELEASES 150,000 EMAILS STOLEN FROM THE DNC AND WEBSITES ASSOCIATED WITH THE CLINTON CAMPAIGN.

JULY (LATE)

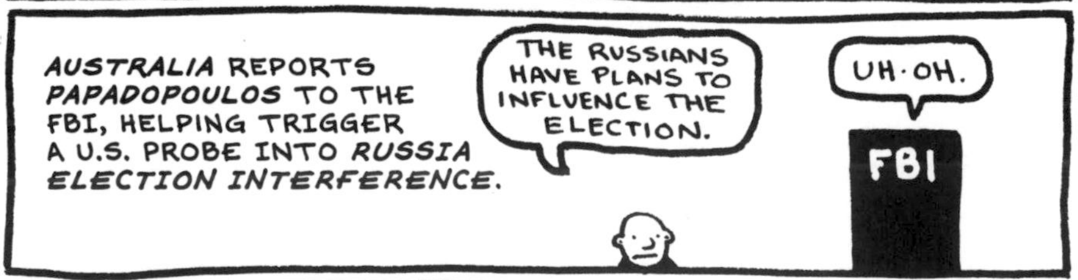
AUSTRALIA REPORTS PAPADOPOULOS TO THE FBI, HELPING TRIGGER A U.S. PROBE INTO RUSSIA ELECTION INTERFERENCE.
THE RUSSIANS HAVE PLANS TO INFLUENCE THE ELECTION.
UH-OH.
FBI

JULY 27

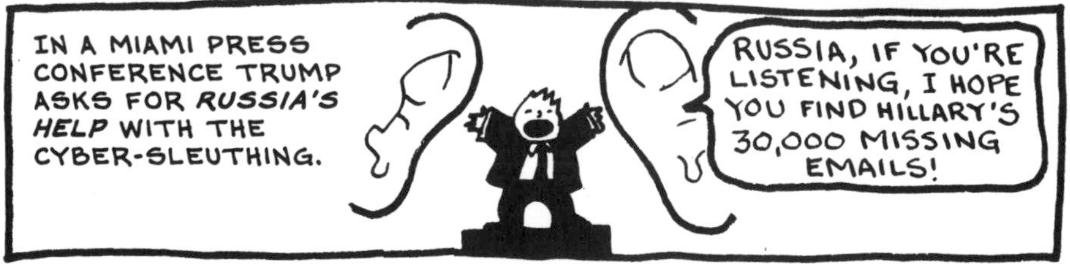
IN A MIAMI PRESS CONFERENCE TRUMP ASKS FOR RUSSIA'S HELP WITH THE CYBER-SLEUTHING.
RUSSIA, IF YOU'RE LISTENING, I HOPE YOU FIND HILLARY'S 30,000 MISSING EMAILS!

Rob Goldstone: British publicist, former tabloid journalist
Don Trump Jr: Donald Trump's son, trustee and executive VP of the Trump Org.
Jared Kushner: Trump's son-in-law, senior White House Advisor, Jan 2017-

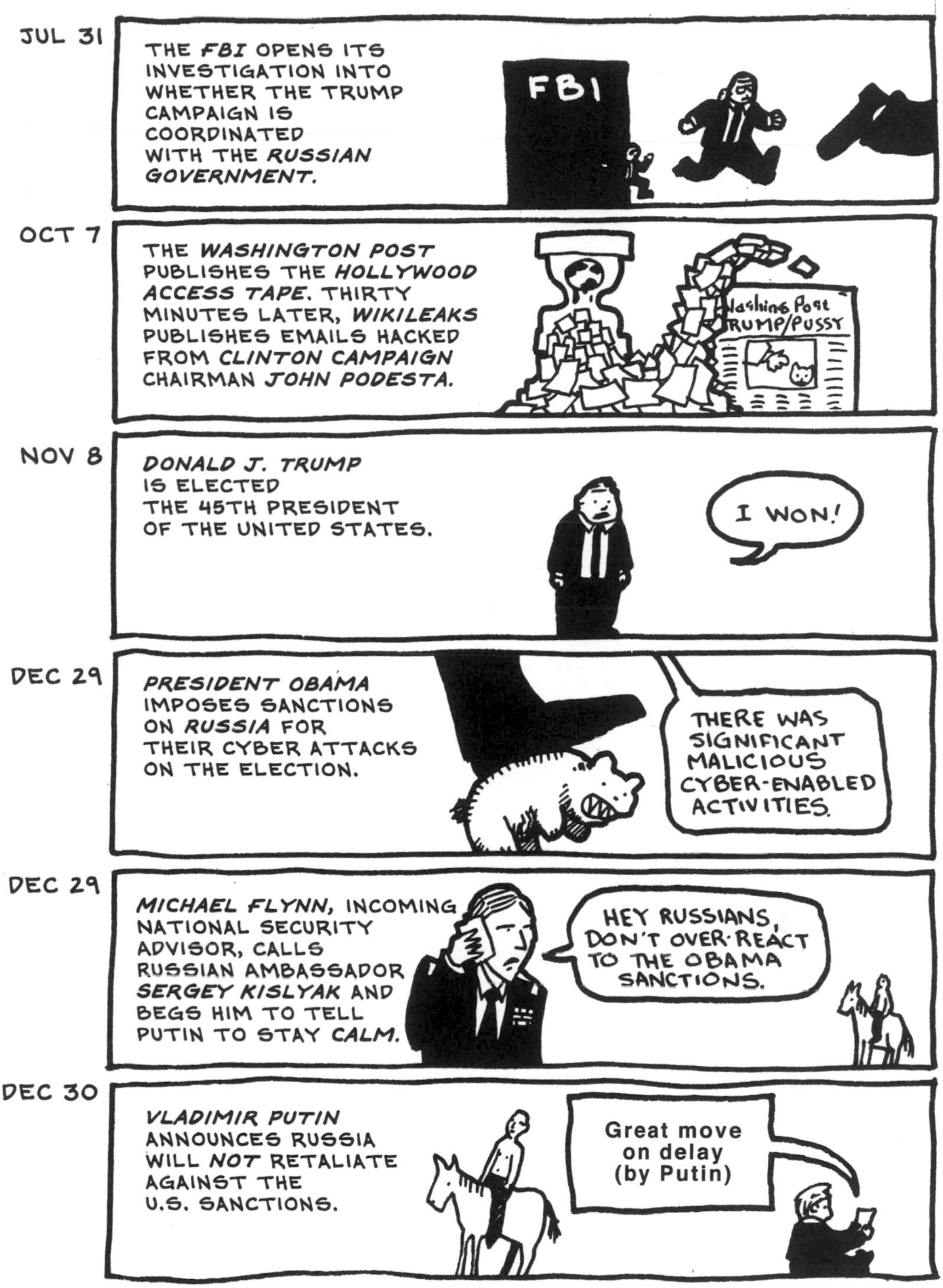
JUL 31
THE FBI OPENS ITS INVESTIGATION INTO WHETHER THE TRUMP CAMPAIGN IS COORDINATED WITH THE RUSSIAN GOVERNMENT.
FBI
OCT 7
THE WASHINGTON POST PUBLISHES THE HOLLYWOOD ACCESS TAPE. THIRTY MINUTES LATER, WIKILEAKS PUBLISHES EMAILS HACKED FROM CLINTON CAMPAIGN CHAIRMAN JOHN PODESTA.
NOV 8
DONALD J. TRUMP IS ELECTED THE 45TH PRESIDENT OF THE UNITED STATES.
I WON!
DEC 29
PRESIDENT OBAMA IMPOSES SANCTIONS ON RUSSIA FOR THEIR CYBER ATTACKS ON THE ELECTION.
THERE WAS SIGNIFICANT MALICIOUS CYBER-ENABLED ACTIVITIES.
DEC 29
MICHAEL FLYNN, INCOMING NATIONAL SECURITY ADVISOR, CALLS RUSSIAN AMBASSADOR SERGEY KISLYAK AND BEGS HIM TO TELL PUTIN TO STAY CALM.
HEY RUSSIANS, DON'T OVER-REACT TO THE OBAMA SANCTIONS.
DEC 30
VLADIMIR PUTIN ANNOUNCES RUSSIA WILL NOT RETALIATE AGAINST THE U.S. SANCTIONS.
Great move on delay (by Putin)

Michael Flynn: Trump's National Security Advisor, Jan-Feb 2017
Sergey Kislyak: Russian senior diplomat

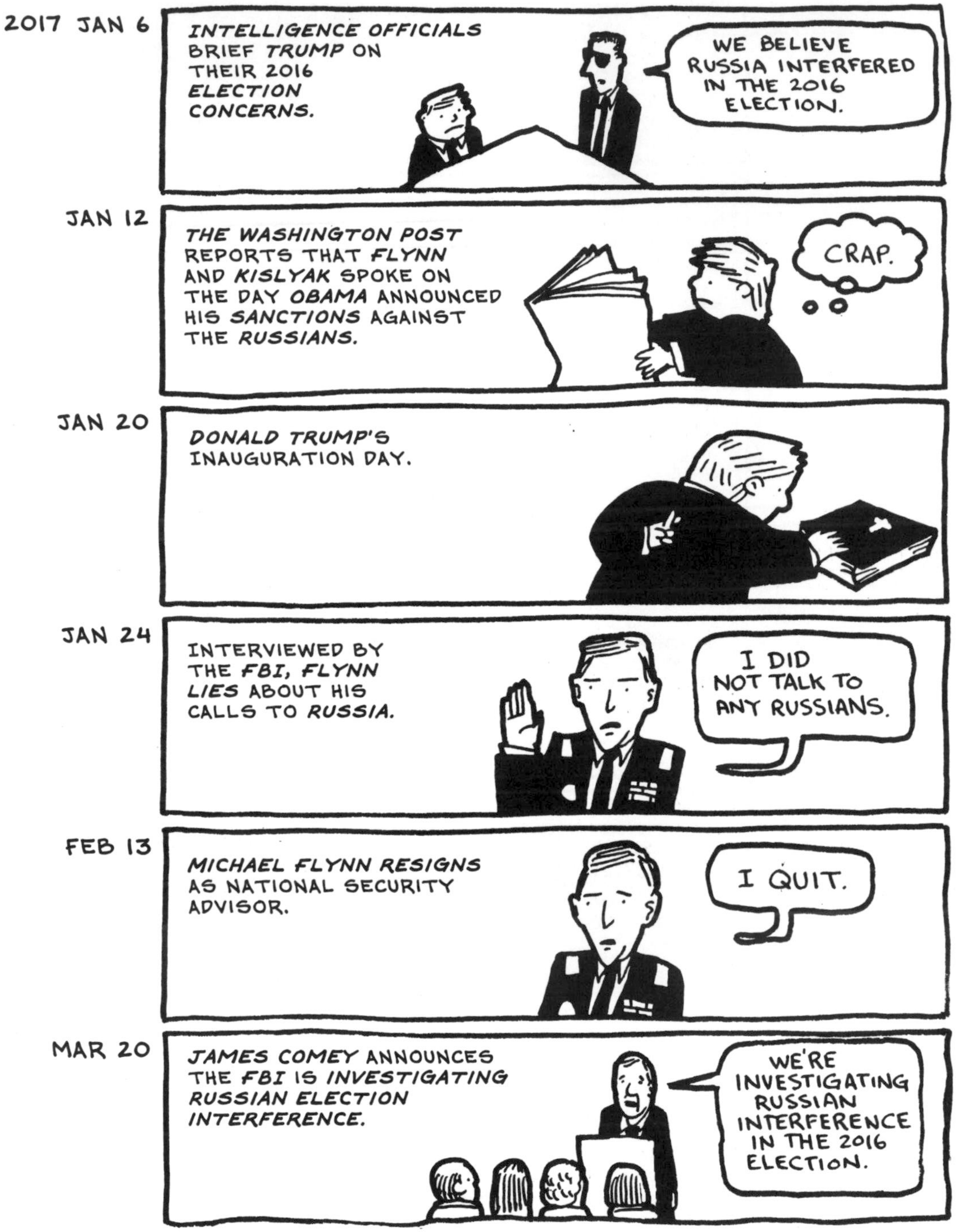
2017 JAN 6
INTELLIGENCE OFFICIALS BRIEF TRUMP ON THEIR 2016 ELECTION CONCERNS.
WE BELIEVE RUSSIA INTERFERED IN THE 2016 ELECTION.
JAN 12
THE WASHINGTON POST REPORTS THAT FLYNN AND KISLYAK SPOKE ON THE DAY OBAMA ANNOUNCED HIS SANCTIONS AGAINST THE RUSSIANS.
CRAP.
JAN 20
DONALD TRUMP'S INAUGURATION DAY.
JAN 24
INTERVIEWED BY THE FBI, FLYNN LIES ABOUT HIS CALLS TO RUSSIA.
I DID NOT TALK TO ANY RUSSIANS.
FEB 13
MICHAEL FLYNN RESIGNS AS NATIONAL SECURITY ADVISOR.
I QUIT.
MAR 20
JAMES COMEY ANNOUNCES THE FBI IS INVESTIGATING RUSSIAN ELECTION INTERFERENCE.
WE'RE INVESTIGATING RUSSIAN INTERFERENCE IN THE 2016 ELECTION.

James Comey: FBI Director, 2013-2017

MAR 26

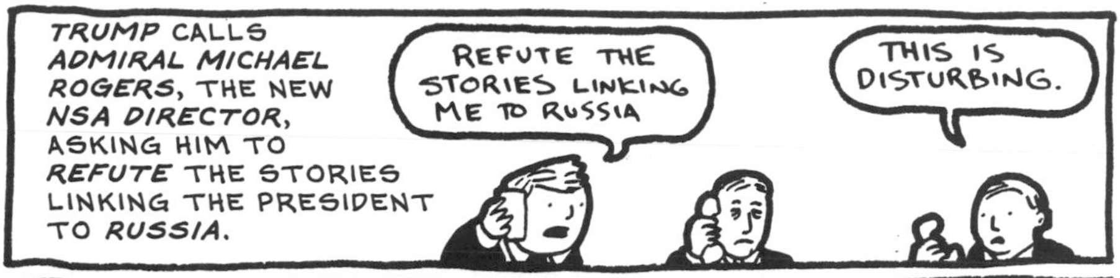
TRUMP CALLS ADMIRAL MICHAEL ROGERS, THE NEW NSA DIRECTOR, ASKING HIM TO REFUTE THE STORIES LINKING THE PRESIDENT TO RUSSIA.
REFUTE THE STORIES LINKING ME TO RUSSIA
THIS IS DISTURBING.

MAR 30

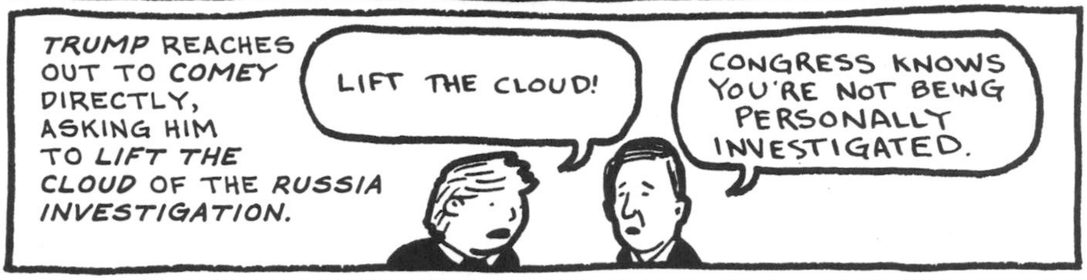
TRUMP REACHES OUT TO COMEY DIRECTLY, ASKING HIM TO LIFT THE CLOUD OF THE RUSSIA INVESTIGATION.
LIFT THE CLOUD!
CONGRESS KNOWS YOU'RE NOT BEING PERSONALLY INVESTIGATED.

MAY 9

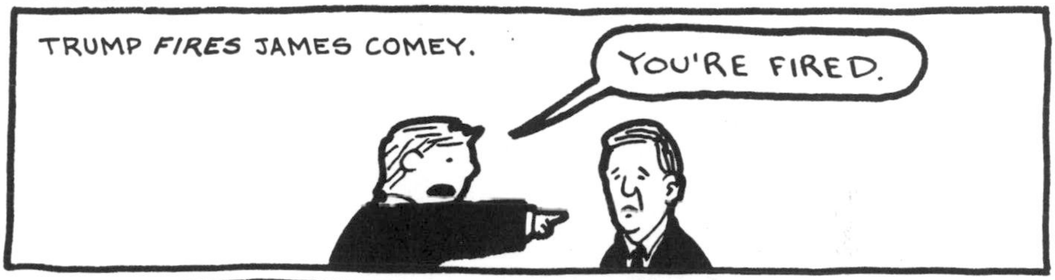
TRUMP FIRES JAMES COMEY.
YOU'RE FIRED.

MAY 10

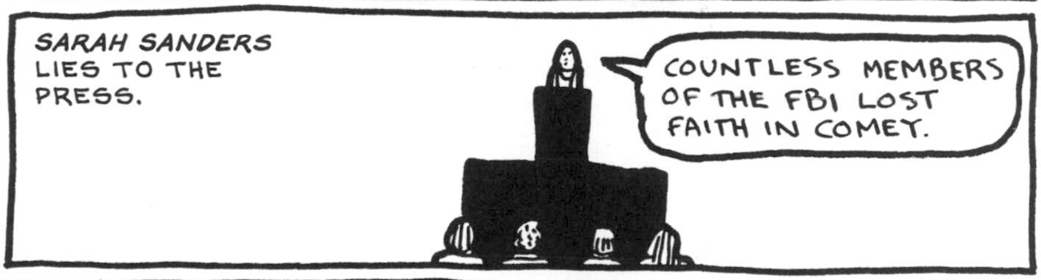
SARAH SANDERS LIES TO THE PRESS.
COUNTLESS MEMBERS OF THE FBI LOST FAITH IN COMEY.

MAY 17

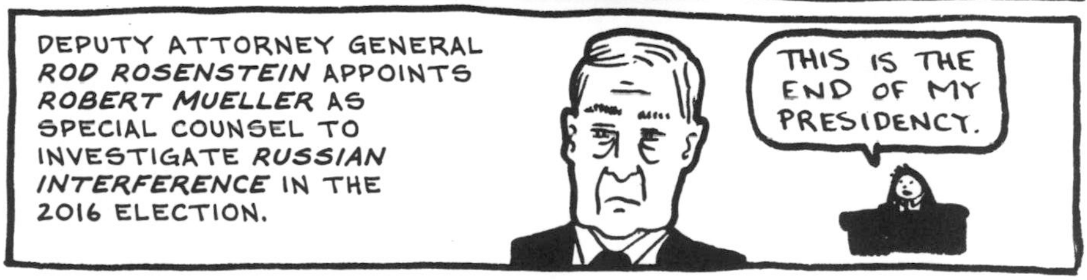
DEPUTY ATTORNEY GENERAL ROD ROSENSTEIN APPOINTS ROBERT MUELLER AS SPECIAL COUNSEL TO INVESTIGATE RUSSIAN INTERFERENCE IN THE 2016 ELECTION.
THIS IS THE END OF MY PRESIDENCY.

JUN 9

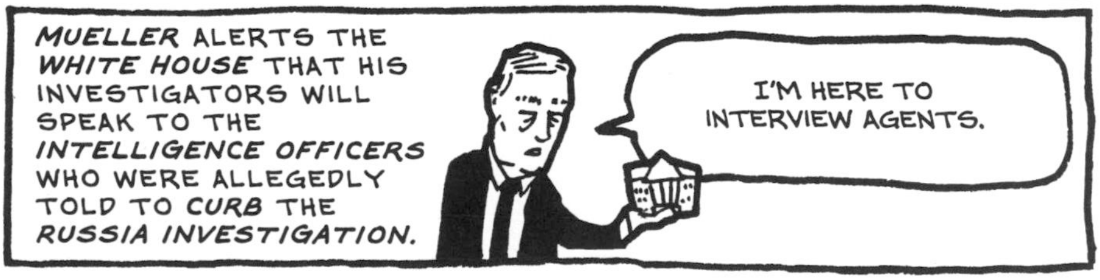
MUELLER ALERTS THE WHITE HOUSE THAT HIS INVESTIGATORS WILL SPEAK TO THE INTELLIGENCE OFFICERS WHO WERE ALLEGEDLY TOLD TO CURB THE RUSSIA INVESTIGATION.
I'M HERE TO INTERVIEW AGENTS.

Michael Rogers: National Security Agency director, Apr 2014-May 2018
Sarah Sanders: Press Secretary, May 2017-Jun 2019

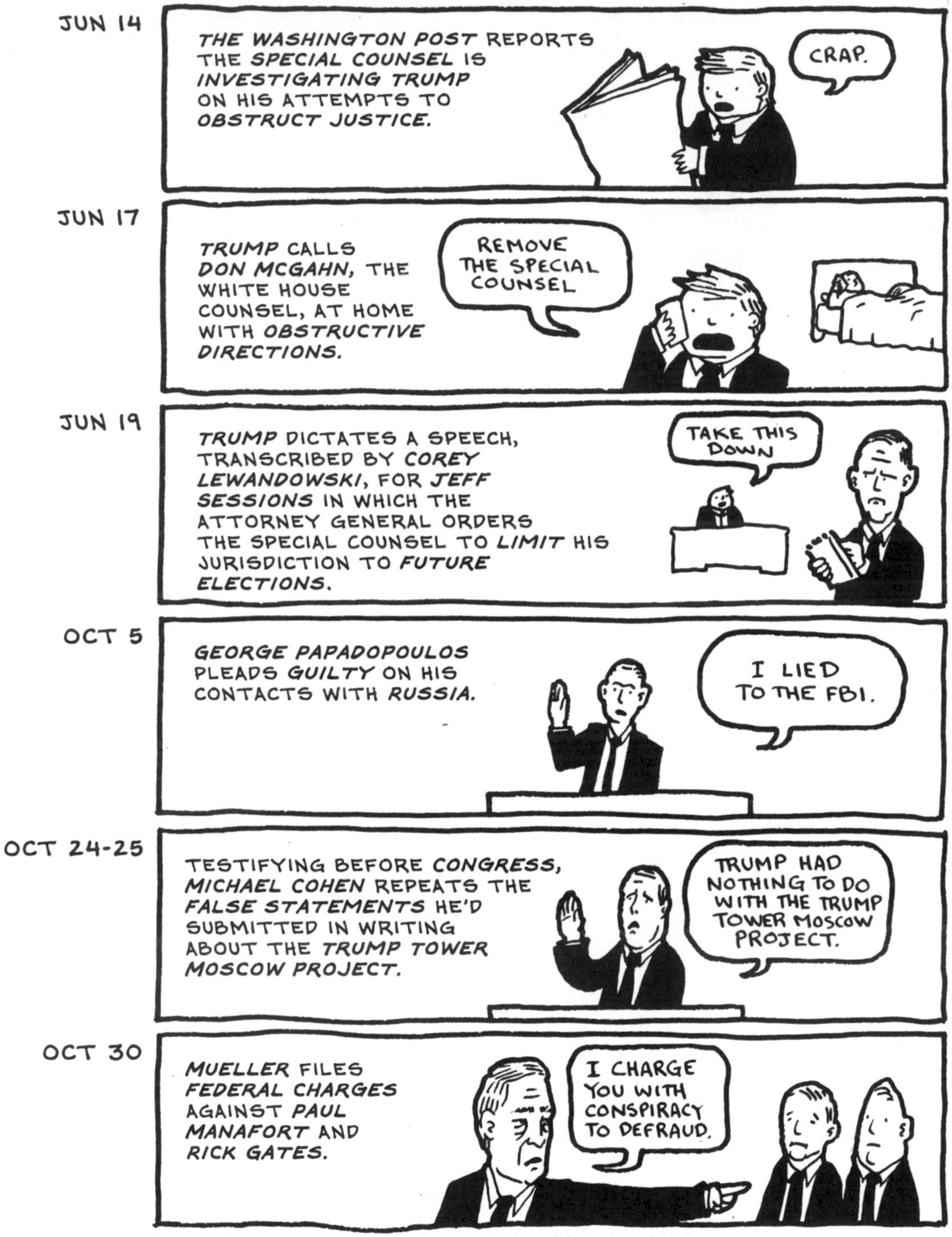
JUN 14
THE WASHINGTON POST REPORTS THE SPECIAL COUNSEL IS INVESTIGATING TRUMP ON HIS ATTEMPTS TO OBSTRUCT JUSTICE.
CRAP.
JUN 17
TRUMP CALLS DON MCGAHN, THE WHITE HOUSE COUNSEL, AT HOME WITH OBSTRUCTIVE DIRECTIONS.
REMOVE THE SPECIAL COUNSEL
JUN 19
TRUMP DICTATES A SPEECH, TRANSCRIBED BY COREY LEWANDOWSKI, FOR JEFF SESSIONS IN WHICH THE ATTORNEY GENERAL ORDERS THE SPECIAL COUNSEL TO LIMIT HIS JURISDICTION TO FUTURE ELECTIONS.
TAKE THIS DOWN
OCT 5
GEORGE PAPADOPOULOS PLEADS GUILTY ON HIS CONTACTS WITH RUSSIA.
I LIED TO THE FBI.
OCT 24-25
TESTIFYING BEFORE CONGRESS, MICHAEL COHEN REPEATS THE FALSE STATEMENTS HE'D SUBMITTED IN WRITING ABOUT THE TRUMP TOWER MOSCOW PROJECT.
TRUMP HAD NOTHING TO DO WITH THE TRUMP TOWER MOSCOW PROJECT.
OCT 30
MUELLER FILES FEDERAL CHARGES AGAINST PAUL MANAFORT AND RICK GATES.
I CHARGE YOU WITH CONSPIRACY TO DEFRAUD.

Don McGahn: White House Counsel, Jan 2017-Oct 2018
Corey Lewandowski: Trump campaign manager Jan 2015-Jun 2016
George Papadopoulos: Trump's Foreign Policy Advisor, Dec 2015-Feb 2016
Rick Gates: Trump's Deputy Campaign Manager, Jun 2016-Aug 2016

DEC 1

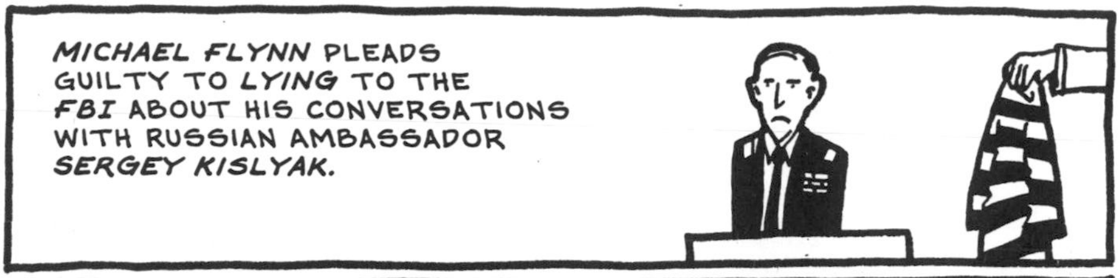
MICHAEL FLYNN PLEADS GUILTY TO LYING TO THE FBI ABOUT HIS CONVERSATIONS WITH RUSSIAN AMBASSADOR SERGEY KISLYAK.

2018 JAN 12

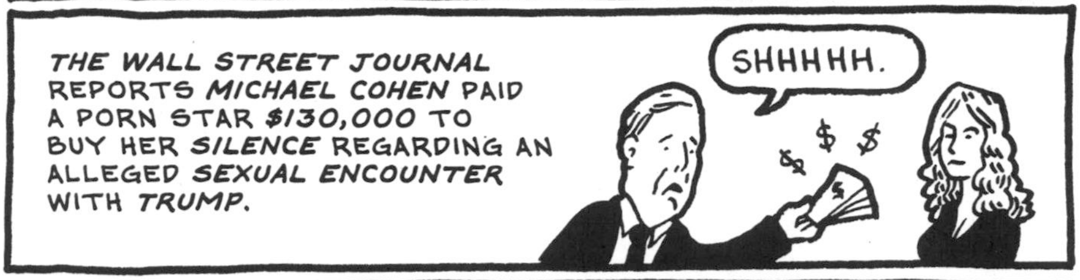
THE WALL STREET JOURNAL REPORTS MICHAEL COHEN PAID A PORN STAR $130,000 TO BUY HER SILENCE REGARDING AN ALLEGED SEXUAL ENCOUNTER WITH TRUMP.
SHHHHH.

FEB 16

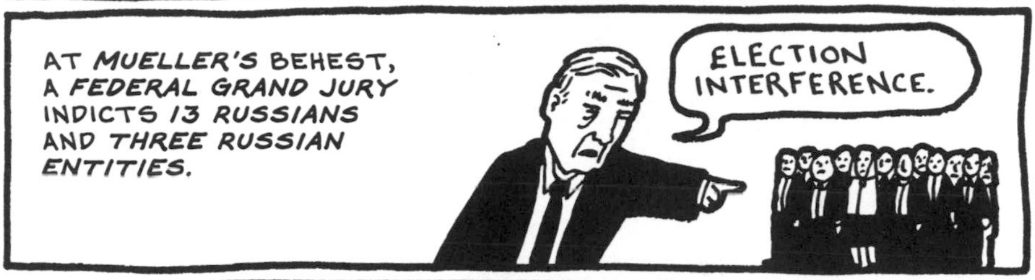
AT MUELLER'S BEHEST, A FEDERAL GRAND JURY INDICTS 13 RUSSIANS AND THREE RUSSIAN ENTITIES.
ELECTION INTERFERENCE.

FEB 22

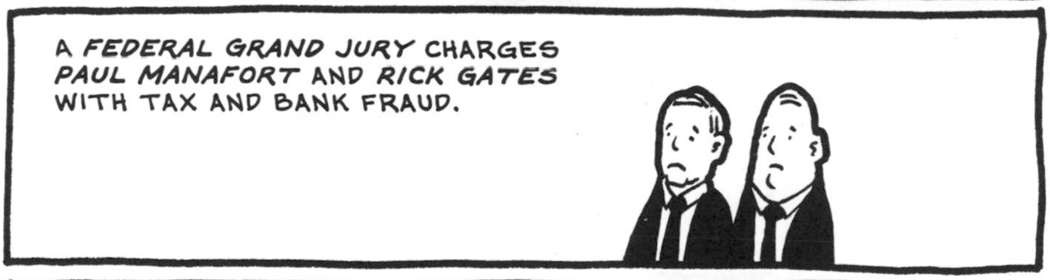
A FEDERAL GRAND JURY CHARGES PAUL MANAFORT AND RICK GATES WITH TAX AND BANK FRAUD.

FEB 23

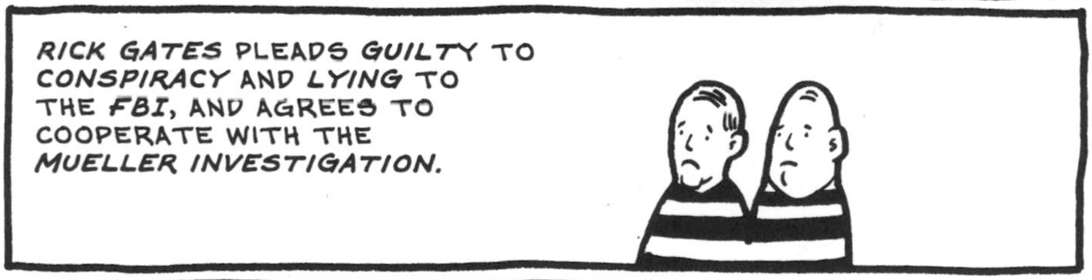
RICK GATES PLEADS GUILTY TO CONSPIRACY AND LYING TO THE FBI, AND AGREES TO COOPERATE WITH THE MUELLER INVESTIGATION.

APR 9

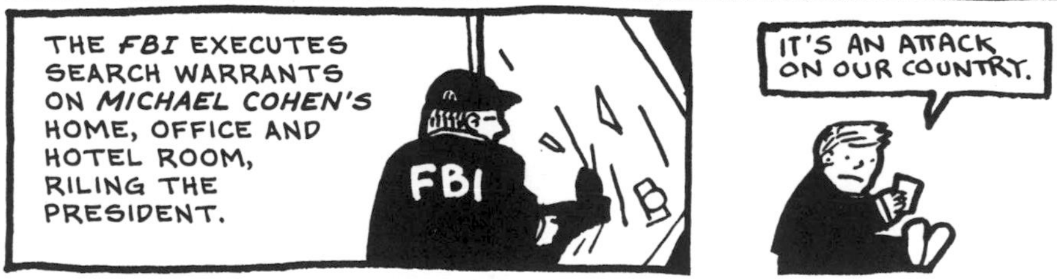
THE FBI EXECUTES SEARCH WARRANTS ON MICHAEL COHEN'S HOME, OFFICE AND HOTEL ROOM, RILING THE PRESIDENT.
FBI
IT'S AN ATTACK ON OUR COUNTRY.

JUN 8

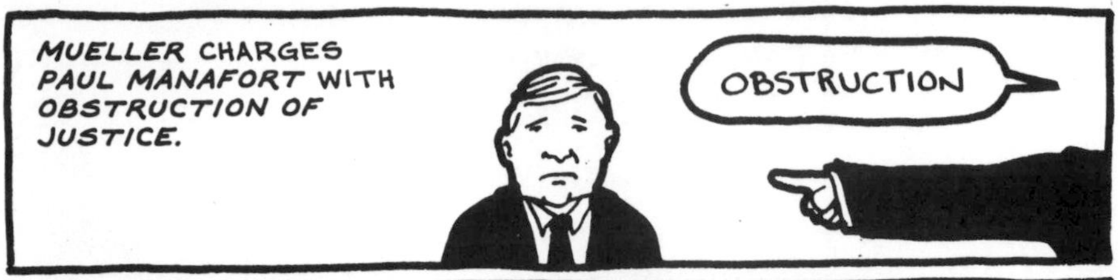
MUELLER CHARGES PAUL MANAFORT WITH OBSTRUCTION OF JUSTICE.
OBSTRUCTION

JUN 15

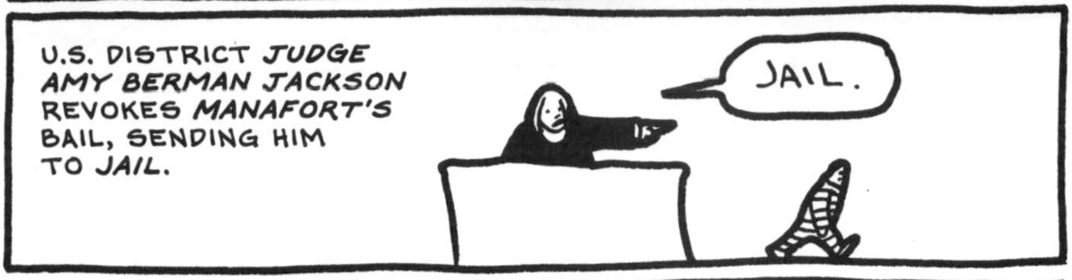
U.S. DISTRICT JUDGE AMY BERMAN JACKSON REVOKES MANAFORT'S BAIL, SENDING HIM TO JAIL.
JAIL.

JUL 13

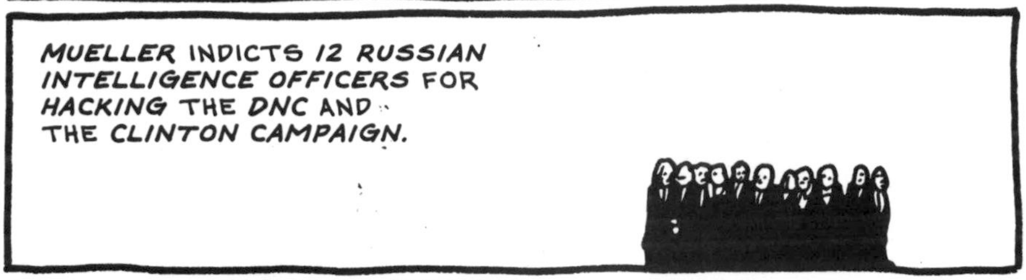
MUELLER INDICTS 12 RUSSIAN INTELLIGENCE OFFICERS FOR HACKING THE DNC AND THE CLINTON CAMPAIGN.

AUG 21

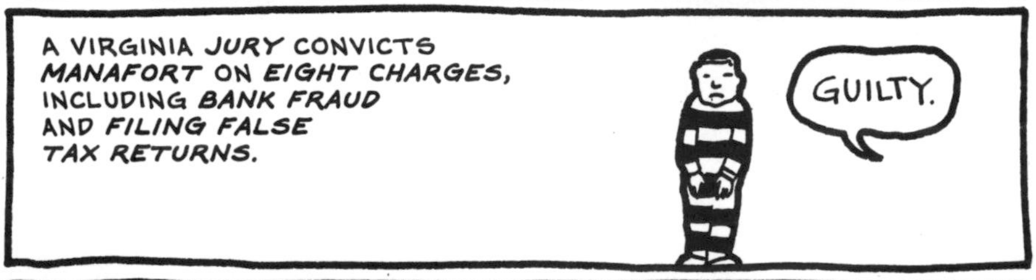
A VIRGINIA JURY CONVICTS MANAFORT ON EIGHT CHARGES, INCLUDING BANK FRAUD AND FILING FALSE TAX RETURNS.
GUILTY.

AUG 21

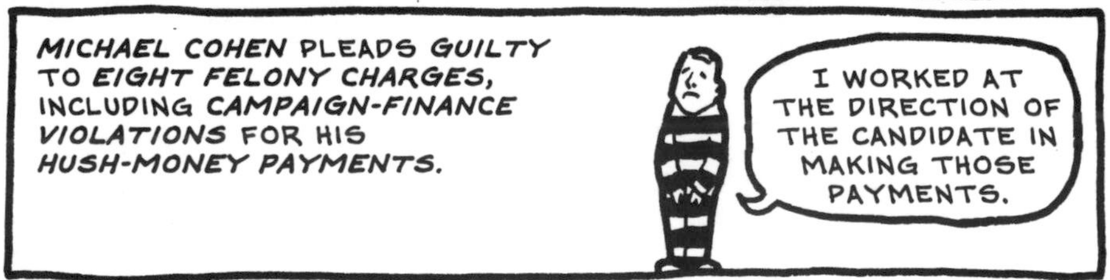
MICHAEL COHEN PLEADS GUILTY TO EIGHT FELONY CHARGES, INCLUDING CAMPAIGN-FINANCE VIOLATIONS FOR HIS HUSH-MONEY PAYMENTS.
I WORKED AT THE DIRECTION OF THE CANDIDATE IN MAKING THOSE PAYMENTS.

AUG 31

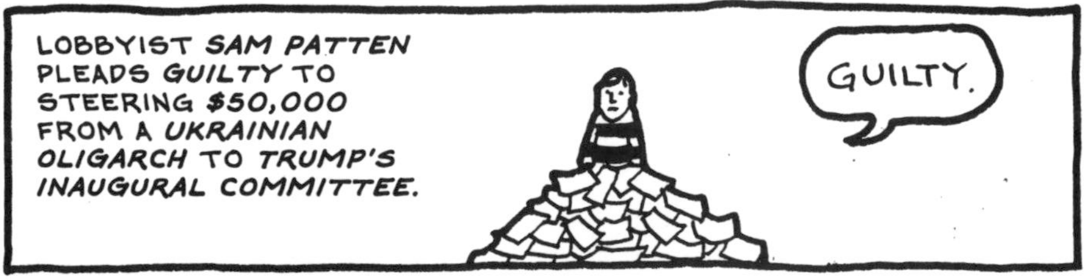
LOBBYIST SAM PATTEN PLEADS GUILTY TO STEERING $50,000 FROM A UKRAINIAN OLIGARCH TO TRUMP'S INAUGURAL COMMITTEE.
GUILTY.

Judge Amy Berman Jackson: Presided over Manafort and Gates criminal cases
Sam Patten: Washington lobbyist, connected to Cambridge Analytica

NOV 7

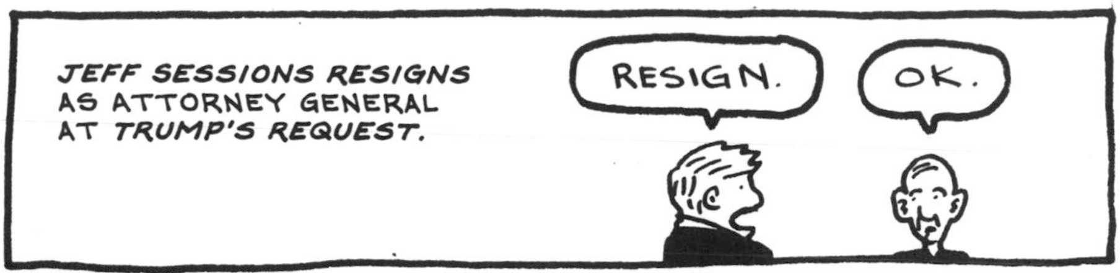
JEFF SESSIONS RESIGNS AS ATTORNEY GENERAL AT TRUMP'S REQUEST.
RESIGN.
OK.

NOV 14

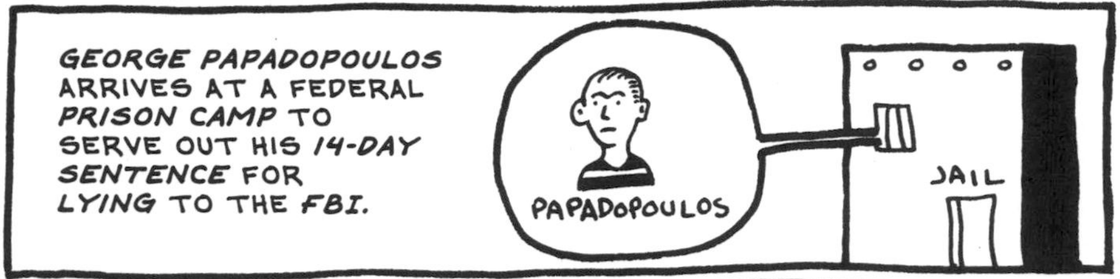
GEORGE PAPADOPOULOS ARRIVES AT A FEDERAL PRISON CAMP TO SERVE OUT HIS 14-DAY SENTENCE FOR LYING TO THE FBI.
PAPADOPOULOS
JAIL

NOV 20

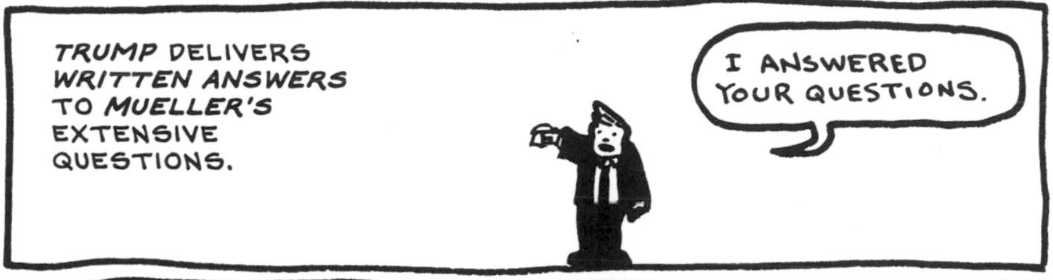
TRUMP DELIVERS WRITTEN ANSWERS TO MUELLER'S EXTENSIVE QUESTIONS.
I ANSWERED YOUR QUESTIONS.

NOV 26

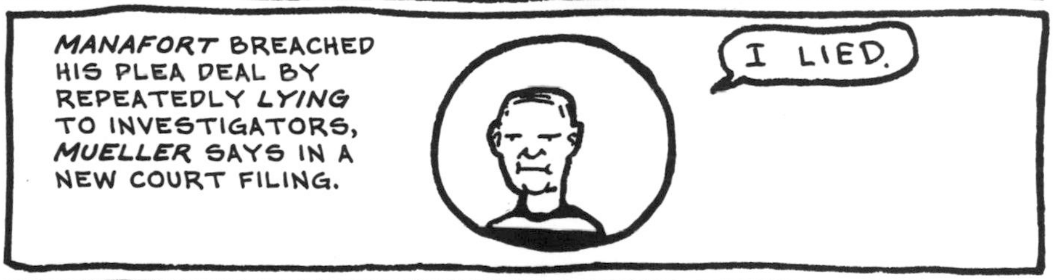
MANAFORT BREACHED HIS PLEA DEAL BY REPEATEDLY LYING TO INVESTIGATORS, MUELLER SAYS IN A NEW COURT FILING.
I LIED.

NOV 29

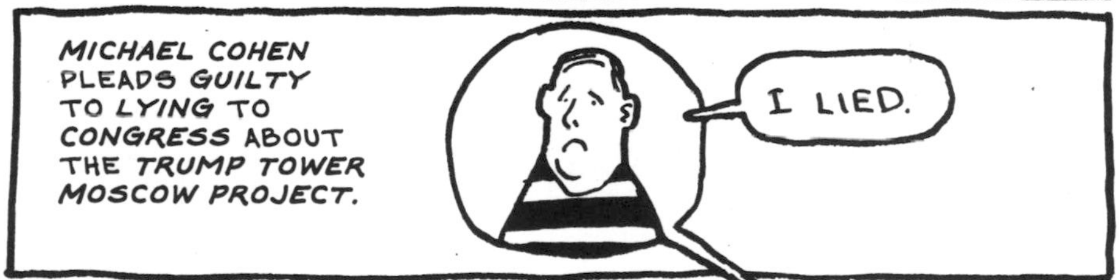
MICHAEL COHEN PLEADS GUILTY TO LYING TO CONGRESS ABOUT THE TRUMP TOWER MOSCOW PROJECT.
I LIED.

DEC 12

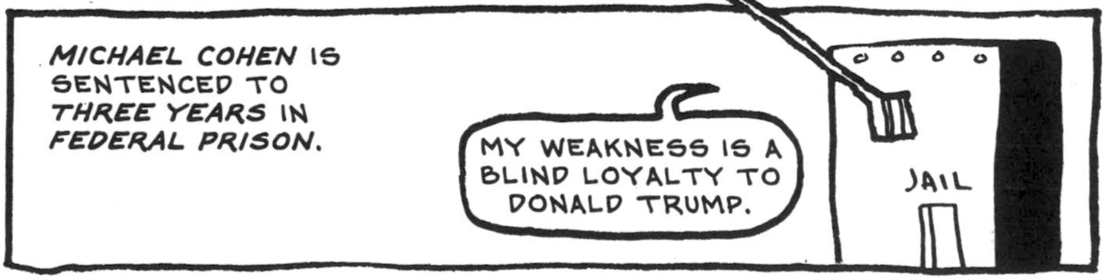
MICHAEL COHEN IS SENTENCED TO THREE YEARS IN FEDERAL PRISON.
MY WEAKNESS IS A BLIND LOYALTY TO DONALD TRUMP.
JAIL

Jeff Sessions: Attorney General, 2017-2018

DEC 16

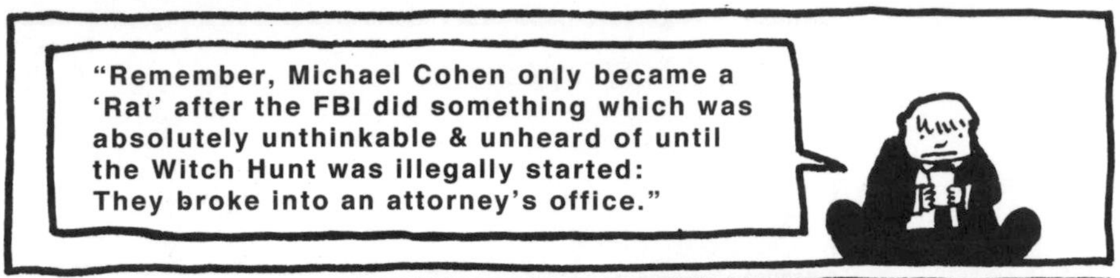
"Remember, Michael Cohen only became a 'Rat' after the FBI did something which was absolutely unthinkable & unheard of until the Witch Hunt was illegally started: They broke into an attorney's office."

DEC 18

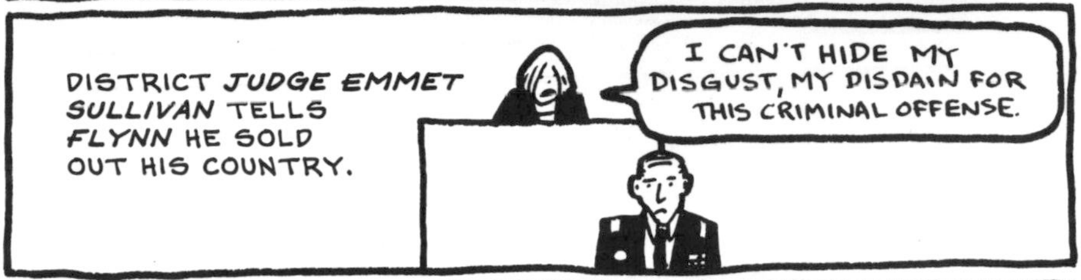
DISTRICT *JUDGE EMMET SULLIVAN* TELLS *FLYNN* HE SOLD OUT HIS COUNTRY.
I CAN'T HIDE MY DISGUST, MY DISDAIN FOR THIS CRIMINAL OFFENSE.

2019 JAN 20

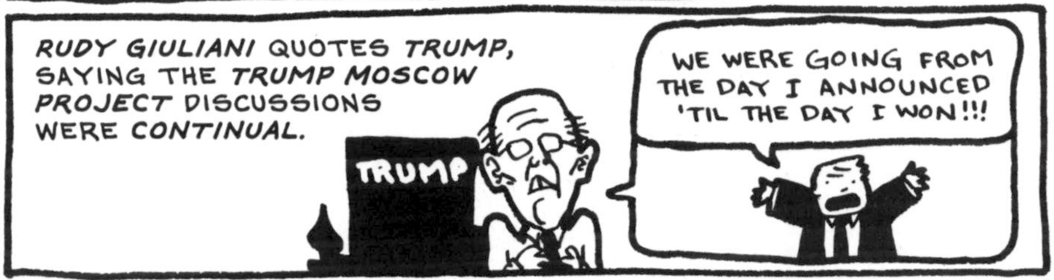
RUDY GIULIANI QUOTES *TRUMP*, SAYING THE *TRUMP MOSCOW PROJECT* DISCUSSIONS WERE *CONTINUAL*.
TRUMP
WE WERE GOING FROM THE DAY I ANNOUNCED 'TIL THE DAY I WON!!!

JAN 25

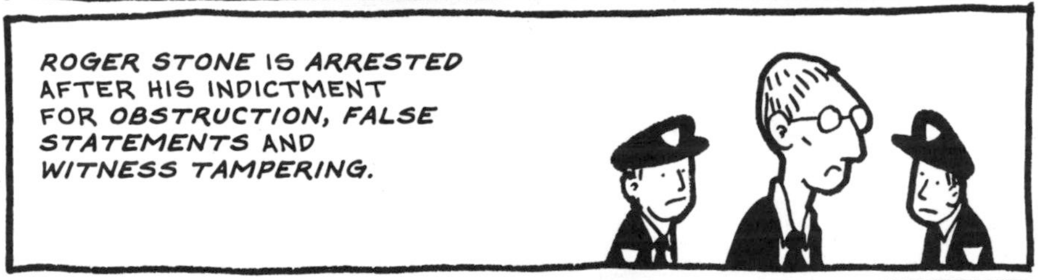
ROGER STONE IS *ARRESTED* AFTER HIS INDICTMENT FOR *OBSTRUCTION, FALSE STATEMENTS* AND *WITNESS TAMPERING*.

FEB 14

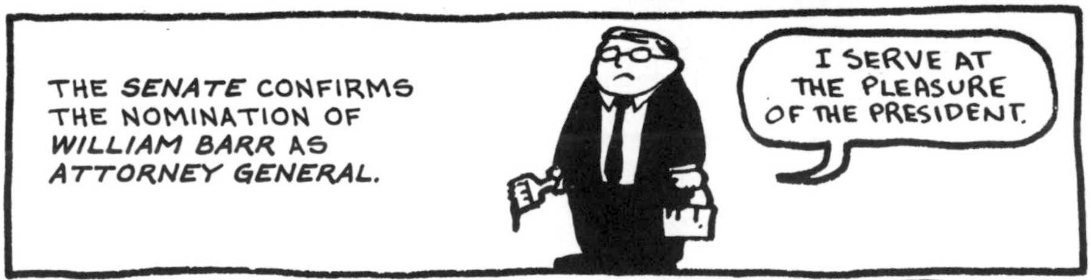
THE *SENATE* CONFIRMS THE NOMINATION OF *WILLIAM BARR* AS *ATTORNEY GENERAL*.
I SERVE AT THE PLEASURE OF THE PRESIDENT.

MAR 22

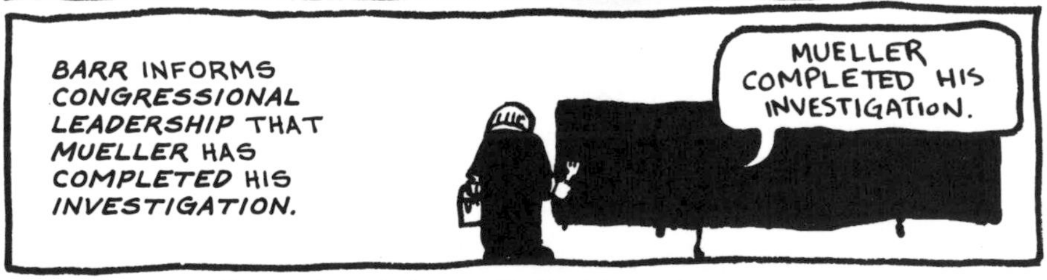
BARR INFORMS *CONGRESSIONAL LEADERSHIP* THAT *MUELLER* HAS *COMPLETED* HIS *INVESTIGATION*.
MUELLER COMPLETED HIS INVESTIGATION.

Judge Emmet Sullivan: Presided over Michael Flynn's case
Rudy Giuliani: Attorney for Donald Trump, Apr 2018 -
Roger Stone: Political consultant
William Barr: U.S. Attorney General, Feb 2019 -

MAR 24

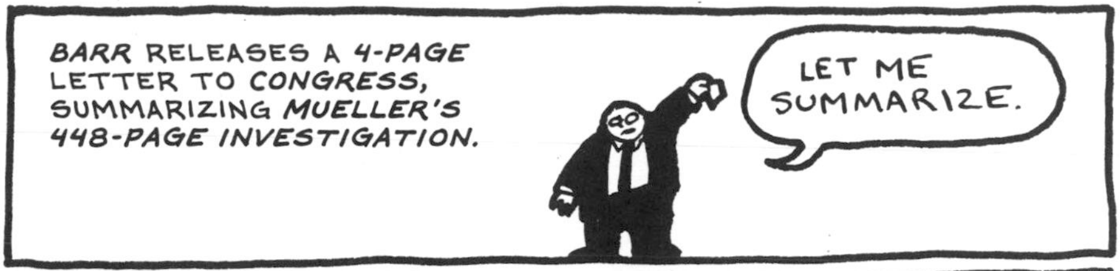
BARR RELEASES A 4-PAGE LETTER TO CONGRESS, SUMMARIZING MUELLER'S 448-PAGE INVESTIGATION.
LET ME SUMMARIZE.

MAR 27

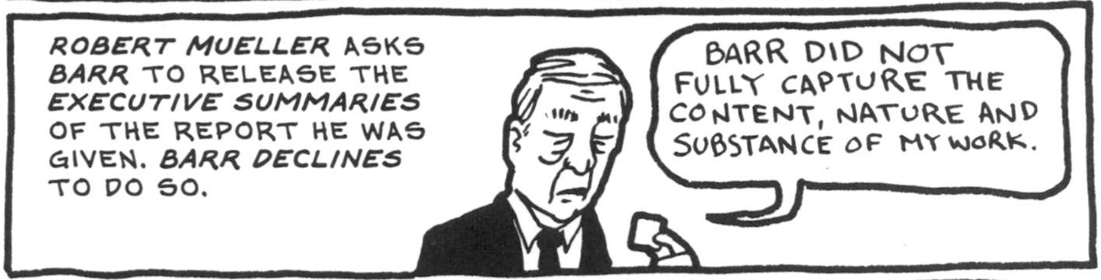
ROBERT MUELLER ASKS BARR TO RELEASE THE EXECUTIVE SUMMARIES OF THE REPORT HE WAS GIVEN. BARR DECLINES TO DO SO.
BARR DID NOT FULLY CAPTURE THE CONTENT, NATURE AND SUBSTANCE OF MY WORK.

MAY 29

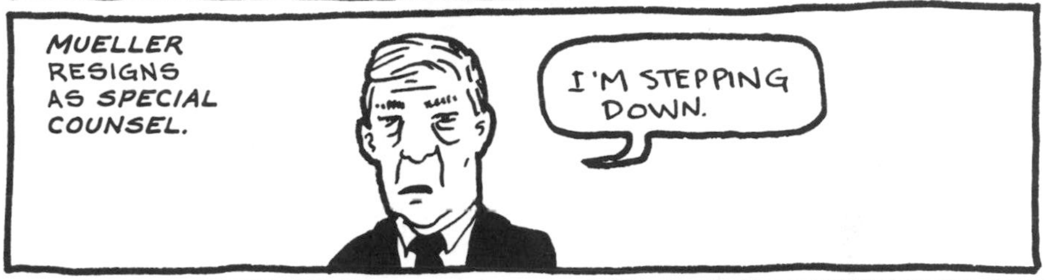
MUELLER RESIGNS AS SPECIAL COUNSEL.
I'M STEPPING DOWN.

JUL 24

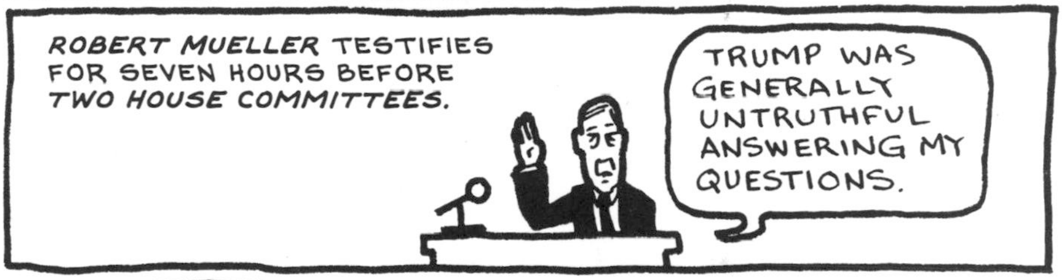
ROBERT MUELLER TESTIFIES FOR SEVEN HOURS BEFORE TWO HOUSE COMMITTEES.
TRUMP WAS GENERALLY UNTRUTHFUL ANSWERING MY QUESTIONS.

JUL 25

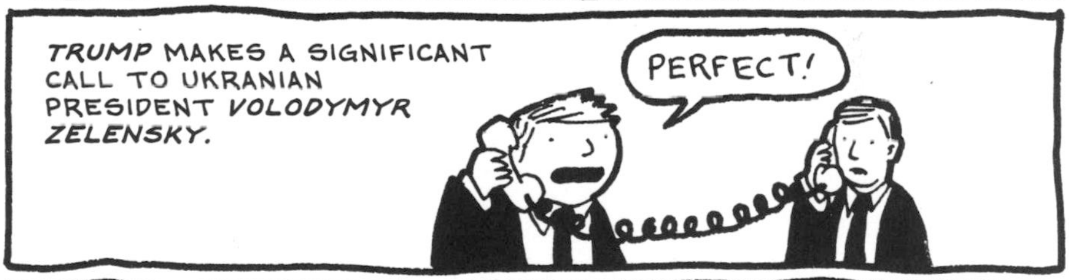
TRUMP MAKES A SIGNIFICANT CALL TO UKRANIAN PRESIDENT VOLODYMYR ZELENSKY.
PERFECT!

AUG 12

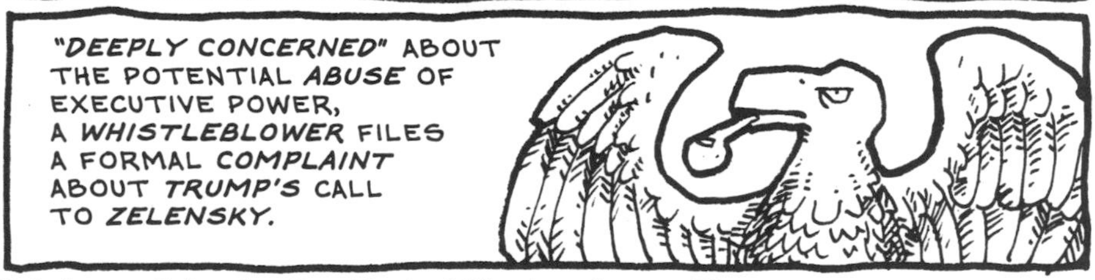
"DEEPLY CONCERNED" ABOUT THE POTENTIAL ABUSE OF EXECUTIVE POWER, A WHISTLEBLOWER FILES A FORMAL COMPLAINT ABOUT TRUMP'S CALL TO ZELENSKY.

Volodymyr Zelensky: President of Ukraine, former TV star and comedian

DEC 18

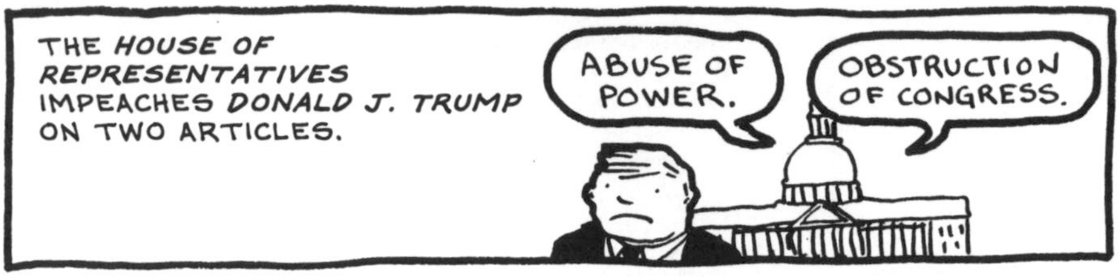
THE *HOUSE OF REPRESENTATIVES* IMPEACHES *DONALD J. TRUMP* ON TWO ARTICLES.
ABUSE OF POWER.
OBSTRUCTION OF CONGRESS.

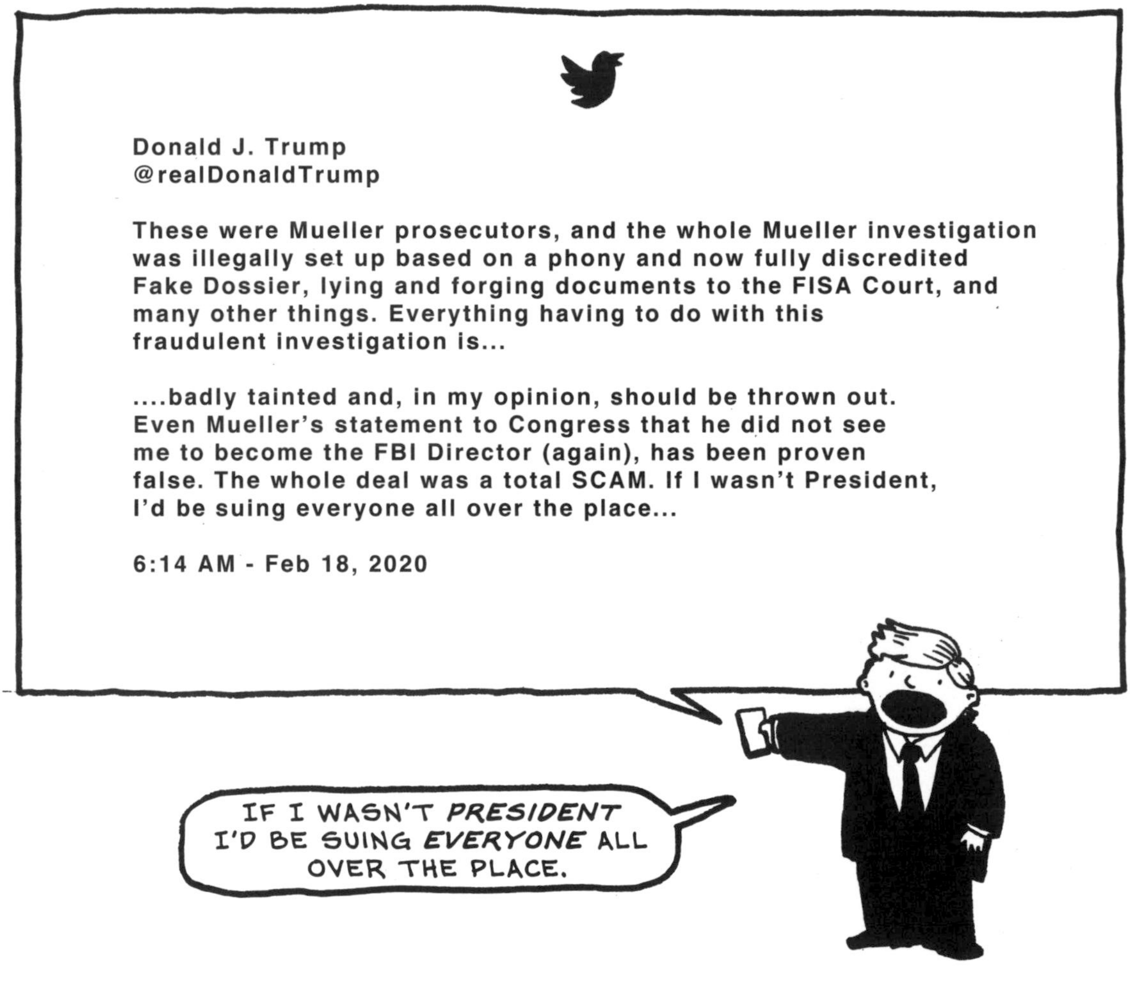
Donald J. Trump
@realDonaldTrump
These were Mueller prosecutors, and the whole Mueller investigation was illegally set up based on a phony and now fully discredited Fake Dossier, lying and forging documents to the FISA Court, and many other things. Everything having to do with this fraudulent investigation is...
....badly tainted and, in my opinion, should be thrown out. Even Mueller's statement to Congress that he did not see me to become the FBI Director (again), has been proven false. The whole deal was a total SCAM. If I wasn't President, I'd be suing everyone all over the place...
6:14 AM - Feb 18, 2020
IF I WASN'T *PRESIDENT* I'D BE SUING *EVERYONE* ALL OVER THE PLACE.

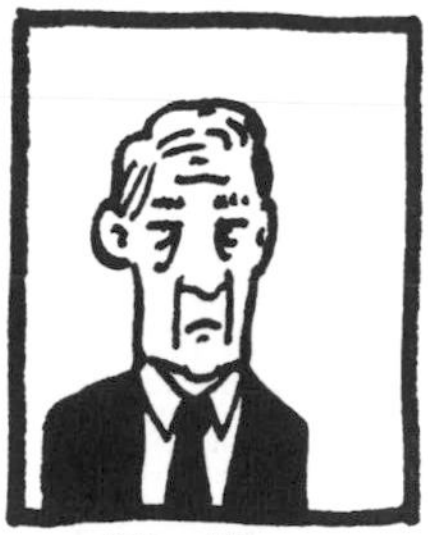

Mueller

Special Counsel, 2016 election investigation

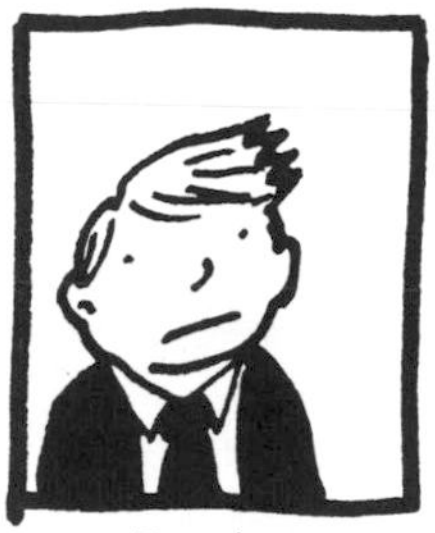

Trump

President of the United States

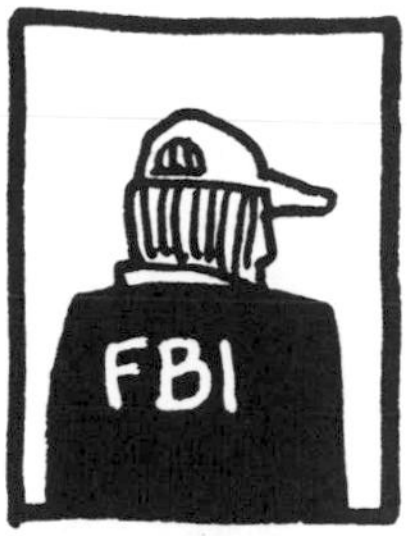
FBI

FBI

Federal Bureau of Investigation

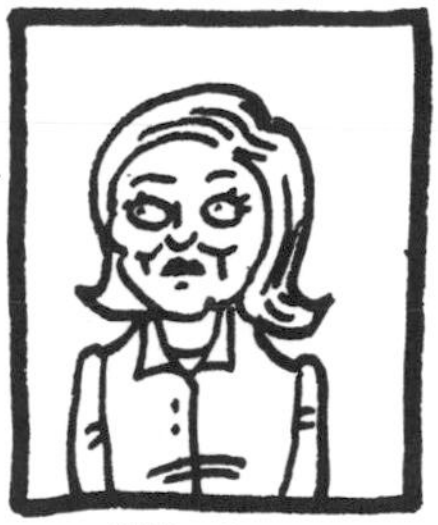

Clinton

Candidate for President of the United States, 2016

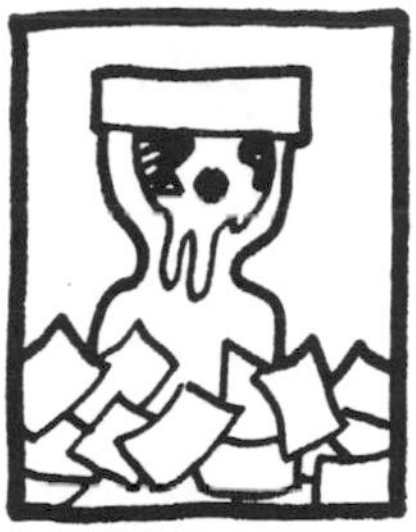

Wikileaks

Publishes news leaks provided by anonymous sources

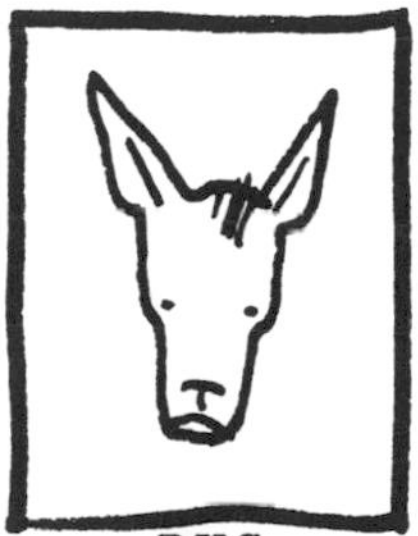

DNC

Democratic National Committee

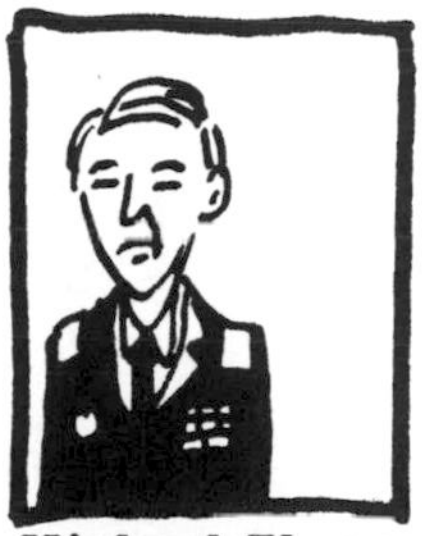

Michael Flynn

National Security Advisor, 2017

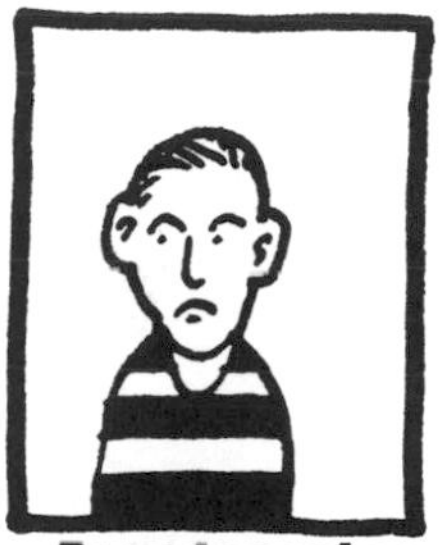

Papadopoulos

Trump's Foreign Policy Advisor, 2016

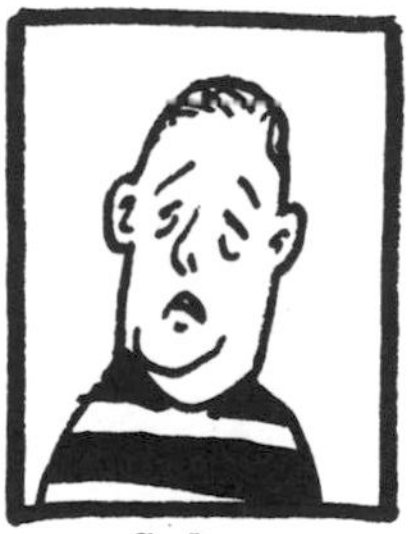

Cohen

Trump's personal counsel, 2006–2018

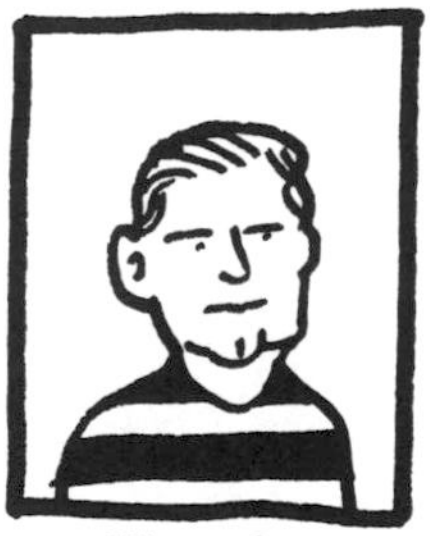

Manafort

Trump Presidential campaign team, Jun–Aug 2016

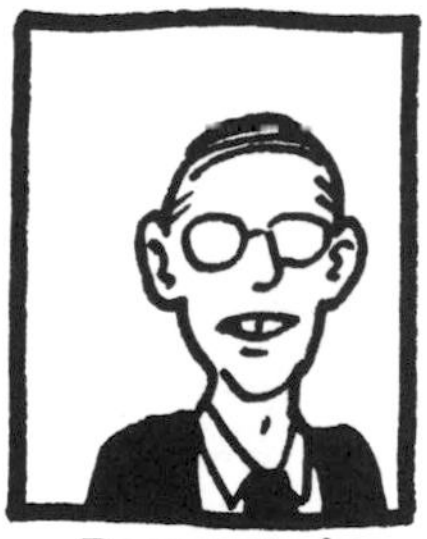

Rosenstein

U.S. Deputy Attorney General, Apr 2017–May 2019

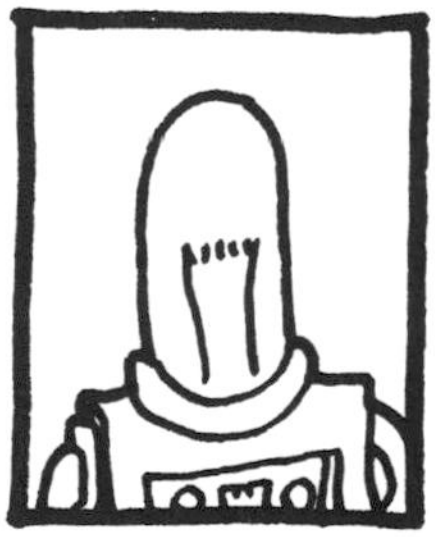

IRA

Russia's Internet Research Agency

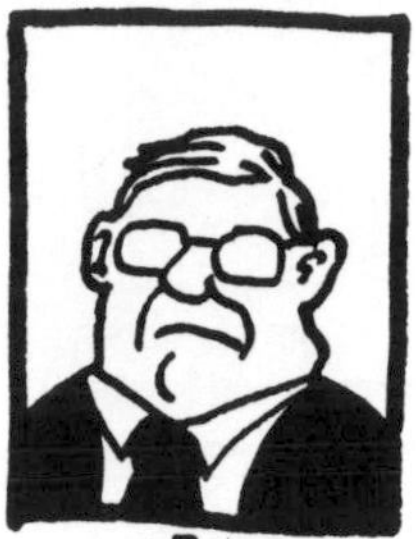

Barr

U.S. Attorney General,
Feb 2019–

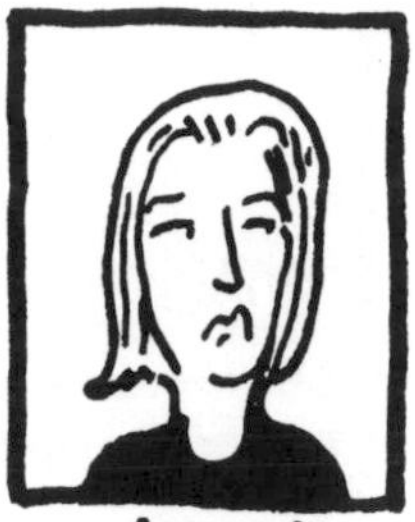

Assange

Cofounder of
Wikileaks

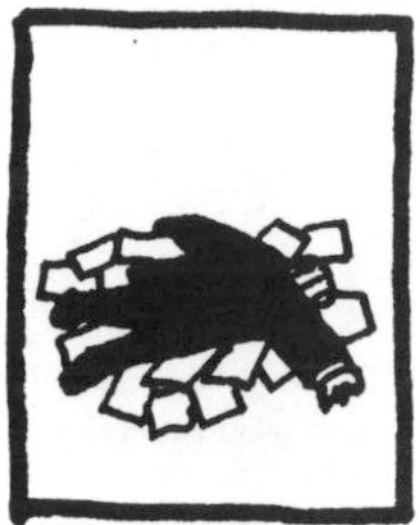

Seth Rich

DNC employee.
Murdered Jul 2016

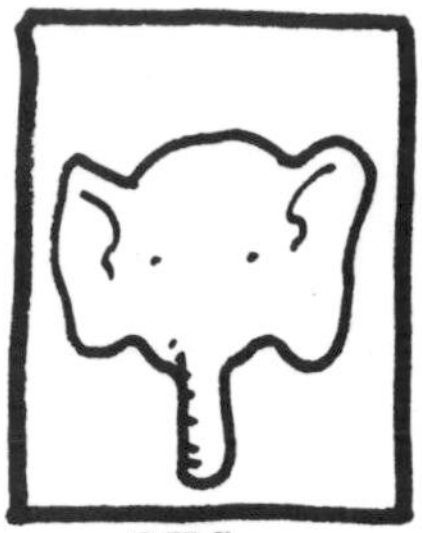

RNC

Republican
National
Committee

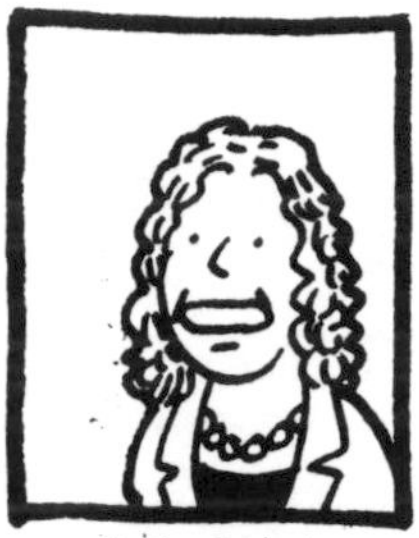

Schultz

DNC chair
2011–2016

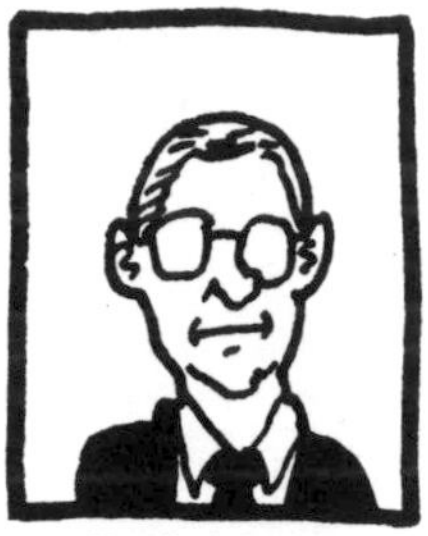

Podesta

Chairman of
Hillary Clinton's
2016 campaign

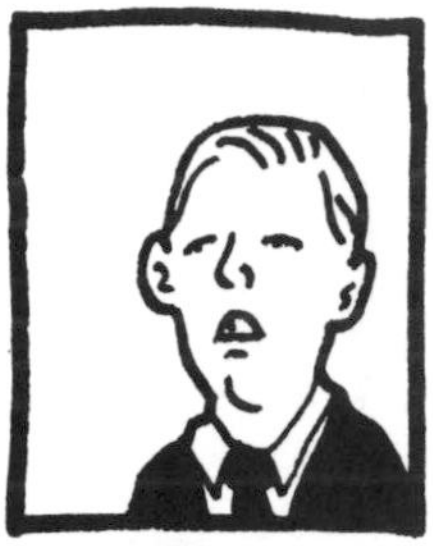

Eric Trump

Donald Trump's son

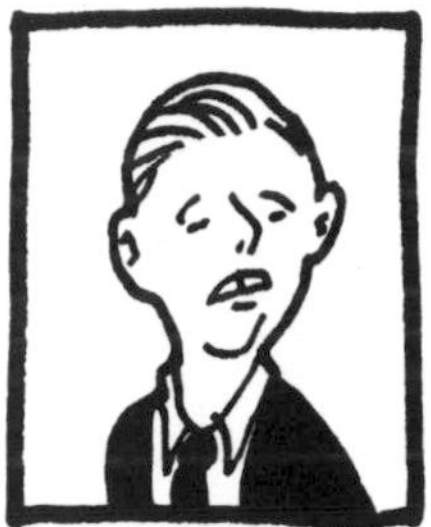

Don Trump Jr

Donald Trump's son

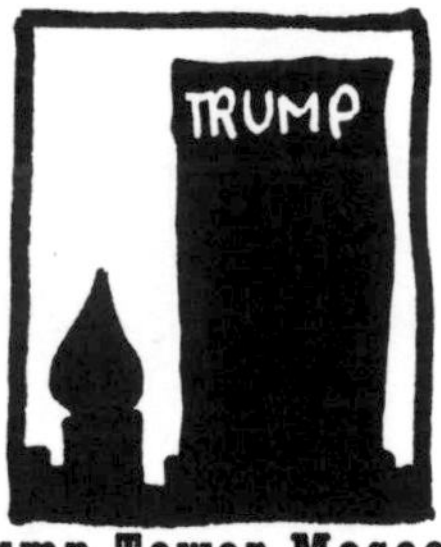
TRUMP

Trump Tower Moscow

Proposed skyscraper
in Moscow, never built

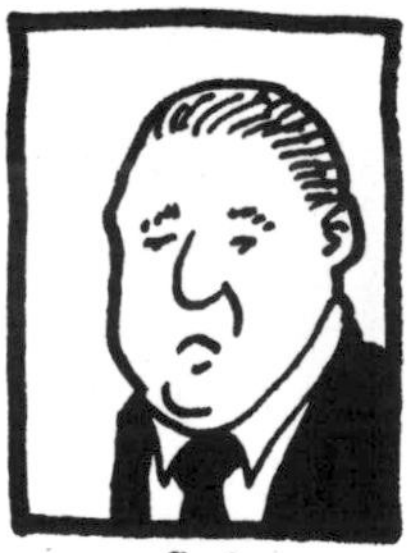

Sater

Russian developer,
Trump advisor,
FBI informant

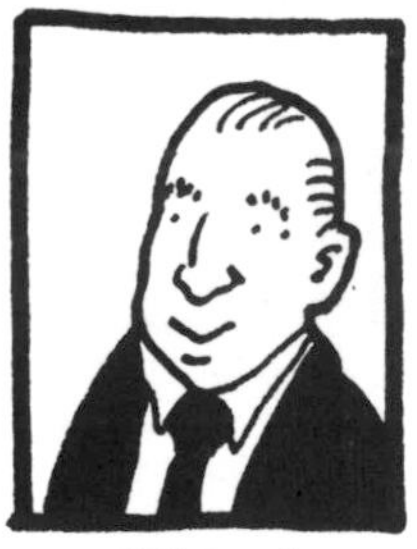

Mifsud

Director, London
Center of International
Law Practice

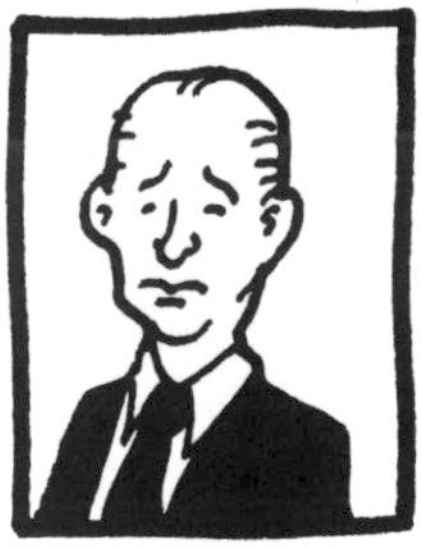

Putin

Russian leader,
1999–2036

Goldstone

British publicist,
former tabloid
journalist

Kaveladze

Russian
real estate
developer

Veselnitskaya

Russian
real estate
attorney

Akhmetshin

Russian military
officer, lobbyist,
billionare, mobster

Kushner

Real-estate developer
married to
Ivanka Trump

Ivanka Trump

Daughter and senior
advisor to
Donald Trump

Hope Hicks

White House
communications
director, 2017–2018

Yanukovych

Ukraine President,
2010–2014

Deripaska

Russian
industrialist
billionaire

Kilimnik

Russian
political
consultant

Gates

Trump's Deputy
Campaign Manager

Roger Stone

Political consultant

Judge Jackson

Presided over
Manafort and Gates
criminal cases

Dmitriev

CEO Russian Direct
Investment Fund

Nader

Blackwater lobbyist,
U.A.E. liaison

Prince

Blackwater CEO

Gerson

Hedge-fund manager,
Jared Kushner's friend

Bannon

Brietbart News. White
House Chief Strategist,
Nov 2016–Aug 2017

K.T. McFarland

Deputy National
Security Advisor, May
2017–Feb 2018

Priebus

White House
Chief of Staff,
Jan 2017–Jul 2017

Obama

President of the
United States,
2009–2017

Sally Yates

Acting
Attorney General,
Jan. 20–30, 2017

Kislyak

Russian
senior diplomat

Comey

FBI Director,
2013–2017

198

Spicer

White House
Press Secretary,
Jan 2017–Jul 2017

Pence

48th Vice President of
the United States

Sessions

Attorney General,
2017–2018

Stormy Daniels

Adult film star
and director

Roy Cohn

Joseph McCarthy's
chief counsel for the
McCarthy hearings

Pelosi

Speaker of the House,
2019–

McGahn

White House Counsel,
Jan 2017–Oct 2018

Annie Donaldson

Deputy Counsel
to the President,
Feb 2017–Dec 2018

Ledgett

NSA Deputy Director,
2014–2017

NSA

National
Security Agency

Stephen Miller

Trump's senior policy
advisor, Jan 2017–

Chris Christie

Head of Trump
transition team

McCabe

FBI Deputy Director,
Feb 2016–Jan 2018

Sanders

Press Secretary,
May 2017–Jun 2019

DOJ

Department of Justice

Ruddy

FOX commenter

Lewandowski

Trump's
campaign manager,
Jan 2015–Jun 2016

Porter

Trump's
Staff Secretary,
Jan 2017–Feb 2018

Emin Agalarov

Russian pop singer

Aras Agalarov

Russian billionaire
businessman and
developer

Gucifer 2.0

Russian hacker
credited for the stolen
DNC documents

DC Leaks

Political leaks
publisher, front for
Fancy Bear, a Russian
espionage group